CW01066871

Battleship HMS King George V entering Rosyth Royal Dockyard (Sir Muirhead Bone)

The Sea
Our Heritage

British Maritime Interests
Past and Present

JEAN CANTLIE STEWART

MA, DIP.ED, BARRISTER-AT-LAW OF MIDDLE TEMPLE

Rowan Books

Jean Cantlie Stewart is the author of five books, a children's story and a book on education published under a pen name, a medical biography of her grandfather – to be translated into Chinese – and a book on law, a recommended university text. She has also written magazine articles and a booklet on Scottish government. She comes of a naval family, sailed in her youth and has always had a keen interest in the sea and maritime matters. Research for the present book has taken seven years and after the composition was completed special thanks must go to the following people for their generous help in advising on factual accuracy: Mr. Robert Allan, Scottish Fishermen's Federation, Dr. G. E. Aylmer, historian and formerly Master of St. Peter's College, Oxford. Vice Admiral Sir Peter Berger, Sir Alexander Cairncross, economist, author and Chancellor of Glasgow University, Mr. Jack Daniel, Director General Ships, Ministry of Defence, Mr. Nick Granger, Ship Builders and Ship Repairers Association, Mr. Eric Grove, author and lecturer at Hull University, Captain J. H. F. Houghton, Member of the Honourable Company of Master Mariners, Rear Admiral Philip Marrack, former Director of Naval Ship Production and Director of the Dockyard Department, Captain John Moore, formerly Editor, Jane's Fighting Ships, Captain James Pack, formerly Director of the Royal Naval Museum, Captain Richard Sharpe, Editor, Jane's Fighting Ships.

First published in 1993
Revised edition 1995

© JEAN CANTLIE STEWART
ISBN 0 9509932 3 9 (pb)

Published by Rowan Books, Keith, Banffshire

Typeset by XL Publishing Services, Nairn
and printed in Great Britain by
Ipswich Book Company, Suffolk

CONTENTS

ILLUSTRATIONS

Frontispiece Battleship HMS King George V entering Rosyth Royal Dockyard
Opposite page 1 East Indiaman (E.W. Cooke)
Between pages 40 and 41
The Great Ship Race from China to London. The Taeping and the Ariel off the Lizard, 1866, tea clippers built in Greenock (ILN)
The Auxiliary Screw Iron Ship Somersetshire for the Australian Trade, 1867, steam clipper built on R. Itchen (ILN)
Carronade, 1779 – traversible firepower at point-blank range (E.W. Cooke)
HMS Invincible – warship of the iron-clad fleet, 1873 (ILN)
Between pages 104 and 105
(Above) Trading barge – still in use in 20th century (E.W. Cooke); (below) Fishing smacks unloading their catch (E.W. Cooke)
Steam ship Ormuz of the Orient Line, 1887, Adelaide to London 27 days (ILN)

SS Caronia of the Cunard Steam-Ship Company, 1947, built on the Clyde by
    John Brown (Alasdair Macfarlane)
MV Melbourne Star of the Blue Star Line, 1947, refrigerated meat ship built
    in Belfast by Harland & Wolff (Alasdair Macfarlane)
Between pages 152 and 153
Britain's little ships on night patrol. Motor Gunboats at high speed returning
    to base at dawn. World War II (C.E. Turner)
Convoy at sea between sunset and darkness, August 1941, seen from the AA
    platform of a corvette, Canadian steamer in the foreground (C.E. Turner)
Malta Convoy under attack, September 1941. HMS Prince of Wales in the
    foreground (C.E. Turner)
The Second Sea Lord presenting awards to Allied Naval Officers, World War II
    (Sir Muirhead Bone)
Between pages 216 and 217
(Above) Stationers' Guild Ceremonial Thames Barge (E.W. Cooke); (below)
    North East sailing collier unloading in London (E.W. Cooke)
The Victory, forty years old at Trafalgar, but modernised in extensive refits
    (E.W. Cooke)
Torpedoed oil tanker, 1941 (Sir Muirhead Bone)
Small craft fitting out; trawlers being prepared for Coast Patrol, August 1940
    (Sir Muirhead Bone)

Acknowledgement of Illustrations
Reproductions of C.E. Turner and Sir Muirhead Bone by permission of the
Illustrated London News, the Tate Gallery, Aberdeen Gallery and Imperial
War Museum; engravings by E.W. Cooke reproduced from a collection of
prints published by Masthead in 1970; line drawings by Alasdair Macfarlane,
published by Brown & Ferguson, 1986; unsigned wood engravings and line
drawings from the Illustrated London News (ILN) by permission of the
Guildhall Library and National Library of Scotland; further assistance and
photographs provided by the National Maritime Museum, Bonhams, and Colin
Denny. Line drawings in the text by Lucy Duke (LD); Warships of the Grand
Fleet from the Laws of the Navy by R.A. Hopwood illustrated by Ronald
Langmaid.

All reasonable steps have been taken to trace copyright, seek permission to
publish and express acknowledgement.

FOREWORD AND ACKNOWLEDGEMENT

The purpose of this book is to ask the questions: what is a maritime policy; what part did such a policy play in the life, development and survival of Great Britain and what part should it play in future. A maritime policy is one connected with sea, ships and deep sea trade – in war it becomes a maritime strategy. A land-locked nation does not require a Navy or a Merchant Navy. An island nation does. Britain, being an island, must have a maritime policy or perish. A channel tunnel can provide an outlet for only a tiny proportion of her trade. She must export and import to and from the widest possible number of countries. Although now a high proportion of passengers, mail and freight goes by air, nevertheless the volume of trade only represents half a percent of the volume of exports and imports, and, however the balance alters, it will never be cost effective to send plant, machinery, raw materials or heavy commodities by air. It thus remains true to say, 'The sea is Britain's lifeline'.

Yet, during the last three and a half decades, this statement of the obvious has been in doubt. The number of ships in the British mercantile marine sailing under the Red Ensign has dropped by five sixths. Ships flagged out under the flag of a foreign country can never provide the same income or security for the country as ships under a national flag. For the first time in the history of Britain, encompassing medieval times, the bulk of her trade is now, even on short hauls to the continent, carried in foreign ships. Meanwhile the number of surface ships in the Royal Navy is only five vessels more than the number of surface ships required to fight one vital convoy through in World War II.

The average reader may ask the question, 'What does this matter?'. There are many answers and all that anyone can do is give the most important and let the story of an island race tell the rest.

First, for financial reasons – present policy means that Britain is paying for most of the transport of her goods in foreign currency, which increases her current account deficit. If she transported the goods herself she would be paying in pounds sterling. Likewise if, as heretofore, she engaged more extensively in cross trades, carrying goods for other nations and sailing under her own flag she would be earning valuable foreign currency to balance her books.

Second, for strategic reasons. The Royal Navy requires sufficient ships to defend the realm, to escort convoys in time of war and defend its vital interests. In times of conflict it depends on the Merchant Marine to provide both ships and men to carry and escort personnel and goods across the oceans. If ships are flagged out to foreign nations there is no guarantee they will be available in emergency and likewise if a high proportion of crews are foreign the numbers of trained British Merchant Navy personnel ready in time of war for service in the Royal Naval Reserve or in the Merchant Navy are too small for the safety of the realm.

Third, in order to obtain overseas orders shipbuilders must have a home market to supply and because the number of British ships sailing under the Red

Ensign has dropped to such dangerously low levels, shipbuilding and repair yards in the United Kingdom have either been closed or sold to foreign nations. In an emergency, without shipyards or skilled workforce, Britain could not replace losses at sea and thus could not defend herself for more than weeks. In both world wars the turning point in the battles of the Atlantic was the moment when replacements exceeded losses.

Fourth, for commercial reasons. Although Britain grows a higher proportion of her temperate foodstuffs than she did fifty years ago, she remains a nation which cannot feed itself and must import food, raw materials (and now machinery), and must earn her living by exporting manufactured and processed commodities. Our ancestors recognised the connection between the effectiveness of an export drive and the identity of the ships which carry them, while a ship which carries British goods is unlikely to go the other way in ballast. Almost within a century Britain has passed from a policy of complete protection under stringent Navigation Laws to one of total abandonment, with consequent damage to her trading current account.

Fifth, Britain enjoys a status in the world, in banking, law, insurance, brokerage and commerce, which is accorded to her on account of her maritime strength and interest. These marine financial, legal and insurance services, inter alia, on which Britain also depends for her living, will wither away unless supported by a flourishing merchant fleet.

In short, the moment the British, an island race, who have always earned their living from maritime trade, cease to wish to sail out into distant seas, Britain will wither and decline. The sea is her natural habitat; it surrounds, comforts, guards and beckons her. From it, all through her history, she has drawn her strength.

When I wrote these words it was my intention to restrict the contents of a small book to the decline of the Merchant Navy and the consequent maritime and commercial decline of Britain. A publishing friend persuaded me to extend the remit to the Royal Navy and, having done that, I decided to complete the picture by adding shipbuilding and repairing and marine financial services. The moment I started to write of the Navy I was in the company of ghosts. At Rosyth, where my father was Admiral Superintendent from 1939 until leaving to run the four Indian dockyards in 1944, we were surrounded by guests, many of whom walk out of these pages of naval history as heroes: Captain Kerr, who went down on the Hood, who stayed with us for months when his ship was being refitted, and who said, when everyone was dismayed by the fall of France, 'No. It will be much better to be alone. We don't have to depend on anyone but ourselves'; Captain Vian, who, when his destroyer Cossack was being refitted at Rosyth, said at dinner that he would give me a polo pony, adding when he saw my grateful pleasure, 'But you'll have to arrange the transport. It's in Malta' – there was hardly one dangerous mission in the Mediterranean, and many elsewhere in which he was not involved; Captain Barry of the Queen Elizabeth who sent a Christmas message home to my young brother on Forces Favourites, before she was sunk in Alexandria, and who was responsible for training the submariners for the attack on the Tirpitz; Admiral Sir Charles

Ramsey, C-in-C, Rosyth, later the Commodore of the first convoy to lose no ships except stragglers, which received a special mention from the War Cabinet; Admiral Sir Wilbraham Ford, that wise and gentle man who came from Malta in 1942 to replace him; Admiral Brodie, an old family friend and also latterly a convoy Commodore, a quietly courageous man, whose deep religious faith had been strengthened by the message he had received from his twin brother T.S. that he was all right minutes after he was killed taking the first submarine into the Sea of Marmara in World War I; Captain Donald Macintyre, a hero of the Atlantic War and also an old family friend who had played golf as a boy with my mother at Elie, a ghost for me from a later period, who 'vetted' speeches and letters I wrote on the Navy and whose splendid and out-of-print books have provided inspiration. He drove himself in severe ill health to alert the British public to the peril to which they were exposed without an adequate Navy to protect them.

Lastly I would remember the Merchant Navy steward, who came to us as an 'extra' to help my father's steward and who, having been sunk three times and having spent on each occasion long periods in the water, plodded round the dining room table as an old white haired man, although he was barely fifty. We did not have many weapons from 1940 to 1943 and not enough ships or aircraft. It is obvious from the pages that follow that the Admiralty used to the maximum the good placement of naval officers and men, the right man for the right job, but it is almost incredible to believe that, in the same way as Churchill fought the war with the English language, the Lords of the Admiralty fought the war likewise with people's names. Yet it is tempting to think that it must have been so, for the name of this steward was Freeman – the choice a constant reminder to the naval officers he was serving at table of the great debt owed by the nation to the Merchant Navy – past the bounds of measurement. Aged beyond his years, he had been at all times, in the words of King George VI, a 'Free man' with civilian status to come and go as he pleased.

What I did not know then of all these splendid ghosts was that we would never in our life time see their like again.

I would like to take this opportunity to acknowledge the tremendous debt that I owe in publication of this book to so many naval and other friends and helpers, past and present, who have given unremittingly of their time to try and eliminate the inevitable errors that seem to occur in any endeavour of this nature which one undertakes. If any are left they are all mine. Also, as always, I owe a debt beyond repayment to all the librarians, north and south, who have given me support and help in finding the right books and papers from which I have drawn my knowledge. It has been a truly gigantic task and I hope it may be some use to those people who wish to understand more about the sea and Britain's great maritime past – and future – and may also be of some interest to others who are already specialists in the subject. Above all I hope it may be of interest to that most elusive section of the public – the 'general reader'. If he or she were to become interested once more in the sea that surrounds us Britain would indeed have nothing to fear.

CHAPTER I

THE GENIE'S LAMP
THE FOUNDATION OF BRITISH MARITIME INTERESTS

The story of Britain's maritime development is usually seen on a rising curve until the 1890's and in decline after 1918, but half a century before that date events occurred which put its future in some doubt. To see these matters in perspective it is important to sketch in broad outline the historical background in which they were set.

The sea is both a friend and a master. It carries a nation's commerce over the oceans, yet its storms can submerge the ships, which seconds before were enjoying its support. So an island like Britain, with harbours and bays to encourage trade and travel by means of a merchant marine, lies open without a navy to conquest. In early days the British Isles were invaded by Angles, Saxons, Jutes, Vikings and Danes, until King Alfred built a fleet to blockade the Danes into Northumbria and saved his kingdom of Wessex. At that time the people of England earned their living mainly from the land, so ships were not in plentiful supply. No sooner had Danes and Saxons learnt to live together than a further wave of Viking invaders gave victory to Canute of Scandinavian origin, who developed maritime trade and built a navy of 40 ships for his protection. After time restored the English line to the throne, the nation was conquered by William of Normandy, since whose reign there have been no further full-scale resisted invasions of Britain. Nevertheless some have sailed, troops have landed, major amphibious forces have assembled across the Channel and expeditions have been made to Ireland to restore the Catholic dynasty to the English throne. In spite of a powerful administration, strengthened by feudalism, local government and the common law, William the Conqueror still needed all naval resources to repel the Danes. In those days fleets of fighting and merchant ships in Europe and the Mediterranean were almost indivisible, and 20 ships were requested by the King from three coastal ports – Hastings, Romney and Hythe – to which were added two more – Dover and Sandwich – known as the Cinque Ports, which became responsible for a permanent contribution to naval forces. Vessels did no fighting; they transported soldiers to land battles and only occasionally did the soldiers fight at sea. In succeeding centuries the Plantagenet Kings, who, through inheritance and Henry II's marriage to Eleanor of Acquitaine, owned extensive lands in Western France, used their own ships and galleys to carry soldiers, but were reliant also on merchant vessels for crown service to repel invaders and mount expeditions. Henry's son Richard I raised a naval force of 100 crown and merchant ships to transport his army of Crusaders to the Mediterranean. In his brother John's reign lands in northern France were lost, but John's son Henry III was triumphant at sea, when a French squadron of naval ships was defeated in the Channel by an English fleet of 40 ships, composed of royal and merchant vessels.

Until the fourteenth century English merchant ships played a minor role in the movement of world trade. Wool and tin were the chief exports, for the manufacture of English cloth was still in its infancy. The movement of trade across the world was mostly by overland caravan routes leading to ports on short sea routes, such as those of Venice and Genoa in the Mediterranean and of the Hanseatic League on the northern shores of Europe. Boats were partially dependent on oared propulsion and did not venture into the oceans. As fear of invasion subsided and sea power was maintained in home waters, English trade increased and was liberalised. Edward III encouraged foreign traders to come ashore to buy wool and later cloth and to sell their goods, instead of doing so only on board ship, and these inland bases, where they were also taxed, became known as 'staples'. Similar depots were established by the English on the continent – in Calais, which Edward seized from the French during the Hundred Years War and later in Antwerp and North Germany. Sufficiently strong at sea to protect herself from foreign armies, England became involved in wars with France in 1337, when Edward, whose lands in Guienne were under pressure from the French, turned the tables and invaded France – even claiming the throne – while keeping open the wool and cloth trade with Flemish burghers. His son, the Black Prince, mustered 400 ships, of which half were merchantmen, to transport soldiers to victory at Crecy, but despite this most of the English territory in France was lost, except for Calais and part of Gascony south of Bordeaux. Nevertheless, English sailors demonstrated their superiority at sea, winning the naval Battle of Sluys in 1340 and developing a reputation for courage and seamanship. The year 1347 saw the first complete roll of ships to be called upon in emergency – a mixture of King's ships and merchant vessels, of which Yarmouth provided the largest number from her herring fleet, while Cornwall and Devon produced a supply of experienced mariners.

There was of course a drawback in using so many merchant ships to supplement the navy in war, for when peace returned commerce and carriage of trade were unavoidably damaged. Competition in the sphere of shipping was meanwhile coming from the continent, where the increasing power of the Hanseatic League adversely affected English trade. This commercial and shipping organisation owed its origin to a treaty signed in 1241 between the cities of Hamburg and Lübeck, which not only gave each other protection from pirates, but saw the financial advantage of creating a monopolistic trading partnership. They were joined by others – Flanders, Norway and Russia – and only ships owned by the League could carry the trade of member nations. A number of cities refused to bow to this monopoly, chief among which was Bruges, and their merchants continued to import goods in their own ships. During the fourteenth and fifteenth centuries the League increased its powerful trading network – privileges were granted to it in England and the numbers of its ships and trading houses grew, but by the middle of the fifteenth century other nations, including England, had also begun to develop restrictive shipping laws. When Elizabeth met rivalry from the League, she carried competition across to the continent and set up a mart in Hamburg. By 1600 the power of the League was passing and in 1852, following the Repeal of the British Navigation Laws, its main trading house in London became Cannon Street Railway Station.

As the fourteenth century ended, Richard II saw the danger into which the country was drifting, with a weak navy and its carrying trade in the hands of foreigners. To pay for a navy he, therefore, encouraged greater trade, while putting a tax on foreign ships coming into English ports. 'All merchants, aliens of what realms, countries or seignories… which be of amity to the King and of his realm, may from henceforth safe and surely come within the realm of England and in all cities, boroughs, ports… within the Realm.. and abide with their goods and all merchandises under the safeguard and protection of the King, as it shall please them, without disturbance or denying of any person'. At the same time Richard tightened up discipline in the navy, ordering that mariners who left the King's service without leave would have to pay back part of their wages and be imprisoned for a year. When this tax and fine did not bring anticipated financial rewards he introduced the first Navigation Act of England in 1381, 'To increase the Navy of England, which is now greatly diminished, it is assented and accorded that none of the King's liege people do from henceforth ship any merchandise in going out or coming within the realm of England, but only in ships of the King's liegance'. If they did so they would forfeit their merchandise. When Richard saw that this Act restricted commerce and that he did not have sufficient ships to carry all the trade of England, including the coastal carriage of coal, he allowed goods to be transported in foreign vessels if there were no English ships available ('in default of English ships'). In order to provide sufficient vessels for his purposes he improved royal and merchant shipbuilding and created the first permanent post of Lord High Admiral in 1391.

Although it is claimed that Richard II's policy was not effective nor consistent, nevertheless by Henry IV's reign the guardianship of the sea was mainly entrusted to merchant vessels and in 1406 a law required shipowners to maintain certain ships at readiness for emergencies, interchange between royal and merchant navies being still taken for granted. English ships were typical of the broader beam characteristic of northern fleets. They were propelled by wind with single masts and ranged in size from 20 to 200 tons. By 1420 the two masted ship appeared, followed by the three masted, and soon the mainmast and then the foremast began to carry top as well as main sails. By now European vessels were becoming more seaworthy, with sharper bows and increased tonnage and the English were making longer trading voyages into the Mediterranean and the Levant. When Henry V re-opened the Hundred Years War with France and temporarily restored Normandy to the English Kings by his victories at Barfleur and Agincourt, claiming a right of inheritance to the French throne, the success of his military expedition was greatly due to his command of the Channel. This he asserted with a vast fleet of naval, merchant and chartered foreign vessels, with guns for the first time mounted on naval ships of which the largest were over 1000 tons. Just as Venice, Genoa and Scandinavia had claimed dominion over the Adriatic, Liguria and the Baltic Sea respectively, the English now claimed limited dominion over the North Sea, as well as over the Channel and part of the Atlantic between North Cape and Cape Finisterre. Parliament referred to them as the 'Lords of the Sea'

– a meaningless title, which provided a sad prelude to Henry VI's loss of all English lands in France at the hands of Joan of Arc (with the exception of Calais) but one which was later re-asserted by Charles II, just a short time before he lost Tangier.

Defeat in France brought anarchy, faction fights and civil war to England. For thirty years the country was torn apart by the Wars of the Roses, as the houses of Lancaster and York vied for the throne. The accession of the Tudors marked the transition from medieval to modern history and, because of the lost lands on the continent, gave a new impetus to England's maritime trade. Henry VII's reign brought increased commerce, based on the manufacture of woollen cloth and clothing and carried to the ports by pack horses. For this trade a large merchant navy was required and when need arose for more ships in the King's navy, Henry, like previous Kings, passed Navigation Acts to increase the size of the merchant marine. Parliament enacted that, since the navy had fallen into decay, wines from Guienne and Gascony (once English possessions) should only be brought in English ships and, when this did not prove sufficient to stimulate English shipping and shipbuilding, a further Act stated that, 'Natives shall not freight or charge alien's ships if English ships may be had. No merchandise to be carried out or brought in if he may have sufficient freight in ships or vessels of the deynseyns of this realm in the same port where he shall make his freight'. With Calais now the only trading foothold left in France Henry entered into commercial agreements with Iceland and Denmark and looked for new trading opportunities overseas. He gave bounties (or subsidies) to shipbuilders who would build vessels over 100 tons, so that, with a plentiful supply of new ships, England was placed in a good position to take part in the voyages of discovery. With the benefit of increased trade carried in English ships, the English were fast becoming professional freight carriers, carrying other nation's goods as well as their own and earning foreign currency in so doing.

In 1490 the first English consul was appointed to a Mediterranean port. European trade was now taking to the oceans. These were the great days of seaward expansion by many countries. Christopher Colombus and Vasco da Gama were both embarking on voyages and pushing back the frontiers of the maritime world in the name of the Portuguese and Spanish Kings. The discoveries were remarkable and productive – Africa, the West Indies, the Cape of Good Hope, the crossing of the Equator and later Panama, India and hosts of islands in east and west. In 1493 the Pope set his seal on these discoveries by creating vast monopolies in the name of the Roman Catholic Church. He divided the newly discovered territories between Spain and Portugal – sending the Spanish west to the Americas and the Portuguese east to India and the spice islands, giving them a virtual monopoly on the route round the Cape of Good Hope. The English resisted this authoritarian and exclusive division of trade. Having traded in the Levant since the Crusades, they arrived in South America (where William Hawkins, having crossed from Guinea in Africa, reached Brazil in 1530) only to find the Spaniards regarding the territory as theirs and refusing to allow any interchange of goods. Undeterred they set out to navigate northern routes to the East. Willoughby explored the North East Ocean towards the Pole, calling in on Norway and wintering in Lapland where he died. Chancellor, his second in command, sailed through the Barents Sea and reached Archangel, where he established the first English trade with Russia, leading to the appointment of a Russian ambassador to London in 1557. On the way home from his second journey he was shipwrecked and died on the coast of Scotland. John Cabot, possibly the greatest of the three, discovered Newfoundland with its rich fishing fields. He was one of the founders of English maritime strength, hoping to open up a north west passage to India. Under his guidance sailors and entrepreneurs formed the Company of Merchant Adventurers – leading exporters of woven cloth who claimed to have been trading since the thirteenth century. With his son Sebastian appointed as its first Governor, the Company aimed to make England into a depot for foreign produce and her ships into leading carriers of other nation's goods, 'Intent to carry a good quantity of wares and make other nations weary of so doing, so that we can command their commodities and other nations may be served by us'. When later the mercantile policies of Spain in the Netherlands and the Hanse towns in Germany sought to exclude English cloth from their markets, a number of other trading corporations were founded, including the Eastland, Muscovy, African and Levant and later the East India Company, all of which secured English markets overseas and owed their success to the spirit of adventure among capitalists and sailors alike.

Although still dependent upon their merchant navies to defend the realm, Henry VII and Henry VIII introduced differences between the two fleets and built more royal ships. The fishing ports were the great providers of ships and men, with fishermen joining the navy during hostilities and their womenfolk taking their place in the boats. Nevertheless Henry VII provided a career structure for his officers and mounted anti-personnel guns on the upper decks of his warships, while Henry VIII inherited 7 royal ships from his father and had nearly 60 naval ships in commission at the end of his reign, including galleons, galleasses and pinnaces. Although tempted to follow a continental policy by his military victory over the French in 1513 and by Wolsey's ability to play off the potentates of Europe against each other, Henry had a great interest in shipbuilding and overseas trade and justly earned the title of the Father of the English Navy. In 1513 he founded Trinity House, to examine officers and petty officers and supply seamen for his ships and fifty years later this body became responsible for providing navigation lights and buoys. Like his father, Henry VIII passed a law enacting that the wines of Guienne and Gascony should be brought in English ships and in 1531 he re-enacted the Navigation Acts of Richard II and Henry VII. This Act was required because the Navy was, 'Marvellously decayed' and the, 'Living of mariners impoverished in such wise (that) within a few years there shall be few Englishmen that shall be expert in the seas to the great peril of this realm and the decay of the people'. In 1540 he confirmed the Acts again and imposed duties on aliens bringing in goods, even in English ships, although the powerful Hanseatic League was excluded from these provisions. In the recital Henry spoke of this measure being, 'Requisite, necessary and commodious for the entercourse and concourse of merchants transporting and conveying their wares and merchandise and a great defence and surety of this realm in time of war, as well to offend as to defend'. Like Richard II he thus linked trading duties paid by aliens to the provision of an English Navy, for which he drew up regulations to improve management and discipline, replacing the Keeper of the King's ships with a Navy Board, which, together with the office of Lord High Admiral, was the foundation of the later Admiralty.

After Henry's death the chartered companies continued to expand in the reign of Edward VI – during which the Muscovy Company received its charter – but under the rule of Mary and Philip of Spain there was a virtual standstill in maritime affairs. Calais, the last trading foothold on the continent, was lost and there was more interest in burning Protestant heretics than in maritime matters. 'Not over motivated by national pride, Mary cared only for the souls of the English and believed they would be safer in Italian and Spanish hands'. It fell to Elizabeth to rekindle the spirit of adventure in the English people and create a new age of literature, learning and sail. Having spent a period of her childhood in the Tower, she saw the importance of the Channel both for defence and trade and did not take long to throw down the gauntlet to foreign states. They were told that, whereas England had never excluded their vessels from British seas, Spain and Portugal were now attempting to do this in the areas which the Pope had given them. On account of this exclusion foreign vessels must honour the flag in the waters surrounding Britain. In 1558 Elizabeth repealed the Navigation Laws, which she said had made other nations 'aggrieved', so that, 'They have made like penal laws against such as should ship out of their country in any other vessels than of their country'. In their place she passed another Navigation Act, laying down that, 'If there is no restraint made of English ships', no person shall, 'Embark, ship, load or discharge by way of merchandise any wares, merchandise (pitch, tar and corn excepted) out of or into any ship or bottom of which the Queen or her subjects is not the proprietor or Master'. 'If they do this then they can pay Aliens' Customs'. She thus placed foreigners and subjects alike on the horns of a dilemma. They were free to use foreign ships, but, if they did when English ships were not under 'restraint', they would pay duties. Later, wishing to increase the number of mariners in the Navy and recognising the close ties between the fishing industry and the Queen's and Merchant Navies, she tried to stop fish being carried out of English waters by her subjects and sold back again after being salted by the Dutch at a profit, but this Act was repealed when Elizabeth helped Holland in its struggle to become an independent Protestant nation. While insisting on the English right to prevent neutrals succouring an enemy, Elizabeth's policy was not to be drawn into continental wars beyond safeguarding her own shores and trade, but her support for the Protestant cause led to the Merchant Adventurers being invited to return to the Netherlands in 1587, from whence they had earlier been driven by the Spaniards.

Meanwhile Elizabeth's chief adviser, William Cecil, one of the wisest and subtlest men on whom any monarch of Britain has relied, warned the Pope that he had no right to divide the world into two monopolies, excluding other countries from trade and handing captured crews over to the Inquisition. With the days of the oared galleys passing, merchant ships were growing larger and more seaworthy, with lower bows, allowing them to sail closer to the wind. The English answer to this exclusion therefore was to send their sailors, superior in gunnery and in managing their faster, more weatherly ships, into the South Atlantic where they harried the Spanish gold and silver trade. The prizes they captured went into both government coffers and into the pockets of those who took the prizes. By this time Spain had annexed Portugal and the inevitable clash of interests that followed these voyages escalated first into a trade and then a political war. The Spaniards placed an embargo on English goods (of which cloth still formed a predominant part) and the English retaliated by sacking cities in Spain and the Spanish West Indies and seizing all kinds of booty and treasure. Bred to the ocean, Drake fired the imagination of the English people by his exploits and seamanship. He had a great love of adventure, mingled with hopes of wealth, and a fervent patriotism, both of which he conveyed to those under his command. When hostilities broke out after the death of Mary Queen of Scots robbed Philip of a focus for his Roman Catholic ambitions, the opposing fleets were different in style and composition. The victorious English fleet contained many ships supplied by merchants of the City of London and by Francis Drake and other entrepreneurs. The Spaniards had 24 galleons, 40 great ships (converted merchantmen), 4 galleasses, 25 store ships and 30 smaller vessels, providing twice the tonnage of the 197 English ships, which were made up of: 34 Queen's ships, 10 from the service of the Lord High Admiral, 32 of Drake's ships, 38 supplied by the City of London, 61 coasters and volunteers and 22 victuallers and other vessels. The Armada highlighted not only the different battle performance of the larger Spanish ships and the low-charged heavily gunned English ships, but also of the English Naval and Merchant ships. From now on a greater division appeared between the two English navies and between the personnel serving in them. Although there were permanent Navy and Merchant Navy men, there were also many who served in the Merchant Navy in peace and the Navy in war. The regular officers of the English Navy provided the leadership of the oldest families of England, which blended well with the expert maritime skills and ability to lead of yeomen like Drake, whose love of exploration took him on round-the-world voyages. This lure of discovery and reconnaissance was shared by many of his contemporaries. Another famous yeoman sailor, John Hawkins, discovered Sierra Leone and made voyages in the 1560's to the Spanish Main and Florida, where he played a part in establishing the nefarious slaving trade. Several years later Frobisher and Davis both attempted to reach India via a western northern route and discovered Hudson's Bay. After the Armada victory England truly became the mistress of the seas, with the Elizabethans seeking trading links with many countries, including Persia, Turkey, Syria, Goa, South America, Africa, the Moluccas, Java and China.

Elizabeth understood the importance of international trade, realising that wealth was not just money, but the accumulation of heritable and moveable capital and the circulation of commodities. The City of London saw the value of expanding this trade to the East and in 1600 the East India Company was given its charter, with trading stations in Madras, Bombay and Calcutta. In the East Indies English merchants met the Dutch, who, although arriving four years later, sent out ten times the number of merchant vessels over the next seven years. Dutch ships were better equipped and needed only one third of the English crew; their charts were the best in the world and they were importing, re-exporting and carrying European trade over all the oceans, with their shipyards building 1000 ships annually. They were engaged in driving the Portuguese out of the Moluccas and out of their valuable trade with Japan and were making themselves the leading naval and trading power in the Eastern Seas. Meanwhile the English were meeting with mixed success. One expedition was massacred in the Red Sea, another was successful with the Moghul Emperor of India, where trade was established and early in the seventeenth century an Englishman obtained a footing in Japan, which, although lost on his death, contributed to the establishment of trading relationships in the area. In 1619 the English and Dutch made good their differences and signed a treaty of friendship, allowing their two East India trading companies to act in concert, but, despite competing successfully with the Portuguese in the Persian Gulf, the English were again out-manoeuvred by the Dutch in the East Indies, where many were murdered, so that withdrawal from the area was seriously considered.

By now in England the glories of the Elizabethan reign had faded into the languid and vacillating laissez faire of the early Stuart period. Sir Walter Raleigh reported the depressed state of the merchant marine, in which there only 10 ships of over 100 tons. Nevertheless, at the Union of Crowns James I brought to England a knowledge of the long tradition of Scottish maritime trade based on her seaport burghs. The chartered companies, including the newly formed Hudson's Bay in Canada, increased their scope at this time and the Merchant Adventurers moved towards a policy of freer trade. But James did not appreciate that to engage in commerce world wide it is necessary to have both merchant and naval ships and with only 27 operational ships in the Navy, many in need of refitting and others laid up with shipkeepers, piracy was on the increase and the English were unable to protect their trade from the Dutch. Elizabeth had opened the English fishing grounds to everyone and the Dutch were also making incursions into the rich Scottish and English fishing grounds, increasing the scope of their salt fish industry. Because of its newly found independence Holland was taking over much of the commerce of Antwerp and the carrying trade of the Hanseatic League, as well as moving into the Mediterranean and the Far East. Amsterdam was also becoming a centre of finance, with the Dutch buying commodities cheap, storing them and selling them at a higher price. It was a veritable 'golden age' and artists, writers, philosophers, scientists and jurists set the stage for Amsterdam to become the Venice of the North. It seemed that everywhere the naval, merchant and fishing fleets of Holland carried all before them. Meanwhile Stuart settlements were replacing Elizabethan exploration and the British were moving westwards to the Americas, where settlers arrived in Virginia in 1607, in Bermuda and in New Plymouth, whither the Pilgrim Fathers sailed in 1621. With the accession of Charles I to the throne this outflow of settlers increased, as did also the precariousness of Britain's maritime situation, with even command of territorial waters successfully challenged. Although Charles re-introduced bounties for shipbuilding and built a few prestige ships, his autocratic rule, imposed without recourse to Parliament, not only drove more emigrés across the Atlantic, but caused the Navies of Britain to fall into further decline. When, in frustration at Parliament's determination to maintain its control over the public purse and the rights of citizens, he imposed a tax of 'Ship money' on the maritime towns to pay for the Navy without recourse to Parliament, and then extended it country wide in 1635, the Civil War was not long in coming.

In its first battles the Navy – Protestant, unpaid and unfed – declared for Parliament and, although later a quarter of the Navy returned to the King and Royalist privateers harried Parliamentary commerce, by 1649 Royalist resistance at sea collapsed. Nevertheless the statutes of the Long Parliament and the Interregnum show the danger to Britain from foreign intervention and the need to provide naval and military defence for her towns. Oliver Cromwell appointed Generals as Commissioners to the Navy, to whom the Admiralty and Navy Board were responsible, but, there being so few warships, he had to rely mainly on Merchant Navy privateers to keep safe the English seas. These privateers, appointed by the Lords Commissioner, were allowed to keep their prizes, except for one tenth of the value, which had to be given to the Admiralty. They also acted with the Navy in defence of convoys and gave protection to fishermen. Once the Civil War was over the Commonwealth government set about rebuilding Britain's trade and her Navy. In order to restore her shattered commerce Parliament protected the manufacture of cloth and passed a new Navigation Act in 1651, which sought to secure British trade for British ships. The Act disallowed more than one re-exportation of goods coming from overseas, even if they came in British ships. This drove a wedge into the Dutch emporium and commodity market, and established the principle of Continuous Voyage, by which the British during the next centuries tried to deprive the Dutch of their valuable neutral carrying trade during wars, when the Dutch claimed a right to disregard blockades. The British insisted that the ultimate destination of the cargo must be considered rather than ports of call. This Navigation Act – which was re-enacted and extended to exports by Charles II when the monarchy was restored in 1660 – was to last for 200 years. It differed from the previous Navigation Acts in a number of important respects and contributed to the causes of three Dutch Wars, which spread into the reign of Charles II. Frequent attempts had been made by the Stuart Kings to enforce previous Acts but these present provisions were more far reaching. No goods from Asia, Africa or America were to be imported into Britain except in British ships and the same rule applied to Europe – with the exception of ships belonging to the country where the goods were grown, produced or manufactured. Salt fish must be imported and exported only in British ships. Even foreign goods brought into the country by British ships had to come only from the country of growth, production or manufacture or from the port to which they were first shipped. An exception was made for Mediterranean goods and for Spanish and Portuguese goods from the Plantations or Dominions, provided they all were shipped in British ships. The coasting trade also was not to be open to strangers.

Meanwhile government coffers were drawn upon to rebuild England's maritime strength. By the end of the Commonwealth and Protectorate half the income of the government had been spent on shipbuilding and the creation of a modern Navy, into which Oliver Cromwell introduced a permanent naval establishment with a father-to-son professional officer class and new Fighting Instructions. The Navigation Act itself might have been sufficient cause for war with Holland, but in addition the Dutch sympathised with Royalist exiles, while the English insisted on the right of search in the Channel and the need for the Dutch to acknowledge the flag. The English had, moreover, an enviable advantage in the Eastern cross trades, for they carried thither cloth to sell, whereas the chief export of the Dutch was still herring, which now had to be transported from Britain in British ships. In the First Dutch War the English Navy fought valiantly, formalising the line of battle ahead and the first clashes exposed Holland's weakness. Her trade was out of proportion to her size and the English set on her slow and cumbersome convoys as they came up the Channel. English ships besieged Amsterdam for a month and brought her close to ruin. The Dutch in defeat agreed to salute the English flag, pay for fishing rights and accept the provisions of the Navigation Act, but Cromwell allowed them to export fish in foreign ships for three years. Cromwell's Puritan faith and support of English traders and colonists then led him into conflict with Spain, during which English naval ships entered the Mediterranean Sea and Blake sacked Santa Cruz, while English troops seized Dunkirk, turning England away from the Elizabethan policy of not becoming offensively involved in wars on the continent.

Charles II's accession ushered in a period of English political manoeuvring among the more powerful continental nations and an expansion of settlements and maritime commerce, the latter of which had suffered during the wars. His Navigation Act confirmed the provisions of the 1651 Act, but went further, laying down that no goods were to be imported or exported into or out of British possessions overseas, except in British ships and with a master and three quarters of the crew British. The same proviso about the nationality of the crew applied to British ships importing American, African or Asian goods. No foreign goods could come into the country in any ship, other than British, unless they came in ships owned by the countries where the goods were grown, produced or manufactured or by the country exporting. Even foreign produce in British ships had to come from the country of origin or from the port where they were first shipped. Like Cromwell, Charles intended to prevent other countries ferrying goods from different places in the world, storing them to increase their value and re-selling them. The coastal trade was again to remain British. Between now and the end of the century there was a progressive drop in cloth exports and an increase in re-exports of one third. This second Navigation Act could not have pleased the Dutch any more than the first and, although England had by now been established as the leading naval power, it was at such ruinous cost that Charles II could not maintain the position. Despite the Restoration Parliament funding the Royal Navy and Charles raising a maritime regiment, there was insufficient investment and much neglect. Ships rotted in port and seamen were unpaid. When, with commercial rivalry continuing overseas, the Second Dutch War broke out the English were initially successful. Although the Dutch had the French as passive allies, New Amsterdam was captured and re-named New York. Then the Plague struck in London, with sailors dying in the streets, followed by the Great Fire, which brought British commercial life to a standstill. The country was virtually bankrupt and fearful lest the French were implicated in some treachery. While the Treaty of Breda was negotiated, the Dutch swooped down on the English coast, attacking ships and ports in the Thames and Medway and sending fire ships into Chatham. Peace terms allowed the English to keep New York, but the Dutch and their German allies were in return to be able to import goods into Britain in their ships and Charles had to accept the Dutch definition of goods liable to seizure in war, thus enabling them to operate their neutral carrying trade to belligerents during hostilities. With the concept of blockade thus virtually ruled out, it did not seem likely that he would accept this position for long.

Charles was on the horns of a dilemma. Parliament favoured Holland and of the potential protagonists France was the most dangerous. Consequently after peace was signed England joined Holland and Sweden in an alliance to contain her. But Charles, who had sold Dunkirk to the French, was beholden to them for brokering his marriage to Catherine of Braganza of Portugal. From her he received in dowry Bombay and Tangier, the latter giving him a naval and trading base in the Mediterranean, until it was abandoned for reasons of economy and because the port was too open. Moreover, Charles had been reared in the Catholic court of Versailles, rich in all the cultural and military arts, to the prestige of which Louis XIV's minister Colbert had added a large and efficient Navy of 120 ships of the line. Smarting under the terms of the Tready of Breda, Charles still considered the Dutch to be England's greatest commercial rivals, while Louis, who had invaded the Low Countries, thought they were out to monopolise world trade. With great duplicity, after promising Louis in a secret treaty of Dover to become a Roman Catholic in return for funds for the Navy and soldiers for a standing army, Charles signed an open treaty of the same name with France to partition Holland, dropping out of the war when revolution restored his kinsman, William of Orange, to power. The Dutch cut their dykes and kept the enemy at bay for six years, before peace was concluded, but Amsterdam's wealth was slowly drained away. In 1677 Charles' niece Mary married William of Orange, creating a bond of friendship between the two countries, and when Charles, in the absence of legitimate children, was succeeded by his Roman Catholic brother James II, the 1689 constitutional revolution deposed James and brought the Protestants William and Mary to the throne. With Britain and Holland thus united for a period of years, London increasingly took over from Amsterdam during the next century as the centre of navigation, commerce and finance.

Although by this time other countries had taken to the sea, Russia (under

Peter the Great), Sweden, Denmark and France, none could rival the seaworthiness and seamanship of the British ships and sailors, nor the growing power of the City of London as a centre of maritime trade. There were, during the eighteenth century, many developments in maritime finance and commerce, which, combined with reforms in the merchant marine and improvements in navigation, contributed to Britain's leading position. In 1689 Lloyd's Coffee House opened in London, moving to Lombard Street in 1691. This was a meeting place of shipowners, shipmasters and merchants, where there were auction sales, shipbroking transactions, exchange of shipping news and marine insurance. An attempt in 1696 to provide regular bulletins of ship movements was initially short lived, but Edward Lloyd supplied his customers with intelligence sent in by shipping correspondents at the ports and a paper called Lloyd's List re-started in 1734. This published the arrival and departure of ships and provided sufficient material for their insurance and subsequent registration. Meanwhile legislation covering sickness, recruiting and pay improved the lot of seamen in the reign of Mary's sister Anne. Disabled merchant seamen entered Greenwich Naval Hospital and in the next century anchored their own hospital ship Grampus (later Dreadnought) off Greenwich. In both Navies the importance of training boys was recognised. The Marine Society was founded in 1756 and boys were recruited from this and other philanthropic organisations. Pepys, who had introduced examinations for promotion into the Royal Navy, had started the practice of sending midshipmen to sea and in Queen Anne's reign, boys, known as apprentices-at-sea, were also bound into the merchant service. Improvements were made in the navigation of ships – lighthouses lit by coal fires had been built on cliffs and rocks in the sixteenth century, but many more now appeared round the coast, together with buoys to mark port entrances. These remained the responsibility of Trinity House, which had supervised navigation since 1563, or of the Commissioners for Northern Lights.

Louis, frustrated by Charles' and James' inability to convert their subjects to Catholicism, viewed with growing anxiety the strength of a united Protestant Britain and Holland. He, therefore, landed James in Ireland to head a Celtic army, with French arms and officers. Ireland fell, with the exception of northern strongholds, placing Britain in greater peril than at the Armada and, although William defeated James at the Battle of the Boyne, these events led to a century of conflict between the two countries, which included landings in Scotland of James' son, the Old Pretender, and of his grandson, the Young Pretender. Britain and France were now to be at war for approximately 60 out of the next 125 years. The British aim was to preserve the Protestant succession and to prevent French hegemony in Europe, her dominance of continental and colonial markets and her control of the Netherlands and Rhine Delta, upon the freedom of which Britain depended for her security and trade. When war broke out to defend the Spanish Netherlands from France, Holland was again vulnerable on land to France and subsequent battles with the dykes cut impoverished her wealthy commerce. The French Navy was larger than the combined fleet of Britain and Holland, but, after initial setbacks, including a French victory off Beachy Head and the landing of invasion forces in Devon,

THE GENIE'S LAMP 13

the Royal Navy seized the initiative, cut Louis' supply lines to Ireland and destroyed much of his fleet in port. The French now had to rely on privateers – like the famous Jean Bart – to harry Allied shipping, which they did so successfully that the Allies had to concentrate forces on convoy protection and set up a board of trade to liaise between merchant shipping and the Admiralty. While the Dutch continued to press their wish to trade freely during the war, the English insisted on a blockade, including that of grain, which the Dutch re-exported, and this had to be partly enforced by privateers and by increased naval presence in the Mediterranean. Dutch losses at sea, combined with the threat to Holland on land, caused increasing trade and wealth to trickle away from Amsterdam to London, where William's ability in strategy and adminis-tration, together with a new feeling of democracy in the nation and the stimu-lation of wealth caused by the founding of the Bank of England, were all attracting capital investment.

On her accession, Queen Anne faced the danger of Louis XIV placing his grandson on the vacant throne of Spain, 'If the French monarchy continues master of the Spanish monarchy, the balance of power in Europe is hopelessly destroyed and he will be able to engross the trade and wealth of the world'. With the French invading the Spanish Netherlands, Marlborough won victories on land, while the Royal Navy was supreme at sea, displaying the same skill and determination as in Elizabethan days, blockading and harrying the enemy coast, and capturing Gibraltar with the Marines. In partnership with the Dutch, the Navy provided over 40 escorts in a compulsory convoy system, with ships carrying such imports as sugar, timber, coffee, tobacco, rice, cotton and silk and exports, which included cloth, coal, wheat and manufactured goods. Escorts were ordered not to chase the enemy out of sight of the convoy, but losses could not be avoided and in the consequent commercial depression in Holland Dutch merchants sought to continue, as far as possible considering their position as belligerents, their neutral carriage of enemy goods in time of war – even to the extent of including arms. By the War of Austrian Succession, which ended with the Peace of Aix-la-Chapelle in 1748, leaving the borders in the New World undetermined, this arangement resulted in two thirds of French trade being carried in neutral ships, so that their merchant marine could virtually remain in port and a blockade could not be maintained. Faced with this impasse at the start of the Seven Years War in 1756 the British drew up the Rules of War at Sea, laying down that neutrals (which the Dutch had become) could only carry trade in war which they carried in peace and that all cargoes in transit to an enemy were liable to seizure, including grain, as was also contraband going anywhere in any ship. The right of search was to be enforced on single ships and those in convoy. With these Rules in force, the British blockade was soon successful. The Dutch, however, had lost trade and foreign currency and were indignant. Attempting to placate everyone, Britain passed an Act of Parliament in 1759, bringing the activities of her own numerous privateers within limits set by the authorities and by the decisions of the Court of Admiralty, as to what was and what was not contraband and legitimate prizes of war.

Although the Seven Years War established Britain in Canada, Senegal, St.

Vincent and Tobago and made her the leading power in the East, its peace left France with a strong Navy. Britain was fortunate to have Lord Anson as First Lord of the Admiralty, for he raised the Royal Navy to a state of great efficiency, and brought the Marines under Admiralty control. Like Drake, he accomplished a round-the-world voyage, ending his accomplishment solo and encouraging others to follow his example in a new age of discovery. In 1764 Captain Byron, a midshipman in Anson's voyage, visited and surveyed the Falkland Islands controlling Cape Horn (the West Islands of which the British settled in 1765) and sailed on round South America to Chile. Four years later Captain Cook, a genius navigator, who buoyed General Wolfe's channel in the St. Lawrence River during the Seven Years War, set out in the Endeavour to discover, 'The existence of a vast southern continent'. Having first charted the coast he landed in New Zealand and sailed on to Botany Bay and New South Wales. On his second voyage he landed again in New Zealand and discovered the Pacific Islands, but on his third expedition to discover a North West Passage through the ice starting from the Canadian side, he was killed by islanders in Hawaii. Information from these voyages gave Britain a lead in chart making, collection of data, nautical surveying and methods of calculating longitude. In 1795 the first hydrographer was appointed to the Royal Navy by the Admiralty, responsible for the production of charts, nautical almanacs, and timetables of tides and races. which were to provide the best coverage of the world's oceans in the centuries to come.

Despite these long voyages undertaken by naval and merchant vessels and the extent of Britain's peacetime commerce and carrying trade, which doubled in the first half of the eighteenth century, the ships were small and her Merchant Navy only rose to 2½ million net tons by 1814, by when she was importing raw materials and grain. The 100 or so ships of the East India Company were the largest, rising from 600 tons in 1640 to 1000 tons in 1787. They could be employed as men of war, the status of their officers being comparable to those of the Royal Navy. In other areas ships ranged from between 200 and 250 tons, rising to 500 tons in the Atlantic and Baltic by the end of the century. In the West Indies there were 700 ships; Canada had 600; there were 800 engaged in the Baltic trade; 400 in Spanish waters and 200 in the Mediterranean. Whalers were employed in the Arctic, South Atlantic and South Pacific and deep water fishing vessels in the Newfoundland cod industry, while large numbers of small inshore vessels fished nearer home. The British coastal trade was also extensive – Newcastle alone, which had an extensive coal trade to London and elsewhere, had 500 ships of 200 tons. In 1760 the Lloyd's Register Society was founded to help marine underwriters assess the maritime risks they were asked to insure. The first Register of Shipping was published in 1764 and it clearly indicated the condition of ships by grading them A, I, E, O, U – A being the best and U the worst. Equipment, masts and rigging were later graded by numbers, hence the term A1 which first appeared in 1775. In addition to this in 1786 a Navigation Act was passed by which all vessels over 15 tons had to be registered on the official British Register. Types of ships included barques, brigs, brigantines, schooners, ketches, luggers and doggers. During wars Lloyd's was influential in getting the Convoy Acts passed and Lloyd's List furnished the Admiralty with news of victory or defeat and recorded the loss of ships. Members of Lloyd's also undertook marine insurance, but this part of the organisation – Lloyd's Underwriters – formed a rival establishment in 1769 in Pope's Head Alley and moved five years later into the Royal Exchange. Although, after the crash of the South Sea Company in 1720 Parliament had passed a Bubble Act, granting charters to only two assurance companies, Lloyd's, being simply a group of individuals, who pledged the whole of their private estate as security, was expressly not prohibited by this legislation and members continued to insure clients. Also starting as a coffee house in London in the eighteenth century was the Baltic Exchange, through which ships were chartered or bought and cargoes were placed. Originally known as the Virginia and Maryland this coffee house changed its name to the Virginia and Baltic in 1774 and then to the Baltic Coffee House, when its first rules were written – much of its trade at that time being concerned with tallow from the Baltic.

In the eleven years of peace between the end of the Seven Years War in 1763 and the start of the American War of Independence, during which France, Spain and Holland joined forces with America, the Navy was run down by Lord North who believed it a luxury. Nevertheless, the figure is given of 58 ships of the line and 198 frigates at the start of the war. Most RN sailors in times of conflict came from the merchant marine and between 1774 and the end of the war naval personnel increased four times, while from the start to the end of the French Revolutionary and Napoleonic Wars there was an increase of more than five. Because of the unpopularity of blockades, which brought shortages to other countries as well as to the belligerents, neutral opinion was by now not working on Britain's side and she found herself in great danger with neutral states forming the League of Armed Neutrality, insisting on trans- porting all goods anywhere in time of war and even indulging in the coastal trade of blockaded nations. Since one third of British ships were colonial built, the Navy Board had to charter 300 merchant vessels and rebel naval strength was considerable. Their ships were operated by expert privateers, of whom the most famous was John Paul Jones, the father of the US Navy. No sooner had Britain conceded independence to the rebellious colonies, than France's support for the American upheavals backfired upon the House of Bourbon and turned the French system of government on its head. The Revolution of 1789, with its terrible excesses, was answered with attempts by other European states to quell it – in which Britain did not join – but French fears of foreign interfer- ence provoked them into invasions of the Rhineland, the Netherlands and Savoy, with offers of assistance to revolutionaries. This was a challenge to Britain's security, but, although a British expeditionary force landed on the continent, it was driven from the Netherlands and the French were victorious in Holland and Italy, with Napoleon, 'The sword of the revolution', setting out on his conquest of Egypt, in which he was foiled by Nelson at the Battle of the Nile. The coalition formed to curb Napoleon's onslaught melted away, and Britain was left, after Austria's defeat, to face his might alone, imposing another unpopular blockade, met again by the League of Armed Neutrality composed of her erstwhile friends. They insisted that only arms should be subject to embargo at sea, but the Younger Pitt repudiated this and said, 'Anything giving succour to the enemy'. With Spain joining forces with France and Napoleon vowing he would close every port to the British, the war on trade at sea escalated and, with three quarters of the French officers executed in the revolution, Napoleon had to rely on privateers to man his ships. Britain's answer to this threat was threefold. First, she set up a Prize Court in 1789 to inject justice into decisions regarding blockade, contraband, joint capture and Continuous Voyage – the British arguing that a ship must come only to the place of import, while neutral nations, led by the Danes and the Dutch (who had become French satellites), maintained they could make calls on neutral or belligerent ports. Second, Parker and Nelson were sent to Copenhagen where they destroyed the Danish fleet in 1801 and forced them to come to terms. Third, Britain again made convoys obligatory by passing further Convoy Acts.

A shaky peace intervened, but in 1803 war resumed, with Britain once more alone while the continent accepted France's recent conquests. Napoleon was crowned by the Pope as Emperor of the French, with members of his family appointed rulers in many capitals and the Electors of the German states transformed into Princes in the Confederation of the Rhine. An armada assembled to transport his army over the Channel, but the Royal Navy barred its way and after defeat at Trafalgar plans for invasion were dropped. Helped by the Danes and Norwegians, the French harried British shipping with their privateers, and the British, who also employed privateers operating under Letters of Marque, imposed an ever tightening cordon of blockade, denying the continent produce from West and East. Nevertheless, ships were not sunk at sight and there were no barbarities, and, while thousands of British merchantmen were captured by the French, British yards built so quickly that by the end of the war the merchant marine was larger than at the beginning. In 1806 Napoleon enforced his Continental Blockade with soldiers in the ports, but the British found other overseas markets and, having seized Heligoland, smuggled in goods both there and through Schleswig-Holstein, so that their exports actually increased. Meanwhile, with their own people short of bread, the British imposed more stringent rights of search and seizure under Orders in Council and the Navy set out again for Denmark, where they forced the Danish fleet to surrender lest it fall into the hands of France. By 1807 almost every nation on the continent was either defeated or cowed, or as in the case of Russia in alliance, and Britain, because of her insistence on rights of search for deserters and contraband, was being led into conflict with the Americans, who were developing a lucrative carrying trade and fitting out French ships in their yards. On June 18th 1812, one week before Napoleon set out on his disastrous march to Moscow to punish the Czar for abandoning his Continental Blockade, America entered the war against Great Britain, employing not only her Navy, but launching three military attacks on Canada. By the time Napoleon was defeated at Waterloo Britain had therefore acquired a new rival at sea. It is also claimed that she had lost friends in Germany, for Napoleon had undermined the cohesion of the German States and, although Prussia had been an ally at the end, she had also intermittently favoured France. Now, having been given, at Castlereagh's request at the Congress of Vienna, the Western Rhinelands, on the borders of Holland, containing vast mineral resources to act as a counter poise to French power, Prussia saw her opportunity to consolidate the German states under her suzerainty by means of a pincer movement and a customs union. Meanwhile, the German states, having endured the privations caused by the French and British blockades, saw France restored and allowed to keep Alsace. Both these outcomes were a recipe for future conflict.

Jealousy now crept into Britain's relations with Europe and America, who felt that she had expanded her own trade and inhibited theirs. Triumphant at sea and possessing a chain of islands with which to protect her trade and merchant shipping she was imposing the Pax Britannica. More states began to look with suspicion upon the British Navigation Laws, feeling that it was this protection that had made her rich. They did not consider her sole stand against Napoleon, from which they had benefited, her strength at sea, her mineral resources, the skill of her people, her industrial lead and her political stability. From 1815 until 1830 the relationship between Britain and America continued to be under strain. Although trade was opening up between the Americans and Canada, the USA gave more privileges to Spanish and Portuguese ships than to British. Each country wanted to retain its own trade, while being let into the trade of the other. In 1817 the Americans passed Navigation Laws, excluding foreign ships from their ports, in retaliation for the British Navigation Laws, and the West Indies became a battleground for this trade rivalry. In 1830 the British allowed the Americans to export and import goods in their ships to and from British ports and a degree of harmony returned, but, when American shipping began to increase at a faster rate than British, questions were asked in Parliament as to why the British mercantile marine was slipping behind. 'The character of British merchant shipping has declined – that of foreign shipping has improved' ran a comment replying to a Foreign Office circular of July 1st 1843. America had splendid harbours, good seamen and better education for her mariners. Why should not British mariners have proper qualifications and a knowledge of stowage and cargo, of exchange and other commercial matters? In 1847 a proposal was made to establish a Board of Commercial Marine within the Board of Trade and Palmerston ordered a Commission to inquire into British shipping. Under the influence of Adam Smith's laissez faire policy as set out in the Wealth of Nations, the politicians were moving towards Repeal of the Corn and Navigation Laws, disregarding his warning about the importance of the latter to the defence of Britain.

For the first time since the Tudors, and indeed since the initial attempt at protection of Richard II's day, the British merchant marine was to be left without a shield against foreign competition. It was argued that, once free trade was established by the Repeal of the Corn Laws allowing imports of corn to flow into the country unrestricted by tariffs, it was inevitable that shipping would follow. But the one does not necessarily follow the other. Imperial Preference

of the 1930's and the EC common agricultural policy are examples of protectionism, yet the carriage of British goods has been free for a century and a half.
Conversely, if British shipping were to be restricted it would not follow that
the goods carried would have tariffs. Certainly the early trading 'regulated'
companies, such as the Merchant Adventurers, trading in Holland and North
Germany, or the Eastlands company trading in the Baltic were protectionist at
a time when British goods were mainly carried in British bottoms. Although
the Merchant Adventurers were free to trade as individuals and were democratic in their election of officers, they were restrictive in commercial practices
and monopolistic in trading areas, regarding commerce as an exclusive profession and accepting entrance by patrimony, apprenticeship and fee. Also
monopolistic were the joint stock companies, such as the East India, Hudson's
Bay and South Sea, in which merchants raised capital, took shares and traded
in the company's name. The East India and South Sea companies even gave
loans to the government in return for exclusive trading rights, the former not
giving them up until 1833, the latter collapsing in the South Sea 'Bubble'
because of lack of commercial opportunities. But the common factor in all
their practices was that trade was protected by price and availability of goods
and by restrictions on shipping. Ships sailed in convoy not only to protect them
from pirates, but also to limit the goods carried and so regulate trade.

Because of this link between protectionism of trade and shipping, it was
perhaps understandable that a number of Members of Parliament in 1848
thought the one followed the other and that the internationalisation of shipping
would lessen the risk of conflict at sea. Shippers, shipowners and shipbuilders
on the other hand argued that protection of shipping had been in place before
the formation of mercantile companies and that by repealing the Navigation
Laws with the Corn Laws Britain would be starting on a voyage into unchar-
tered waters, with foreign countries and the Excise and Customs as the only
beneficiaries (smuggling to avoid tariffs had become a lucrative way of life for
many aiming at respectability and wealth). They argued that throwing open all
British shipping unilaterally was a radical act of faith with unknown outcome,
neither wise nor justified by facts. With the hindsight of history, it stands to
reason that a nation which offers some protection to its shipping will enjoy the
benefits of a larger Merchant Navy than one that does not. Although it is true
that when British shipping was thrown open to the world her Merchant Navy
increased in size, two factors should be borne in mind: first, that the British
Empire then straddled the globe and second, that, starting in the days of John
Cabot, British ships had not only carried their own goods but the goods of
other nations. The carrying trade is like a genie's magic lamp or a ring in a
fable — it brings wealth, influence and prestige to whoever holds or wears it.
For centuries, in common with other states, Britain had protected her shipping
from foreign competition and hostile navies, but now, believing that she had
more than her fair share of the world's markets, she gave the right to ship her
goods and those of her Empire to other nations to make of it what they would.
The next chapter tells the story of how and why she opened her carrying trade
to others — the rest of the book records what they made of it.

CHAPTER II

'THE DAY OF DUPES'
REPEAL OF THE NAVIGATION LAWS

The Repeal of the Navigation Laws has been overshadowed by the question of free trade and the Repeal of the Corn Laws. In 1846 Sir Robert Peel's Conservative Party, reacting to the distress in Ireland and to the pressure for free trade (coming primarily from Manchester with its German immigrant cotton workers and to a lesser extent from Birmingham), introduced a Bill into the House of Commons, which relinquished duties on corn and a number of raw materials and reduced tariffs on others. Thus the Act was in place in time to bring cheap food to British workers, before they were subjected to the revolutionary pressures sweeping through Europe in 1848. Although the Bill passed its first two readings, this attack on the landed aristocracy and agricultural interests of Britain cost Peel the leadership of the Party, which split into two wings. The government fell. The Whigs (or Liberals) came in under the premiership of Lord John Russell, who steered the Bill through its final reading. The following year the Liberal government, having suspended the Navigation Laws, set in motion legislation for their Repeal.

The move caused considerable commercial panic. Regulations governing British shipping were complicated, altered piecemeal for many years. Internal shipping – coastal and Empire – was in British hands, with only one quarter of the crews in the Empire trade allowed to be foreign, while India – not being a colony – was excluded from such restrictions. Exports from Britain could be carried by foreign shipping, but imports into Britain or the Empire were restricted to British ships or ships of the producer or of those nations enjoying rights under reciprocal treaties. This meant that no produce of Asia, Africa or America could be imported into Britain via Europe. In the years leading up to 1847 reciprocal treaties increased in number and complexity, with alterations waiving restrictions being made by Orders in Council. Countries enjoying degrees of exemption included America, Prussia, Russia, Denmark, France, Sweden, Norway, Mexico, a number of German states, such as Hanover, and the Hanseatic Republic of Lübeck, Bremen and Hamburg. There were many anomalies: Russian corn could come to Britain in Russian ships, but not if first landed in Prussia; a consignment of cotton shipped to Le Havre, but not wanted for sale there, because of political upheavals in France, could not, it seemed, be shipped to Britain. Voices raised at home for Repeal were the same as those for free trade, while the foreign clamour was led by Prussia and America.

British shipowners answered calls for Repeal by saying they would have to invest in foreign ships and crews and build ships in Danzig to cut costs. This would bring decline to British shipping and shipbuilding, affecting the Royal Navy. Meanwhile, with warehouse fees cheaper abroad, merchants would have to store goods there as well, spelling commercial disaster. By 1847 the Americans were promising reciprocity if the Laws were repealed, a promise they had little intention of honouring. Press reports spoke of the commercial treaty made by the Americans with Hanover and soon to be made with the Rhine Provinces, which – perhaps recalling the dangers of the recent US alliance with Napoleon – may, 'Have been in no small degree instrumental in disposing the British Government to this wise measure'. Not everyone saw the matter in this sanguine light. It was pointed out that every nation protects its shipping by inserting insidious clauses into its legislation and treaties. Indeed, 'It has been through the operation of our navigation system entirely that the maritime power of this country has been raised to its present height, that the country has been defended and all the evils, which would have resulted from its being made the theatre of war, have been providentially averted'. The government prevaricated. In March 1847 it stated it was not in favour of Repeal; yet, in answer to a parliamentary question, it appointed a Commons Committee, which, taking evidence from 25 witnesses in favour and 9 against, was naturally charged with imbalance. Its work was not finished when the House rose and its evidence not properly presented. The matter seemed shrouded in secrecy and in the summer a US press report took the British public by surprise, 'This will be the greatest stride yet taken by free trade and it is not to be doubted that all Europe will follow the example of Great Britain. Repeal by Great Britain of the laws restricting the trade of the USA with her colonies will be far more beneficial to this country than any commercial treaty ever made by our government'. There were many in Britain who agreed that the USA would be the greatest beneficiary from Repeal. During the 1830's there had been serious problems of violence from US freebooters and revolutionary radicals along the border of Ontario during the rebellions in Upper and Lower Canada and in the West of Canada the Oregon Dispute had only recently been settled, so that good relations with the USA were of paramount importance.

In November 1847 the government stated in the Speech from the Throne that Her Majesty's Government, 'Recommends to the consideration of Parliament the laws which regulate the Navigation of the UK with a view to ascertain whether any changes can be adopted'. The House of Lords reacted at once and in February 1848 appointed its own Committee to take evidence. Lord Hardwicke attacked the whole idea of Repeal, 'If we let the US into our colonial trade we will be ruined.' In prophetic language he warned the Peers that if British trade and shipping were opened up to foreign competition, 'You must consent to give up the building, fitting and equipment of ships'. Shipowners would have to be permitted to go to cheaper foreign yards and consequently UK merchant yards would be reduced in number and efficiency. The government would also be bound to admit foreign seamen, 'Their lordships should remember that the military and commercial navy of this country are one and the same, that the mercantile navy is the marine militia of the state'. Lord Ellenborough speaking for the government struck a sombre and familiar note. The government, he said, intended to legislate whatever the findings of the Committee.

Britain's maritime supremacy, so high in every nation's regard after the defeat of Napoleon, had now been affected not only by envy, but by doubts about her recent acquisitions in the Far East and resentment at her long drawn out naval enforcement of the abolition of the slave trade, which brought her great unpopularity. The name of William Wilberforce and the date of the abolition of slavery in the Empire are known – what is less known is that the nefarious trade continued for many decades afterwards, in spite of Britain policing the seas round the west coast of Africa to prevent blockade running and to free imprisoned Africans. Debates in Parliament in 1846 show concern at the loss of British lives, both in sporadic fights and by tropical disease – one ship losing 110 out of a crew of 160 in six months. It was also a costly business. Pleas were made in Parliament by men dedicated to stopping the slave trade, who nevertheless pointed out that Britain was suffering many casualties and great expense, as well as grave unpopularity among a number of states. The USA was giving her every assistance and France and the Netherlands were moving towards support, but some states were almost hostile. 'Our humanity', said Lord George Bentinck, 'is very dearly bought'. He told Parliament that traders were battening down hatches to escape observation during search, so that hundreds of Africans were dying on the voyage and the number reaching their destination – 60,000 to Brazil alone in one year – in no way represented the number that set out. Blockade-running ships, operated by individuals of many nationalities including the British, who had once been leading players in the trade, were being designed and built in a number of countries.

It was against this background of international resentment, jealousy and criticism, in a clamour whipped up by the revolutionary unrest sweeping the continent in 1848, that the government, backed by a petition from 297 people in the City of London, signed by the Governor of the Bank of England and his Deputy, proposed the Repeal of the Navigation Laws to the House of Commons. The aim of some Members was a hoped for increase in wealth. The motive of others was pure unselfish philanthropy. In March 1848 almost every capital of Europe and every German state was in turmoil. The uprisings were led by two separate factions: middle class liberals, seeking democratic government through new assemblies and parliaments, and radical revolutionaries, spurred on by Communists and calling for improved conditions for workers. Britain had escaped revolution, and so, disregarding the part played in preventing it by intellectuals and lawyers, who had anticipated the Chartist Movement and brought enlightenment and education to the masses, these Members felt, as foreign nations did, that she must make concessions, because she was an old and wealthy country with colonies and world wide trading interests. In the pages of Hansard the characters come to life, bringing home to the reader the maxim, 'Plus ça change, toujour la meme chose'. It is there, in the Chamber of the House of Commons, that the story unfolds.

The Conservatives condemned the Bill outright and, after the formality of the first reading, Mr. Herries, for the Opposition, moved a resolution on May 29th 1848, 'To maintain the Navigation Laws subject to any modification, which could obviate inconvenience, without endangering Britain's national strength'. He stated that, although British shipping would lose all protection by Repeal, shipowners were still to be subjected to the same onerous provisions and burdens as under existing UK. legislation, placing them at a disadvantage with 'unqualified competition'. 'Who gave Prussia', he asked, 'a just claim – or any claim at all – to insist upon our making so enormous a concession as is involved in the total repeal of our Navigation Laws?'. Prussia already had the greater advantage under her present reciprocal treaties with Britain and between the two countries there was a great trade imbalance; Prussia was the least liberal nation in the intercourse of trade and British manufactures were almost excluded; her exports to Britain were lumped in with Germany's, but together they exported to Britain a figure, 'Greater by an enormous amount' than Britain exported to Prussia. What right had she to threaten Britain and why should she be listened to, for these threats could not affect Britain in the same measure as the Repeal of the Navigation Laws? The USA had never made threats, but she, 'Never made any proposition to any other country, without having previously ascertained that she would herself be a gainer by it'. He reminded the House that US promises to open her colonial trade if Britain would open hers were valueless, because, 'The US has no colonial trade'. He quoted Mr. Huskisson, a free trader, as saying that, 'The British commercial marine is the foundation of our naval supremacy', and Adam Smith, another free trader, who said, 'The authority of Britain depends on her maritime authority. Strip her of that and she would be a third or fourth rate power'.

For the government Mr. Labouchere, President of the Board of Trade, said the measure was necessary not only for the general and commercial benefit of Britain and for her military greatness, but because the colonies, deprived of protection in British markets by the Repeal of the Corn Laws, were finding the Navigation Laws an increasing burden. He claimed that British shipping in the previous two decades had grown faster than that of America; Prussia, he said, had promised that after Repeal she would enter into trade with Britain on equal terms and he believed her. He was confident the new measures would enable Britain to compete on favourable terms with other countries – particularly in trade with the Far East. It was inconceivable that, 'This country, with its seafaring population, its abundant harbours, the genius of its people, long inured to navigation and commerce, and its expanding trade, could dwindle away from the maritime greatness it had hitherto maintained'. Turning to ship-building, he said that if Britain could not compete with other nations in that industry, there was no field in which she could compete with them. He made the proviso, however, that all these hopes depended on, 'Tranquillity at home and abroad'. Tranquillity abroad was, of course, in the succeeding century, the one thing that Britain was denied. A number of back benchers supported the government, pointing out that goods would be cheaper if freight costs were cut and expressing little sympathy with the shipowners, 'With British superfluity of capital, low interest rates and colonial possessions, if they could not compete they were not up to much'. Others expressed grave anxiety, 'If Britain could not compete with US shipping now in China (tea for London was carried in American ships) how could she do better with protection gone?' Prussia had made no concessions to the British, and since a reciprocal treaty had been signed between them her tonnage of trade with Britain had doubled, whereas

Britain had seen hers halved. 'The very nations who are taking our carrying trade away are those who rejected our manufactures in order to establish their own'. Moreover, Britain would have to maintain a much larger Navy now that its links with the merchant marine were to be broken.

Mr. Gladstone gave his support to the measure and said he was ready to consider extensive change, 'The more free and unrestricted the application of competition the better will trade be conducted'. Since Prussia was a first class commercial power, Britain should trust and trade with her. At the moment British ships could go to Prussian ports, but Prussian ships could only enter UK ports if they came from Prussia. Britain should act on the foreign desire for Repeal and free the colonies from restrictions before they also complained. Australia should choose her own freight and not have exports of wool tied to British ships. If Cuban sugar came to Britain in US ships, then why not Jamaican sugar as well? Since shipowners had benefited from recent increases in trade, shipping should now be opened up to further competition. The invention of steam placed Britain at an advantage and, when it came to defence, Repeal of the Navigation Laws would act as a, 'Benign contagion' and would, 'Much strengthen the bonds of amity which unite different countries and diminish the frequency of wars'. Mr. Gladstone died without seeing his forecast proved so tragically wrong. He believed that Repeal would lead to an increase in British commerce and navigation; he was not afraid of 'cheapness' in competitors, but rather of those countries which had 'Capital, enterprise, industry and intelligence', in any of which Britain could beat all comers. Stating that, 'In fair and just competition the British would never be left behind', he warned that the, 'Shipowner must not be made to fight with one hand tied behind his back'. He listed what he saw as 'needless fetters': impressment into the Navy, the number of apprentices the shipowner had to carry, high charges for lights and pilots, discouragement from building abroad, import duties on timber for ships built in the UK and the need for the shipowner to man them with a three quarters British crew. With prophetic accuracy, he stated, 'If you continue legal restrictions of that kind he will not register his ship as a British ship'. Turning to the situation of British seamen, he pointed out that not only was he subject to competition from apprentices, but was liable for service in the Navy, and, although he must contribute from his small wage to the Merchant Seaman Fund, he received a tiny pension and was left little more than a pauper. Drawing attention to high freight insurance on British ships, he called for swift, careful carriage of cargoes in order to reduce it and for reductions in foreign customs duties, which should be evenly levied on all shipowners. Although he looked forward with 'ardent hope' to other nations following the British lead and saw no dangers to British interests from Repeal because, 'They were too extended to be damaged', he, nevertheless, accused other countries of, 'Selfish and narrow views', and hoped they would reciprocate and open their trade. He did not favour government proposals to reserve the right to retaliate by Orders in Council if they failed to do so. He saw no contradiction in his own preference for treaties of reciprocity, while at the same time being prepared to go forward unilaterally (even as regards the coasting trade) if that was what the government wanted. He relied on the pious hope that, having done the right thing themselves, the British would be given equally generous terms by others. Reassuring himself of the advantages Britain possessed as an island, he pledged support for the Bill.

When the debate resumed, Lord George Bentinck spoke for the Opposition. He had become Leader of the break-a-way Protectionist Tory Party in the Commons, which, having toppled Peel, then reabsorbed the mainstream Tory members. He had retired in December 1847, having handed over the leadership of the Party to Mr. Disraeli. He was the champion of the mariners of Britain, by whom he was beloved, and his contribution to the debate was prophetic. It is worth, therefore, departing for a moment from the Chamber to sketch the character of this man, who believed so passionately in British maritime interests. He was one of the most colourful Members, who ever sat in the House of Commons. 'During three years (of his leadership) under circumstances of great difficulty', wrote Disraeli in his biography, 'he displayed some of the highest qualities of political life'. He had good looks, intelligence, courage and capacity for detail, combined with quick apprehension, clear judgement, energy, perseverance, love of truth and lack of personal vanity and ambition. He was the only leader of the Tory Party to have his biography written by his trainer and his family said they never could remember whether he gave up racing for politics or politics for racing, his early death depriving him of any enjoyment from the second change. Horses were his great love and when young he rose at dawn, took the train to Andover to hunt, returning to the House, 'Still in top boots, with a great coat flung over his scarlet hunting coat'. Disraeli said, 'He regarded the House as a club, yet possessed a great and peculiar influence over it'. He took the same concerned interest in the well-being of his horses and the racing public as he took in the future of British mariners. He owned a stud of 200, inventing the first horse box, pulled by dray horses, to end the tiring walk between fixtures. He was a renowned turf reformer, establishing proper starting arrangements by imposing fines on unpunctual Clerks of the Course and ill-disciplined jockeys. He introduced saddling enclosures and the cantering of properly numbered horses before the stands, which he provided for the public's safety and enjoyment. He tried to eradicate fraud, by weighing-in jockeys and ending the custom of winning owners rewarding judges. The Goodwood course was made at his instigation and he helped to plan the new Derby course in better view of the stands, moving a motion to adjourn Parliament for Derby day in 1848. In order to fit these activities into his Parliamentary duties he worked 16 hours a day. Suddenly, at the age of 44, he saw the Tory Party being taken down the radical road of Peelism. The Protectionist wing of the Party had been prepared to support Peel's policy until they realised that the abolition and reduction of tariffs were permanent. Then the 'Army' abandoned its 'Emperor' and Lord George flung himself into, 'Rallying the broken and dispirited forces of a betrayed and insulted party'. He accepted leadership only, 'Until someone more suitable could be found', making it a condition of acceptance that he would vote on matters of religion according to his conscience. He sold his stud of race horses in order to devote money and energy to, 'The commercial, maritime and defence interests of his country', rightly anticipating that the Repeal of the Navigation Laws would follow within two years.

Lord George opened by defending British shippers and seamen from charges of carelessness and bad character, which government speakers said prevented them from obtaining freight. The American ships, which obtained freight from Rio on the date mentioned, were, 'For the African coast slavers no doubt...Americans have means of obtaining freights which are not consistent with the honour and morality of Englishmen. ... Good gracious. Are we to condemn the seamen of England, because they have not French manners, because they do not possess the grace of the Italians!' As for the government's claim that the recent increase in British tonnage had surpassed that of the USA, he showed how the two sets of figures had been calculated upon different measurements – one new, one old. If measured by the same formula US shipping had increased by 58 percent, compared with a British figure of 24 percent. The government claimed that Britain had nothing to fear from US rivalry in her colonies, but already, with inter-colonial trade partly thrown open, the US in 1846 carried five times the West Indian freight carried by British ships and eight times the freight carried by foreign shipping in the Spanish colonies. 'When therefore America proposes to foreign states to divide with them their colonial trade we can judge well which party will get the larger share'. Jamaica now realised that, as the result of Repeal, cheaper slave-grown Cuban sugar, finding its way into the UK, would deprive West Indians of any benefit from cheaper freight.

Lord George derided the City of London petition, which claimed the Navigation Laws were the only impediment to international trade, preventing export of cotton from India and transferring its culture to the USA and Brazil. Surely they were over-hopeful when they said that after Repeal more loans would be given to British merchants than to foreigners and there would be more money for social projects and the prevention of crime. Indeed, it was more likely that 'numberless operatives' in the cotton industry, 'Would be transported. Nay, deported' overseas, to escape unemployment. Mr. Gladstone, said Lord George, was ambiguous – the broad brush in favour of Repeal, the detail for the status quo. Referring to the lack of reciprocity to the Repeal of the Corn Laws – he asked why nations should be more generous now in response to this second unilateral action. He challenged Mr. Gladstone's claim that the British lead in steam vessels would lessen competition, for in 1847 seagoing steamers launched in New York exceeded total UK tonnage in that year. Likewise Board of Trade figures used to prove that British unprotected trade had increased more than protected trade were gross errors; the same ships had been counted twice and coastal and overseas trade confused. 'Why not take the steam boats from London to Margate equally with the steamboats from Dover to Calais?' It was the, 'Iron hand of unqualified competition', which some Members advocated, that, 'Ground down wages and turned men into paupers. 'It is protecting duties that raise the price of the produce and the price of produce creates competition in labour, which raises the wages of labour. Remove the protection and it leads to diminution of wages of labour'. Lord George put his finger on a fundamental economic truth – citizens can have cheap bread or high wages, but they cannot ever have both.

He asked why, if Repeal of the Corn Laws had brought lower wages, the government should be making more Repeals without reciprocity, 'Are we to drive the sailors of this country to seek protection in a foreign country and under a foreign flag? The country that protects them and the flag that flies over them will become their country and flag and they will not be likely to come back in time of war to fight the battles of a country that neglected them in time of peace...In the same way we shall lose our shipwrights...Is it a time to discourage those classes – when thrones are tottering, when empires are dissolved, when the whole of the continent of Europe is in commotion? For whose good is it? For the good of the foreigner?' It was claimed that the British Navigation Laws were preventing change in the commercial policies of Prussia and the German states and that their removal would bring about, 'A reduction in the tariffs which press most heavily on British produce'. But 'Germany had already got all she wanted in the Repeal of the Corn Laws, without giving anything in return', and the answer of Prussia and the German League had been to raise duties on British iron and steel. He made a comparison with 1842 when, under a similar Prussian threat, Lord Aberdeen wrote that the British Government, 'Would learn with deep regret of the intention of Prussia to adopt measures so opposite to the enlightened principles which she has constantly professed. If (British) endeavours meet with no reciprocity and only lead to increased restrictions it may be necessary for the British Government to have recourse to retaliatory measures'. (At this time, Britain was re-negotiating reciprocal treaties with Hanover and the German maritime states, which had set up their own maritime customs union to prevent being sucked into Prussia's Zollverein (or economic union), the ultimate aim of which was political domination from Berlin). Lord George asked why in 1842 Britain took care of her national interests, whereas now the government said, 'If Prussia threatens, we must give in for fear of the consequences.. Now that she (Prussia) has invaded territories, which by treaty England is bound to defend, is this the time for England to cringe and crouch to her dictates?' (He referred to Schleswig-Holstein and Denmark, the invasion of which had upset the newly constituted Frankfurt Parliament* and the Four Treaty Powers). Acknowledging the rising greatness of the USA, he pointed out that she already had a large share of British colonial trade, for which she had given nothing in return. America would not let Britain into her extensive coastal trade, whereas Repeal would extensively damage British shipping and fishing interests. The British should ask the USA to give them as many free imports as they were giving her, before they gave away free trade with their colonies. The same argument applied to the US virtual monopoly with Cuba, whence the British had to go in ballast if they wished to bring home sugar. What

* This was an elected body, whose constitution had been drawn up by a self appointed Committee meeting in Heidelberg, Germany. [A Companion to German Studies A. Ramrn, Methuen, London 1972 Chapter 4 Making of Modern Germany 1618-1870.]

chance, he asked, would England have in the carrying trade there? 'None whatever'.

It was said that one of the reasons for Lord George's early death was that he never took food during the day before making a speech because it would sap his oratory. The result was a pent up energy breaking into the climax of his speech with a shaft of light, a style followed by Disraeli in the years ahead. Speaking with eloquence of the 'Mariners of England', he accused the Manchester School of claiming that, 'The trade of this country is not indebted to shipping for her manufactures'. 'But', said Lord George, 'manufactures and commerce are so closely bound up together that neither can flourish unless the other prospers'. In the course of the whole debate he had not heard one argument about the fate of the quarter of a million British seamen and their wives and families. 'I think, Sir, that now is the time above all others when we should foster the commercial marine of England. Not because I am one of those who thinks that the Repeal of the Navigation Laws would for the purposes of tomorrow strip our mercantile navy of all its power and utility in manning the RN but because I am of the opinion that the effect in a few years would be to diminish that mercantile navy, which has always been and must continue to be the chief support of the Royal Marine'. Two fifths of the RN came from the merchant marine and he asked the House whether it would want to increase the Naval Estimates to provide the 40,000 extra men who would be required to fill the gap. 'Not that I am one who fears for this country. I have as much confidence in the vigour, energy and gallantry of her defenders as any other man, and when the struggle comes I will not believe that they ever will be found wanting; but if we are not to be found wanting for the struggle we must be found prepared for the emergency. The great security for peace is great providence for war and the greatest providence for that, with our insular position and our extended colonies is and ever must be, the strength and attachment of our seamen to their native country; but if the iron hand of competition is to be put upon them and they are to be ground down to cheaper wages, if they are to be driven from their homes to seek asylum in foreign countries, then indeed shall I fear for my country. "England never did nor never shall, Lie at the proud foot of a conqueror, But when it first did help to wound itself'. But if we discourage and dishearten our seamen – injure them in their pockets, wound them in their feelings, and show them that in time of peace we are indifferent and careless of them – shall we be able to press them into our service in the day of difficulty and danger? I fear not, Sir; but let us cherish our brave seamen; show them that alike in peace and in war we will provide for them; that we scorn to weigh in the balance with the comforts, prosperity and happiness of our gallant defenders the miserable saving of 2/6p a ton upon our shipping and the one eighteenth part of a farthing per pound on our sugar and coffee, and then we may again as heretofore boldly challenge and safely defy all the nations of the earth:-

'Come then ye nations,
Shroud old Ocean with your hostile sails;
By her own sons, defended and beloved,

England shall stand unshaken and secure,
And only fall when time itself expires'.

When Lord George died at Welbeck just over two months later 'From nine till eleven o'clock on the day his death was announced all the British shipping in the docks and the river from London Bridge to Gravesend hoisted their flags half mast high and minute guns were fired from appointed stations along the Thames. The same mournful ceremony was observed in all the ports of England and Ireland, and not only in these, for the flag was half mast high on every ship at Antwerp, at Rotterdam, at Le Havre', and at Cherbourg and Bordeaux. He had been last seen alive leaning against a gate on the way to a friend's house, within sight and call of estate workers, who thought he was reading and did not wish to disturb him. He had been taken ill and, in keeping with his courage and independent spirit, did not ask for help, but relied on his own powers of recovery. He was found after dark too late to save him. He had, for the past year, spoken of premonitions of death and had sought a suitable candidate to whom to hand on the leadership of the party, but no one wanted the task, 'Nothing but pinching adversity', he wrote to a friend, 'will bring such men to a proper sense of duty'. Towards the end of 1847 the Roman Catholic Irish Bill and the Bill for Jewish Disabilities came up in the Commons and, as he had forewarned, Lord George voted with his conscience, which was always for tolerance. With Parliament going into Christmas recess and thus lacking friends round him, who might have dissuaded him, he wrote a letter of resignation. When Parliament reassembled in January 1848 he walked into the Chamber with Mr. Disraeli, ostentatiously took his seat one row back and indicated to Mr. Disraeli that he should remain where they had habitually sat together– on the front opposition bench. It was in this way that Mr. Disraeli became leader of the Tory Party in the House of Commons, while Lord Stanley led the Party in the Lords.

Summing up for the Opposition, Disraeli told the government they were moving in a vicious circle in which the benefit of one interest (free trade) was to the injury of another (British shipping) which could in turn profit at the cost of a third. Instead of the government's promised advantage he forecast universal disaster. Relying on figures provided by a well known shipping expert, he claimed Repeal, 'Would depreciate shipowners' property by 30 to 40 percent, that it would drive purchasers of ships to foreign countries, that all artisans concerned in the trade must suffer very severely'. He had listened with regret to criticism of British mariners and captains – they were not 'drilled slaves', but had been raised in a country with free institutions and liberal principles, and their behaviour compared favourably with that of operatives in one of the textile mills, where soldiers had been on the premises for 6 months. It was argued that if the British coastal trade were thrown open to competition foreigners would be deterred by language difficulties, but no seaman was allowed to be a captain in Scandinavia who did not speak English. It was argued that if the British seaman competed successfully in the unprotected export trade, why should he be protected in the import trade. 'I deny', he said, 'that in the export trade he competes with the foreigner with advantage. No evidence had been put forward to prove this fact...Every member of the House knows that practically all our export trade is in the hands of foreigners'. If the USA ordered iron in England it was fetched in US ships; if the French ordered coal it was fetched in French ships. Disraeli put his finger on the fact that a ship going one way with freight takes cut price cargo on the other voyage rather than go in ballast.

It had been claimed, said Disraeli, that in Rio and Trieste British shipping carried all before it, but, from House of Lords Committee evidence, he showed that if the inter-colonial shipping was removed from the totals, Britain was just holding her own against foreign competition in Rio, where she only had one quarter of the US share, while in Trieste there were practically no British ships clearing except to Brazil. The government also claimed that the increase in British tonnage coincided with the start of treaties of reciprocity, but this was not true. Members had filled, 'Their goblets from the tainted fountain of the Board of Trade', which took exports and imports separately for 1824 and compared them with 1846 when they were added together. The colonies did not require a wider choice of shipping; protected British ships ensured transport, in spite of the fact that from Australia one third returned in ballast. With regard to the 'long haul' from the Far East, British goods were cheaper and fresher, and therefore Britain had become the emporium of the world. The Le Havre cotton had been given publicity out of all proportion to its importance – the reason it could not be sold in England was simply the depressed state of the market. The Navigation Laws were designed to prevent a third power taking over entirely the lucrative indirect carrying trade (which is where the wealth has always lain)and Disraeli said he had heard no argument by the government as to why Britain should break this age old safeguard.

Turning to the behaviour and policy of foreign states, Mr. Disraeli said the government would not confirm that Prussia had used a 'menace', but they admitted, 'They had been warned' and that the Prussian Minister, 'had delivered a threatening notice to the government'. With what, asked Disraeli, could Prussia threaten Britain. Prussian ports were of no use to the British. Either they had insufficient draught or they were shut for half the year by ice. Because of Prussian exclusion from the open sea, 'The motives for their invasion of Denmark might be inferred'. He paid tribute to the, 'Spirit and energy (with which) that gallant little nation had opposed their unscrupulous invasion'. He pointed out that, 'If the Prussians could get possession of the ports in the North (of Germany) then they would be able to manage the President of the Board of Trade... But why should Britain listen to them now?... This bugbear is to frighten us into changing the ancient maritime charters of this country', at a time when Prussia could not currently retaliate in any way whatever. As for the USA, 'They will give little if we give little, but I defy them to give us much if we give them much'. He reminded Ministers that they should, 'Make themselves masters of the difficulties they would encounter', instead of acknowledging that they were, 'Totally ignorant of the consequences'. 'It would be better', said Disraeli, 'to keep the present system until Ministers (were) more familiar with the facts. This is trifling with the national interest in a reckless manner...for nothing is more fatal than the recklessness of ignorance'. Referring to the present revolutionary upheavals all over the continent and comparing them with the tranquillity at home, he was surprised that the member for Manchester, 'Had described the present age as one of commerce, peace and internal improvements. My only idea of them is a band of Communists tearing up a railway; with Naples in a state of siege; Paris in insurrection; Vienna in revolt; Berlin barricaded; with four pitched battles fought in Europe in eight weeks, and the Baltic and the Adriatic alike blockaded. I do not pretend to that prophetic power which the Honourable Gentleman and his (Manchester) School so pre-eminently possess; but in reading the past we may sometimes find some guiding admonitions for the conduct of the present. And certainly in reading our annals I find no reason for withdrawing my allegiance from that arm of military power, which, in this country, has at the same time created empire and cherished liberty. Amid the fall of thrones and the crash of empires around us I know of no circumstances more remarkable than that strange anarchy and that mysterious demoralisation, which have lately fallen upon those vast armies, which were once considered the best mainstay of power and authority. I cannot help thinking, when we have heard the startling accounts of those hosts of France, Austria and Prussia, which have deserted their masters in their hour of need – I cannot help thinking that an Englishman must have remembered with pride and perhaps satisfaction that our legions reposed upon the waters'.*

Sir Robert Peel reminded the House of the benefits that had come from cheaper corn flowing into Britain without duty and the reduced tariffs on raw materials – how famine had been averted and commerce increased. The hopes of peoples lay with free trade. The only argument, which would alter his opinion about Repeal of the Navigation Laws, would be one showing that it would undermine the defence of the country and this the opposition had not proved. If they could show that the British merchant marine depended upon government 'encouragement' and could not survive international competition without it then their arguments and demonstration of Adam Smith's caution would be valid. But they could not and therefore the case for Repeal on the grounds of increased commerce and wealth was made. (One problem in a democracy is that it is impossible to prove such a case in future context, since it depends on imagining a set of circumstances as well as presenting proven facts). Casting accurate history aside Sir Robert claimed that the Navigation Laws only dated from Cromwell, who had brought them in to ruin Dutch trade, and that now, instead of being adversely bound like the British, the Dutch were free to carry goods to the USA. He gave an assurance that the British coasting trade would not be thrown open (an empty promise) and rejected all idea of reciprocal treaties, warning that the exclusion of other nations from British shipping would lead to retaliation and trade wars. Pointing to the recent increase in British tonnage and numbers of seamen, he did not say it had occurred when

---

* Marx was expelled from Brussels in 1845. The first Communist League was formed in 1847. The first Communist Manifesto was published in 1848.

British shipping was protected, nor that there had been an accompanying increase in world tonnage. Claiming that half the capital in shipping had been lost in the past 25 years, he did not take into account the boom in shipbuilding after the Napoleonic Wars, when fortunes were made. Condemning the impressment from the Merchant to the Royal Navy, he forecast that Britain's shipping would always be able to compete internationally, because of her favoured position as an island and the progress of steam power. Relying on the evidence to the House of Commons Committee given by a Captain of a US liner, he discounted the threat from US shipping and said that US ships should be admitted to British ports on the same basis as those from Canada. Differentiating between reciprocal treaties conferring 'most favoured' status and those only extending reciprocal privileges – he agreed with Mr. Gladstone that he did not favour restrictions being re-imposed by Orders in Council, preferring assessment during a temporary duration of Repeal. He was convinced that future increases in tonnage would depend not on the Navigation Laws, but on the wider prosperity of commerce. Navigation Laws were undesirable, because for one thing they made the colonies subservient to the interests of the mother country. He ended with a quotation from Mr. Huskisson on the benefits of competition and free trade – an unfortunate choice, because Mr. Huskisson, in an adjacent passage, spoke also of, 'Advantages which must be reciprocal'.

In summing up for the government, Lord John Russell was more outspoken. He criticised Lord George's, 'Peculiar line of argument', and, 'Narrow confined views'. Also attributing the Navigation Laws to Cromwell, he was convinced they conferred no benefit on England. He saw no danger of another mercantile marine threatening that of Britain, which had extensive capital, abundant iron and copper, and a labour force of quality and skill, capable of high productivity. There was nothing to fear from competition. In the port of Hamburg in 1846 there were 995 British ships compared with 12 American. Since reciprocal treaties had done Britain no harm, Repeal of all the Navigation Laws would do no harm either. The Royal Navy did not depend for its strength on the merchant marine, 'No more fallacious mode of keeping up the strength of the Navy ever was invented than obliging a shipowner to have a certain number of apprentice boys on board his ship'. By removing the Navigation Laws, 'You will draw closer the bonds of amity with foreign nations, which are ready to act in bonds of amity and friendship with you and you will thus give a proof that you are equal to the destinies that await you'. The destiny which awaited British seamen in two World Wars was one about which he could never, even in a nightmare, have dreamt.

When the government won by 117 votes Repeal seemed inevitable. At the Second Reading on March 9th 1849 Mr. Herries, for the Opposition, informed the House that 30 towns with shipbuilding connections had sent petitions against Repeal, including one from Northern Ireland. St. Andrews had signed on behalf of the Fife shipbuilding burghs. London had provided 27,000 signatures, Liverpool 24,700, The West Indies also had decided against Repeal, recognising that cut price freight would aid the importation into the UK of

Cuban slave grown sugar and Canada was of the same persuasion regarding its grain. The government did not know whether it was taking the step unilaterally or in the hope of reciprocity. The majority of foreign states whose opinion Lord Palmerston had sought had replied that they would do nothing now. The Germans and Prussians said they would wait for a central government to be established in Germany; Hanover said it could not enter into separate commercial agreements (by 1849, Hanover, despite signing a reciprocal treaty with Britain in 1845, had succumbed to pressure and the loss of its trading partner Brunswick and, against its wishes, had been sucked into the Prussian Zollverein); America and Austria had not answered; Belgium had said 'No' – it must act in the interests of its own people; France was polite but had put a tax on salt coming in foreign ships. 'Were Ministers alone wise and all the rest of mankind unable to see their own interests?' Mr. Herries disagreed both with the originator of the Bill, Mr. Ricardo, Member for Stoke-on-Trent, who thought a commercial marine not essential for a great naval power, and with the government, which said the Navigation Laws impeded commerce, were not necessary for a thriving maritime marine and could be repealed without threatening national safety.

Mr. Gladstone, who no longer had Lord George to challenge his statistics or 'ambiguity', claimed that after 1790 British shipping had increased faster than American, (in fact, there was no increase in British shipping between 1815 and 1835, whereas US shipping, design and tonnage had dramatically improved, but after 1836 British tonnage had risen faster). He repeated his hope for reciprocity once Britain acted unilaterally, but because of defence implications he did not want to drive a hard bargain with shipowners, who should be freed from impressment and other duties. He thought the keenest competition would come from the USA and the Baltic, but with her small population, Norway could not be a serious challenger, (in fact, in the 12 years after Repeal US tonnage doubled and Norway's advance was 'just as marked'). He repeated his preference for relaxing the Laws by Orders in Council for reciprocating states, in which case the coastal trade could be given away also, but said again that if the government was determined to repeal unconditionally he would back it. 'Let us not be alarmed by vague and dreamy vaticinations of evil'. Sadly the prophecies of evil were, in the next century, to become the hideous reality of which the Opposition had warned.

At the Committee stage in June Mr. Disraeli poured scorn on the government, which had tried to include in the Bill foreign and interport coastal trade and then had withdrawn those provisions on the advice of the Revenue (who thought them too complicated). He derided Mr. Gladstone, who had suggested one important change – to divide Britain's Empire trade into external and internal, opening the latter only to reciprocating foreign countries, and then had withdrawn all his amendments, saying they did not have sufficient support and he did not want to embarrass the government. 'I was almost reminded of that celebrated day in the French Revolution when the nobles and prelates vied with each other in throwing coronets and mitres to the dust as useless appendages! I think that day is still called the day of dupes.....I am persuaded that what has taken place tonight will give rise to very serious and mournful considerations... The legislation has been precipitate and ill-advised, (the British people) have been sacrificed not to necessity foreseen long years ago by great statesmen and regulated by master minds... but their fortunes have been destroyed and their positions in life deteriorated because suddenly, abruptly, without thought, with great precipitation, in a hurried, blundering and hasty manner, you have passed laws which have most perniciously affected the great interests of this country...Their destinies have been dealt with...by men who on every occasion have come forward to catch the breeze of the moment and who have been ready to attempt legislation without making themselves master of the subject they attempt to legislate on. When you act in this manner, and create such a feeling in the minds of a people, I tell you you do more than injure and destroy the material interests of a nation – you lay the foundation of a stock of political discontent, which will do more than diminish the revenues of the kingdom and the fortunes of its subjects, which may shake the institutions of the country to their centre'.

In the House of Lords the Bill had a much stormier passage than in the House of Commons. Whereas evidence to the Committee of the House of Commons was not on oath, the 40 shipbuilders, shippers and merchants giving testimony to the House of Lords were all sworn and Mr Joseph Allen, writing from Greenwich Hospital, compiled a book publishing this evidence. 31 of the witnesses, who represented interests in the UK, West Indies, Australia, Canada, South America and the Middle and Far East, were against Repeal, two were in favour (one of whom was a naturalised German), five were indecisive, two, including a German from Hamburg, gave dire warnings about retaliation if Repeal was not carried through. One witness said that British manufacturers and consumers would suffer just as much as the maritime industries. 'I very much question', said another, 'whether the continental nations, made up of fraternity, will give England credit for philanthropy'. A shipbuilder forecast the progressive decline of British navigation and the rapid increase in that of foreign nations who would undercut British prices. 'I should think it an act of folly if the Navigation Laws were repealed for a British shipowner to register his ship as British if he could possibly avoid it'. The two witnesses warning of retaliation stressed that there were great feelings of nationalism among the Committee Members appointed by the 1848 National Assembly at Frankfurt, three quarters of whom were protectionists and who were trying to force Spain and Holland to retaliate against Britain if Hamburg ships were not admitted on the same footing as theirs. Mr. Mitchell, MP backed this evidence and confirmed that Prussia 'Could almost compel Hamburg to retaliate'. By means of its recently created Zollverein Prussia was exploiting the move towards the consolidation of the German states, started by Napoleon in his Confederation of the Rhine, and putting pressure on them through the Frankfurt Parliament to co-operate. It was also pointed out by witnesses to the House of Lords Committee that the USA had stricter Navigation Laws against Britain than against any other country, whereas US ships could carry their goods to UK possessions overseas, lift exports from there for foreign countries, and import their goods into the UK tariff free. These were considerable concessions, but the reader will recall that Britain had only emerged decades earlier from a world war, in which the USA had backed France in a conflict sparked off by restrictions on shipping, in which, without Napoleon's march to Moscow, the outcome might have been different. Indeed, the results of that conflict were still being felt in Canada, where US freebooters, declared illegal by their government, were backing French secessionists north of the border. In the House of Lords the Bill was only carried by ten votes and would have failed without proxy voting. Lord Brougham poured scorn on statistics, proving anything when divorced from sound principles and reasoning, 'We have conquered Napoleon because of the Navigation Laws'. Lord Stanley said the Bill discouraged maritime employment and would reduce the strength of the merchant marine and of the Royal Navy, 'Which was the main foundation of the greatness of this country and the surest defence of its independence', but Lord Lansdowne, speaking for the government, said that British success and prosperity were not a consequence of the Navigation Laws, but were due to British commercial genius and enterprise.

When the Bill returned to the Commons for the Third Reading in April 1849, Disraeli made a last appeal for a change of heart. Free trade had not yet proved its worth and there should be hesitation, 'Before we incur the additional expense of raising a costly capital upon what may be a column of very ill fashioned design'. The government rested its case for Repeal on three grounds, commercial inconvenience, colonial discontent and foreign menace. The shipowners were not obdurate, as Mr. Gladstone claimed; on the contrary Disraeli quoted from their Report to show they would consider anything, 'Not involving a fundamental principle'. Colonial discontent with the Navigation Laws was past – it was a market for their corn and sugar that Canada and the West Indies wanted. As for foreign menace, what Prussia was really saying was, 'If we succeed in our foreign policy, if we secure the harbours of Schleswig-Holstein, of the North Sea, of the Elbe and by the favour of England become an important maritime power then we shall be prepared to open negotiations with you and we shall then stand upon our right'. The government had, 'Thrown dust in the eyes of the people and their representatives', unsettling issues so that they could settle them again in their own way. They claimed the issue was, 'Progress or reaction'. Was it, 'Progress to paradise or progress to the devil'? What did the government mean to accomplish? At least the aims of the Manchester School were intelligible: 'They tell us they want to overthrow the Church, to destroy landed tenure, to change the whole constitution of the land and to do many other things besides which may be perilous, perhaps fatal to this country'. There was, he said, 'A great statistical conspiracy which has for so long tampered with the resources and trifled with the fortunes of a great country'. He reminded the House of one solemn fact – that, 'If they took all the male operatives of all the factories of Great Britain they would not compare with the number of merchant seamen of England'.

The manufacturing, commercial and maritime interests of an island nation are inextricably interconnected. If one is damaged the others are affected also.

Since these great debates the Empire has gone, transformed into the Commonwealth of nations. 'The British', said Adelai Stevenson, 'have lost an empire and have not yet found a role.' His well known words disguised a more fundamental truth. What they had lost was a carrying trade and they have not as yet found an alternative income. No other country followed Britain in her unilateral declaration of the free carriage of goods, carried into effect in the vain hope of averting national conflicts.

CHAPTER THREE

'BY JOVE WE'LL TRUMP THEM'
HOW BRITISH MARITIME POWER WAS MAINTAINED

The year 1850 marks the end of Britain's traditional maritime policy which, for four hundred and fifty years, lapsing sometimes and being reactivated, was one of protectionism; and begins the progress towards the policy of abandonment, which has now produced the disastrous effect on British maritime interests and the Royal and Merchant Navies that many nineteenth century Conservative leaders predicted. What they did not foresee was the length of time it would take to cause the decline or the peaks and troughs in the shipbuilding industry and in the strength of the Royal Navy, which marked the intervening years – peaks, followed by over-capacity, in periods of political instability and war and troughs in periods of peace. The reason that the effects took so long to materialise and that the Merchant Navy expanded rather than declined in the years following Repeal can be attributed to many factors, a number of which were the result of government action taken to avert the adverse consequences, of which Members of Parliament had been warned.

First, after the post-Napoleonic War depression there was a dramatic increase in world trade, of which British Empire trade formed a high proportion and this was particularly marked in the opening up of commerce with the East, where by the end of the century Britain had 80 percent of the trade with China. Second, as Sir Robert Peel, Mr. Gladstone and Lord John Russell had forecast, the situation was saved for the time being by the geographical position, plentiful natural resources, good fortune, wise planning and skill of the British people. Not only had they iron ore in abundance to build the first iron ships – an iron boat was trading on the Severn in 1787 and Bristol was becoming a leading iron shipbuilding centre – but James Watt of Greenock had invented the steam engine as a method of propulsion. The change from wood to iron was gradual, in 1818 an iron vessel was used on the Forth and Clyde Canal and three years later the next iron ship crossed the Channel, but it was not until after Repeal that iron usurped wood, as steel took over from iron decades later. Meanwhile in 1788 a paddleboat, launched at Dalswinton in Scotland, was fitted with a steam engine and fifteen years later another was successfully tested on the Clyde; but again delays in development followed, with the Forth and Clyde Canal ignoring the work, while the Americans took up the idea and forged ahead – so that for the moment the US merchant fleet increased dramatically in size in comparison with the British fleet. Only when the Comet was launched on the Clyde in 1812 did the British fully understand the importance of their discovery and soon afterwards a British built steamer arrived in Liverpool from the Clyde. With the first Channel crossing by steam accomplished in 1816, a UK coastal steamer service was running by 1830 and soon 45 steamship companies were registered in London alone, with their ships and those from other ports entering all the oceans of the world. Then in 1836 the screw propeller – attributed to a Frenchman and developed by an

Englishman – was patented in the UK, where an experimental vessel received financial help from the government, leading to the first screw steamer crossing the Atlantic in 1843.* Three years later Brunel's Great Britain, screw propelled and six masted, crossed the Atlantic in 15 days. In the decade following the number of British steamers increased nearly four times and, with abundant supplies of iron ore and banks ready and willing to lend, Britain for the moment held her place in world shipping. By 1870 her carrying trade was four times that of her closest rivals and she owned 54 percent of the world's steam ships, rising to 60 percent in 1880 and 63 percent by 1890, after which her share declined.

Third, following upon the recent voyages of discovery and the movement of population caused by the Highland clearances, there was a great increase in passenger traffic and emigration in the nineteenth century to Australia, Canada, New Zealand and other places overseas. Emigrants from the continent sailed from Liverpool and this movement of peoples led to the granting of government contracts to British and Empire shipping companies for the carriage of mail to the continent and Empire and for the carriage of passengers and freight. These mail contracts provided lucrative subsidies for the shipping companies – the value of which was reduced with the changeover to steam – for had the government put them out to foreign tender they would have been undercut and cost the British taxpayer one third less. There were altogether 43 mail contracts for the Empire, of which only 12 were not British. The great steamship companies which won these contracts – of which the first was the General Steamship Navigation Company for mail to the continent – were all built from small beginnings and the stories of the leading firms form a romantic part of British history. Mr. Samuel Cunard from Halifax, Nova Scotia, financed by funds from Glasgow and Liverpool, founded the British and North American Royal Mail Steam Packet Company, which later became Cunard. In 1833 its ship the Royal William was the first vessel to cross the Atlantic under steam and in 1837 the company obtained the government contract for mail across the Atlantic with four steamers, which maintained an average speed of 8½ knots. The first ship built to their design was the Unicorn, the second was the Britannia, launched on the Clyde and propelled by sails and paddle-wheels. Two years later the newly formed Royal Mail Steam Packet Company obtained the government contract to carry mail to and from the West Indies and Central America. At times operating jointly with the Pacific Steam Navigation Company of Liverpool, Royal Mail organised transport by mules and canoes across Panama to establish a mail link between Great Britain and the west coast of America, while the US Pacific Mail Steamship Company carried mail round the Horn. Many other famous British and Empire lines came into being at this time, a number of which were either started by Scotsmen or based in Scotland. One of these was the Allan Line, which began trading in 1818, winning a mail contract and merging temporarily with the

* 4 engineers were involved: Smith and Wilson (British), Sauvage (French) and Ericsson (Swedish).

Montreal Ocean Steamship Company in 1854. An Allan liner was the flag ship of the Tenth Cruiser Squadron, responsible for the northern blockade in World War I. The firm was taken over by the Canadian Pacific Steamship Company, which won the Empire mail contract across the Pacific, also owing its origins to two Scotsmen, who built the famous railway uniting Canada from coast to coast. Founded in 1859 the Anchor Line, with wide interests in both west and east, sent the first ship through the Suez Canal and then combined with Donaldsons, which started in 1855 by chartering, broking and insuring, owning its own ships in 1870. Anchor lost so many ships in World War I that it went into liquidation, but Donaldsons continued, building the Athenia, which was torpedoed with 1,400 passengers aboard within hours of the outbreak of World War II. Other famous names were Alfred Holt, who founded the Blue Funnel Line, Furness Withy and White Star, owned by Ismay, Imrie and Company, which had many of its large, fast ships built by Harland and Wolff in Northern Ireland. It vied with Cunard, with whom it merged in 1934, for top speeds across the Atlantic and was the owner of the ill fated Titanic, which put records before safety.

The American challenge on the Atlantic route began soon after the Napoleonic War with the Black Ball, Red Star, Swallow Tail and Black X Lines. In 1836 the US Collins line was founded, a group of sailing ships, which, when changing to steam, had disasters at sea and, despite winning the Blue Riband* for the fastest time across the Atlantic, was wound up in 1858. In co-operation with the Germans the Hamburg America Line was established in 1856 and North German Lloyd in 1857, but in 1861 the American Civil War took the USA temporarily out of the maritime race, and it was not until the later years of the century that US subsidies and German finance turned these two companies into leading firms. Until 1880 many German ships were built in British yards, but after that date Bismark successfully developed the German shipbuilding industry. Although the British had established a lead, with Cunard winning the Blue Riband in 1856, many countries were vying for first place in the Atlantic race and in 1897 the Germans won the award. It was won back again by Cunard with the Lusitania in 1907 and was then wrested from her by her sister ship the Mauretania. In building techniques, choice and training of personnel, discipline, punctuality, look-outs and soundings Cunard aimed at excellence. The standards of precise timing maintained by these ships were remarkable and in 1966, when sister ships met on schedule sailing across the Atlantic in the opposite directions, the comment to the author by a crew member was, 'You could set your watches by these ships'. Safety was never sacrificed and nothing, not the smallest detail, was ever left to chance.

By the 1830's many steam ships were operating in the Mediterranean and Far East, where the same high standards were the reason for the success of The Peninsular and Oriental Steam Navigation Company, which was started by Mr.

In 1935 – almost 100 years later Harold Hales MP Sole proprietor of Hales Bros, Shippers, gave the Hales Trophy and £75,000 to the winner of the Blue Riband.
[*Blue Riband of the Atlantic*, Tom Hughes, Patrick Stephens. Cambridge 1973.]

Willcox, a shipbroker in the City of London, who began trading in 1815 with himself and an office boy, Arthur Anderson of Kirkwall, Orkney. In 1834 Willcox was appointed London agent of The Dublin and London Steam Packet Company, which carried mail to Ireland, and in this role chartered a ship to run to Spain at the request of the Spanish government. Three years later this firm – entitled P & O by Royal Charter in 1840 – obtained a British government contract for mail to the Iberian Peninsula, including Gibraltar. Shortly afterwards P & O acquired further British government contracts for regular services carrying mail and passengers to India, Australia and the Far East and had 55 ocean going liners by 1855. The East India Company, which had been providing an irregular service to the Far East, lost its trading monopoly in 1833 and finally withdrew from the direct route in 1854. The Oriental Line started in 1839 and concentrated on the transport of mail, passengers and freight to Australia, to which the gold rush began in the early 1850's and whither Brunel's Great Eastern sailed in 1856. All these journeys were a challenge of pure romance, for the 90 mile overland route between Cairo and Suez had to be undertaken in wheeled transport drawn by mules or horses – partly by moonlight – until 1859 when a railway was built. When the Suez Canal was opened ten years later there was a demand for smaller ships, at which time the City Line was formed. There were no coaling stations at ports on the way, often no accommodation for passengers and sometimes no fresh water. Other firms engaged in trade with the East included T and J Harrison, British India, which later combined with P & O, the Cayzer's Clan Line, Bibby's of Liverpool, Swire's China Navigation Company and Jardine Mathieson. Meanwhile, serving the ports on the 'long haul' round the African coast line, the Liverpool based African Steamship Company won a contract in 1851 for mail to West Africa and the Union Steamship Company was formed two years later to carry trade between Britain and the Cape of Good Hope, winning a government contract for mail, troops, passengers and freight. At the end of the century it combined with Sir Donald Currie's Castle Line, which transferred from Calcutta to the South African route in 1872, winning further government contracts – the amalgamated company becoming famous as the Union Castle. Like those on the Atlantic route, some of these lines concentrated more on emigration traffic, others on the two-way luxurious passenger traffic, vying with each other both in comfort and speed.

The fourth reason that the British kept their lead during the half century following Repeal was the demand for specialist ships and cross trading tramps, of which a large number were built in British yards and sailed from British and Empire ports. The former transported raw materials, livestock and commodities such as meat, cotton, wool, palm oil and later oil for fuel. In these fields the British were pioneers, leading the world with the first refrigerated ship in 1879. These specialist shipping lines benefited, as did the cargo and passenger ships, not only from the opening up of trade, but from the liberalisation of British company law, which enabled them to be financed on a joint stock basis. Among them were firms sailing from Liverpool into West Africa to pick up palm oil and others bringing cotton from India and South America to Liverpool for onward transmission to Manchester. Independent traders were owned either by individuals or by partnerships. If they were partnerships, they were governed by the oldest laws of mercantilism, dating back to before the sixteenth century, dictating the number of partners allowed, which had to be a multiple of 64. Ships sailing from Liverpool were often part-owned by the master, while in the East India Company masters had only become salaried in 1815. Many of these independent traders were merchants, not interested in profits from shipping but only in those from the goods they were transporting. Prominent among these were the wool traders of Australia, who were able to make profits and yet keep the price of their wool competitive by operating their own ships outside the big cartels. The large cartel companies encouraged business in a number of ways. Either they agreed to waive primage or commission, provided the merchant always shipped with the same company, or they allowed the shipper to build up a six monthly rebate, which was lost if he went elsewhere. Agreements between these large companies, which became known as conferences, began in the Atlantic in 1869, spread to India and China in the next decade and to Australia and Africa in 1886. Meanwhile, British cross trading tramps, commanded by British captains with navigational and commercial skills, could also be found all over the world, picking up freight wherever it was available. British tramps were the backbone of the shipping industry, often carrying coal out and grain back and engaging in the cross trades in between. Lastly, steaming in and out of British ports, was the, 'Dirty British coaster with a salt caked smoke stack' of Masefield's poem, which was not sacrificed to the 'Iron hand of competition' until five years after the passing of the Repeal Act. For some time to come these vessels still held pride of place.

Another reason that the effects of Repeal were temporarily kept at bay was undoubtedly the will and determination not to be beaten by foreign competition, which was typical, at that time, of the bulldog character of, 'This island race'. Referring in an after dinner speech to the challenge that the American sailing clippers presented, the speaker declared emphatically, 'By Jove, we'll trump them.' The courage, daring and entrepreneurship of the traders, shipowners, shipbuilders, captains and crews of the last century make compelling reading, and particularly is this true of the story of the sailing clippers. The first American clipper was built in 1844, distinctive because of its new long sharp bow and fuller stern. These clippers brought tea from Foochow, Shanghai and Canton to New York via London, where the main tea market was sited, and commodities and raw materials to and from Australia, New Zealand and India at record speed. They were also cheaper to operate than the steamers and did not need to carry their own fuel. The British took up the challenge, motivated not only by the will to win but the will to survive. During the next decades the British and Americans raced each other across the world, timing each contest in hours and minutes with the same nonchalant efficiency as if they had been sailing toy boats on the Round Pond in Kensington Gardens. Large wagers were placed upon the prowess of these vessels and fortunes were made and lost by their victories or defeats. The American ship-

The Great Ship Race from China to London. The Taeping and the Ariel off the Lizard, 1866, tea clippers built in Greenock

The Auxiliary Screw Iron Ship Somersetshire for the Australian Trade, 1867, steam clipper built on R. Itchen

Carronade, 1779 – traversible firepower at point-blank range

HMS Invincible – warship of the iron-clad fleet, 1873

builders, benefiting financially from the discovery of gold in California, increased the size of their vessels and at the start monopolised much of the British carrying trade to China, undercutting their prices. Soon, however, British firms, such as Jardine Mathieson, Hall and Hood of Aberdeen and Scott and Robert Steele of Greenock took up the American challenge. When the gold rush opened up in Australia every available vessel of both nations was used in this trade. The Americans built in softwood, which was light and fast; the British built in oak, which was heavier, but more durable, so that cargoes arrived in better shape. The Americans chalked up many wins; their first clipper, the Sea Witch, was followed by other famous names: Great Republic, Oriental, Challenge, Surprise, Flying Cloud (built by Donald Mackay), Sovereign of the Seas and Marco Polo. But in 1856 Hood of Aberdeen built the tall masted Thermopylae and she made the record voyage from Melbourne to Britain in 60 days in 1869. The Sir Lancelot, launched by Steele of Greenock, was a composite ship, built of wood and iron and spreading 46,000 square feet of canvas, and she made the Foochow to London trip in 89 days, the year the Cutty Sark was built on the Clyde. The Ariel, a composite ship also built in Greenock, reached Hong Kong from London in 80 days and the Alnwick Castle sailed to India in 67 days. The development and perfection of these sailing vessels was not confined to American or British traders. German sailing ships had for more than a century been providing a service to South America, where in 1871 the Hamburg American line began to operate steamships on this route, which has always remained an important part of the German trading empire.

A sixth reason for the maintenance of British primacy in maritime trade was that the British government took action after Repeal to give assistance to shipping and the shipbuilding industry. As Mr. Gladstone had wanted, import duty on foreign timber for the building of ships was removed. Various Acts were passed to improve conditions at sea and the government gave generously to provide facilities for welfare and education. The newly created Merchant Seamen's Fund was expanded and a structure of promotion was introduced, with first and second class certificates of examination awarded for those seeking positions of command. The need for medical attention at sea was recognised and ships' doctors were provided on larger ships. Wage structures were altered, with amounts paid depending upon length of voyage. Ships' logs were kept and inspectors appointed by the Board of Trade to maintain standards. New measurements of ships were laid down and the Plimsoll line fixed to prevent overloading. Comprehensive rules were introduced to prevent accidents at sea, with better training facilities in seamanship and safety. Measures were brought in to increase the efficiency of lighthouses and pilotage – still the responsibility of Trinity House and the Corporation of Northern Lights. All these innovations and improvements required finance, but, as Sir Robert Peel had forecast, there was a flow of capital into the shipping industry after Repeal, stimulated by the passing of the Limited Liability Act in 1862 and by the amalgamation of a number of small firms. In 1884, although the size of the Royal Navy had declined, Britain was building 80 percent of the world's merchant ships and had a large and thriving merchant marine. Then towards the turn of the century came a challenge from the finance houses of America and Germany, which combined in a number of ventures. An American Bank bought White Star and, in conjunction with a German shipping line, formed the International Mercantile Marine (or IMM) in 1902, with which to challenge Cunard's supremacy. Cunard scorned the offers of take-over and in return the government gave the company help to build the Carmania and Caronia which were the first ships to have turbine engines and hydraulic machinery for closing doors. In 1903 the government followed this up with an annual subsidy of £150,000, a further 20 year mail contract and a loan of £2.6 million at two and three quarter percent to ensure that the company remained British and built fast modern liners to be registered in the UK and available to the Royal Navy in an emergency. This intervention was responsible for the winning of the Blue Riband by the two new Cunard liners, Lusitania and Mauretania, in 1907 and 1909 respectively.

The last reason for the maintenance of the British position was the influence of Lloyd's Register of Shipping. Although at the beginning of the century Lloyd's Register created ill feeling by allegedly ranking Thames ships higher than ships from other yards, which sparked off the creation of a second Register published by shipowners, the two merged in 1834 to form the Lloyd's Register of British and Foreign Shipping. In 1837 Lloyd's inspected its first iron ship and in 1855 drew up a Set of Rules for Iron Ships, formulated with the co-operation of shipbuilders. Before long a number of other countries as well as Britain accepted the classification of Lloyd's Register without further inspection for the acceptance of ships on their national Registers. By 1914 the Society was regarded as international and the 'British or Foreign' on the title was consequently dropped. Safety was the hall mark and the aim of the Society. When the iron hull was introduced the expectation of a ship's life was no longer fixed as in the days of wood, and regular surveying became an important part of the work. Now, instead of the different gradings of earlier years, Lloyd's Register accepts only the highest. During the second half of the nineteenth century, Britain's maritime position also brought increased business to the separate insurance Society of Lloyd's – Lloyd's Underwriting – as well as stimulating other marine related financial activities in the city, such as ship broking and chartering, conducted in the Baltic Exchange.

In addition to these and other British advantages, there were also three international events in the second half of the nineteenth century, which gave a temporary boost to British shipping. The Crimean War, breaking out in 1854, led to an increased programme of shipbuilding for both Royal and Merchant Navies, with ships built at record speed to land and supply the far-flung amphibious operation. Then in 1861 the American Civil War began over the twin issues of federation and the slave trade, and in six years of violent conflict much of American shipping went to the bottom of the sea. Lastly, in 1869 the opening of the Suez Canal and the provision of more coaling stations en route to the East brought to an end the days of sail and the challenge of the American sailing clipper. The Crimean War, as always after hostilities, was followed by a glut of commercial shipping and then a depression, with companies and banks failing. Repeated requests were consequently made by shipowners to Parliament for the Navigation Laws to be restored and the government was reminded that France, Spain, Portugal and a host of other countries still allowed Britain no reciprocity in shipping regulations, while the trade of others, like Belgium, was severely restricted. Shipowners pointed out that foreign coastal trade was also withheld by a long list of countries, including France, the Papal States, the Sicilies, Russia, Austria, Spain, Portugal, Greece, the USA, Mexico, Peru, Brazil, Chile, Venezuela and Haiti. Why should Britain, it was asked, continue to lay her coastal trade open to all comers.

The problem for the shipowners was that the figures seemed to tell a different story. In the sixty years from Queen Victoria's accession to the year of the Diamond Jubilee the number of British steam ships went up on a steadily rising graph from 554 to 6655 and, with their size tripling concurrently, now totalled 10 million gross tons. In 1897 just over half of the world's merchant tonnage sailed under the British flag, which, including steam, sailing and Commonwealth vessels, comprised 13½ million gross tons, out of a world total of 26½ million. Just before the Great War, out of a world tonnage of 45,404 million gross tons the British owned 18,892 million and the Commonwealth 1,632 million. But while these figures silenced the critics of Repeal, the percentages for vessels entering British ports steadily dropped after 1886. There were few regular statistics until after 1870, but those that there were show the dramatic increase in world trade, in which Britain shared. In 1837 only 7 million tons entered and cleared British ports, whereas by 1855 the figure was 18½ million and by 1897 80½ million, rising to a total in 1912 of 139 million. The first percentage given for British trade carried by British ships is 59 percent for 1855. The next figure is assessed under the new 1870 measurement and is for British ships entering British ports. In 1874 this was 57 percent and in 1886 62 percent, but in 1911 only 51 percent and by 1914 it had gone down to 46 percent. Until 1911 the German percentage of the total of ships entering British ports remained fairly constant at 7 percent, but the numbers of Scandinavian ships had by 1911 increased to nearly a quarter of the total. Meanwhile the figure for US merchant vessels entering British ports still remained low because of the effects of the Civil War.

Two great challenges to British shipping now lay ahead. Although the losses in the Civil War had, for a time, almost driven the USA out of the carrying trade a resurgence had already begun, together with the development of manufacturing trades on the western seaboard, due to the anticipated opening of the Panama Canal. This incredible feat of engineering, started by the French in the 1880's and finally accomplished by the Americans after the French ran into financial difficulties, was accompanied by heavy loss of life from tropical disease. Yellow fever, carrying with it the risk of madness, decimated workers and the canal was only finished just as World War I broke out. London to Perth and Adelaide was still closer than either of these Australian ports to New York, but New York was now closer to the Far East than London. Until 1914 Britain was holding her own in Eastern trade and London remained the wool market of the world. Almost three quarters of Australia's trade was with the mother country, but the acquisition of the Philippines by the USA gave Americans an increasingly influential presence in the Pacific. Now through the Panama Canal the USA would be able to establish a connection between California and the continent and so enable the Western seaboard to trade more cheaply with European states. Not only were her coal exports threatening those of the UK (in 1912 the UK exported 70 million tons, of which only 20 million went to her ships' coaling stations and the rest to foreign countries), but by the end of the nineteenth century the German invention of the diesel engine meant that ships were turning to oil, of which the USA had vast reserves.

As if this threat to Britain's economic future was not sufficient, a political and economic threat had meanwhile been developing closer to home. As Disraeli warned, Prussia had by now not only absorbed or conquered the German states in a bear-like hug, but was taking to the oceans, first by her absorption of the Baltic Hanseatic ports and later by the opening of the Kiel Canal, which gave her a direct communication to the open sea. Britain had reacted slowly to the growing power of Prussia and Germany and their friendship with Austria. In 1870 had come the first stirrings of unease, reflected in Queen Victoria's letters, which condemn the cruelty of the Prussian troops to the French before the gates of Paris in the Franco Prussian War. In the same year as the Prussian King was crowned German Emperor in Versailles, he ordered the creation of a Volunteer Navy – issuing an invitation to German shipowners to make their merchant vessels part of the German Imperial Navy. As demonstrated by the Napoleonic Wars, countries in control of the central land mass of Europe have an advantage in a global conflict over countries on the perimeter, which can only redress the imbalance by sea power. Thus, when powerful continental nations take to the sea, as the Germans did at this time and the Soviets were to do more recently, followed again by Germany and some of the central powers, the countries on the perimeter are forced to protect their position. Nevertheless, by the second half of the nineteenth century the British had become so over-confident and complacent that, in spite of an increase in armaments by continental countries of 40 percent and in the size of their navies, the threat to Britain was not fully understood until 1879, by which time the numbers of ships in the Royal Navy had dwindled so far that there were not enough to protect Britain, her overseas possessions or her trade. With the carriage of goods internationalised, the need for an effective Royal Navy had become marginalised in government policy, as the Conservatives had warned in 1849. A survey was carried out of the number of British and foreign armoured ships in commission on home and overseas stations. This list, printed in 1880, showed that there were only 4 ironclad ships in the Channel Squadron, with 9 in reserve and 8 unarmoured; in the Mediterranean there were 6 ironclads and 15 unplated; in North America and the West Indies there was 1 ironclad, together with 13 unplated; in South East America no ironclads and 4 unplated corvettes; in the Pacific 1 ironclad flag ship, together with unarmoured sloops and corvettes; at the Cape of Good Hope 11 unarmoured; in the East Indies 12 unarmoured; in China 1 ironclad and 23 unarmoured and in Australia 9 unarmoured. The decision was taken immediately to increase the strength of the Navy, but in 1884 Mr. Gladstone's Liberals were returned to power and progress was made by, 'Hastening slowly'. Gilbert and Sullivan's operetta, HMS Pinafore, therefore drew attention to the danger of there only being brass handles ashore to polish, 'In order to be Ruler of the Queen's Navy'.

Three international events now precipitated action. In 1883 the Germans formed their first military and industrial cartel; in the same year a dispute arose over colonies with the French, who had just almost reached parity with the Royal Navy, and the Americans started to rebuild their Navy. In July 1884 Lord Salisbury spoke about the reduced strength of the Navy in the House of Lords and in September an article appeared in the Pall Mall Gazette, sparking off a series of letters in the Times from distinguished Admirals, pointing out that naval ships were obsolete and in short supply. There were only 24 unarmoured ships for convoy protection compared with nearly twice the number in Nelson's day. £5½ million was immediately awarded to modernise the fleet and before the 1885 election the two political parties entered into a secret agreement not to publicise the need for ships, but to postpone the announcement of a programme of naval shipbuilding until after the election, when the party becoming the government would increase the size of the Navy. In June 1885 Lord Salisbury's Conservatives were returned to power and £21 million was directed to the Navy. This delay accounted for the further drop in British numbers of ships in the published list of 1885, which was accompanied by an increase in French ships on several stations, as well as by the arrival in the Black Sea of 2 Russian ironclads and 11 unplated and unarmoured naval vessels, and 6 armoured and 6 unarmoured Austrian ships in the Mediterranean. In 1887 Lord Charles Beresford presented a memorandum on the state of the Navy, which was accepted by Lord Salisbury, and then resigned as Fourth Sea Lord in order to embark on a crusade in the House of Commons and the country on the need for a more effective fleet. After almost frenetic efforts numbers of ships were back to normal by 1895, by which time there were 86 armoured vessels either building or in commission, compared with the French figure of 63, the US 30, the Russian 45 and the German 34, each of these nations having also an average of between 30 and 40 unarmoured vessels. All that the British had been doing was catching up with the figure they had maintained throughout the century, which was in theory although not in practice the total of the other two largest navies, while bluffing their way through with gunboats, but these peaks and troughs in shipbuilding, forecast by Lord Stanley, were not good for world stability.

Meanwhile the standard of training in the Royal Navy, which had been low at the time of the Crimean War, had continued to sink steadily and did not start to rise until the turn of the century. It was not until after the Russo Japanese War in 1904 that the standards of gunnery began to substantially improve. Equally serious was the effect Repeal was having on the number of trained personnel in the Merchant Navy, upon which the Royal Navy would have to draw in time of war, a danger foreseen by Lord George Bentinck and Mr. Disraeli. The merchant marine had always had at least twice the number of men as there were employed in the Royal Navy and, with impressment finally abolished and recruitment adversely affected, the Navy was now more dependent than previously upon a supply of trained personnel from the Merchant Navy in time of war. Anticipating this the government had not only improved the training of mercantile officers and seamen, but established a proper chain of command, going down through quartermasters, boatswains, carpenters and other specialists (who ranked as petty officers) to able bodied seamen (so called because they had managed sails and lead and could steer the ship) and thence to ordinary seamen. Since Repeal shipowners alone had been responsible for manning levels and some ships were now seriously undermanned. In 1855, with a total tonnage of just under 4 million gross tons, there were 155,610 British seamen of all ranks in the merchant marine, whereas in 1895, with a total tonnage increased by two and a half times, there were now only 15,000 additional seamen to man these ships. The lack of proportionate increase could partly be explained by larger ships, but questions were asked in Parliament, where yet more dramatic figures were quoted. In 1887 it was claimed that there were only 53,000 experienced able seamen – only half of whom had more than four years experience – and 27,000 foreigners. The problem was that, although wages on British ships were higher and food better than on the majority of foreign ships, wages were dropping compared with levels at home and consequently there were fewer men under twenty five. In his evidence to the House of Lords Committee in 1848 Admiral Sir George Byam Martin had warned that not only would British shipowners have to build ships abroad – taking out of commission a number of civilian yards which would be needed in time of war – but they would also have to recruit foreign crews and no longer be able to train apprentices, so vital to the Royal and Merchant Navies in peace and war. Up until Repeal a fixed number of apprentices had to be carried on all merchant vessels, but this had been swept away to enable shipowners to compete with subsidised foreign shipping. The figure for apprentices of 15,074 in 1850 had therefore become by 1894 only 2,164. Recognising the seriousness of the situation, the government now offered an allowance on lighthouse and other dues to shipowners prepared to carry boys, who were physically fit and members of the RNR.

In that same year, one of the lengthiest and most comprehensive Acts ever passed – the 1894 Merchant Shipping Act – consolidated and improved the scope of previous legislation, endeavouring to provide British shipping with an efficient framework to take it into the twentieth century. It was becoming apparent that it was easier to build more naval ships than to recruit more British crews. Unless present trends could be reversed the Royal Navy would have to look elsewhere than to the Merchant Navy for recruits in time of war. It was indeed a tragedy for Britain that the words of Adam Smith had not been understood and heeded during the 1848/49 Debates. 'Defence', he said, 'is more important than opulence... The Navigation Laws are perhaps the wisest of all the regulations of England'.

CHAPTER IV

'A HIDEOUS REALITY'
THE FIRST WORLD WAR

During the controversy in 1884 about the shortage of ships in the Royal Navy it was said that, 'No nation is more difficult to arouse to a sense of danger than the English'. Nevertheless, when in 1895 the Germans created the Pan German League and in 1897 announced a shipbuilding programme for the Imperial Navy amounting to 328 million marks, many countries were alerted to a serious threat. The smaller nations on the perimeter began to build their own fleets, primarily of torpedo boats, and even larger nations like France began to build shoals of TB's. Britain, as well as adding 100 of these little 'mosquitoes' to her fleet, put in hand the building of the powerful Dreadnoughts, which were to render obsolete all other naval ships of the period. The stage was set for international conflict on a grand scale and tragedy was not long in coming. Meanwhile, because of the increase in world trade and Britain's determination to maintain her commercial and maritime strength in the nineteenth century, the number of merchant ships gave the government no cause for concern. In 1914 Britain's Merchant Navy was the largest, most up to date and efficient in the world. Germany's merchant marine was only one quarter of its size and the merchant fleets of the USA, France, Norway, Japan and the Netherlands had each approximately one third of Germany's strength. In 1913 85 percent of British tonnage had been built since 1895, 68 percent since 1900, and 44 percent since 1905. At the outbreak of war Britain had 4000 ocean-going ships, another 500 within home waters taking part in foreign trade and many more vessels engaged between coastal ports or in fishing. Such was the position of the Merchant Navy before the First World War and only a pessimist would then have suggested that the combinations of companies were perhaps becoming too large for healthy competition.

If this was the state of Britain's merchant shipping what was the position of her sailors? Conditions of service varied. In liner companies they were reasonable, but in the tramps, where lack of refits meant mounting problems in the engine rooms (accounting for many convoy stragglers in both World Wars), in some cases living conditions were little short of appalling. Safety and life-saving equipment were in a bad state. The crews' quarters were often damp unpainted pits of squalor with upturned sea chests serving as tables. Fungus was not unknown, vermin was frequent and bedding soaked from dripping deckheads and bulkheads. Food mostly consisted of salted meat, with the biscuits often mouldy, while continuity of employment depended on the master finding sufficient cargo. Deaths from accident and disease (much of it tropical) were far higher than on land and during the 1880's and 1890's St. John Ambulance therefore started conducting lectures in First Aid and Hygiene in Seamen's Institutes at home and overseas. Then, when the Seamen's Hospital Society brought its hospital ship Dreadnought ashore into a wing of the RN Hospital at Greenwich, demand for instruction in tropical disease in armed and civilian services became so strong that Schools of Tropical Medicine were started in London and Liverpool to expand the work of the Edinburgh University students, who trained on the Dreadnought. The British Sailors' Society and the Missions to Seamen were both founded at this time.

Meanwhile, with the historic link between the Royal and Merchant Navies weakened by the Repeal of the Navigation Laws, the nation now regarded the merchant marine solely as a trading organisation, instead of also as a reserve of trained men. In 1850 the Merchant Navy Act had created the Marine Department of the Board of Trade, to which Admiralty powers over the Merchant Navy were transferred in 1856, and this saw its role as one of regulating the life of mariners at sea, rather than acknowledging a wider responsibility of providing ships and trained crews for the Royal Navy in time of war. Efforts were consequently made to create a national Register of Merchant Navy seafarers and this, having been placed initially under the Admiralty, was transferred to Special Superintendents, with the task of improving conditions at sea as well as providing a system of voluntary enlistment into the Royal Navy in war. By 1914 the official Merchant Navy Reserve – known by then as the Royal Naval Reserve – stood at 18,000 men, and in 1913 a separate Register was introduced for British seamen employed in foreign ships. Strenuous efforts were also made after Repeal to make the Royal Navy more self-sufficient in its reserves of trained men. The system of impressment had been replaced in 1853 by 'continuous service', by which men who had left the service were liable for a number of years to be called back should the need arise. Then in 1858 a Royal Commission was appointed under the chairmanship of Lord Hardwicke to look into the most efficient way of manning the Navy, particularly in time of war. It recommended the formation of a Volunteer Naval Reserve, which came into being at the turn of the century and was known as the Royal Naval Fleet Reserve, numbering 24,000 men by 1914. For a small retaining fee men, who had left the service, volunteered to keep their training up to date and return in an emergency. Lastly, the Royal Naval Coast Volunteers, which had started in 1853 to defend the coastline, had become a seagoing force in 1873 and been renamed the Royal Naval Volunteer Reserve. Nicknamed the Wavy Navy, because of the curving stripes on their sleeves, the RNVR reached by 1904 the maximum number allowed by law of 30,000 officers and men, and in two World Wars it shared, in common with the other Naval Reserves, the same conditions of service as the men of the Royal Navy.

In line with the hopes expressed in the Parliamentary debates on the neutralisation of shipping, naval strategy began to alter and in 1903 a Royal Commission took evidence from the Royal Navy on how the supply of food and materials would be maintained in time of war. An Admiral and an MP examined Prince Louis of Battenburg, Director of Naval Intelligence, and the two Commanders in Chief of the Mediterranean and China Fleets respectively and all reported that in their view it was a misconception to suppose that protection to merchant shipping could only be given in convoys and by naval cruisers and destroyers. Increased intelligence would anyway alert the enemy to the convoy's assembly and time would be lost in waiting for escorts. The best defence in their view against detection and destruction was the ship's speed, its alteration of course from regular trade routes and the use of the vast tracts of ocean in which to hide. Since at this time submarines had a very limited radius and low speed and had to be accompanied by a parent ship, the possibility of an effective blockade being mounted against Britain by them or by surface raiders was therefore injudiciously dismissed and instead the maritime policy was promulgated of concentrating force and establishing command of the sea. 'With a strong fleet we find no reason to fear that such an interruption of our supplies would lead to the starvation of our people, nor do we see any evidence that there is likely to be any serious shortage'.

As war threatened thoughts were turned as to how to protect merchant seamen from the privations suffered at the hands of privateers in the Napoleonic wars. Because the greatest danger to seamen comes from the sea itself, a trust and friendship had grown up over the centuries among seafaring people, which it was hoped could be channelled into the alleviation of suffering in time of war. To emphasise its non-belligerent role the RNR was taken off gunnery drill and a Conference on the maritime aspects of International Humanitarian Law was held in the Hague in 1907. Rules were laid down covering the use of merchant ships serving in the fighting Navy. If they were converted into warships – serving for instance as raiders or on blockade – they must bear distinguishing marks; Commanders must be officers of the fighting fleet and the crew must be under military discipline. Soon afterwards it came to light that the Germans were planning to convert a number of merchant ships into armed cruisers and Britain followed suit, converting a number of fast liners, two of which were completed by 1914. At the same Conference the bombardment of civilian towns was outlawed and an attempt was made to prevent mines being used against civilian shipping. The latter, however, had to be abandoned because of the difficulty of proving whether the intended victims were naval or civilian. The Germans nevertheless said they did not wish to see mines used and their spokesman at the Conference stated categorically that 'Sentiments of duty, imposed by the principles of humanity will be the surest guide for the conduct of sailors. The officers of the German Navy I emphatically affirm will always fulfil in the strictest fashion the duties which emanate from the unwritten laws of humanity and civilisation'. Despite these sentiments, when Britain, the USA and Japan wanted to restrict the arming of merchantmen to ships in coastal waters Germany would not agree, and so by 1914 Britain had fitted guns aft to 39 merchant ships, which could be used defensively when a ship was trying to escape.

Since the rules of humanity at sea laid down that ships should not be sunk unless passengers and crews were taken on board, and the limited space on a submarine rendered this impossible, the British refused to take this menace to civilian shipping sufficiently seriously. Renewed efforts were made at the Declaration of London in 1908/9 to outlaw submarines as a means of destroying civilian shipping and had this treaty been ratified as well as signed by all the Powers, it would have been against international law for an enemy raider to sink merchant shipping without warning and without making provision for its crew and any passengers. A neutral ship, challenged and then captured carrying contraband or conditional contraband could not be destroyed, unless all persons had been placed in safety – lifeboats not qualifying unless within reach of land. In order to get agreement the British had signed away the vital principle of Continuous Voyage, which prevented neutral ships calling in at belligerent ports or sailing in safety to neutral ports and discharging cargo for onward transmission to belligerents. The British and French wanted to set out agreed principles of international law, covering such matters as contraband, blockade, Continuous Voyage, the legality of the destruction of vessels and the possibility of setting up an International Prize Court, as had first been proposed at the Conference at the Hague in 1907. Disagreements concerning close or open blockade were resolved by the French defining both as falling within chosen areas of operation, but, although such cargo as arms and uniforms were patently contraband, arguments continued as to whether food going to civilian rather than military consumption fell within the definition of conditional contraband. For four years questions and debates about ratification continued in the House of Lords and House of Commons as to whether, in renouncing the principle of Continuous Voyage, Britain would be giving up the 'quid' without the 'quo' and would be accepting that all food coming to Britain could be ranked as conditional contraband and not just that going to a military base. At last, by an inspired leak from two German Generals, it was realised that the Germans intended to count all food as fair game for enemy raiders. With the Balkan Wars beginning, talk of ratification was consequently dropped, since, once the principle of Continuous Voyage had been abandoned, the Germans would have received the food they wanted by landing it at a neutral port, while that bound for Britain could have been legitimately seized.

By August 1914 the fact had to be faced that Germany had 28 sea going submarines and more under construction and that she was not going to honour promises made about not employing submarines against civilian shipping. Nevertheless, while these discussions continued in Parliament in the years leading up to war, the Colonial Defence Committee remained confident it could defend shipping and the colonies. In 1910 it reported that the fleet would seek out and destroy enemy squadrons, that large fleet battles would decide supremacy at sea and that, although the enemy would use old type cruisers as raiders to prey on merchant shipping, this, owing to Admiralty intelligence, would offer them, 'But slight prospect of any but transitory success'. No words could have been proved more wrong, but the policy was also endorsed by the Committee of Imperial Defence. Naval action in home waters would dispose of the enemy and this would be followed by naval action in distant seas. Too much reliance was placed at this time upon preventing the escape of the enemy into the open sea by a naval screen, a strategy talked about again today. Since so little time elapsed between the two World Wars the experiences of the First War had not been forgotten. 'The sea is too big an area', said Churchill, during the Battle of the Atlantic, 'to seek and destroy the enemy'. He knew that U-boats and surface raiders must come to the convoys and be destroyed there, rather than being sought out in the trackless wastes of ocean. Since by 1914 the close blockade had become too costly on account of mines and submarines, an open blockade could never guarantee that a single ship or submarine would never escape from port. Sir Arthur Wilson, who succeeded Lord Fisher as First Sea Lord in 1910, understood the dual role the Navy would have to play, defending Britain from invasion and shipping from enemy raiders. Nevertheless, with hopes at the start of the war of a new attitude to shipping – due inter alia to steam and the faster flow of vessels – and an over-reliance on naval screens and patrols causing a departure from all previous maritime policy, ships sailed alone in World War I, until catastrophic losses altered the policy to one of convoys in June 1917. Until that date the only protection given to merchantmen was at the point where trade routes converged. Otherwise it was every merchant master for himself and, with their crews, they met the German U-boats on their own. The merchant ships were told to use the ocean as their protection and if ships were sailing together they were told to disperse if a raider was sighted. Both shipowners and masters were opposed to convoys and naval opinion on the subject remained divided. Merchant shipping losses would have been even greater if the Director of Naval Intelligence, Captain Slade, had not set up the nucleus of an organisation for co-ordinating intelligence about Merchant Navy ships with a data of naval, diplomatic, Indian, colonial, and insurance information. This co-ordination of effort saved the country from even greater loss.

It was soon realised that if German promises were not kept then an equal danger would come from laying mines. All Royal Navy and merchant ships would be equally at risk and, because of their size and sophistication, Royal Navy ships would be unsuitable for search. In 1907, Lord Charles Beresford therefore suggested that trawlers should be used for minesweeping instead of warships. Training commenced, first in Aberdeen and then in other ports, and by 1914 the Navy had 7 trawlers under its command and the right to use by charter 82 Merchant Navy trawlers operating from ports right down the east coast of the British Isles. Immediately upon the outbreak of war a secondary fleet was also organised under Admiralty control, which consisted of craft never intended for use in war – not only trawlers, but whalers, drifters, steam yachts, paddle steamers, motor launches, motor boats and other small craft. As far as the British were concerned the First World War was essentially the war of the volunteer. While touring cars were being converted into ambulances and shipped to France, steam yachts, which in that first week of August 1914 had been attending Cowes Week, were being given guns and converted to minesweepers and submarine-hunters.

A war was now to begin, which was the first in history in which civilians were to be claimed as legitimate targets. Nevertheless, it appears that German naval officers started the war at sea with gentlemanly principles, intending to carry out promises that the Rules of Humanitarian Law would be observed, that crews were to be taken prisoner and passengers allowed to go free, unless involved in organised resistance. While, during the advance through Belgium, the German military machine was responsible for brutalities, which, it was said, 'Would have made a Zulu blush', the German Navy on the whole made an exemplary start to the war, with some German officers towing lifeboats to shore. Although shortly after the outbreak of war the Germans sank a French merchant ship with 40 Belgian refugees on board, nevertheless in the first seven months only 232,000 gross tons of civilian shipping were lost and no lives. It was not to last beyond March 1915, when the Princess Victoria and Tangistan were sunk, with all passenger lives lost except one, and by the spring of 1915 ruthless acts to deter British seamen from their duty were being relentlessly carried out, acts which, in fact, had precisely the reverse effect. During 1915 U-boats (and on a few occasions aircraft, including seaplanes and later zeppelins), attacked and sank merchant ships without warning as a matter of routine. Eleven merchant ships were lost in one month in March 1915.

To combat the threat of U-boats and mines, these small merchant, fishing and pleasure boats, which made up a part of the auxiliary Navy, a number of which had been in training before the war, were now assembled into units, each consisting of one yacht, four trawlers and four motor boats. The yacht owners at first joined the Royal Naval Volunteer Reserve and then transferred to the RNR In addition, a motor boat reserve was also built up, which was affiliated to the RNVR. Granton, on the Firth of Forth, became one of the largest auxiliary stations, but soon many of these little vessels were employed in distant seas, as well as home waters – in the West Indies, the Mediterranean and the White Sea – and detached squadrons of six armed anti-submarine yachts were formed, one of which was sent to Gibraltar. Some trawlers in the units were armed, others were unarmed and employed only to ram the periscopes of U-boats. The aim of these little vessels was to ram, shell and drop explosives on submarines. In all, there were 4000 of them, manned by 50,000 officers and men of 'impeccable renown'. Drifters were used to lay protective nets around ports and other sensitive areas in which to entangle U-boats. These vessels were not armed either, but worked at night, using acetylene lamps. By the end of February 1915 nets were in position in the Dover Straits as were also a number of British mines. By September 1914, almost as soon as war was declared, a fleet of 300 trawlers and drifters and 100 motor boats and paddle steamers were trawling for German mines. At first only the coastal waters were mined but soon drift mines were scattered in the Atlantic and Mediterranean and the approaches to Archangel, to which went British and Allied ships with Russian supplies. By June 1915 U-boats were employed to lay enemy mines. The Germans used the ruse of naval bombardment of British ports and coastal towns to lay mines inshore. The purpose of their raid on Scarborough was to entice British squadrons out on to mine fields laid during bombardment, and, although shelling of towns was outlawed by the Hague Convention, this raid was followed by many others including those on Lowestoft and Dover. Great courage was displayed by the men of the merchant marine and the fishing fleets on their minesweepers. During the Dardanelles campaign the Turkish bombardment of the Narrows was so heavy that even at night it was suicide to sweep the mines and, although crews were supplemented with naval personnel, the operation had to be abandoned. Thus Royal Naval surface ships never reached the Narrows and troops had to be landed instead on the difficult terrain of the peninsula, in which operation trawlers were again engaged.

Numbers of merchant ships were requisitioned to carry soldiers and supplies and to act as hospital and store ships, inter alia. Some converted merchantmen were used by both sides in the war to supplement naval forces. The British employed a number of converted liners, together with 8 old cruisers – laid down in 1889 – in the Tenth Cruiser Squadron of 25 ships on Northern Patrol. The Patrol was responsible for the blockade of Germany and again, as in the Napoleonic Wars, Britain acted under Orders in Council. Neutral ships were boarded and sent to neighbouring ports for examination, sometimes under escort. In 1915 alone 3068 ships were intercepted, of which 743 were found to be carrying contraband and suspicious cargoes. The Germans used their converted merchantmen as surface raiders to prey upon merchant shipping and so tighten the stranglehold increasingly imposed by submarines. Whether facing surface or underwater raiders, the majority of ordinary British and Allied merchant ships relied upon speed and the device of suddenly altering course to avoid torpedoes. At the outset most of them were unarmed. By May 1915 only 149 merchant ships were fitted with defensive armament aft, but by 1918 4079 vessels had guns in the rear of the ship. Some crews were given rifles, but these were in short supply. By 1916 ships had also been supplied with devices for making smoke screens. British fishing boats were defenceless and particularly vulnerable to attack and so many were sunk without warning that armed auxiliary patrols (fishing vessels under RN or RNR command) were formed for their protection. British decoy merchant vessels, manned by the Royal Navy were also used to lure U-boats preying on the fishing fleet to their destruction, the lieutenant in the decoy vessel being in telephonic communication with the submarine commander. A number of successful missions were carried out resulting in the destruction of a U-boat, but it was a difficult operation and success was infrequent. (These towed 'C' ships are not to be confused with the 'Q' ships mentioned later in the chapter). The whole merchant marine was now beginning to feel dislike for everyone and every-thing of German origin. Seamen read in their newspapers of outrages and horrors committed by the Germans on their advance to Paris but they saw with their own eyes the sinking of peaceful ships with their passengers and crews.

In May 1915 the Cunard liner Lusitania, the pride of the nation, was sunk with 1198 passenger and crew lives lost. No troops or guns were on board, but many women and children. German sources claimed that she was carrying cases of ammunition. Norway said, 'The whole world looks with horror and detestation on the event'. Yet German newspapers spoke of it as, 'A success the moral significance of which is still greater than the material success', and a medal was struck in Munich to honour the officers and men of the U-boat. Everything pointed to the Kaiser himself being in favour of this action. Then, owing to American pressure, there was a change of policy. The U-boat commanders were told to lay off action in the coastal waters of Great Britain and in the Western Approaches and to concentrate their action in the

Mediterranean where there were no American ships. In February 1916 these orders were cancelled, for the German High Command said it could not win on land if Britain commanded the sea. Then in March the SS Sussex was torpedoed in the English Channel with US citizens on board. The USA issued an ultimatum and again the Germans backed down, giving orders to naval commanders that no ships were to be sunk without first making arrangements for the safety of passengers and crews. The reason for this change of heart was that the Germans hoped at this time for peace on their terms through the initiative of President Wilson. The German naval and military commanders were furious about these new instructions and carried on with the sinkings against official orders.

The Germans then made one of their three great mistakes of the war. Seeking to frighten merchant seamen, they took Captain Fryatt, a British citizen, off his merchant ship, Brussels, having first surrounded it with destroyers. They made him a prisoner, accused him of once trying to ram a surfaced U-boat, which he was entitled to do by the Rules of the Sea, if he was trying to escape capture or sinking. He was court-martialled and not allowed to appoint his own defence. A German officer volunteered to defend him and, although ultimately a member of the US Embassy fulfilled the task, even then the Germans did not follow the rules of international law and permit proper facilities to the defence. He was found guilty and shot by order of Admiral van Shroeder. The execution took place at Bruges, where a memorial was erected to him. Such inhuman behaviour only led to increased resistance by the British. If that was how the Germans were going to behave to the British people then they would fight to the death.

Throughout 1916 and until February 1917 the German Navy tried to get its way with the government in order to force it to revert to unrestricted submarine warfare. Admiral Scheer wanted to do this by keeping the U-boats at home to force the government's hand. Admiral von Holtzendorff did not agree. He wanted to restrict the U-boats to operating in the same way as surface cruisers, whose presence alone gave a warning. The U-boat commanders themselves simply shook off the orders and restrictions and the number of sinkings rose dramatically from August 1916. Out of the gross tonnage sunk in 1916 (1,237,634) a large proportion was sunk without warning. In February 1917 official policy again reverted to 'unrestricted submarine warfare' and by March the amount of British shipping left was barely sufficient to carry vital supplies. April was one of the blackest months of war, 997 merchant sailors' lives were lost and 516,394 gross tons of British merchant shipping went to the bottom, together with 364,633 Allied and neutral. This had the effect that the Kaiser dreaded and in April the USA entered the war and more merchant shipping became available. By the end of that year the figure of British gross tonnage lost for 1917 was 3,729,785 and that for world tonnage 6,235,878. German surface raiders also were now adopting tactics which, infringing the laws of the sea, had been used in the eighteenth century – flying flags of neutral ships or even the Red Ensign as disguises. They excused their duplicity by pointing out that RN ships were also disguising themselves as merchantmen – the Q ships – but the British replied that these were used as decoys against submarines and not against civilians and therefore did not infringe Humanitarian Law. U-boats were also sinking well lit hospital ships in contravention of the Geneva Conventions, and making no efforts to rescue wounded men. The Kaiser's hand was forced. It seemed he had little alternative but to command unrestricted submarine warfare, since after the Battle of Jutland there was disaffection in the German Navy. With the army fought to a standstill – Hindenburg said at the time, 'The position could hardly be worse' – German public opinion demanded the sinkings. On one occasion (when the Huntsvale was sunk off Malta) merchant sailors were horrified as they swam to life rafts to see German officers casually photographing them in the water for media consumption. It was still only too possible in April 1917 that the U-boats might win the war, for even if the British could not be intimidated, terror might be spread among neutral shipping.

 Fortunately, however, British relationships with neutral ships and foreign crews were remarkably good. This friendship was built up by observing the rules of the sea. The destroyer HMS Nymph saved a Chinese crew from a burning ship. The ship was a furnace and rafts were thrown for those who could jump. Nine Chinese were too frightened to jump. At great risk to herself Nymph came alongside and all the crew were saved. Incidents like this helped to maintain good relations with foreign nations. Nevertheless, the situation was becoming daily more brutal and catastrophic. Whereas in the Napoleonic Wars French and British alike had rescued the lives of crews of both naval and merchant ships, all this was now cast aside. One U-boat commander submerged with 19 British sailors on his conning tower. With Germany now short of food the supplies in the lifeboats were seen as booty and on more than one occasion lifeboats were rammed by U-boats in order to take supplies from them. But an extraordinary spirit was being imbued in ordinary travellers. When the City of Birmingham outward bound from Gibraltar was sunk with 170 passengers on board, the captain rose to the surface to hear women singing hymns as they swam in the water.

 In 1917 nearly 4 million gross tons of merchant shipping were lost out of a world total of over 6 million. By March 1917 there was barely enough Allied shipping left to carry vital supplies. The entry of the USA into the war meant that the Allied blockade could be tightened and at last in June 1917 convoys were introduced, at the instigation of Sir Maurice Hankey, with the backing of Lloyd George. Admiral Jellicoe did not agree to all convoys being escorted for another three months and at the end of the year he was replaced as First Sea Lord by Admiral Sir Roslyn Wemyss, who had been C-in-C, East Indies and Egypt. Wemyss had been appointed to Mudros in 1915 to prepare a base for the Dardanelles campaign and then took over temporary command from Admiral de Robeck during the successful submarine campaign in the Sea of Marmara, for which Commodore Roger Keyes as Chief of Staff, was responsible. As the U-boats became more heavily armed, so the weight of guns on merchant ships was increased and by October ships of over 3000 gross tons were armed with howitzers and bomb throwers. The USA and neutral ships manned their guns with armed guards, who were not members of the merchant marine. In the convoys the rear ships were also equipped with depth charges, as were the escorts. By this time hydrophones had been installed in many RN ships. This was a listening device, through which it was possible, provided conditions were favourable, to hear the movement of submarines. Dazzle painting of merchant ships was tried out – to break up outlines by contrasting colours – but it was not successful in confusing enemy raiders. Smoke screens on the other hand were used with increasing frequency and even in convoy merchant ships were instructed to zig zag and make a series of different courses to avoid torpedoes. This also confused the U-boats and made them correct their position, thus using up their batteries which only lasted for two hours under water. Once convoys were adopted it was found that the delays so much feared by shipowners did not come about. The most important component of convoy sailing is disciplined seamanship and again the shipowners were wrong in thinking the masters would not accept this. Before the adoption of convoys these men and their crews had to meet danger alone. Now they were given support and comradeship and if their ships were sunk their chances of being saved were infinitely greater. The success of the convoy proved the undoing of the enemy. It was in Sir Archibald Hurd's words, an example of, 'Scientifically applied energy, seamanlike skill and unconquerable endurance'.

Meanwhile the little ships on patrol had also been fulfilling their task and by this time the flotillas of U-boat hunting trawlers, drifters and motor launches were also armed with depth charges. Whereas the Dover Barrage was a major obstacle consisting of minefields and permanent nets, the port entrances were protected by 132 drifters laying nets every few hours in an operation known as the Suicide Club, because of the dangers from German destroyers and torpedo boats operating from occupied ports. In the last months of the war this operation was undertaken right up to the Belgian coast, while in 1917 boom defences, already laid in the main ports, were extended to other harbours. A total of 11,000 enemy mines had been laid in nearly fifteen hundred groups around the British coast. Trawlers sweeping for these mines were now equipped with otters which were towing devices for cutting through the moorings. During the war auxiliary ships from the Merchant Navy carried men and supplies across to the armies in France and they were aided by the Dover Patrol, which was composed entirely of fishing vessels. In 1917 four fishing vessels were captured or sunk each week.

The British were now going back on the attack and at sea the picture looked a little brighter, although on land, where the Russians after the Revolution were being, 'Chased across Europe like sheep', it was anything but rosy. The entry of the USA into the war, apart from the initial contribution of 100,000 men, did not immediately substantially affect the Allied land forces, which had to wait for victory until the main army arrived the following year, but at sea the situation was different. For one thing American involvement meant that the blockade of Germany could be tightened. By mid 1917 the Germans were sinking all ships, whatever their destination, including a number of hospital ships, and this meant that Allies and neutrals were all facing the same dangers, bringing a great spirit of unity. Of 147 neutral vessels examined by the Northern Patrol in two months in 1917, only two were suspected of carrying illegal cargo and required to be sent for examination. After this, interception stopped and neutrals chose instead to sail to examination ports from which they obtained certificates of clearance. During 1917 the British had been steadily laying increasing numbers of mines and nets close to the Belgian coast, but despite this on February 14th 1918 the Germans penetrated them to make a naval raid on the Dover Barrage, where they sank many drifters and a trawler and damaged others. In April the port of Zeebrugge was successfully blocked by a daring raid organised and led by Admiral Sir Roger Keyes. Two cruisers full of cement were sunk inside the canal entrance to prevent the exit of naval vessels. A simultaneous attempt to blockade Ostend failed, as did Admiral Keyes' later second attempt on that port. All this combined action took its toll of U-boats, whose crews by 1917 were not of such high calibre and were beginning to lose their nerve. By the middle of 1918 the British were nearly making good all the previous losses at sea. The government had not seriously tackled the problem of replacement of ships until quite late in 1917, and even then because of the shortage of steel and skilled labour it was not until well on in 1918 that the number of new ships began at last to match the losses. With the USA in the war more ships were coming on to the Register than were being sunk and in 1918 only 215,784 gross tons of Allied shipping were lost.

Throughout this war of attrition at sea, over 14,000 lives were lost on merchant vessels, 500 on fishing vessels alone. The number of British and Allied merchant ships sunk was 2479, making a total of 7,759,000 gross tons and the number of fishing vessels lost was 675, making a total of 71,765 gross tons. Allied losses were just over 2½ million gross tons, with neutral losses just under that figure. Out of a total Royal Navy strength in 1919 of over 700 ships (including aircraft carriers and auxiliary and catapult carriers but excluding minesweepers and smaller vessels) convoy protection had latterly absorbed over 250 warships and 190 aeroplanes and 300 seaplanes and flying boats, which later became the coastal element of the RAF. In Sir Archibald Hurd's words, the greatest reason for the German difficulties in the Atlantic and on the other sea lanes of the world was, 'The unbreakable spirit of the officers and men of the merchant marine who sailed daily into danger with indomitable courage and no request for recognition or deflection from duty...They insisted to the end upon using freely the highways of the sea without let or hindrance'.

CHAPTER V

'THE STEADY DISCIPLINE OF FREE MEN'
THE MERCHANT NAVY IN WORLD WAR II

The First World War should have reminded the nation that a Merchant Navy provides the vital life line for survival, but, although losses of merchant ships were made good during and immediately after hostilities, the subsequent period of economic slump brought unwelcome changes in Britain's maritime position. In 1919, in spite of the nation's reduced capital assets and liquidity, there was a mini boom with rising wages. The British government had helped to finance the war by issuing Treasury bills and this created post-war speculation and temporary liquidity, financed by borrowing. Many industries were geared to armaments and could not transform quickly to peacetime exports, so that demand exceeded supply, bringing further inflation. Investment in new machinery and equipment was almost non-existent during the war and continued low. Industrialists thought in the short term and the government gave little sense of direction. At the start of the war large profits had been made by shipowners, whose ships had been requisitioned, but from 1915 an Excess Profits Tax was charged and ships were requisitioned at rates laid down by the government in the Blue Book. After the war the mini boom in shipping pushed profits and prices up and increased the number of berths in British yards by nearly a third. The boom, however, was short-lived. In December 1919 the National Government, concerned at the dangerous pressures in the economy, announced its intention to return to the gold standard at pre-war parity when opportunity arose, a policy requiring deflation. When by April 1920 this warning failed to halt inflation, bank interest was raised to 7 percent, public spending was cut and social reforms put aside. At that time unemployment stood at only 2 percent; wages had risen at Trades Union insistence without increases in productivity and this had been accompanied by a shorter working week and a return to pre-war demarcation lines; exports had passed their peak and begun to fall.

This time the deflationary policies took effect. By 1921 there was one of the most sudden recessions in history, with unemployment at 22 percent and wages and prices falling, tied together in a sliding scale. When the bottom of the cycle was reached, the economy began to recover and by 1924 exports were rising to a satisfactory level. A year later, therefore, the government decided there was sufficient strength in the economy to return to the gold standard, a decision taken in the interests of international commerce. Sterling was a reserve currency, traded in by the Commonwealth and other countries, which might wish to convert their sterling balances or trade in another currency, so that a fixed measure of its worth was essential. The nation was not prepared for this second deflationary shock. Wages fell, sparking off the 1926 General Strike, which, collapsing in eight days and leaving the miners, who had started it, to fight on alone, nevertheless cut exports by a third and coal exports, which were starting to recover from the war, by two thirds. Unfortunately the benefits did not materialise and the sacrifice was for nothing. Instead the country moved from a surplus on current account of £104 million to a deficit of £114 million, and reduction in the money supply brought contraction in many industries, including shipbuilding. To make matters worse, in 1930 world trade went into recession and other countries failed to maintain parity with gold. Thus in 1931, in the face of mounting debt and withdrawal of foreign balances, Britain realised she too must again abandon the gold standard, devalue her currency to help exports and return to a policy of Imperial Preference.

During these years of recession, although foreign nations (a number of which had made substantial profits throughout the war and increased the size of their merchant fleets) were now subsidising their Merchant Navies and bringing in restrictions on shipping similar to the discarded British Navigation Laws to increase their share of the world's carrying trade, the British merchant fleet received no protection. Over 3 million gross tons of shipping were laid up and, although in the late 1920's shipbuilding achieved an average annual total of 1.5 million gross tons, compared with 2 million in the year 1911, nevertheless it slumped back again in the early thirties to a quarter of a million and by 1938 stood at only one million. The return to Imperial Preference in 1931 might have brought improvement in shipping and shipbuilding, but it was not until government subsidies came in 1935 that the tide turned. Although in 1937 the gross tonnage of the fleet was the same as in 1914 (20½ million gross tons) and over half the vessels entering and clearing home ports were British, 1½ million gross tons were not registered in Britain; the figure for dry cargo was not as good as that for tankers; there were nearly half a million tons less of ocean going vessels than before the war; the number of firms had shrunk so far that one quarter of total UK tonnage was controlled by five companies and Britain's share of world shipping had fallen by a third. When an accelerated shipbuilding programme was undertaken in response to the Nazi threat an exacerbating factor was that, during the slump, the steel industry had been run down. Out-dated, with insufficient investment, it was unable to respond adequately to the 1936 warship construction programme, just as it had been to the demands for steel in World War I. While the French and Belgians had modernised their steel industries with German reparations, Britain financed her US debt and returned to the gold standard. Naval and merchant shipbuilding was consequently held up by steel shortages and the country had to rely again on imports. Even by 1939 Britain was only producing two thirds of the 1929 output in Germany, where the steel industry had been rebuilt with US loans, given in return for promises Germany failed to keep. With rearmament under way British shipbuilding rallied, rising from one quarter of the world's tonnage in 1932, (compared with a half in 1914), to a third by 1939, by which time British registered merchant gross tonnage was approximately the same as in 1918. These figures, however, hid a problem, which by 1940 reached crisis proportions. Post-war contraction in the shipyards meant that when the industry expanded the pool of skilled labour was too small and, in spite of a large intake of apprentices, this shortage remained endemic throughout the war in a work force which increased in size in the three pre-war years by one third.

Ambitious forecasts were made in Whitehall about emergency shipbuilding in wartime for the Royal and Merchant Navies, it not being realised that, when war came, many skilled men would be employed in ship repairing in naval and civilian yards (10 percent of the Merchant Navy was always undergoing repair) or that vast quantities of imported steel would have to run the gauntlet of the U-boat.

As war drew nearer the danger of the U-boat was again underestimated. Part IV of the 1930 Treaty of London was ratified on November 6th 1937 by 32 nations, including the future Axis Powers – Germany acceding on the 23rd of the month. Whereas the Treaty of Washington, ratified by the USA, Japan and Great Britain, had laid down rules for surface raiders, but had clearly prohibited the use of submarines as commerce destroyers, Part IV of the Treaty of London laid down that, 'In action with regard to merchant ships submarines must conform to the rules of international law to which surface vessels are subject. In particular, except in the case of persistent refusal to stop on being duly summoned or of active resistance to visit or search, a warship, whether surface vessel or submarine, may not sink or render incapable of navigation a merchant vessel, without having first placed passengers, crew and ship's papers in a place of safety – the ship's boats cannot be regarded as a place of safety unless the safety of passengers and crew is assured, in the existing sea and weather conditions by the proximity of land or the presence of another vessel, which is in a position to take them on board'. Because Germany ratified this part of the Treaty, Britain again believed that U-boats would be subject to the same rules as surface raiders and would therefore be restricted to the amount of civilian shipping they could sink. With war coming, the needs for shipping were placed in classes of priority – dry cargo, tankers, troopers, ships for Dominions and Empire and ships for France. There was not enough gross tonnage to fill these needs. Because of the Neutrality Acts the USA would provide no ships, but European neutrals carried almost half the UK and French cargo and the government presumed that Britain would be able to charter. Shipping was not considered by the Committee of Imperial Defence until after Munich and it was calculated that Britain could import 48 million tons of dry cargo in the first year of war, whereas the actual figure was 11 million tons short of this figure. The only requisitioning planned was of liners and passenger cargo ships, 41 of which in the event were converted to armed merchant cruisers (AMCs) and of fishing vessels. As in World War I the latter included trawlers fitted with asdic in place of hydrophones for submarine hunting and others for minesweeping, as well as drifters for laying submarine nets. Other small boats, including some pleasure yachts were also called in. Larger British liners were to serve as troop carriers, the figure being swelled from six to eight by the addition of a French and chartered Dutch liner. The government did not plan at this stage to take further merchant ships into service, but those carrying vital, scarce imports, such as iron ore, timber and wheat were also requisitioned in the early years of war. Some requisitioned ships were manned by the RNR.

The AMCs were initially used for blockade and convoy escort. They were hopelessly outgunned and captains and crews, such as those of the Rawalpindi, under Captain Kennedy's command, or of the Jervis Bay on convoy protection displayed great bravery against overwhelming odds. Captain Fegen, commanding the Jervis Bay in an action on November 5th 1940 with the Admiral Scheer was awarded a posthumous VC for trying to save his convoy of 37 ships, which he was defending as the sole escort. The convoy was ordered to scatter, while he took on the German ship alone. With one leg torn off and the other smashed and 186 of his men killed, he held the enemy at bay for 22 minutes, with dead and dying covering the decks. The Jervis Bay sank, but it saved all but 5 of the merchant ships in the convoy. His citation was for, 'Valour in challenging hopeless odds and giving his life to save the many ships it was his duty to protect'. After this action AMCs were used mainly for blockade duties and replaced on convoy duty by naval ships, which the RN could ill afford. Meanwhile in 1940, under the threat of invasion, 1000 trawlers and drifters were taken into the Auxiliary Patrol to keep watch for German naval forces, until in August Admiral Forbes, C-in-C Home Fleet, urged that trawlers be released back into escort duty. Here in the Atlantic in the first days of war trawlers fitted with asdic sailed in front of the convoys to search for U-boats, until, as RN escorts became more numerous, they moved to the back as rescue ships. Trawlers continued to accompany the majority of convoys, being used also as minesweepers on the Russian route. The large requisitioned liners, steaming at approximately 28 knots, usually sailed alone, being escorted only at the beginning and end of their voyage, although on occasions they had air cover and RN escorts. After fulfilling duties in the East, the Queen Mary started in the Atlantic in 1942, carrying between 10,000 and 15,000 troops at a time, followed shortly afterwards by the Queen Elizabeth. The Queen Mary steamed half a million miles in 6 years and carried three quarters of a million personnel. The Queen Elizabeth was commissioned in November 1940, and undertook similar duties, carrying proportionate numbers of troops and prisoners of war. All ships with a speed of 15 knots and below sailed in convoy from the beginning of the war. They were controlled by the issue of licences, their sailing dates and times being authorised by Navy Control of Shipping Officers. Acts of terrorism against men in lifeboats, as that against the crew of the Greek Peleus, were, with possible exceptions, directed against ships sailing alone. 5 members of this U-boat company were brought to justice by the Germans.

Whereas the First World War was a war of attrition on land and sea, the Second for the Western Allies was a war of attrition at sea. Despite one German lieutenant radioing the position of lifeboats, for which Churchill personally thanked him after he became a prisoner of war, in the first nine months three quarters of a million gross tons of merchant shipping were sunk, almost all without warning. One third of British ships were lost by 1942 and the question remained unanswered as to how this tonnage could be replaced. The answer to build more ships was inhibited by lack of steel and skilled labour, for, in spite of a higher level of productivity than in World War I, even by 1942 Britain built one third fewer ships than in 1913. The alternative to buy or charter from neutral countries seemed impossible, for the Germans were waging a war of fear at sea, sinking on sight neutral ships in British convoys, while neutral vessels sailing independently were examined and, if carrying British goods, were sunk also. All gentlemanly behaviour ended after the defeat of Poland and in November/December 1940 Admiral Dönitz's Standing Order No. 154 was, 'Do not rescue any men, do not take them along, and do not take care of any boats from the ships. Weather conditions and the proximity of land are of no consequence. Concern yourself only with the safety of your own boat'.* (This signal should not be confused with the more strongly worded signal sent by Dönitz after the Laconia was sunk on September 12th 1942 with British troops and Italian prisoners of war on board. On that occasion three U-boats were still on the scene on the 16th using a Red Cross flag when they were bombed by a US aircraft). The countries closest to Germany were the most frightened of her and the Germans made clear that any nation helping Britain by selling her ships would put itself at risk. Britain could have used coercion, for she then classified and insured most of the world's shipping and controlled most of the foreign coal bunkers, but, even if she had been prepared to use these methods, they would not have succeeded because the neutrals could have turned to the USA or elsewhere – although the picture changed after the fall of France. Only the Norwegians and Greeks were prepared to charter a small number of ships on a voyage basis.

In the face of these difficulties imports in foreign ships halved in the first six months of war and, in view of this, Britain decided that the only answer was to bring back some ships from the Empire trade where, in company with foreign ships, they were earning much needed hard currency. The numbers would be few, however, in comparison to needs, and Britain's imports would have to be cut by 10 percent. The Ministry of Food having already made very substantial reductions, now the Ministry of Supply would have to cut raw materials for armaments and other commodities by nearly one quarter. The position was made worse by France's needs for British coal which pre-war she had cut back. The British nearly quadrupled supplies between the first month of war and May 1940, which meant more than doubling the number of ships involved. Even before the invasion of the Low Countries French imports of all goods had fallen by half and, although France was never dependent in the same way as Britain on imports of food and raw materials, nevertheless, after the Germans entered France, nearly one fifth of her wheat production was lost, half her sugar and almost all her coal, iron and steel capacity. In May Britain shipped another million tons of coal to France, but by now her own problems were dire. The shortage of ships was critical.

In April the Norwegian campaign cost the Royal and Merchant Navies further ships, although the loss of German destroyers was more critical to the enemy. Within a week of the attack on the western front in May 1940 – with the Germans again following the Schlieffen plan of World War I, only this time including Holland as well as Belgium – the Allied line had broken. Within three weeks the French army had collapsed and the British army was, in

* P. Padfield. *Dönitz. The Last Furher.* Gollanz London 1984.

Churchill's words, literally, 'Hurled into the sea, with all its equipment lost'. Within six weeks Britain was alone, 'With Germany and Italy at our throats... and Japan glowering on the other side of the globe'. On May 27th the merchant vessels, used to supplement naval craft for the evacuation from Dunkirk, began to gather. 40 motor boats and launches assembled at Sheerness, while, 'At the same time,' wrote Churchill, 'life-boats from liners in the London docks, tugs from the Thames, yachts, fishing craft, lighters, barges and pleasure-boats began to flow towards the sea'. They made up a fleet of nearly four hundred vessels, which ferried back and forth to the ships off shore, carrying nearly 100,000 men. 365,000 men were brought off the beaches under the bombardment of the enemy, with the RAF flying 4822 sorties to the loss of 106 aircraft. 'There was a total of about eight hundred and sixty vessels of which nearly seven hundred were British and the rest Allied'. The Germans saw success snatched from them in what the British regarded as a miracle. A vital factor for success was the holding of Calais and Churchill sent Admiral Somerville to France as his envoy, with instructions that the Green Jackets were to hold it at all costs until the evacuation was complete. Dunkirk cost the British further vital, scarce shipping with which to keep the Narrow Seas safe. Also present in the Channel now were increasing numbers of German torpedo (E) boats operating at 40 knots and accounting for many ships close inshore.

After the fall of France, the Danish fleet came over to the Allies, as did half a million gross tons of French shipping – most French crews returning home after the Armistice, while another half million gross tons of French shipping were requisitioned in British ports. The small Belgian fleet came over and a number of Dutch and Norwegian ships. When foreign crews came into the British merchant marine they were paid more than British crews on an immensely complicated scale. The British also bought half a million dead-weight tons from the Norwegians and one million from the Dutch, leaving both with about one million dead-weight tons each with which to continue trading in the East in hard currency. By the end of the war 8 million gross tons of shipping had come over to the Allies from Norway, Holland, France, Greece, Denmark and Belgium. (Gross tonnage is calculated by cubic capacity of the ship, dead-weight by the weight of the cargo and stores she can carry. Churchill objected to figures coming before him in one form and then another and insisted that the calculations be made to standardise them before they landed on his desk). The increase brought by the addition of these foreign ships was soon to be offset by Italy's entry into the war and the closing of the Mediterranean to trade. The British now had to depend on very long supply routes round the Cape of Good Hope, with some convoys taking many months to reach their destination.

In June the British realised that they would face massive dislocation by the bombing of the docks. A number of retired naval officers had been voluntarily working in welfare organisations in the London docks and, understanding the human problems, could communicate with the men. If London was bombed would the dockers, employed on a casual basis, continue to unload? If, on the other hand, ships were diverted and unloading was transferred west, would the railways stand the strain? The bombing of the London docks began in September, while the increased strain on the ports caused by the fall of France was still being felt. It intensified throughout the winter and spring. In order that ships could be turned around as quickly as possible, crates were piled up quicker than they were being removed, a recipe for chaos. Regional Port Directors were appointed, who, although possessed with numerous powers, were far from dictators in the authority they had to exercise them, needing to persuade rather than coerce. The RPD for the Clyde, and later for all Scotland, was a remarkable man with great tact and human understanding and his ports were so efficiently run that his blue print on how to organise them was used elsewhere throughout the UK. In December the Luftwaffe mined the Thames estuary and in May Liverpool was appallingly damaged by bombers, with a number of other ports being bombed in subsequent raids. In one week of continuous nightly bombing 4000 people were killed in Liverpool, the same number injured and 180,000 houses damaged. Only a proportion of 1 in 11 berths were left in working order, but almost unbelievably the turn around of ships was not slowed down. With more bombing anticipated a Diversion Room was set up in the Ministry of Shipping, so that ships could be sent to safe ports at the end of their voyage. At the Prime Minister's intervention, Inland Sorting Depots were built, the first completed in January 1942.

During the war British losses in merchant shipping were 11,357,000 gross tons, those of the USA 3,334,000 and Allied and neutral 6,503,000. 80 percent of these losses were suffered in the Atlantic. It was here that the largest number of U-boats were destroyed. Casualties in the Merchant Navy were heavy. In 1939 there were 132,000 British serving seamen. By June 1941 this figure was reduced to 108,000. Killed and permanently disabled took 14,400 off the register. The RNR called up just under 7,000. 600 were taken as POWs. Other changes in the figure were caused by some foreign crews leaving and others joining. In the second half of 1941, there was a temporary lull in the Battle of the Atlantic, but by 1942 the figure of killed and permanently disabled seamen had risen to 9 percent, going down in 1943 and 1944 to half that figure. Initially merchant ships had no defence against magnetic mines and their hulls had to be fitted with de-gaussing coils or 'wiped' with a high current passed round the outside. No sooner had that been done that the acoustic mine, detonated by the sound of a ship passing overhead, began to be a greater menace and later again the 'oyster' mine was set off by the pressure set up by a passing ship. Danger from the air – which was increased after Focke Wulfs started operating from Bordeaux – was met by a nucleus of trained gun crews provided by the RN or RNR, supplemented by members of the Merchant Navy (a special corps of merchant seamen gunners), but there were not enough AA guns to go round and the Germans bombed everything in sight including barges and tugs, which could not be defended. The first Oerlikon short range AA guns came from Switzerland and had to be paid for in gold. After the fall of France the supply dried up until alternative sources were found in 1942. The only other effective AA short range gun was the Bofors, also in short supply. Every available weapon in private hands in Britain was called in and Brocks supplied fireworks to try and frighten off attackers with bangs. If it did nothing else it gave crews something to do under attack. Later properly defended merchant ships known as DEMs (defensively equipped merchantmen) were provided with Royal Artillery gun crews, of which there were 14,000 members by 1944. In the first years of war steel was so short that bridges on ships had to be reinforced with sandbags and cement.

In the last ten days of August 1940 22 ships were lost and in one week in October 27 were lost – 20 in one convoy to 6 U-boats. In November 18 fast non convoy ships were sunk. By the end of 1940 2 million gross tons had been lost since the start of the war. Nevertheless faith in the convoy system was constantly reinforced. Out of 47 vessels sunk in February 33 were stragglers or independently routed. These crews faced terrible ordeals, if bombs or torpedoes found their mark death could come suddenly or after days on a life raft or clinging to wreckage in the open sea. Some merchant ships were laden with heavy steel and sank suddenly like stones, giving little or no time to abandon ship. Others carrying oil ignited into blazing infernos and yet others, with 2,000 tons of TNT on board exploded and disappeared in seconds. Until the introduction of rescue ships – initially trawlers and then in 1941 specially adapted passenger steamers with medical facilities – either escorts or merchantmen stopped and picked up survivors. It took iron nerve under air attack to remain motionless while this operation was under way, and in the case of slow steaming merchant ships, these Good Samaritans had then often to be left to find their own way home. The odds against rescue were at first three to two, then in 1941 they shortened to evens and after that improved in the Atlantic, where the first continuous escort was introduced for HX129 in May 1941, but remained under evens for the overall figure, because the Arctic convoys had fewer rescues and survival time was very short even on a life raft or in a lifeboat. In 1941 the most pressing need was for rafts and life jackets which could be worn continuously in dangerous waters. Recruitment of crews before the war had been by captains of ships but in 1939 men were recruited by the Minister of War Transport into a seamen's pool. It was still on a voyage basis in the early days of war and until June 1941 only half the total of British seamen were of call up age, so that they were free to abandon their calling at will. The temptation to do so must sometimes have been very strong. They had no service training, they wore no uniform and they could not be accused of desertion. Although from 1941 they had to register under the Registration for Employment Order and their time ashore was cut, they remained civilians until the end of the war.

Soon, in order to avoid the U-boats, Atlantic convoys were routed north into the fogs and icebergs, where in winter storms it was difficult to keep station. Of the 24,000 merchant seamen sunk in 1940 just under a quarter perished mainly due to the coldness of the water. Many of the masters were men over 60, some were more, other masters were as young as 27, one cabin boy who, with the ship sinking, threw secret papers over-board was only 15½. One quarter of the men serving at the outbreak of war either did not live to see the end or led permanently damaged lives, many having been sunk and suffered exposure or extreme heat a number of times. What was the secret of their morale? Although not in an armed service they shared their privations with the Royal Navy. 21 of the Commodores responsible for passing on escort orders died during service. Many were retired Admirals and Merchant Navy officers well over 60. On a Russian convoy Commodore Dowding (a Merchant Navy Officer), a steward and a cabin boy shared a raft of barrels for 3 hours before being picked up. Upon arrival in Murmansk Dowding went almost straight back on an escort vessel to look for stragglers. When a US crew was considering abandoning ship they were told by the RA gun crew, 'It is our duty to stand fast and take defensive action until the ship sinks'. The crew remained on board. But while example lights the flare path, the courage and generosity of giving came from the men themselves. These captains and crews were imbued with an extraordinary devotion to duty. 'Unable to hit back they waited to be bombed or watched torpedoes travelling towards them or felt the ship shudder as the bombs burst round them,' while all the time the convoys kept on, 'With dogged determination and remarkably little confusion'. Although convoys were sometimes brought almost to a halt by escorts or merchant ships going to the rescue of stricken vessels, picking up survivors, or trying to get ships in tow, it was very rare even under the heaviest attacks for convoy orders not be carried out. These were free men, under no naval discipline, who gave their service willingly. 'No demands involving unusual risks... were ever refused'. In the spring of 1941 a questionnaire was sent to them to discover the state of morale. Conditions of service on the tramps were little better than they had been half a century before. Yet the men had great pride in their profession, the freedom of the sea was in their blood and they understood the peril in which their country was placed. The attempt failed. 'Everyone was willing to answer the inessential questions. They grumbled about food; they realised, they said, what it would mean if Britain were defeated; they had not been approached by enemy agents; they had listened to Haw Haw at the beginning of the war because they thought him funny, but he did not seem funny any longer. The rest is silence'.*

By February 1941 imports to the UK fell to 31 million tons, the same figure as in 1917 when the population was much smaller and by summer the shortage of shipping was desperate. The UK hoped for US merchant ships, perhaps as many as 1 or 2 million gross tons under Lease Lend, but although 50 destroyers and 2 million tons of welcome US cargo arrived in the UK the merchant ships did not materialise. Britain therefore suggested requisitioning foreign ships in South American ports, but, perhaps unsurprisingly, this idea did not appeal to the USA. As the year went by, the Americans generously provided some fast merchant ships for conversion to aircraft carriers, and by December 1941 1 million gross tons of merchant shipping materialised, including some Norwegian ships for which the USA paid in hard currency. By now the supply of fresh vegetables and fruit to the UK had stopped – most of them anyway had come from the continent – and animal feeding stuffs had been almost elimi-

* C. Behrens. *Merchant Shiping and the Demands of War*. HMSO, London, 1955

nated, leading to a halving of the pig population and a drop in poultry of a third. In any disputes between Ministries Churchill insisted that food was not cut further – in order to maintain the, 'Staying power, resolution and stamina of the people'. Instead, fewer men were taken into the Army, saving on clothing and weapons, and there were further cuts in imports of steel and iron which meant fewer ships and armaments. With twice the number of ships lost in 1940 and 1941 as were being replaced by building, the Germans scented victory, but by the end of 1941 the help coming from the USA tilted the balance the other way and the situation in the Atlantic improved.

Meanwhile, overseas the British shipping position was complicated. India, Egypt and other countries required grain, coal and fertilisers. Australia required phosphates from Egypt. South Africa had rice to export, but needed coal. The port of Freetown was short of water which had to be sent in tankers. The cost of freight soared. The shipping crisis came to a head in 1941 when British troops were engaged in Egypt, Greece, Iraq, Syria and Persia. Troops had to be transported and in some cases evacuated, POWs had to be brought out. If cargo ships were withdrawn from convoys in order to carry troops imports would have to be cut further and in May 1941, in spite of Churchill's priorities, food rations in Britain were reduced. Likewise, if merchant ships were built in British yards, escort vessels could not be built. The Prime Minister would not take an American 'No' for an answer to his requests for help, but only one out of the promised six troop carriers crossed the Atlantic before the attack on Pearl Harbor. Meanwhile a food crisis was breaking out in the Middle East. By now the Ministries of Shipping and Transport had become the Ministry of War Transport and the British set up a Middle East Supply Centre in Cairo with a Permanent Representative from the Ministry. This Centre supplied essential goods to Egypt, Sudan, Palestine, Transjordan, Malta, Cyprus, Turkey, Greece, Yugoslavia, Ethiopia, Eritrea and later to Aden, Syria, Lebanon, Iraq, Persia, Saudi Arabia, French Somali land, Cyrenaica and Tripolitania. Throughout the area decisions of the Supply Centre's administrators were reached by committee and compromise. Countries were encouraged to do all they could to help themselves, but the Centre controlled all the shipping and built up emergency food supplies, many of which had to be shipped round the Cape and across the Indian Ocean. The British were over-hopeful about persuading countries to introduce rationing, forgetting that their own people were, 'Literate, obedient and wanted to win the war', but the fact that they could rush supplies to places with shortages, where hoarding was starting, did in fact, prevent famine. One key to the problem was clever loading of ships, for instance a ship carrying vehicles could carry sacks of coal between the wheels. As a number of British ships were withdrawn from the Indian Ocean and Far East cross trades, the Norwegians and Dutch stepped in to this now lucrative business. Differences of opinion arose as to what were luxuries, for what the British now regarded as a luxury other countries regarded as essential.

In June 1941 the Germans attacked Russia and, as in World War I, there was need to supply her with armaments, food and raw materials. The first convoy, sailing in August from Loch Ewe, was led by a Union Castle ship. In the initial agreement the Russians undertook to provide ships, but they did not have sufficient and the bulk of the task fell to the British. Aid, which came increasingly also from the Americans via British ports, was given freely without question of payment. By December 1941 750 tanks, 800 aircraft, 100,000 tons of military equipment, 1,400 vehicles and other supplies had been landed at Murmansk, carried by 41 British and 7 Russian ships, sailing in 8 convoys. The casualties did not start until 1942, by which time the Americans were providing more merchant ships than the British. The escort ships were almost all British, although there were a few French and Polish crews. It is said that survivors of sunk vessels could only live for one minute in that ice-cold water, although undoubtedly some survived longer. Lifeboats were trapped in the ice and in one lifeboat adrift for 24 hours 5 out of 15 men were dead when picked up. There were extraordinary escapes. After the PQ 17 disaster, the story of which is told in Chapter X, a RNVR lieutenant, in command of an icebreaker trawler, led three US merchant ships north into the ice packs, where he ordered all hands to paint the ships white in order to lie undetected from the air until rescue arrived! 'There were many long drawn out ordeals of terror for only in the last few seconds of the dive could enemy bombers be shot down'. Eye witness accounts describe how, 'Many did collapse and lay in extremities of fear, while others displayed a cool courage and heroism probably never to be equalled by any civilian service'. Some ships, particularly minesweepers and trawlers acting as minesweepers, had to remain for long periods in the White Sea ports, where the only anchorage made available was within range of German bombers. By December problems were multiplied by the increasingly chaotic conditions of Murmansk port, where there were no heavy cranes, railways were not always connected with quays and ships were iced in because icebreakers did not arrive. The Russians had little mechanical sense and employed gangs of emaciated convicts to unload, who, in Stalin's regime, were shot if they collapsed at work or came forward to get the pig swill from the British ships. Knowing that Hitler was maintaining his war machine with millions of slave labourers taken from occupied countries, fed on the most meagre rations and disposed of as soon as they failed to be of use, the British came home from Russia very concerned about these sights, but realising they must keep them in perspective. 'Have I not reason to lament', mourned Wordsworth in a poem at the time of the French Revolution, 'What man has done to man'.

Such was the situation in the world in December 1941, when the whole of the Far East erupted with the Japanese attacks on Pearl Harbor, Hong Kong, Malaysia, the Philippines and other islands. Some vessels were ordered to leave Hong Kong in time, but most were intercepted and crews and passengers taken prisoner. With the fall of Singapore more merchant ships were lost and this was followed by the bombing of Darwin, the threat to India and the closing of the Bay of Bengal to British shipping. Ports further west became clogged up with vessels arriving from the Far East and needing repair – 60 percent of which required urgent attention and supplies. Even by June 1942 78 ocean-going merchant ships still lay idle for these reasons – sometimes as many as 25 at a time outside South African ports, where employees had not yet caught the sense of urgency that gripped workers in the UK and US, where minutes counted. Ports in the Far East still in Allied hands were in the same chaotic state as UK ports in 1940. Supplies and the normal routing of scarce vessels were hopelessly disrupted. Rationing was required, but the government of India was not sufficiently strong to impose it, nor the people sufficiently disciplined to accept it. The challenge faced by the British seemed, 'Beyond the wit of man'. At the same time as facing these emergencies, they were trying to fight a war with tremendously long lines of communication and construct bases, pipe lines and emergency dry and floating docks thousands of miles from home. Yet, in the words of the official record, 'The task was undertaken and undertaken successfully... for the British had by now developed the art of management and the will to move mountains'. Britain chartered all the ships she could, and, in company with the USA, requisitioned others and together the two nations made themselves responsible for supplying and feeding the free world.

Now followed the most critical fifteen months of the war at sea in three spheres of conflict. The Japanese were in control of islands within 300 miles of Australia and were threatening India. There was a dearth of naval ships and, with the failure to evacuate the British and Commonwealth fighting men from Singapore, the USA and Australians bore the heat of the day in defence of Australia. The shortage of merchant ships had also reached a crisis. The British, having first ferried troops from Colombo, lent their fastest passenger liners to the Americans to transport troops from the USA to Australia, a task undertaken in half the time required by ordinary merchant vessels. The Mediterranean was virtually closed to merchant shipping except for convoys to Malta, which had to be fought through and the Battle of the Atlantic had reached a dangerous phase. In the first 8 weeks of 1942 80 Allied merchant ships were sunk, and the number was rising dramatically. 'The only thing that ever frightened me during the war', said Churchill, 'was the U-boat peril'. 2½ million gross tons of shipping were repaired in the first 6 months of 1942, but this absorbed half the UK shipyard workforce, who were then not able to build new ships. By now, however, a close friendship had developed between Roosevelt and Churchill. The President realised the continuing desperate need for ships and an agreement was reached by which the UK would concentrate mainly on building naval ships and the USA would supply most of the replacements of merchant ships. This was an unfortunate arrangement in its post-war implications, but Churchill was right in thinking that the only way for the British to ensure sufficient supply of warships was to build them themselves. The US Service Chiefs were not in favour of the President's decision to put American merchant ships under the civilian War Shipping Administration in Washington and this body never acquired the same standing as the Ministry of War Transport in London. In spite, therefore, of a Combined Shipping Adjustment Board set up concurrently in 1942 in London and Washington, the US Armed Services appropriated 56 percent of US merchant ships and a high percentage of new shipping coming from US yards. This acute shortage of ships explains why the British Service Chiefs were unenthusiastic about the US offensive in the Solomons in 1942, knowing how many ships it would absorb. With the President and Prime Minister deciding to concentrate first on winning the European War, they would have preferred that, for the moment, the Japanese be held in a defensive ring.

In 1942 British losses of merchant ships over gains shot up to 1,362, while US gains over losses were 2,663. Even after March 1943, by which time the Battle of the Atlantic was virtually won, this disparity continued, for British net gains for the next nine months were only 719, while US gains for the whole year were 9,221. These figures tell the story of the British predicament. Britain was increasing her output of naval ships but only at the expense of her launchings of merchant vessels. It was also becoming apparent that the USA could give less help in the Atlantic than she had done in 1941, since her escorts were required in other spheres. Moreover the US Navy could not be persuaded to introduce convoys in inshore waters until May. Despite improved radar, more anti-aircraft guns and the use of torpedo nets on long booms fixed to merchant ships to give increased protection, losses on the far side of the Atlantic to British ships were unsustainable and would soon be threatening morale. To counter this there were many improvements in life saving equipment. Red lights in jackets, protective clothing, pumps and special rations for lifeboats were all being supplied and soon orange coloured smoke signals were provided to attract the attention of friendly aircraft. Although losses in the Far East were fewer – 151 Allied ships were sunk between September 1942 and February 1943 of which half were British – nevertheless the shipping position was equally critical. Because of the shortage of British vessels Britain was having to rely on scarce Dominion ships to fill the gap and on British military transports, which were now also carrying civilian goods and engaging in the cross trades before returning home. Discussions on how to solve the problem went round and round. There was no satisfactory solution. Could UK supplies be cut further? By 1942 UK imports had fallen to 22 million tons and in November were 30 percent less than in October. Could the number of military vehicles for the Middle East be cut? Too late it was discovered that there had been an over-supply. What was the risk of famine in India? There were insufficient statistics to forecast. It was clear that if things had not improved by mid 1943 a number of UK factories would have to be shut. As ever, the darkest hour comes just before the dawn. No sooner had these dire thoughts been considered than Britain broke out of the defensive net. In August 1942 came the famous relief of Malta – Operation Pedestal – followed in November by the 'Leap in the dark' – the invasion of Vichy French North Africa, code-named Operation Torch.

The naval story of the amphibious landings is told in Chapter XIII. In all of them the Merchant Navy played a vital role. No one knew to what extent the French would resist and how fast the Axis Powers would get their troops to the battle front. In the event French resistance lasted only days, but the campaign continued until May, when Axis troops surrendered to the 8th Army. Operation

Torch was one of the greatest Armadas in history. The distances travelled were immense and the organisation required formidable. British ships came from the UK and rendezvoused at and set out from Gibraltar for Algiers and Oran. US ships crossed the Atlantic to Casablanca. With the relief of Malta, Allied aircraft could now fly from its airfield to attack Rommel's supplies and submarines could use its harbours.* 240 British merchant ships were escorted to and from Gibraltar by 94 Royal Naval vessels, 112 US merchant ships from America by 75 ships of the US Navy. All the Merchant Navy crews who took part in the amphibious landing and support of the expedition were volunteers. It was hoped that the merchant ships would be able to return to the UK with imports, but instead they had to turn around immediately and get back to the battle area with much needed supplies. On New Year's Day the Naval Commander – later Admiral of the Fleet Viscount Cunningham of Hyndhope – sent a message to the officers and men of the Allied merchant fleets. He paid tribute to their outstanding bravery and skill which, he said, had only added to the great admiration he already had for their work. Victory would be due, 'In no small measure to the courage and tenacity with which the merchant vessels of the Allied nations had kept the sea open in the face of continued and savage attack... The Navy, Army and Air Force alike know how much they depend on your efforts'. By the end of six months no fewer than 1,000 ships had sailed from the UK for North Africa, carrying either troops or supplies.

The cost of success in the Mediterranean was, however, borne by increased strain in other areas, particularly the Atlantic. Ships and aircraft, including auxiliary aircraft carriers had to be withdrawn from convoy routes just as the battle seemed almost won. The Sierra Leone passage in the Eastern Atlantic, leading as it did right down the enemy coast within a short distance of their strike aircraft was considered, without carriers, to be too dangerous for convoys to undertake. Therefore ships outward bound to Africa, Suez and beyond had to sail in convoy to the Azores and then proceed independently. Vessels homeward bound sailed from the Cape or West Africa to Trinidad or New York – sometimes going right down into the South Atlantic to escape U-boats. They returned in the Atlantic convoys, a journey adding nearly 5,000 miles to their normal route. This was a heavy burden on crews and the Prime Minister realised that relief must come soon. 1942 was a year of heavy gales, terrible weather and huge seas, 5½ million gross tons of shipping were lost in the North Atlantic, 646 vessels and 8,000 seamen – nearly half a million gross tons were sunk in November alone.† The Allies were by now facing a shortage of trained personnel to man new ships. Safety regulations for survivors had again been improved: equipment was being provided for making drinking

* S.W. Roskill. *The War at Sea 1939–45*, Vol II, Chapter XIII. HMSO, London, 1954. Page 312 and 322

† Summary of Appendix O. *The War at Sea* [Vol. II] S Roskill. HMSO London 1954. 1942 N. Atlantic 5½ million gross tons. S. Atlantic ½ million. Indian Ocean ¾ million. Pacific ½ million. UK and Mediterranean ½ million. Total 7¾ million.

water from the sea and 3 radio officers were designated for each motor boat – to give the greatest chance of summoning help. Nothing, however, could disguise the essential need to sink more U-boats. At the Casablanca Conference in January 1943 the Allies decided to make defeating the U-boat their first priority.

As 1943 dawned, it seemed, nevertheless, that the British and the Americans had promised greater commitments at Casablanca than it was likely they could fulfil. Churchill knew and told the President that what Britain needed was a solemn promise from the USA about what share of its merchant shipbuilding programme Britain was to get in 1943 and 1944. The North African operation was still absorbing large numbers of merchant ships, 92 sailed in February, 75 more in March, 38 in April. On account of losses in the Atlantic imports to the UK in January fell to half the figure for January 1941 and 42 percent less than January 1942. The British were now eating deeply into their stocks of food and half of their stocks of raw materials were gone. Loans to the USA of British merchant ships for the transport of US troops for the invasion of North Africa meant a reduction of 17 percent in British merchant ships, and this figure was calculated after taking into account the US ships on loan to the UK. The Queen Elizabeth alone made 30 Atlantic crossings from this time onward, carrying US and Canadian troops to Western Europe. In July came a further demand for merchant shipping for the invasion of Sicily. 'Measured by the strength of the initial assault, it breaks all records for amphibious operations', – wrote the US naval official historian. Including merchant ships Admiral Ramsay had 795 ships under his command, and Admiral Hewitt – the US Admiral – 580. In the words of Lord Leathers, Minister of War Transport, 'Merchant shipping has become a fourth service as far as combined operations are concerned'. Rear Admiral Sir Philip Vian, who was escorting the convoys, wrote in similar words to the masters of the Allied merchant ships, 'A great part of the success is entrusted to the well proved steadfastness and seamanlike skill of the Merchant Navies of the Allies, whom I am proud to have under my command in this momentous task'.

The problem was, however, that there were too few merchant ships to go round and there seemed no answer to the shortage, unless the USA could be persuaded to give the British a larger supply of their new ships. In these critical circumstances the Prime Minister saw no alternative but to halve the cross trades in the Indian Ocean, where there were anyway insufficient naval ships to give protection, and get ships home at once after their first consignment had been delivered. But famine was now threatening in India, Ceylon and East Africa, where the main naval base of Kilindini was in danger, and there were fears that it would spread to Rhodesia, Mauritius and the Seychelles. When it finally struck in Bengal it was not so much because imports were cut – for this was only by 3 percent – but because, without similar stocks to those held by the British in the Middle East and with no Ministry of War Transport Representative to organise distribution, there was panic buying and hoarding, which sent the supply system into turmoil. The rice eating population preferred to starve rather than eat wheat and vice versa. The Prime Minister was faced with a tragic dilemma and an 'insoluble conundrum'. With the date for the invasion of Normandy now provisionally fixed, Churchill considered that it would be dangerous to cut UK imports further. In 1943 they had been held at 26.4 million tons, but cutting them further, he said, would reduce the efficiency and will power of the British people so that the invasion of the continent would be launched from a disintegrating base. Would not the people of India, if Britain was defeated, face an even bleaker future?

While these events were taking place in the Mediterranean and Far East, the Battle of the Atlantic had reached a critical stage in March 1943. The story of the last months of the Atlantic struggle fought out in terrible weather and huge seas is told in Chapter X. In the same month the Prime Minister sent his Foreign Minister to Washington to tell the Americans yet once more how drastically UK imports had been cut – to one quarter of their pre-war level in the last four months. Churchill pointed out that British ships were operating in all the danger zones, that Britain had supplied half the cargo tonnage for the North African campaign, not to mention a percentage of the troop tonnage and, when the agreement had been made for Britain to build naval ships and the USA to build merchant ships such a situation had never been envisaged. The US merchant fleet was increasing, while the UK fleet had dwindled. 'We cannot live hand to mouth', wrote Churchill, 'on promises limited by provisos', and this sentence was followed by a threat that British merchant ships would be withdrawn from present military services, 'Even though our agreed operations are crippled'. There was an immediate response – the President promised 2 million gross tons of shipping for British needs. These new US ships, called SAMs, were handed over to Britain in monthly batches until 182 of the promised 200 had arrived. The President wrote, 'You in your country reduced your merchant shipbuilding program and directed your resources more particularly to other fields in which you were more favourably situated, while we became the merchant shipbuilder for the two of us...' He recounted how the US merchant fleet had become larger and would continue to increase rapidly, while 'On your side the British merchant fleet has been steadily dwindling... It has shrunk to something between 6 and 9 million dead-weight tons since the war began.' The President went on to point out that, owing to the recent very high losses of ships, the British now had a pool of trained crews, whereas the USA had a shortfall. The British should therefore man the new ships to be transferred. His offer was most generous, but the USA was not speaking with one voice. Some groups were more pro-British than others. When Churchill at once and with a certain degree of craftiness, diverted some new ships to the Far East cross trades to avert further risk of famine in India, there were ready critics on US Committees, who thought this was a threat to the post-war trading future of other nations. The ships, however, were not withdrawn and the USA increased its shipment of grain and fertilisers to the Middle East to take the strain off the British. While the British criticised the extravagant demands on merchant ships made by the US Service Chiefs, stressing to them the need to send military and civilian cargo together, the USA continued to say that the UK did not need to import so much food.

In September 1943 came amphibious landings at Reggio and Salerno, again drawing into the Mediterranean merchant vessels needed in other spheres. In his Christmas Day broadcast King George VI spoke directly to the men of the Merchant Navy, paying tribute to their long drawn out vigil on the oceans of the world. 'From the Master in command to the boy on his first voyage, you have worked together with the steady discipline of free men who know what is at stake. Your reward is the consciousness of duty done and the affection and respect of all your countrymen'. Then in January British and US troops were landed at Anzio, where a narrow beachhead, supporting soldiers dug into trenches and in the greatest peril, was maintained from the sea for 4 months, placing great strain also upon the sailors of the naval and merchant ships. Churchill thanked the merchant seamen, 'Whose losses have been greater in proportion than those even in the Royal Navy. We never call upon them in vain'. Finally, on the 6th of June 1944 came the invasion of Normandy, the final climax of sea power. Within Operation Neptune, 7,000 ships of all sizes and types sailed to France (or like the block ships for the Mulberry harbours were towed over the Channel to be sunk on arrival). Naval vessels and landing craft apart, it included 736 auxiliary ships and 864 merchant ships, as well as numbers of smaller craft. 'When volunteers were asked for D-day, pretty well all the seamen in the United Kingdom must it seemed have volunteered'. By this time organisation and drill were almost perfect. Master mariners were party to all consultations with military authorities and the Sea Transport Division. Vehicles came out of the ships with drivers and full petrol tanks in the order required for battle – something upon which Churchill had insisted and for which detailed plans of cargo holds were drawn, with wooden scale models of the vehicles requiring shipment. More coasters were used than ocean going ships, because they could get close in shore and if necessary be beached. The larger and ocean going ships, which transported vehicles and tanks across the Channel, discharged their cargo over the side under enemy attack and returned for another load. The operation involved 5 percent of the British merchant fleet, with two thirds of the merchant ships British, since the USA did not have sufficient troopships or any coasters. In 1940 Churchill had promised the continent that the British would return to liberate them. Now, in company with the Armies and Navies of the Commonwealth, the Americans and the Free Forces of the Allies, they had kept their word. In his Christmas Day message of 1944, King George VI spoke thus of the Normandy landings, 'The greatest combined operation the world has ever seen, perhaps the greatest it ever will see. The three fighting Services and the Merchant Navy worked as one vast complex, but perfectly constructed machine and won a resounding victory'.

With hundreds of ships to fit out, repair and supply and floating harbours to construct as well as the usual unloading of imports, the ports took a greater strain than in 1940. The USA said the solution was to cut UK imports further. Although the Prime Minister refused, saying that ships should be loaded with proper regard to the destination of cargo which would save time, this time the USA won its point. The Ministry of Food was told to cut down on stocks in preference to the Ministry of Supply, since, if the invasion went well and there were insufficient raw materials in Britain, she could not switch over to a peace time economy and if it went badly the USA, 'Would be in no mood to help anyway'. Once established the Allied Army had to be supplied from the sea while the people in the liberated areas had to be fed, all of which required further shipping. At this stage the USA was less interested than it was later in civilian needs and saw as its first duty the protection of US lives and the supply of military requirements, so the Prime Minister again resorted to veiled threats. If the USA cut back on British imports, he would not only cut military supplies to India, which would mean fewer ships carrying civilian supplies in the cross trades, raising once more the spectre of famine, but he would also cut down on British supplies for civilian needs in Europe, which would have equally disastrous consequences. This brought a reaction and at the end of 1944 the President ordered that the US Services must be less extravagant with merchant shipping, of which they had 6 million gross tons, much of it used for storage and diversions instead of allowing it to be released back into civilian service after unloading. At the Argonaut Conference in January 1945, the US Services asked for the authority to 'clear' this shipping for civilian needs, but the British Service Chiefs, siding with the civil authorities, stressed the humanitarian principles for which the war was fought, and succeeded in changing the wording from 'clearance' to 'prior consultation'. Meanwhile, with the British dry cargo fleet now down to only 15 million gross tons, the Prime Minister again pressed for US military supplies to be shipped with civilian ones, sticking to 26 million tons as his bottom figure for British imports. The USA said that figure was too high, but by now another friendship had developed, this time between the civil staff of the War Shipping Administration and the British Merchant Shipping Administration in Washington and at the last minute the USA relented and imports were increased. Since, however, stocks had been dispersed the British received instead all sorts of luxury goods – which the children of the time remember – such as tins of sweetened condensed milk, not seen since 1939, and dried bananas. This welcome relief was, however, followed by greater stringency, for during the next few months the Prime Minister lost the argument and imports went down in 1944 to 25.1 million tons. Nevertheless, Britain could and did somehow supply grain to India and the Middle East.

In 1943 at the height of the convoy war, a book on the Merchant Navy was edited by Sir Archibald Hurd. The debt they were owed by the whole world was, he wrote, beyond repayment, 'Their bravery and endurance are beyond praise. Their ships may be sunk under their feet, they may suffer desperate privation and misery in open boats, but no hardship deters them from setting forth in another as soon as opportunity occurs. Their steadfast courage stands star high'. The Germans had spoken of the 'madness' of crews of ships sailing alone, who, with their ships' back broken and low in the water radioed their position and fired back with their inadequate gunnery until ammunition ran out. It was not 'madness' but devotion to duty and intrepid courage. There were incredible feats of endurance – on deck, in lifeboats and in the sea – and outstanding examples of seamanship, like that of the Llangibby Castle, which, crippled by enemy action, sailed 3,400 miles without a rudder, later taking part in the landings in North Africa and Normandy. As the war progressed trials and tribulations were increasingly shared by Americans, Norwegians, Poles, Dutch, French and many others, to whom the Merchant Navy Memorial at Tower Hill pays tribute, commemorating the names and nationalities of ships sunk in both World Wars, together with their gallant crews. Perhaps, however, the saddest stories of all came from the Far East, where there were incidents of the Japanese machine gunning and ramming lifeboats in acts of terrorism. Here, as in the First World War, ships often sailed alone and disappeared without trace, with their Commonwealth and Chinese crews. The courage and self discipline of these men, afloat for days or weeks in open boats, beggars all description. Many died. Through waters not very far from these Captain Scott sailed to the South Pole half a century earlier and wrote these words before his death. 'If things have not turned out as we expected we have no cause for complaint'. It was the patience and loyalty of these Merchant Navy crews in all the oceans of the world, which, together with their courage, were their most remarkable attributes. Lord Mountevans, (Admiral Sir Edward Evans), who had accompanied Scott as far as his last base camp, was one of the contributors to Sir Archibald Hurd's book. 'Our enemies', he wrote, 'had all the advantages in their favour except one. This was the spirit of the brotherhood of the sea, which in past centuries, led to the suppression of piracy and slave trading and to the charting of the oceans, so that men of all races might go down to the sea in ships and do their business in great waters. Historians have praised the daring courage and resourcefulness of the Elizabethan sailors after the Virgin Queen had declared the seas open to the seamen of all maritime nations. But nothing has happened in the past 1,000 years which compares with the dauntless courage, endurance and skill of our merchant seamen who stood up without flinching or complaining to the onslaught of the pirates of the twentieth century'.

CHAPTER VI

WHO PAID THE BILL?
LEND LEASE AND ITS AFTERMATH

If the inter-war recession in shipping and shipbuilding had such serious repercussions on the supply of merchant vessels in World War II, its effects on the Royal Navy were certainly as serious and were exacerbated by the signing of the Treaty of Washington in 1922, under which Britain had to scrap a large number of Dreadnoughts and cut her naval shipbuilding programme in the slips. With the effects of the Treaty rendered more severe by British financial stringency and the desire for disarmament, the strength of the Royal Navy was thus severely depleted. Then in 1931 the seriousness of her economic position led to a decision, taken with regret, to abandon her post-war policy of free trade, which Lord Salisbury believed in so passionately as a means of averting war, as well as of promoting wealth, and return to Joseph (and now his son Neville) Chamberlain's policy of Imperial Preference, imposing tariffs on imported goods from outside the Commonwealth and targeting exports to Dominions and Colonies. At the start of the twentieth century the Conservative and Unionist Party had been split on this issue. Lord Salisbury, who retired in 1904, had seen free trade as an instrument of peace, and issued repeated and prophetic warnings about the division of the world into trading blocks and the race into armaments, whereas Joseph Chamberlain, who divided the Party then led by Arthur Balfour, saw Imperial Preference as a way of helping Britain's economy and did not see the danger of erecting tariff walls in the face of German exports, whose aggressive expansion threatened Britain's overseas markets. For free trade to flourish all nations must play the game on equal terms and these were absent before and after the First World War – in 1904 Britain faced high tariffs in the USA, Russia, Germany and France and in 1914 a German firm was even given the contract for rewiring the British Embassy in Peking.

Once Imperial Preference was in place in 1931 economic recovery began and continued. Then in 1934 came the need to re-arm in the face of the mounting Nazi threat. As John Kennedy points out in his book WHY ENGLAND SLEPT Britain had been the only major power to reduce her armament appropriations between the years 1926 and 1932. She had deluded herself into thinking that by disarming unilaterally she was leading the world to multilateral disarmament, just as she had done over the Repeal of the Navigation Laws. In 1932 a Disarmament Conference was called from which Germany withdrew in 1933, after Hitler became Chancellor, backed by leading German financial and industrial institutions. During 1932 defence expenditure went down in Britain, France, Italy, and the USA, while remaining stable in the USSR. In Japan, which had invaded Manchuria in 1931, it rose by 52 percent. In Germany it increased by 3 percent, but this was followed by a rise of 27 percent in 1934, and 85 percent in 1935. Meanwhile. in the USSR expenditure on defence jumped in 1934 by 223 percent. The Second World War followed, for which

Britain was very much less prepared than for the First, with a repeat of her post-war economic problems and debts, this time of greater magnitude, more humane and unselfish solutions and direr long term economic and financial results. All the weaknesses in Britain's inter-war industrial strategy were highlighted by re-armament, for without steel a nation cannot build the vital components for peace or war. With shipyards idle inter-war, there had been insufficient investment and the number of skilled men in the naval and merchant shipyards was down to dangerously low levels. Britain entered the Second World War with her financial and industrial might depleted, her Merchant Navy less easily replenished and her Royal Navy weakened by cuts and cancellations in defence spending.

In these circumstances it was not surprising that by May 1940 her need for more naval ships was desperate, in order to form a shield against the invasion of her extensive coastline, and to escort convoys across the Atlantic and other oceans of the world. Even before the fall of France Churchill was urgently asking Roosevelt for 50 destroyers, motor boats, flying boats, 100 aircraft, anti-aircraft equipment, munitions and steel. Through his American mother Churchill understood both American generosity and self-interest and he thus always presented his case from the American point of view. He pointed out that in the case of an Allied defeat the USA would be faced with a Nazified Europe, intent on world as well as European conquest, and that the USA itself would not be safe from Hitler's aims. 100 Italian submarines would soon be in the war to augment the U-boat fleet. 'If American assistance is to play any part it must be available soon'. On June 4th Churchill spoke to the British nation in these words: 'If, which I do not for a moment believe, this island or a large part of it were subjugated and starving, then our Empire beyond the seas armed and guarded by the British fleet would carry on the struggle until in God's good time the New World, with all its power and might, steps forth to the rescue and liberation of the old'. Lord Lothian, the British ambassador in Washington, warned that these words might encourage those Americans who thought that, if Britain went under, the Royal Navy would cross to them. Churchill immediately told Lord Lothian to quash the idea of any such outcome.

In the same month Churchill asked again for destroyers, promising to return them at six months notice, if only they could be delivered soon. With the fall of France the whole weight of German armour would be thrown against Britain, provided Hitler could first win command of sea and air. Again he warned that, if Britain were defeated, a Nazified Europe would be stronger than the USA, adding that a puppet British government might hand over the Royal Navy. This last fearsome suggestion came back to haunt Churchill, for, before handing over the destroyers, Roosevelt tried again and again to extract promises, which, because they would have tied his freedom of action in a moment of crisis, Churchill resolutely refused to give. British morale, he told Roosevelt, was concentrated and dependent on the fact that, in Queen Victoria's words, the country, 'Was not interested in the possibility of defeat'. In August, when the destroyers were still not forthcoming, Churchill instructed Lord Lothian, British Ambassador to Washington, to tell the USA that, in the event of defeat, America would never be able to pick up the debris of the British Empire, but would risk instead being outmatched by the Axis Powers at sea. He told Lord Lothian to point out that British islands and naval bases would certainly be seized by the Nazis and would threaten the security of the USA. 'If we go down Hitler has a very good chance of conquering the world'. The old but reconditioned destroyers might, he instructed Lord Lothian to suggest, be traded off in exchange for a lease to the USA of vital bases in the West Indies and Bermuda.

On July 31st Churchill told Roosevelt by letter that in the last ten days four destroyers had been sunk and seven damaged and that without the extra US destroyers the war might be lost. Joseph Kennedy, the replaced ambassador to London, had already reported that it was. The bases and islands to which Churchill referred were of great strategic defence value to the Americans. They would be the stepping stone by which America could be attacked from Europe. Regarding the 50 destroyers he commented that there was, 'No comparison between the intrinsic value of these antiquated and inefficient craft and the immense permanent and strategic value afforded to the USA by the enjoyment of the island bases'. For one thing they defended the Panama Canal. The two leaders were under different pressures. Churchill had to present the leasing of the bases to Parliament as necessary for the security of the world. Roosevelt had to persuade Congress it was a good bargain.

At last, on September 2nd came the simple exchange of letters between Cordell Hull and Lord Lothian. 'In view of the friendly and sympathetic interest of His Majesty's Government in the United Kingdom in the national security of the United States to co-operate effectively with the other nations of the Americas in the defence of the W. Hemisphere, His Majesty's Government will secure the grants to the government of the United States freely and without consideration of the lease, for immediate establishment and use of Naval and Air bases and facilities for entrance thereto and the operation and protection thereof on the Avalon Peninsula and on the Southern Coast of Newfoundland and on the east coast and on the Great Bay of Bermuda'. Then, in Cordell Hull's grateful acceptance of this 'generous act' it was promised that the USA would transfer fifty destroyers from the reserve fleet in Philadelphia to the United Kingdom. Although they were old and needed much unenvisaged maintenance and, although it may seem now a small contribution in comparison with the size of the Royal Navy at that time, nevertheless it was a most welcome gift and contributed more escorts than the present destroyer and frigate strength of the Royal Navy (there no longer being any larger ships except the carriers). Moreover, the immediate handing over of the bases meant that the USA established an air base on Bermuda, which aided British convoys.

Nothing more could be done until the Presidential election in November 1940. Both candidates, Wendel Wilkie and Franklin Roosevelt, were now committed to giving aid to Britain and to the struggle for the preservation of justice and freedom of law. At this time Britain was still paying for everything she had received from the US – except for the destroyers which were paid for by the leases – but now all gold and dollar reserves and overseas investments were gone, with the exception of some $2,000 million investments not as readily saleable and some gold, carefully hoarded in a South African vault. ''We felt', said Churchill, 'as if we were on a desert island on short rations which we must stretch as far as we could'. He describes in his history of the war how from May onwards the government had, 'Followed a simple plan, namely to order everything we possibly could and leave financial problems on the lap of the everlasting Gods'. It was this 'simple plan' which, after the war, led to many shortages and financial problems which have still not properly been resolved. Did the world owe Britain an obligation for her heroic and at that time solitary stand against Hitler or was she to be left in 1945 to pick up the remaining debts which had fallen from that all providing lap?

In December Churchill wrote to Roosevelt again, saying that, although the danger of invasion had passed, the immense losses to merchant shipping posed a new and mortal peril. In the First World War the French, Italian and Japanese Navies had fought with the British (and later the USA), but now Britain fought alone. If the French Navy were to pass into German hands – Vichy France had so far managed to resist this, although the bulk of the French Navy had not joined De Gaulle – then West Africa would follow suit. Churchill now became bolder, knowing that the sending of destroyers had already compromised US neutrality. He asked if US naval forces could escort British convoys on their side of the Atlantic and whether Eire could be persuaded by the US to open her ports to RN ships. At this time Britain was excluded from Eire's ports, which continued throughout the war, and on account of resulting losses in the Western Approaches could only access via the North Western Approaches. He pointed out that Britain urgently needed more aircraft as well as ships, artillery and tanks. All her reserves were now gone. She could not pay the contractors to whom she owed money. If she was to be stripped to the bone, (again Churchill appealed to American self interest), then she would be of no use to the USA after the war as an importer of American goods, which would cause massive US unemployment. Roosevelt brooded and then decided that the solution was to lend or lease the required equipment. By a 1892 statute it was possible to lease American Army equipment for a maximum of five years. 'Give us the tools', Churchill said, 'and we will finish the job'.

In March 1941 the leases of the bases were formally drawn up for 99 years – in the Avalon Peninsula, Newfoundland, the Great Bay of Bermuda, the Eastern side of the Bahamas, the Southern coast of Jamaica, the Western coast of St Lucia and of Trinidad, Antigua, and British Guyana. These were to be given 'In exchange for naval and military equipment and material which the US government will transfer to HMG'. From now on anything needed by Britain – the arrangement was not confined to armaments but included oil, raw materials and food – was to be either leased or lent. It was the most remarkable gentleman's agreement in history, made on what might be called 'the old boy network'. Succeeding generations should know how it came about and how it worked to defeat the cruellest tyrant who ever came to dream of world conquest in modern, or indeed medieval, times. Churchill recounts how, when all was arranged, he was able to witness once more the extraordinary combination of generosity and self interest of his American cousins. On the one hand the US War Department ordered equipment it did not need in order to pass it on to the British, while on the other the US sent a ship immediately to pick up the last British gold in South African coffers and UK negotiators were appointed to arrange the sale of remaining British investments in the USA. Thus, although Britain was the only nation in the free world who fought the war from start to finish, for four fifths of the time she fought it, to a notable extent, on American money.

In June 1941 Hitler attacked Russia and she became Britain's ally in the struggle against the Axis Powers. On August 14th 1941 Churchill and Roosevelt met in mid Atlantic to sign the Atlantic Charter. The fact that Russia was not democratically governed made it all the more important to formulate the visionary aims of the Allies at such a time. The principles of the Atlantic Charter were later embodied into the constitution and aims of the United Nations, respecting the rights of all people to choose their own government and have their sovereign rights restored. Nations should abandon force and promote peace on land and sea, so that men should no longer suffer from fear and want. Both nations bound themselves not to seek territorial changes, which were not in accord with the wishes of the people concerned, and to further equal access on the part of all states to raw materials, trade and full collaboration in economic fields.

The commitment in the final paragraph of the Atlantic Charter to free trade was developed further in a Mutual Aid Agreement signed between the US and the UK on February 23rd 1942, two months after the attack on Pearl Harbor and US entry into the war. In this document it was stated that it was, 'Expedient that the final determination of the terms and conditions upon which the government of the UK receive such aid and of the benefits to be received by the US in return', should be, 'deferred until the extent of the defence is known'. As a preliminary agreement the USA would continue to supply to the UK defence articles, services and information, which the President authorised. The UK would do the same for the US, 'In so far as it may be in a position to supply'. This was the start of UK Reciprocal Aid, which was more extensive than is sometimes admitted. The UK bound herself further to return all defence articles not destroyed, lost or consumed, which were not of use in the defence of the USA or the Western Hemisphere. Then came a sentence which developed further the spirit of the Atlantic Charter and bound both countries to certain post-war economic policies, 'In the final determination of the benefits to be provided to the USA by the UK in return for aid... terms and conditions shall be such as not to burden commerce between them and the betterment of world wide economic relations. They shall include agreed action to eliminate all forms of discriminatory treatment in international commerce and to the reduction of tariffs and other trade barriers'.

By summer 1942 Russia's position was desperate, Stalingrad was under siege, her armies were falling back and Moscow was threatened. Aid from Britain to Russia started in August 1941, and on July 14th 1942 both countries undertook formally to give one another military and other aid during the war.

The Russians were not in a position to help Britain except by valiantly contin-uing to fight against the Axis Powers, pinning down German troops on the eastern front, but military supplies of all kinds were transported through Arctic waters and later overland through Iran. The amount of British aid has remained undisclosed – the Foreign Office Files are not opened until 1994 – but the US contribution to Russia is put by some economists at £2.35 billion, which may seem high, when compared with aid to Britain under Lend Lease estimated at £6,700 million*. Against this latter figure should be set off the £1,300 million given to the USA in UK Reciprocal Aid – including help with atomic discov-eries and plans for new aeroplanes – which reduced the total to just under £5,500 million. A further £5,500 million had been paid by the British for mili-tary and other supplies in money or transfer of assets before September 1940 and it should be borne in mind that Britain also paid for Lend Lease by the transfer of her island bases. No one should ever underestimate the generosity of US giving, but what may have been as serious to British interests as the leas-ing of the bases was the inference in the Mutual Aid Agreement that the British would not return to Imperial Preference after the war. Article VII stated that there would be, 'Agreed action' by both countries 'to the elimination of all forms of discriminatory treatment in international commerce'. No time limit was set and the matter was long disputed afterwards, Churchill trying to resist pressure, the US pressing for abolition. Although Imperial preference might have been whittled away anyway by shortage of dollars and weakness of ster-ling the question as to the extent of the sacrifice remains unanswered.

In 1944, as victory came closer, the US, UK and European governments met to discuss the financial future of the free world. It was felt that the rigidity of the gold standard – tying paper currencies to a rare metal – had caused a lack of flexibility in world markets, which, together with the problems caused by countries going back on and coming off the gold standard at different times, had contributed to, if not been the cause of, the depression of the 1930's. Now at Bretton Woods a compromise was agreed, by which the dollar would be pegged to gold at 35 dollars an ounce and other currencies, which had all been adversely affected by the war, would become convertible to dollars as soon as possible after peace came. London was seen as the financial centre of Europe and sterling was to be re-established as an international reserve currency, with London as the exchange market. The International Monetary Fund and World Bank were set up, the first to provide short term loans, the second as the lender for long term developments, particularly to poorer less developed countries. Lord Keynes wanted these institutions to have their own lending currencies but it was agreed instead that the founding nations would contribute part in their own currencies and part in gold or dollars. States with deficits or surpluses in their trade would be required to bring their current accounts into balance to avoid strains being cast on the world economy.

* Britain did not switch to the US definition of a billion until 1974, after which Department of Trade figures show a thousand million as a billion, although the British measure is still used as well in other contexts.

When peace came British hopes and the role that she was expected to play were greater than the contents of her national purse or the physical strength and energy of her people. War torn continental Europe had been ravaged – psychologically, physically and economically – by German occupation. Hordes of slave labour had been taken from other countries to Germany to work in munitions. 30 million persons had been forcibly dispersed and 7.5 million coerced into the German labour force. Food and raw materials had been confiscated and taken to Germany. It has been estimated that $42 billion were diverted to Germany in various ways. The horrors and deprivations that Europe faced can never be under-estimated. 'Over wide areas', said Churchill, 'a vast quivering mass of tormented, hungry, careworn and bewildered human beings gape at the ruin of their cities and homes and scan the dark horizons for the approach of some new peril. Among the victors there is a babel of jarring voices; among the vanquished the sullen silence of despair'. Nevertheless, occupied Europe was not in debt, for, apart from her brave resistance network and welcome volunteers serving in Allied forces, her role had of necessity been mainly passive. France, for instance, in 1945 had substantial reserves and no indebtedness.

Meanwhile, for six years Britain had been a desert island, overworked, overstrained and short of proper food. 42 percent of her workforce had been in the armed services, and only 2 percent of the rest had been working in peacetime exports, which in 1944 were only 28 percent of their pre-war level. The release of men to the services had been achieved by others working massive overtime (many working 63 hours a week, not including travelling time), the return of retired workers and the recruitment of 2 million women to munitions. One bizarre statistic of the war is that 1.3 million German women were still employed in domestic service, showing how little disruption there was until 1944 in the ordinary way of life of the upper and middle classes. Although British casualties had not been as catastrophic as in the First World War, her stock of capital fell in the Second by nearly twice as much (28 percent compared to 15 percent) and on external account there had been a net sacrifice of nearly £5 billion in assets disposed of or debt contracted. Food, which had been cut at intervals during the war, was again under threat of further cuts, which even the ascetic Stafford Cripps felt were impossible. The nation was virtually bankrupt, with material things lost, although this was off-set by the joy of being able to rest upon its oars, safe from fear of death or slavery. So serious was the position that Arthur Bryant wrote in a newspaper article in the summer of 1946 that if Britain went down, 'It will create a vortex in which the whole of civilisation will crash'. The continent naturally expected Britain and the USA to give a lead back to peacetime sanity, with financial and moral help in reconstruction. This was greatly needed, for the standard of living in France had fallen by 50 percent and similar figures applied across Europe. Nevertheless, because of UK financial problems, world wide commitments and calls upon her purse, it was the British who, in 1949, returned to dried eggs, queues and rationing after a happy, well-fed holiday on the continent, their pockets emptied of their £25 travel allowance. This impression is borne out by statistics, for by 1948 the French output had risen again to its pre-war figure. John Colville reports in his diary ON THE FRINGES OF POWER how Churchill, mindful of the debts Britain was incurring, prophesied gloomily about a lower standard of living after the war for the British people. Nevertheless, to maintain morale and give the nation the will to win through those dark days of siege, which required hope and courage, the assurance had been given that there would no return to pre-war unemployment, but instead a post-war welfare state, outlined in the Beveridge Report and now called by some writers in derogatory terms a 'New Jerusalem', in which no one would want for housing, health, education or basic living requirements. Just as Churchill promised the people of the continent that the British would return and liberate them, his government also assured the British people, through whose steadfast courage – together with that of their Allies – the promise to the continent was honoured, a decent standard of living for all. At the time this welfare had not been costed and now here was 'the rub'.

Two days after the Japanese war ended the newly elected Labour government was told by the Americans that Lend Lease would stop within two days and Britain must pay for or return the goods already in the pipeline, in accord with the President's promise to Congress. History cannot tell us whether, if Roosevelt had lived or Churchill had been re-elected, Lend Lease might not have been replaced by another generous and temporary financial arrangement to help Britain over the crisis she faced. The world never understood why the British voted out so great a leader, to whom the world was deeply grateful and whose National Government had been most ably advised throughout the war. The USA was under no obligation to finance the setting up of a welfare state by a Labour government, which planned a massive programme of nationalisation. Members of Congress had not been in Britain between 1940 and 1945 and could not understand the reason for the Beveridge Report and the assurances about the 'New Jerusalem'. In August the Labour government, faced with debt and no promise of aid, went cap in hand to the USA hoping for a grant. Imports stood at 60 percent of their pre-war level, but outgoings in foreign exchange were running at £2,000 million a year and income from exports, invisibles and the US forces stationed in Britain came to less than half that amount. Even with a quick build up of exports the dollar deficit would still be vast and, with an economy geared to such an extent to armaments, it was difficult to see how this could be achieved. Lord Keynes said it was a financial Dunkirk, but the country was unable to take it in and the government felt unable to tell the truth, lest it cause a run on the pound. People were suffering from exhaustion and the myopia of siege mentality, which gripped the nation long after the war ended and manifested itself in disciplined acceptance of controls and pride in hardship, which, together with the current belief in socialist centralisation, blunted the impetus of entrepreneurial endeavour.

Calls on Britain's purse seemed limitless. Not only had she to pay for garrisoning and policing trouble spots all over the world, but she had also to garrison and feed the West Germans at the same time as introducing bread rationing at home on July 21st 1946. By this time, according to the Times newspaper, shiploads of wheat and barley had been diverted from the UK to Germany, yet the British people seemed unaware of this. There was no resentment, people had got used to accepting things and it was natural that they should feed their erstwhile enemies. In six years of war the country had been superbly run. Savings had been high – there was nothing to spend money on – and weekly wage rates had kept up with prices, but not outrun them, although, owing to overtime, earnings had risen by half as much again. The British had never allowed themselves to think beyond the end of the war and, having disciplined themselves not to complain, had not noticed the run down in the country's infrastructure and in the machinery for peacetime exports. Only in shipbuilding, aircraft and munitions had there been investment, much of it due to Lend Lease. Now the country was faced with worn out plant, damaged buildings and bomb sites transformed into car parks, standing empty because of rationed petrol, which all required money and raw materials for replacement, restoration and redevelopment, as did also the expensive welfare state with its legal safeguards to ensure democracy. The socialist principle was that the rich would pay, but no one is rich in a country which cannot pay its bills.

There were differences of outlook across the Atlantic about aid. Lord Keynes was the negotiator. He saw that the USA was likely to regard Britain as any other European country, but Britain's external debts were vast as the result of her expenditure on the war. No other country faced such a situation. Even the US overseas expenditure had been less. The British felt they were owed some recompense for the wartime distortion of their economy, but the USA thought they had been sufficiently generous in Lend Lease. Instead of a grant Britain was offered a loan of £3.75 billion at 2 percent, repayment of which was to start in five years and be spread over 50. Lend Lease debts of $65 million were added to the loan. The interest was generous, but the loan was subject to no discrimination against individual US imports (which meant importing US films as well as butter) and to full convertibility of sterling through the London exchange within two years. What the USA wanted was access to the sterling area on equal terms. Although, taken as a group, the sterling area was solvent, the US had ended the war as the only exporter of many vital commodities, including food, which could only be paid for in dollars. The Labour government considered the option – nicknamed 'starvation corner' – of making the country independent of the USA, but decided it was politically and economically impossible. Lord Cobbold, Governor of the Bank of England, expressed himself as being against convertibility in the Bretton Woods sense and tried unsuccessfully to persuade the Americans to allow sterling to be convertible in the hands of the holders, so that it could be spent anywhere, and not as laid down in Bretton Woods, which would expose the UK to heavier demands for foreign exchange. This implied a system of transferable accounts, as was later adopted – 'Moneys would only be convertible to the currencies of countries, which have themselves accepted convertibility'. At the same time he advised the Labour government that if they would desist from so much public expenditure, much of it on the welfare state and nationalisation, which could not endear them to the USA, the Americans might give them better terms.

Again his words went unheeded – the government pressed on with their social-ist programme (1947 was the year in which most of their legislation was passed) but, realising the gravity of their economic situation, they were humbled into accepting a waiver clause, which they said was not what should be expected from a victor nation, that if Britain's current account deficit fell below the pre-war average for a period of five years no interest would be charged on the loan. The debt owed by Britain – a victorious nation – to a number of countries in the sterling area alone, notably Egypt and India, plus the funds required to pay interest on the American loan added up to what the Russians were claiming from Germany, but did not in fact receive in repara-tions from East Germany. The Conservative Front Bench abstained when acceptance of the loan went through Parliament and many Conservatives voted against it.

In the five years between 1945 and 1950 there was an improvement in Britain's current account, but also a continuing dollar drain, as Lord Cobbold had predicted. Although imports were held to well below the pre-war figure, there was no hoped for dollar flow from other countries into London to pay for food and raw materials from the US and the interest on the resulting dollar deficit had to be financed, absorbing 80 percent of the loan. This predicament had not been anticipated at Bretton Woods, when the seriousness of Britain's post-war debit position had not been understood, nor the fact that many conti-nental countries, although ravaged by war and with assets stripped by occupy-ing forces, had, nevertheless, since 1940 been earning money from their colonies' exports, from shipping and other overseas ventures and were in credit when peace came. Also, unlike Britain, these countries were not respon-sible for clearing up German labour camps and ravages of war and occupation, for rehabilitating refugees and displaced persons, for feeding Germans and giving a lead in providing contributions to set up institutions, such as the IMF, the World Bank, and UNRRA. They were thus able to spend more of what they had internally and could convert their surpluses into dollars as opportunity arose, causing a strain on sterling.

In spite of these difficulties the sun shone in Britain during a wonderful summer in 1946. The war was over, hopes rose and exports improved. The euphoria was short lived. In Britain, as on the continent, the coal industry was unable to meet the increased domestic and industrial demands for energy in one of the worst winters on record. 'We face an emergency', said Attlee, 'of the worst gravity'. Thousands of coal wagons were stranded in the snow. The shortage of fuel in Europe reached crisis proportions. Instead of rising to meet it coal output fell everywhere, due to lack of investment, dilution of skilled labour and insufficient nourishment of the workforce. Truman offered to divert US ships with coal to British ports, but Attlee turned down the offer, because he said the need for coal in Europe was just as pressing. Governments realised that it was no use asking for higher production from people chronically under-fed. The embryo of the Marshall Plan was conceived during that cold winter of 1947, although General Marshall did not make his famous speech until June 1948 and the first generous interim American aid did not arrive in Europe until

December of that year.

Meanwhile, the deadline given by the USA to Britain for the convertibility of sterling was fast approaching. All through 1947 Belgium had been converting her large sterling balances to US dollars to the tune of £200 million. Norway, Ireland and Germany had been doing the same. The French alone – to their great credit – borrowed from the UK in sterling and repaid in dollars. There had also been an outflow of capital in loans from the UK to the sterling area, which meant that countries outside Europe had convertible sterling balances, in addition to the existing large holdings accumulated by India and Egypt during the war. In July sterling became convertible, but within five weeks convertibility had to be suspended, causing the USA to halt payments on the loan. The Cabinet was divided on what action should be taken. Dalton wanted to cut imports and overseas expenditure and increase exports, making the UK as independent as possible of the USA. Bevin said 'No'. The British must first stop paying dollars to feed and help the Germans before they imposed further rationing on their own people, (during that year £60 million had gone in 3 months on feeding the fused UK and US zones). Fortunately negotiations led to US understanding of the so-called temporary nature of suspension and loan payments were unfrozen. Nevertheless the decision was made to cut UK calories, and Attlee suggested selling art treasures. In August the government brought back controls of labour and everyone of working age had to have a job. All this affected the morale of the nation. Many British people blamed socialism for these stringencies and the government again felt it could not tell the public the truth for political and financial reasons. It was indeed a bizarre situation in which to find a victor nation, without precedent in history.

A Government Economic Survey in mid 1945 had warned of the dangers in these words, 'It is no exaggeration, but a sober statement of fact to assert that our external problem after this war will be at least as considerable as that of Germany after the last war'.

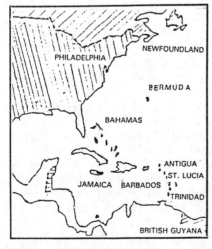

CHAPTER VII

'A STAR WAS LOST'
BRITAIN'S POST-WAR ROLE

While Britain struggled through these financial maelstroms, events in Europe and the world were moving quickly. They were events which led Britain to question her maritime policy and to move towards greater European integration. The idea of a united Europe was fostered by the Marshall Plan (or European Recovery Programme), which was undertaken by the USA between 1948 and 1952 and went to eighteen European countries. But for the generosity of the United States, said Churchill in his Zurich speech on the 19th September 1946, 'Which has now realised that the ruin or enslavement of Europe would involve its own fate as well, the Dark Ages would have returned in all their cruelty and squalor. They may still return'. Churchill's ideas on post-war Europe, incorporated into this speech, included the vision of a 'European family of nations', with – as the first practical step – a Council of Europe with supreme Judiciary and economic and social committees, inter alia. This had birth at a gathering led by Churchill in 1948 in the Hague – home of the Court of International Justice – out of which grew the European Movement and Council of Europe in Strasbourg, a consensus of free states with common adherence to justice, human rights, democracy and the rule of law. In this speech Churchill called for a Europe, 'United in the sharing of its common inheritance', in which France and Germany in partnership would play a leading role, although the German states might take their seats individually. Placing upon Germany the responsibility for the, 'Crimes and massacres' of the twentieth century, 'For which there is no parallel since the Mongol invasion', and which arose from the Germans', 'Vain passion to play a dominating role in the world', he called for an act of 'blessed oblivion' or forgiveness and for a 'European family' to be built within a new fabric – 'A structure under which it could dwell in peace… as free and happy as Switzerland is today'. He did not see this European group conflicting with the United Nations – quite the reverse – and envisaged a number of, 'Broad natural groupings', the USA, the British Commonwealth of Nations, the USSR, who would be, 'The friends and sponsors of this Europe'. Meanwhile, with the war still whirling round them, the Benelux countries planned in 1944 a zero tariff union which was put into practice in 1948 and formalised as the Benelux Economic Union in 1953. It is clear from this speech that Churchill believed in a united Europe, but did not see Britain entirely within this interlinked system, 'The English speaking world', he said to John Colville in November 1940, 'Would be apart from this, but closely connected with it and it alone would control the seas as the reward for victory… England and America would have equal navies'. Churchill knew, as all British statesmen have known, that it was in Britain's – and America's – interests to have a stable Europe in which one state or alliance did not dominate the smaller nations, but he knew also that, being an island with a large population and few natural resources, Britain depended upon exports for her survival. He therefore pictured for her a continuing maritime role, which, opening up in 1485, had been undertaken in particular after the Congress of Vienna when – with a few exceptions – it had kept the world at peace for over half a century. He did not foresee that there would be no reward for victory, only debts and responsibilities with no money to pay for them.

The Marshall Plan was conceived during the long cold winter of 1946/7, but it was the British cabinet decision in February 1947 that it could no longer aid the Conservative government of Greece or supply help to Turkey that, in the face of mounting Soviet threats, forced the Americans to act. Truman addressed Congress in March 1947, at which time he feared Germany and Austria might join the Soviet bloc. The USA, he said, would support free peoples anywhere resisting attempted subjugation, external or internal. By the time interim aid was sent in December the position all over Europe was critical. Marshall Aid was given primarily to help war torn Europe, but also to contain the threat of Communism arising out of devastation. The Soviets were entrenched in Eastern Europe, they were still in Iran and wanted bases in Turkey. The Americans wished to avoid the mistakes which they thought, 'Had perhaps brought about World War II'. They believed they had lost the opportunity after 1918 to lead the world into a better era; they felt that they should not have retreated into isolationism, followed selfish economic objectives, refused to ratify the Treaty of Versailles, turned their back on the League of Nations and failed to provide the military power to contain the aggressors. During the Second World War, they, therefore, asked themselves what policies they should pursue towards Germany. Churchill believed victors should be magnanimous – Napoleon had chosen to be imprisoned by the British because he thought them most likely to treat him kindly – and he said to John Colville on the same occasion in 1940 that, although Prussia should not be allowed to have an army for 100 years, the German states should not be included in this ban; there should be no war debts or reparations, only the Nazis and Gestapo should pay and suffer for their misdeeds. Nevertheless, he faithfully promised in his Zurich speech that the Germans would be deprived of all power to ever again wage another war of aggression.

In 1944 Roosevelt's Secretary of the Treasury, Henry Morgenthau, was quoted as saying that Germany should be severely punished, her economy forcibly held down and her resources used for the rehabilitation of her former enemies. Other Americans argued that this would impose severe strains on the US economy, of which Germany was a natural trading partner, and that Germany's talent for industrial production and advance should be rebuilt and channelled into peaceful aims. With the war over it was clear that neither the Soviet Union nor France, both of whom had suffered a number of times at the hands of German invaders, favoured this idea. The US administration was itself divided. The State Department wished to restore France to its leading role; the Army – in which General Marshall had been Chief of Staff – wished to build up Germany and this view prevailed. The British promise to the French in 1940 that their nationhood and world role would be restored was absolute, but the British Government also realised the need to restore Germany to her central position in Europe and believed that to deprive the Germans of the rights and standard of living that they expected would be an error. Thus in meetings under the Allied Control Commission in Berlin in December 1945 Britain insisted that German steel capacity should be fixed at 11 million tons annually, 3 million tons more than the US proposal, double that of the Russian, almost double that of the French, and well above the European average. A compromise was reached between the two extremes and at a meeting in Moscow in April 1947 General Marshall and Ernest Bevin, the British Foreign Secretary, agreed to remove all restrictions on German production in the American and British zones. The decision was crucial for Europe, Germany was to be forgiven and treated as an equal partner.

The USA generously offered the Soviet Union and Eastern Europe participation in the Marshall Plan, but they withdrew into their own economic alliance, from which they threatened Western Europe with Communism. In view of this, the USA was confirmed in her belief that West German participation was vital to European recovery and decided to over-ride French fears and rebuild Germany as a bulwark against the Soviets. To allay the anxieties of the American people, the aims of the Plan were publicised as being to, 'Prevent the resurgence of an aggressive Germany'. Headed by Secretary of State W. Averell Harriman and mainly composed of industrialists, cotton brokers, academics, bankers and labour leaders, its Committee felt that to appease tax payers the USA had spent too little on Germany since the war. Truman wanted Under Secretary of State Dean Acheson to head the aid agency, but Congress chose Paul Hoffman, a motor car manufacturer, with Harriman as Paris representative. Although totals for aid were assessed nationally it was distributed on a regional basis, since the USA envisaged a Europe crossing frontiers with no national constraints. Britain received in dollars: 3.17 billion, France 2.70, Italy 1.47, Germany 1.38, the Netherlands 1.07, with the other 13 participants receiving lesser amounts. 70 percent of the aid was spent in the USA, which had the supplies that Europe required; half was shipped in US ships; over a third was spent on raw materials and semi-finished products, just under a third on food, animal foodstuffs and related commodities. In 1947 the combined industrial and agricultural production in Europe was only 70 percent of pre-war levels, but by 1952 both were up by 35 percent and 10 percent respectively. Marshall Aid ensured European recovery and out of the Plan was born the Organisation for European Economic Co-operation, (the last part of its title now changed to Development).

Even well-informed people in Britain are not aware that they received Marshall Aid. This is because it had a negative effect, in the sense that rationing of food, clothes, petrol, coal and other commodities and import controls on raw materials continued, although supplies were not cut further. On the other hand its positive effect was felt on the economy, for between 1947 and 1949 British exports rose by 60 percent and it seemed Britain was on the road to recovery. 'Don't be too hard on yourselves', a German pastor said to the writer in 1966, 'We spent our Marshall Aid on new machinery, you had to spend yours on food'. He might have added, 'And on feeding us', but he was too young to remember. Then, as light appeared at the end of the tunnel, the Soviet threat obscured it again, rearmament began in the USA and the UK and a disproportionate amount of Marshall Aid had to be spent by the British on defence. In April 1949 the USA, UK, Canada and most recipient countries joined together for mutual defence into the North Atlantic Treaty Organisation, West Germany joining a year later at unit level, again with France opposing. At first America had only two divisions on the continent, little more than a skeleton force, but Britain gave a lead in stationing forces and the USA followed suit. With limited funds for the armed services, the UK had to channel more resources than were traditional into military rather than naval estimates. Then, at the outbreak of the Korean War in June 1950, the Americans generously assumed responsibility for the post-war Alliance and expected Britain to co-operate. US military aid to her Allies was accelerated, so that by the final year of the Marshall Plan it supplanted economic aid and became known as the Mutual Defence Assistance Programme. Britain's burdens now multiplied almost beyond the spirit of her people and certainly beyond her purse. With the USA just holding on to the only beachhead in South Korea, the Royal Navy in the Far East was put at the disposal of General MacArthur and in August the first British troops landed, soon joined by contingents from other nations. Meanwhile Britain put in hand the highest rearmament programme possible without cutting rations, requisitioning factories and directing labour. Misunderstandings arose about who was paying the bill. The UK thought that the USA had agreed to pay half the increase in the armaments programme, whereas the USA, seeing sterling reserves rising, wanted to supply finished armament products. Meanwhile, the military situation in Korea improved so far that General MacArthur chased the enemy over the 38th parallel without consulting the Allies, bringing China into the war, whose forces threw back those of the West. The world hung on the brink of renewed conflagration and the USA was reported to be considering dropping an atom bomb. Attlee flew to Washington, where he agreed to raise the amount to be spent on rearmament to nearly £5 billion over a three year period.

By this time the defence programme was having a disastrous effect on the British economy and exports were under severe strain. Military requirements made demands in many areas – engineering and metal goods in particular – and one third of the motor car industry was involved in defence. In 1951/2 Britain swung through 700 million dollars from credit to deficit in a balance of payments crisis which led again to cuts in imports, control of raw materials, prices and dividends and the allocation of skills at labour exchanges. Production was hampered by shortage of steel and loss of Iranian oil, so that, in such trades as shipbuilding and ship repairing, the lack of raw materials led to an official policy of 'Go Slow' to prevent depleting vital supplies and yet keep men employed in line with wartime promises, a policy of enforced 'idling' which contributed in some measure to the birth of the 'English disease'. Some economists believe that it was rearmament falling disproportionately upon the British, compared with her continental neighbours that led to her economic decline. Why did the British Government fall in with US demands? Because without US help the British would have been left alone to face the might of the Soviet Union across a defenceless Europe. During the summer of 1950 the peoples of the continent were still remembering with horror their nerve shattering experiences recently endured and eyeing with fear the new enemy behind the 'Iron curtain'. One British cabinet minister thought the Russians intended to force the West into rearming to paralyse and embitter its peoples. The British were not embittered, but their economy was threatened with paralysis. The Americans, in spite of bountiful generosity in sending food and clothes parcels long after the war ended, did not understand the deadening effects of continuing wartime controls and shortages in Britain, from which, until the Korean war, people hoped they were escaping. In 1953 the Ministry of Materials and Ministry of Supply were still supervising the distribution of over 270 scarce commodities.

Meanwhile, on the continent, 'There were no debts, no liquid liabilities, no military and economic obligations, no feeding of the Ruhr, no establishing of law and order, no responsibility for refugees, or setting up the administrative machinery and economic life of a defeated nation'. Although a substantial amount of housing stock was destroyed by Allied bombing and the German defence of their Nazified homeland, nevertheless in 1945 Germany was left with 80 percent of industrial plant and 10 percent more capacity than in 1936. Many financial houses and industries had been placed underground and/or moved to occupied Europe, where they co-operated with the SS. Speer did not obey Hitler's orders on retreat so that, although many buildings and factories were destroyed, much plant was left intact. Meanwhile the USA and Britain, in a reversal of wartime policy motivated by the precariousness of the international situation, restored to their positions almost all the financial and industrial leaders. Some were let out of prison after serving only a few years of their sentences and a number of Nazi officials were re-employed to fill minor official posts in the new federal system, set up to prevent dictatorship. Perhaps only recently has the full extent of the involvement of a number of banks and industrial cartels in facilitating Hitler's rise to power become known to the general public. While Russia removed plant and took immediate reparations from East Germany, where she centralised power in a system of government requiring fewer officials, the USA and UK took little in reparations and only after recovery, so that by the early 1950's Germany's industrial assets were back to pre-war levels, and by 1951 German industrial production was 50 percent higher than in 1936. Thus, while Britain was coping with financial crises, rearming and restricting imports of raw materials, the continent of West Europe was keeping its concentration fixed on production and investment in industry, aiming a measure of its output to the home market and cushioning the huge current account deficit necessary to achieve growth out of capital given in Marshall Aid or earned during the war from overseas assets, shipping or other sources.

There was another factor also not working to Britain's advantage. The USA wanted to encourage further liberalisation of European trade, lower tariffs, easy currency exchanges and the breaking of bottlenecks, both for her own commercial advantage and to prevent war. and once again she wanted Britain to give a lead. Britain saw, in Mr. Gladstone's words, that in keeping the European union together 'You neutralise and fetter and bind up the selfish aims of each. The only object for which you can unite together the Powers of Europe are objects concerned with the common good of all', but she tempered Gladstone's optimistic liberalism with the realism of Disraeli, Salisbury and Churchill, who understood Britain's economic dependence on wider overseas markets. Britain also did not wish to jeopardise her position as head of the sterling block by integrating her economy with that of the continent. These fears were justified by events, for, although British exports, having dramatically increased since 1945, were five times those of France in 1947 and in 1951 were still twice those of France and Germany added together, nevertheless the liberalisation of European trade, which she was promoting, was not to her advantage. Between 1947 and 1952 European trade grew in value by 70 percent but one third of the increase went to Germany's profit, with Britain only benefiting by 5 percent. The early 1950's were seeing continental Europe rising like a phoenix from the ashes, exerting as many efforts on her own behalf towards the liberalisation of internal trade as were being promoted by the USA and UK. In May 1950 came the Schuman Plan and France, having found she could not prevent the build up of Germany or her entrance into NATO, decided to throw in her lot with West Germany, hoping in this way to influence her and prevent further war. By the time the Benelux countries formalised their tariff union into the Benelux Economic Union in 1953, France and Germany had already formed with them the European Coal and Steel Community two years before, with its registered office and High Authority originally sited in the State Bank of Luxembourg. Both these organisations joined together, with Italy as the sixth member, to sign the Treaty of Rome in 1957, giving birth to the European Economic Community.

Britain was asked to join the European Economic Community at the time of the Schuman Plan and the matter came up for debate during question time in the House of Commons. The British government replied that, while warmly welcoming European unity, Britain must retain her economic freedom and could not join a supranational state. At that time Britain produced more coal and steel than any other country in Western Europe, but the six EEC countries added together produced slightly more coal and twice the steel. Britain realised that European cartels would increase in strength and number, for there was to be a Common Organisation for Ruhr Coal, a Steel Cartel in Brussels, and a French Technical Association of Coal Importers. As reported in the House of Commons on the 21st of February 1955, the prices of their products were, 'Strangely similar'. Under the Allied Control Commission this concentration of industry in the German Ruhr had been prevented, which accounted in some measure for the lead in British coal at this time. While the British government agreed after the formation of the Coal and Steel Community to lift restrictions if Germany and France wanted it done, both government and Parliament were concerned at the possibility of the renewed formation of cartels, which would dominate European trade. These misgivings were voiced in the House of

Commons. 'To prevent the possibility of economic struggles again leading to war, particularly in the case of Germany, sooner or later we shall have to look into the question of this concentration of power in single concerns in Germany, particularly if those single concerns remain largely under the control of individual German groups,... which we in this House remember'. The High Authority of the Coal and Steel Community was by 1952/53 responsible for one quarter of the loans granted to Community industrial firms and had reduced interest rates from 9½ to 7 percent, making steel cheaper. Meanwhile the USA was engaged in providing a loan of 100 million dollars to the High Authority, which enabled it to guarantee further industrial loans. This created problems for Britain, for in the early 1950's she was dependent upon her exports of steel. Taking imports into account, she exported in 1954 2½ million tons and 4 million tons of finished products and by 1953 she had already become uneasy at a world increase in steel output of 10 percent, most of which, since US output had dropped, had come from the continent. During these debates in the House of Commons Mr. Harry Legge-Bourke gave a visionary warning that, when an international bureaucracy is set up, there is a tendency for it to become more important than the subject it is dealing with, and likewise that the importance of the delegations attending may come to outweigh the interests of the people who sent them.

Britain now had a trading bloc on her doorstep, planning to surround itself with a wall of tariffs, which would eventually make her economic position and that of other European states harder. She responded by forming the European Free Trade Area – a consensus of independent states engaging in free trade – comprising Britain, Switzerland, Norway, Sweden, Denmark, Eire and Austria (who joined afterwards). The success of this group was immediately apparent and by 1989 their members enjoyed a higher standard of living than those in the EEC. In 1958 the United Nations answered the threat to the spirit of the Atlantic Charter from a 'fortress Europe' by launching a programme of free trade through the agency of the General Agreement on Tariffs and Trade (or GATT), which was thus given a second birth after an abortive attempt to form an International Trade Organisation in 1947. The present efforts to secure agreement for international free trade in the Uruguay Round of the GATT talks, and the dangers, if not successful, of the world sliding back into economic power groups, possibly leading as before to conflict on a world scale, have their roots in the last century. Lord Salisbury spoke frequently and eloquently of free trade in a world of few barriers and voiced in the Times of 10th November 1897 the hope, 'That the Powers may gradually be brought to act together in a friendly spirit on all questions of difference which may arise, until at last they may be welded together in some international constitution, which shall give to the world a long spell of unfettered, prosperous and continued peace'. This belief in the benefits of free trade as a means of maintaining peace was expressed again in the Atlantic Charter and Mutual Aid Agreement of World War II.

All this time Britain – despite her rearmament and involvement on the continent – was still pursuing her traditional maritime policy and her trading account was improving. A Conservative government had been in power for 6 years, controls were going and she was starting to concentrate on her own recovery, a picture confirmed by statistics. In 1956, 54 percent of vessels entering and clearing British ports were British or Commonwealth, compared with the same percentage(for British vessels only) in 1939 and a lower percentage of 46 for 1914. Likewise, the number of vessels of over 500 gross tons stood at 3,041, which is approximately equal to the figure of 3,071 for 1939,* while the total of vessels was 13,232 compared with 12,500 for 1935 and 1911. Meanwhile the gross tonnage of the UK merchant fleet was standing at nearly 18½ million gross tons, with a further 3 million for the Commonwealth, comparing well with just under 17 million for the UK and 2 million for the Commonwealth in 1939, and 19 million and 1.6 million for the UK and Commonwealth respectively in 1914. Turning from shipping to trade, the ratio of manufactured imports and exports in 1957 showed the required proportion for British economic health – one unit imported to every three exported – the £927 million imported manufactured goods for 1957 being one third of the £2,754 million exported. Disregarding invisibles, there was a total deficit for that year between exports and imports of only £899 million, comparing favourably with a deficit of £226 million for 1911, when the value of money was greater. The 1911 figure shows the destination of the exports – £295 million going to foreign countries and £158 million to the colonies, of which goods to the value of £89 million were re-exported to foreign countries. Thus only 15 percent of exports went to the Empire and were not re-exported, showing the true position of Britain's trade – even then the majority of exports, either directly or through the colonies, went to foreign nations. She was, therefore, right to regard with deep anxiety tariff walls erected around a neighbouring trading group of which she was not a member.

Britain was now to enter a period of uncertainty and maritime decline, which contributed to plunging her trading account into the red in the 1960's and 70's, leading inter alia to the devaluation of the pound in 1969. By the end of the decade starting in 1956 only 41 percent of vessels entering and clearing British ports were British and Commonwealth, 13 percent down on the 1956 figure. Apart from her military commitment of land forces to the defence of the continent, the creation of the Common Market in 1957 and the consequent formation of the European Free Trade Area (EFTA), there were other reasons why Britain at this time turned her face away from her natural, historic habitat – the sea. The first was Suez – President Nasser's nationalisation of the Canal in 1956. Justified or unjustified, Britain and France mounted a successful sea and air operation, and pulled out, against a background of Soviet threats, American disapproval and pressure on the pound. Their desire for wanting action was understandable. France had built the Canal, Britain was a shareholder and had recently withdrawn troops from the Zone, Middle East affairs were menacing. The Prime Minister, Mr. Eden, had reason to know that dictators feed on success. He had resigned as Foreign Secretary in 1937, because

* or 3,573 and 3,603 in another table.

sanctions were not applied after Mussolini's invasion of Abyssinia. With the operation halted, the Allies handed over to a United Nations force, acting for the first time in a peace-keeping role, and President Nasser remained in power. Churchill was reported to have said, 'I should never have dared. But if I had dared I should never have dared stop'. Why did Britain and France stop? Soviet reaction was a threat, but the shadow of Bretton Woods hung over the Western world, for Britain had not honoured her 1945 promise to make sterling fully convertible by July 1947. She did not do so until 1958 (and even then citizens did not have free access to foreign exchange), France, Germany and other members of the European Payments Union acting together at approximately the same time. Unconsulted over Suez – and with Britain buying alternative Venezuela oil, for which she needed dollars – was Secretary of State Dulles tempted to remind Britain that nine years after her first attempt she was still unable to expose the pound to the chill wind of the market? Was the lesson taught by Suez that it is no use engaging in costly overseas operations from a debtor position, however worthwhile the purpose – in this case to safeguard and keep open the sea lanes of the world? The USA was soon to discover that maintaining the balance of power between warring states of unequal strength is expensive, for she also suspended convertibility in the 1970's. Now, with the dollar no longer pegged to gold and the world trading precariously on paper, dominated for the time being by the yen and mark, the Gulf crisis has introduced the principle that countries benefiting from world stability and the rule of international law should contribute towards the sacrifices necessary for their maintenance. Long before that, however, the British, realising they were playing third fiddle in a world dominated by two super powers had begun to lay up their ships to their own loss and that of other nations.

Meanwhile, creating a second factor, the shipping and shipbuilding programme of the world was thrown into confusion after Suez by nations building larger and swifter tankers to sail round the Cape and so avoid the closure and uncertainty of the Canal. This, coupled with its later re-opening, led to threatened over-capacity and dangerous fluctuations in world tonnage. These two problems were to return again in later decades, with the reduction of oil production, the rise in its price and the second closure of the Suez Canal for eight years in the 1960's and 1970's, together with an increase in the laying of oil pipe lines. Because Britain was over-committed to the tanker trade, this was seriously to affect her shipping and shipbuilding programme in the years to come, while the situation was exacerbated by large bulk carriers which had transported oil, moving to dry cargo and creating over-capacity there. Also in 1956 and introducing a third factor, Japanese shipbuilders, who had been challenging the British for markets the year before, began with US aid to expand their programme of prefabricated shipbuilding and in that year exported a greater tonnage than all Britain's launches put together. During 1957 and 1958 this challenge from the East dramatically increased and, in common with growing numbers of other countries, including Germany and France, Japan provided cheap loans and subsidies to shipbuilding companies to enable them to capture world markets. British shipbuilding was now under serious threat.

The Suez crisis also contributed to a change in the attitude of the French, making a fourth factor. While Britain deliberated over whether to apply for membership of the Common Market (would she be overwhelmed by the agricultural wealth of the 'fair land of France' or the industrial muscle of Germany?), France put an end to her weak post-war governments and voted for General de Gaulle as President. He was a patriot, who restored France's self-confidence, but forgot his obligations to countries which had rescued his – seeing only the dangers of domination of world markets by the US dollar. He withdrew the French from Algeria and NATO (although not out of the Atlantic Alliance), shipped gold from Fort Knox to France to strengthen her financial position and risked the break up of Canada and offence to Britain by emphasising the uniqueness of French-speaking Quebec. The USA, who had been pressing Britain to give a lead in Europe since 1947, saw great dangers in this increasingly anti-American attitude, which had its roots in an earlier decade. Remembering the number of times that continental Europe had opted for bureaucratic authoritarianism and the suffering to which it had led, she thought Britain would exert a restraining, democratic influence within the EEC and this was in line with Britain's own historical policy – never to allow a power block to develop on the continent without keeping the scales of power finely balanced. Thus, under the leadership of Mr. Macmillan, Britain applied for entry in 1963, endeavouring to negotiate terms for her imports of raw materials and food from the Commonwealth. Her application was turned down by de Gaulle, because she was not sufficiently 'European' – he was reported to have said he wanted her in 'naked' (without overseas interests) – and she thus received a second knock to her prestige, taking a further toll of her self confidence. The depreciatory, good natured humour, persisting since wartime, began to change to barbed satire directed at an Establishment, which seemed unable to steer a successful course between the rocks. By being too magnanimous in victory had Britain let down her own people? What was going to be left for her in this melting pot of uncertainty?

The Commonwealth countries, which stood loyally by the mother country throughout her EEC application, now realised that, since she might try again, they must plan their own economic survival, Australia and New Zealand in the Pacific Basin, Canada in a free trade area with the USA. This was the period of Mr. Macmillan's 'Wind of Change' in Africa. With dependencies also influenced in some degree by Britain's decision to apply for EEC membership, Britain then began an accelerated retreat from Empire, producing a fifth factor, turning her from overseas commitments and markets. All over the world national feelings were being aroused and people wanted control over their own destinies, leading to political agitation and in some cases to violence. Sometimes withdrawal left continuing stable communities, but in other instances internal strife and insufficient numbers of indigenous trained staff meant that political agitation erupted again and removed the very freedom to which people had aspired. Britain made no attempt, as France was doing, to tie these fledgling economies to the mother country, in which case, as well as trading agreements, some form of contractual shipping preference could have continued. Instead, in keeping with the spirit of the Atlantic Charter, she left them free to plan their own destiny (as in the case of India, which reserved her coastal trade after independence) holding them together by friendship within the Commonwealth family of nations. As the Union Jack dropped from one flag pole after another and the colonial administrators packed their bags, the last tied shipping contracts fell away; the emerging countries began to build or buy their own merchant fleets and the saving to the Treasury of paying for peace-keeping forces was off-set by the loss of availability of raw materials and markets for British goods shipped in British ships.

Despite these problems, all still seemed reasonably well to the British people in the first half of the nineteen sixties and even by 1966 it seemed the sun shone, although the better informed spoke of Britain's large population and lack of raw materials. The devaluation of the pound in 1969 was blamed on the Labour government and the people voted Conservative in 1970, convinced that better days lay ahead. Meanwhile deliberations about the EEC continued – those who argued to go in did so for political and defence reasons, those who argued to stay out did so on historic and economic grounds. 'How can it work', they asked, 'when continental countries will want us to buy their manufactured goods and, for our survival, we need to sell them ours?' The British who visited the leafy boulevards of Strasbourg or sipped wine in the elegant cobbled squares of Brussels or Luxembourg, the three homes of the legislative, administrative and judicial organs of the EEC, surely did not go shopping with their own money, for here the cheap imported food and clothing available at home were oceans away. Britain was on the horns of a dilemma. It was argued on one side that if she went in her historical liberties could be compromised by joining a centralised bureaucracy without the same common law and democratic safeguards, which she had always enjoyed and jealously preserved. It was said on the other side that, since the Luxembourg compromise (upon which the French had insisted), which allowed nations to require unanimous voting in the Council of Ministers, her sovereignty would be assured. Certainly it seemed that if she entered she could lose much needed and valued Commonwealth connections, of which Churchill had spoken with warmth, and could see her vital fishing industry, already under threat, further eroded. On the other hand if she stayed out she faced tariff walls and would be unable to influence the powerful political and economic forces growing in strength across the Channel. Meanwhile all this uncertainty was having its effect, for not only was she losing Commonwealth and other overseas markets to the USA, Germany and Japan, but her ratio of manufactured exports and imports slipped during the decade from the necessary three to one towards the ratio of one for one. In this anxious situation the government cast round for alternative means of livelihood and North Sea oil was discovered at this critical time. When Mr. Heath applied again to the EEC in 1973 this was soon to come on stream and by the 1980's Britain had become one of the largest oil and gas producers in the world.

This time Britain's request for membership was successful, making a sixth factor turning her eyes landward from the ocean. In 1971 over half her trade was deep sea (or long haul), whereas by 1986 this had been reduced to just over a quarter, lessening her need for ocean going ships. Even with the substantial income coming from oil and gas predictions about Britain's economic situation within the EEC have been to a considerable extent confirmed. Although immediately after the war Britain exported more to Europe than she imported, the balance had soon swung the other way and was to gather pace until German reunification, which has temporarily altered the balance. In 1988 Britain's exports to the whole world were £82.1 billion and her imports £106.6 billion. Within this figure, her exports to the EC were £41.1 billion, with imports of £56 billion and her exports and imports to non EC countries were £41 billion and £50.6 billion respectively. (Figures from the Department of Trade and Industry). This expressed in percentage terms meant that Britain's deficit with the rest of the world was 18.9 percent, compared with 26.6 percent with the EC. Seen in this light the 15 percent of exports going to and remaining in the Commonwealth in 1911 becomes more significant. Just over half of Britain's trade is now with the EC, with all of whose members she is in deficit, except for Spain and Eire (who both want a political prize from her, in the shape of Gibraltar and Northern Ireland). The deficit has been most marked with Germany, with whom it was in 1989 (expressed in US dollars) $8 billion. In 1988 Germany's surplus with all other members of the EC stood at $35 billion, a figure which had increased by $16 billion since 1985. On the other hand, Germany has allowed the Netherlands to maintain a substantial and continuing surplus and, although the USA was in deficit with her by $9 billion in 1988, this figure only increased in the same three year period by one ninth. For the moment, however, this whole situation has been thrown into the melting pot by German reunification and, because of this significant but short-lived variation, Britain's deficit with the EC in 1991 was reduced from £14.9 billion in 1988 to £1.9 billion in 1991, while, due to the US recession, that with the rest of the world has increased.

While all these events were taking place, Germany, as Disraeli had forecast in 1848, had started to build up a maritime carrying trade, which affected British shipping, particularly on short sea routes. As before the two World Wars, the USA provided German shipping companies with loans of millions of pounds, enabling her to make a new start and the West German government followed this up with low interest loans, so that by 1957 Germany possessed a growing modern fleet of 3.6 million gross tons. Soon 30 or more countries were operating similar shipping subsidies and were once more introducing flag discrimination and entering into treaties restrictive of shipping. Britain refused to join in such practices, but watched countries such as Japan, Germany, Holland, Scandinavia, Greece, Italy and Russia begin to build up lucrative carrying trades. This renewed foreign competition based on subsidies and cheap loans is the seventh factor in Britain's declining maritime position. The figures for British vessels entering and clearing British ports steadily dropped from 41 percent in 1966 to an average of 38½ percent in 1976 (32 percent for imports and 45 percent for exports) and has gone on down to 24 percent for dry cargo and 25 percent for tankers in 1986 and 18½ percent for the total in 1990.

At the same time the number of British registered merchant vessels dropped from 2319 in 1966 to 1573 in 1976 and to 481 in 1991. Lloyd's Register shows a similar reduction for vessels of over 100 gross tons – from 5508 in 1956 to 4303 in 1966 and then from 3549 in 1976 to 2256 in 1986.* Gross tonnage has also fallen dramatically from 18½ million in 1957 to 11½ million in 1986 and only 3 million in 1990. Soon it will be reduced to zero unless drastic measures are taken to stop it, and, as the last ships flag out or are sold and the last ship-yard closes, the fact must be faced that Britain no longer has a maritime policy for peace nor a maritime strategy for war. Knowledge of the sea appears neces-sary for proper understanding of the problem – for during the years when the Prime Minister had maritime experience, either under sail or in the wartime Navy the drop was within the range of 2 percent, instead of the average of 7.6 percent. Whereas in 1966 the Norwegians were the chief competitors (and since 1988 – with the introduction of the second Register – have more than doubled their merchant fleet), in 1976 it was the Germans who were carrying 10 percent of British trade, which figure by 1986 had risen to 17 percent of British exports and 15 percent of imports, with the Dutch lying second at 9 percent and 6 percent respectively. Thus by 1986 two continental countries were together carrying more British trade than the British themselves and the leading European competitor was a part of that country which was reported to have used 'menace' to make the British end their Navigation Laws. Even the most liberal minded of Members of Parliament in 1848 might have thought there was a degree of self interest in her demands.

Looking beyond Europe to the world, as Britain withdrew from the ocean going passenger trade and deep sea hauls, she was replaced by the East Europeans and Japanese respectively. Although in 1945 the USSR had only 2 million gross tons of merchant shipping, she started to build after the Cuban crisis and within a forty year period by 1985 she had 24.74 million with 7,154 vessels of over 100 gross tons, while the Japanese, whose defeat in World War II has been partly attributed to their lack of sufficient merchant shipping, had just under 40 million gross tons, with 10,288 ships of unspecified size. Although it looked at the end of the war as if the USA intended to take over much of the British carrying trade, by 1985 US tonnage had halved to 19½ million, with 6,447 vessels of over 100 gross tons. Other totals for merchant fleets for 1985 were: the Norwegians 15 million, the French 8, the Germans 6, and the Netherlands 4, while in the whole post-war period the Greeks have multiplied their merchant fleet by ten and a number of Middle East countries have begun to own sizeable fleets.

The carrying trade is a valuable asset, but when accompanied by aggressive marketing policies, it bestows wealth and control over commodities, which, unless accompanied by open handedness, can endanger world commercial stability. The expansion of German and subsequently Japanese exports have been faced a number of times in the last two centuries with serious conse-quences. Trade imbalances were ruled out by Bretton Woods and the

* or 2,888 in another table.

International Monetary Fund, because of the chaos into which they throw world markets. Countries with surpluses were told to correct them and the European Payments Union, set up with British backing after the war, provided a collective pool to give trade deficit countries time to pay. Although budget deficit nations in the EEC are told by Brussels to correct them and there is provision under the Treaty of Rome to aid countries with balance of payments problems, there are no such directions to nations with trade surpluses, although it is relatively simple to put them right by spending more public money on infrastructure and related social matters or encouraging demand or raising the value of their currency. The problem is that if action is not taken political power is drained away from weaker nations to those with stronger economies. The USA has had limited success in explaining this to the Japanese, but, if, before unification, such measures were suggested to a member of the West German Bundestag, they were treated with derision. How long will the peoples of the continent be content to see German economic and consequent political dominance grow until it is impossible to roll it back? The recent closely fought referendum results in some member states have given the Commission in Brussels an answer. Perhaps the British idea of teaching people to play games in order to observe rules, to play as a team, to learn how to win and lose and not take unfair advantage, rather than always wanting to win may in the end be the solution, for everyone cannot be a winner. 'After you Claude', 'No, after you, Cecil', were catch phrases in the wartime Tommy Handley show, representing the need to see the other person is all right before looking to your own affairs, a Christian philosophy of co-operation out of fashion in a world dominated by selfish material gain.

CHAPTER VIII

'BUT WHEN IT FIRST DID HELP TO WOUND ITSELF'
THE BRITISH DISEASE?

Those people who felt that Britain had carried an unfair share of burdens on the post-war stage were balanced by others who thought she had temporarily lost her political path. Gratitude for her wartime courage and exertions and admiration for her respect for liberty were turning into different emotions as the continent watched English football hooligans clashing in their cities and read of industrial strikes (which, despite the frequency of Lowland Scottish leaders became known as the 'English disease'). The candle, whose flame of freedom had kept alive the hopes of many through dark days, was flickering for reasons people did not understand. Nations on the continent, defeated and invaded and provided with financial help by victors and liberators had by now successfully engaged in productive revolutions to rebuild economic strength. The Germans concentrated on the social market and the French on the removal of bottlenecks and reduction of time spent waiting between trades, while Britain, who had won from victory freedom for herself and for the world, together with unwanted debts, was still displaying the qualities of doggedness and obstinacy, which Dr. Johnson said, were maddening in peace and magnificent in war and was engaged in a social revolution to redistribute the almost zero wealth she had left. Harold Wilson when Prime Minister told her that the world did not owe her a living, but there were many people in Britain who did think the world owed them more than debt and decline, particularly in shipping and the shipyards, for this workforce had shared in large measure the inter-war depression and long hours of work in wartime and it was at sea that the greatest civilian casualties and sufferings had been endured. 'England', said Pitt in 1805, 'has saved herself by her exertions and will I trust save Europe by her example'. Lord Lothian said the same in his American speeches in 1940, but in 1815 the valour of her sacrifice was rewarded by the normal fruits of victory and not by the unhappy vicissitudes of fortune that followed 1945.

It was as if the British had been prepared to wait for better times for themselves until the mid 1950's and then, when nothing appeared on the horizon except further financial problems and calls upon their strength, the country began to tear itself apart. Helped by the moderate leadership in the National Union of Seamen of Tom (later Sir Tom) Yates, who was fourth in line from its founder, Havelock Wilson, (under whom the NUS, having accepted a cut in wages, had refused to join the General Strike), the whole of the shipping industry was relatively strike free until the mid fifties. But the 1957 strike in the shipyards – when the government intervened to get the skilled men a higher wage – did nothing to dampen appetite for higher pay or discourage weak management. Post-war wage demands throughout all industry were always pitched at 2 percent or more above the rate of inflation, so that, while wage earners got richer, the country became poorer. Unlike the position immediately after World War I, when a National Government imposed a sliding scale for wages and prices, there was in every instance a party in opposition prepared to offer a, 'No incomes or prices policy' in order to gain power. Neither party would consider a national government and the people played one side off against the other. The nation refused to understand that if a person goes on taking seven chips out of a box and putting in five eventually there will be nothing left. The catch-22 alternative for management of either giving increased wages or suffering prolonged strikes did particular damage in the maritime, as compared with other, industries for here lack of downward pressure on costs was multiplied by the number of links in the chain – stretching from the building and operation of ships to the crucial handling of goods on the quay side. Increases in outgoings were handed on to those shipping the freight and were reflected overseas in the ultimate price of the exported goods. In 1960 there was an unofficial strike sparked off among the shipboard catering crew, after which hours were cut and wages increased. Dissident seamen, who had broken away to start a new reform movement, were elected to the executive committee of the National Union of Seamen, where they took a militant line. In 1965 hours of work in port were again decreased except in exceptional circumstances and disputes over this led to the disastrous seamen's strike of 1966 after which – with the number of vessels under the Red Ensign already declining – nothing maritime in Britain was ever the same again. Wages went up without increased productivity. Cunard and other shipping companies could not afford to maintain their passenger fleets and many firms went under. Attempts to answer the problem were made in the Merchant Shipping Acts of 1970 and 1974, which put seamen on a similar footing to workers in other industries, a move of doubtful wisdom because of the unique nature of life at sea. Faced with the need to reduce costs on all vessels – either by making faster voyages or reducing crews or employing cheaper foreign labour – many companies began to sail ships under flags of countries with lower taxation and wages, no national insurance contribution and less stringent standards of manning, qualifications, training, safety equipment and welfare. Shipping companies were also affected by strikes in the shipyards and docks, which were aggravated by demarcation issues and multiplicity of unions. Wartime promises enshrined in legislation to uphold skill privileges were being interpreted as the right not to cross demarcation lines, while in the docks, with the port authorities supplying labour ashore and the stevedoring companies, employed by the shipowners, providing labour on board ship, areas of work were largely controlled by different unions. No national or industrial leader appeared able to sound the necessary note to ensure co-operation. No doubt the politicians did not mean to create weak management, but they certainly contributed to it and management itself became increasingly remote from its workforce. The reasons for this divorce between leadership and led are explored in greater depth in the chapters on shipbuilding. It seemed that the Greek myth telling that when the gods distributed gifts the British were given foolishness might after all be coming true. The people appeared to believe that money grew on trees.

With so many industries nationalised, or, like the ferry service, partially nationalised, the issue of public spending was also a matter of controversial political debate. In the crucial year 1957 three cabinet ministers, wishing to see economies, resigned from Mr. Macmillan's government. If public spending increases investment and national wealth the higher interest paid on the nation's debt is easily serviced from this increase, but if it leads only to inflation and devaluation, then the nation's currency is debased, with the result that prices in the shops rise and a wave of strikes follow. (The increases in the price of food after joining the EEC sparked off a similar wave of strikes in 1973). In the post-war period Britain had not the liquidity to subsidise in the same liberal manner as her competitors, but the question must be asked whether UK subsidies to the shipping industries provided long term profitable investment. First, lame duck industries of national importance were taken under the government wing and debts written off, perpetuating inefficient management, but even if public money had gone directly into capital plant it was essential to have harmony in industry for benefit to accrue and this harmony after 1960 was absent in sections of the maritime industries, particularly in ports and shipyards. Second, although in 1961 the government provided £24 million to Cunard to build the Queen Elizabeth II and three years later the Shipbuilding Credit Act enabled UK companies to get 80 percent of the cost of a new ship in low interest loans, (with writing off provisions and cash subsidies), in 1966 these benefits were extended to foreign companies, provided they remained on the British Register for 5 years. The result was that the British merchant fleet increased by half by 1973, throwing the British share of world shipping temporarily out of balance. If public money is spent, expenditure must be planned with vision and supervised with care, fine tuning the economy as a musician would tune the strings of his violin. In the nineteenth and early twentieth centuries subsidies and low interest loans were given to shipping companies to build and keep on the British Register fast, seaworthy ships and this money was spent in the shipyards by shipping managers, who ensured they got value for money. There was no reason why this practices should not have continued under scrutiny, nor why the reforms called for in 1848 should not have been borne in mind – to put British shipping companies and seamen on the same footing as their competitors. There could have been help with seamen's pensions, social service payments, tax exemptions and other incentives employed by countries overseas to encourage mariners to stay at sea and to reduce the overall operating costs of companies in which they worked.

Perhaps the question that requires to be asked is whether government subsidies in the UK are as carefully monitored as they are on the continent and in Japan. Germany, France, Belgium and Japan all have credit institutions, which operate between the lending banks and the government and these are staffed by specialists with industrial expertise. Some economists claim that governments and investors in these countries think and invest long term, with continuous, linked financial and industrial advice and help, whereas Britain lacks long term vision in her investment – both private and public. Is this true? Certainly the doubling up of financial functions is not as unusual on the continent, where the

*(Above) Trading barge – still in use in 20th century; (below) Fishing smacks
unloading their catch*

Steam ship Ormuz of the Orient Line, 1887. Adelaide to London 27 days

SS Caronia of the Cunard Steam-Ship Company, 1947, built on the Clyde by John Brown

MV Melbourne Star of the Blue Star Line, 1947, refrigerated meat ship built in Belfast by Harland & Wolff

state bank of Luxembourg is also merchant, deposit and current account. This would not be acceptable in the UK or the New World but in 1944 the Canadians got round the problem by creating a specialist Industrial Development Bank to grant low interest loans to industry. Belgian, French and German post-Napoleonic financial institutions and industrial banks were given fresh impetus by Marshall Aid, which was channelled through them into industry. The first industrial bank – the Société Générale – opened in Brussels in 1822 and this was followed by the French Crédit Foucier and Crédit Môbilier, which, although the latter collapsed in 1867, acted as prototype for the Kreditbanken in Germany and the Industrial Bank of Japan, which opened in 1902. These banks of the nineteenth century were followed by the Special Credit Institutions of the twentieth century, whose role varies according as to whether or not there is a firm industrial banking base in the countries in which they operate. Subsidies and low interest government loans are channelled through these financial institutions to industry under the guidance and control of industrial experts, who insist on gains in productivity. Professor Yao-Su Ho of Hong Kong University insists that they can 'Orientate investment according to national priorities...The advantages of using credit institutions rather than relying on direct government intervention are that political interference, bureaucratic delays and administrative inefficiency are reduced'. The Professor goes on to point out that a Minister answerable to Parliament for the policy of his department has not the expertise or incentive to monitor the investment he has authorised. On the other hand the UK policy for subsidising industry – broadly common also to the USA – does prevent the formation of interlinked banking and industrial cartels, which helped to finance Hitler and were the subject of warnings in the House of Commons in 1955. To allow banks to channel public funds where they wish and not to have them under proper parliamentary control undermines democracy and leads to bureaucratic authoritarianism. But surely the inventiveness and political know-how of the British could find a compromise between the requirement of specialist industrial expertise to supervise the distribution of subsidies and the need for parliamentary scrutiny. In the last century the UK system seems to have worked competently. Perhaps ministers then had a deeper, wider knowledge of their departments or there were more specialists in Parliament and fewer junior ministers, ensuring that the views of informed constituents could lend greater weight to parliamentary debate. Perhaps the civil service was more responsive to public need in its advice to politicians. Alternatively, it may be that government nominee industrialists, who are currently put on to the boards of subsidised industries, have lost 'the smell of the salt' and are too removed from the skills and problems of the shop floor to resolve the confrontation and engender the trust necessary for progress. Could it be on the other hand that the shipping firms themselves did not take proper advantage of the opportunity offered, allowing foreign firms to make better use of the facilities ? Whatever the reason the problem needs to be urgently addressed, for other countries, as before the war, have spread their subsidies successfully across the board to help shipping companies to lower operating costs, maintain crew levels and promote training, whereas in the UK subsidies have either been withheld or poured out so liberally that they have distorted the balance of the industry.

The war should have taught the British that training is the most vital of all factors related to survival and success and nowhere is this more important than at sea, where dangers from winds, waves, rocks and races require orders to be quickly and correctly carried out. Instead, there was in post-war Britain a lack of discipline at home and school, leading to hooliganism in leisure-time and lack of industrial discipline, attention to detail and quality on the shop floor. Again the excuse can be made that on the continent a greater degree of structured family life continued throughout the war, whereas in Britain, 'No country in the history of mankind ever mobilised itself to such an extent', increasing its workforce by 2 million. With fathers away, and mothers in industry, older children were caught up in the commitment to win the war, creating a spirit of youthful independence, which in post-war Britain was then diverted into a drive for equality in education rather than quality. Although technology was the key to the future, arguments in favour of the tripartite system of education (grammar, technical and vocational) were rejected in favour of a bipartite system (grammar and vocational) and then, when, despite generous funding, the latter was claimed a failure, all children were thrown together into huge multi-ability Comprehensive Schools, while the continent continued with traditional systems and methods. Nowhere was the effect of this modern approach to education felt more acutely than in the maritime industries, which had depended for generations upon a disciplined environment from which to draw recruits. Four hundred years ago, when Scotland earned her living from the soil and from the sea – where she fished and over which she carried her trade – John Knox introduced into his first system of state education in the world the teaching of maritime skills for all pupils except the most academic. In the eighteenth century in England schools for seamen were opened in Rochester, Fleet Street and Greenwich. The first training ship was started in 1786 by the Marine Society on the Thames off Deptford Creek and a year later Trinity House opened an onshore school for sailors in Hull. Most of these shore based schools run by charitable trusts were later taken over by Local Authorities. In the middle of the nineteenth century further pre-sea training ships were commissioned and these, together with the shore based schools, are closed now, except for the Indefatigable, which is a shore based independent school in Anglesey run by the Liverpool Seamen's Trust. Meanwhile the Merchant Navy Acts of 1850 and 1854 brought into being Schools of Navigation, a number of which – having been taken over by Local Authorities in 1908 – are still in operation as marine departments of further education institutions. In 1859 and 1862 the Officers' Training Ships, HMS Conway on the Mersey and HMS Worcester on the Thames were commissioned – John Masefield trained at Conway, which was aided by the Shipping Federation. After World War II the 13-year-old entry to these officers' schools was changed to 16 (as it was at the RN College at Dartmouth) and a new school was opened at Warsaash, Southampton, which provided a 9 month course for officer recruits at 16 years of age. However, the number of recruits dropped steadily, the lure of the sea after school being unable to compete with the higher wages paid on land and grants for further education. Meanwhile, although engineers (key men since the introduction of steam) were paid higher wages than seamen, their training was still mainly through shipyard apprenticeship, and, as shipbuilding declined, so did shortages of recruits arise. In 1965, with government backing, the Merchant Navy Training Board established new course in maritime skills, including two university and two polytechnic courses in nautical science, and lectures were provided for masters, engineers, radio operators and navigators leading to the national certificate and Department of Transport examinations.* Despite this injection of intellectual content nothing can compensate for the loss of good in-service training – HMS Worcester was closed in 1968, HMS Conway in 1974. On the Worcester site the Inner London Education Authority built The Merchant Navy College, but this was shut in 1989. The Royal Naval School, HMS Ganges, has also been closed, which, although preparing boys for the Navy, did provide some recruits for the Merchant Navy as well. Meanwhile Pangbourne, which opened in 1917 to prepare boys to become officers in the Royal and Merchant Navies, has become a school of general education. Among sea schools still in existence are the London Nautical School, formerly run by ILEA, which is now a grant maintained secondary school retaining a strong nautical core programme and the National Sea Training Trust's College at Gravesend. While the Shipping Federation has always trained a high percentage of recruits, it has now had to take on far more of the financial burden of training its officers, technologists and seafarers.

The question should be asked whether the lack of entrants closed the schools or the closure of the schools accelerated the drop in recruits. The government was warned that the change to the 16-year-old entry would cause a decline in applications, but it did not heed the warning. The closure of so many schools means that shipping companies, searching for recruits as officer cadets and crew apprentices, are dependent now on young people with a very different background of training from that which produced the seafaring population of long ago. After the war 60 percent of crews were under 35 years of age and one third of recruits left within a year. With the Merchant Navy Schools shut, employers can no longer provide the high standards of nautical, technical and character training, by means of which these schools turned out the finest officers and crews in the world. Anyone who sailed with Cunard or P & O or any of the other leading shipping firms knows how close in discipline, maintenance of safety standards, time keeping and other maritime expertise the ships of these and other companies were to the standards of the Royal Navy, with which so many of their men served in time of war. Yet successive British governments have apparently taken for granted the maritime skills and instruction to which the debates in Parliament in 1848 referred. Now, when it is really

* University and College Courses in Nautical Studies are now being offered at: the University of Wales, South Tyneside College, Southampton Institute of Higher Education, University of Plymouth, Liverpool John Moores University, Glasgow College of Nautical Studies, inter alia.

too late, government help has been given in the Merchant Shipping Act of 1988 to companies to assist them with training programmes. The figures tell their story. In 1975 2315 cadets came forward for training, by 1987 there were only 160.* By then, with the fast turn around in port quashing any idea that young people might go to sea to see the world – round which it is now possible for a ship to go in 86 days – there were only 35,000 British seafarers in the Merchant Navy, compared with 105,000 in 1951 and 54,000 in 1971, while the figure for 1991 is 6,051 officers and 12,981 ratings on board Chamber of Shipping Member Company vessels. Although it must be borne in mind that the place to train seamen is deep sea and that is where the British have lost most ships, nevertheless, by 1991, with government help given to shipping companies for training under the 1988 Act, the figure for cadets was up to 428. Not only does the UK have very few ships under the British flag, it has also very few sailors to sail them.

Faced with higher operating costs, remoter management, worsening industrial relations, subsidised foreign competition, lack of monitored government help and falling standards of training the decline in the number of British ships – a fleet of 'unrivalled supremacy' in 1959 – gathered momentum in the 1960's, was reversed by a huge increase in investment, mostly in the tanker fleet in the late 1960's and early 1970's and then accelerated quickly down in the late 1970's and 1980's. The first ships to be affected were the passenger liners. Although the 1.5 million gross tons of passenger shipping lost in the war were made good by 1962, nevertheless four years earlier the number of passengers crossing the Atlantic by air had exceeded those going by sea. Taking their place came the cruise ships, which increased in number by 25 percent during the following decade to become one of the greatest contributors to foreign currency. All other sections of the merchant marine were hammered – even the off-shore oil industry fell to a great extent into the hands of the Norwegians – and the oil companies began in the 1970's to flag out and to charter ships rather than to own them. By 1984 BP owned only one third of the tankers it possessed a decade earlier. On short sea routes roll-on, roll-off ferries took over from cargo ships, while the container ships, which originated with the US military, replaced the cargo liners on the longer hauls. As the demand for container ships grew during the 1960's four British shipping companies: P & O, British & Commonwealth, Blue Funnel and Furness Withy joined together to form Overseas Containers, which planned to provide the same through service – terminal to terminal, using ship, train and lorry – as had been planned in the early 1900's by IMM. This company, together with Associated Container Transportation, enabled the UK to maintain a level of 10 percent of the world's ocean container fleet compared with 4 percent of world seaborne trade in general.

Although Britain was not as much to the fore in a number of these developments as she had been in the last century – for instance she was not in at the birth of the latest refrigeration boom – nevertheless she pioneered the liquid gas containers, currently built by Kvaerner on Clydeside. Meanwhile, the bulk

---

* Or 93 in another table.

carriers of grain, bauxite and other materials, spearheaded by the Swedes, pushed out the dry cargo ships, including the tramps, which for a hundred years and more were the prime currency earners of the British merchant fleet. Despite world tonnage doubling since the war, dry cargo only increased by one half, so that tramps were anyway under pressure before the arrival of the bulk carriers and container ships. Advances in technology enabled the building of larger ships, which – using a smaller crew per tonnage – are more economical to run, and new techniques allowed deeper loading, increasing dead-weight tonnage by 5 percent. These ships required greater capital investment and so the liner conferences and consortia of shipping groups were given a new impetus, pushing the little ships further on to the side lines. These agreements about shipping routes are criticised because of their monopoly, but the argument is that they enable shipping to be rationalised, so that there is not an over-supply on popular routes and an under-supply – or none at all – on less popular ones. It is, however, difficult to get agreement world wide to prevent domination of the market by over-large cartels and a compromise worked out by the United Nations Conference on Trade and Development to protect free carriage of goods has not yet been confirmed by Brussels. The change-over for Britain from Commonwealth to EC trade after 1973 meant further cutbacks, reducing 'long haul' cargoes. Recognising the need to halt this decline the government gave help in the 1988 Act towards the transport of seamen engaged in deep sea trades, but it was too little and too late – the decline had gathered a momentum of its own.

Large numbers of British merchant vessels engaged in the carrying trade have now been 'flagged out', (flying the flag of another state or a dependency with less stringent standards), and are in competition with ships still on the British Register. Restrictions against flagging out were slowly lifted after 1951, although not entirely removed until 1959. The flagging out, which followed, was temporarily halted by investment and depreciation tax allowances, but in 1984 the government withdrew the 100 percent depreciation allowance on ships and replaced it by one of 25 percent, with the result that during the 1980's the momentum of flagging out became almost unstoppable. Of ships over 100 gross tons, there were in 1991 481 directly owned UK vessels of 4 million gross tons under the UK flag, 71 vessels of 2.8 million gross tons under the Crown Dependencies, 86 vessels of 5 million gross tons under the British Dependent Territories and 147 vessels of 3.6 million gross tons under the flags of the rest of the world. The problem is not confined to Britain. It is estimated that 44 countries currently fly flags not representing the nationality of the owners. Favourite flags for the British are Hong Kong, Gibraltar, Bermuda and Liberia. The results of flagging out are far-reaching. First, with a flagged out fleet the links between the Royal Navy and Merchant Navy are broken and the availability of merchant ships in an emergency is seriously affected;* flagged out ships cannot be relied on to enter war zones and if one comes under fire the

---

* In the Falklands campaign the proportion of British to foreign merchant ships was 3 to 1, and in the Gulf War only 5 out of 146 transport ships flew the British flag.

remainder may refuse to go on. Second, not only is the training and recruitment of RNR volunteers seriously threatened, but a large proportion of crews are foreign. The right balance between national and foreign crews is a matter of complexity and importance and one, which to a great extent, is still unresolved. Third, the decline of British registered ships has a wider spin off, causing ship-yard redundancies and closures, so that in war the nation could not replenish her fleet or feed herself or bring raw materials or reserves of men or equipment to her shores. Fourth, the ripples go wider, for, apart from the maritime invisi-bles, such as insurance, chartering, registering and broking, which make greater contributions to the economy than people realise, there are industries, such as compass making and rope manufacture, which rely wholly upon thriv-ing shipping and shipbuilding companies for their survival. Fifth, although in 1988 British shipping produced £3.8 billion in gross profit (£4 billion in 1990), from this figure has to be deducted the overseas costs, reducing the profit to £2.7 billion net, 56 percent of which comes from cross trades, 18 percent from the carriage of exports, 16 percent from passenger traffic and 10 percent from chartered vessels. £1 billion a year is also saved on average on the import bill. Much of this profit in foreign currency has now to be earned by a flagged out fleet and, whereas in a British flagged fleet shipping costs are a domestic charge, in a flagged out fleet a proportion of operating costs are deductible in foreign currency and so reduce the over-all benefit to the trading account. Moreover, British freight carried in foreign ships has eventually to be paid for in foreign currency, while the potential carrying trade of foreign goods lost to competitors is foreign currency lost to Britain. It is a situation in which doctri-naire thinking has dominated the need for practical solutions.

What meanwhile has been the fate of the smaller craft that ply around British shores – the coastal traffic and the fishing boats – the 'dirty British coaster' of Masefield's poem, with its cargo of coal, iron, lead, firewood and tin trays? The British coastal dry cargo fleet almost halved between the end of the war and 1960, owing to a reduction in the coal trade and the greater use of road traffic. Britain's share of her own coastal traffic, which accounts for 32 percent of shipping passing through her ports, is now only 60 percent – although the Department of Transport gives 72 percent as UK total earnings from the trade. At last, under the 1988 Act the British government has reserved the power to ban foreign ships from UK cabotage, unless there is some measure of reciprocity from other nations and this has brought a response from the EC. These coastal ships were in the main traditionally owned by small firms, and, when the argument turns to the fishing vessels, the reader is presented with an industry, which, like agriculture, is almost 100 percent based on family units. Here there is no 'us or them', no strikes for higher wages, no demarcation disputes, no remote management. These men are all entrepreneurs, with their skills mainly taught father to son. If extra training is required the industry is broadly satisfied with government schemes, for in a small boat a man either learns fast or stays ashore. Only in the matter of public spending have the fishermen been affected by any of the problems known as the 'English' disease. Here it is perhaps possible to detect the same spending spurts and periods of non-intervention on the part of government, illustrated inter alia by the story of the scrapping grants given in the first half of the 1980's to distant water vessel owners on the Humber and criticised by the Public Accounts Committee, because the boats subject to grants were sold by companies to fishermen abroad, so making double payment. It may not be surprising that the government is reluctant to repeat the performance but it cannot support an argument that the fishermen lack self reliance.

How has this capacity for initiative and entrepreneurship helped the fisher-men in their fight to keep afloat in the EC fishing 'Pond'? It is worth looking at this matter in some detail for it has a direct bearing on how far Britain has been responsible for her own decline. The Department of Transport gives the figure of 11,000 boats for the fishing fleet, upon which the monarchs of earlier centuries relied for the sailors for their navies and from which the Royal Navy once commandeered thousands of ocean going trawlers and drifters in two World Wars. This figure includes 9,000 boats of under 40 feet in length, which can only operate in fairly calm waters close to land. The old trawler fleet virtu-ally disappeared overnight with the end of distant water fishing. The larger boats are now seine net, which fish for white fish, or purse seine, which fish for herring and mackerel, and refrigerated trawlers, to be found only in certain areas. Beam trawlers, which fish off south west England and in the North Sea, are dominated by the Dutch and Belgians, who own and operate most of the boats, under the cloak of beneficial UK ownership. The comparative figure for 1980 was 7,000 boats, of which 4,500 were under 40 feet in length and 2,500 were middle and distant water. In percentage terms boats of over 40 feet have gone down by 20 percent, while those under 40 feet have doubled, showing the extent to which the inshore industry has been allowed to grow and the amount of over capacity in the present UK fleet. All through history fishing has provoked great controversy, partly on economic grounds and partly because of the defence potential of men and vessels. Some British monarchs and statesmen were, like Elizabeth and Cromwell, flexible in pursuit of wider aims, whereas the Stuarts raised great hostility by rigorously enforcing national fishing grounds to augment the auiliary Navy. Since 1945 there has been a vicious circle of over-fishing, which in EC waters is partly caused by the use of certain types of nets and trawls. So serious is the threat to stocks that fishing for herring was temporarily banned in 1965 and between 1977 and 1982, and fishing for cod was recently cut back so far after an OECD Report that fishermen reached their quota months before the end of the year, thus effecting a virtual ban. 80 percent of the EC catch comes from the North East Atlantic, where in Greenland, the Faroes and Iceland fishing contributes 90 percent of exports. Low and falling yields are particularly bad in the North Sea, where Norway, with its large indus-trial fishing complex, did not enter the EC in 1973, fearing its fishing grounds – the largest in Europe – might be eroded. In Norway fishing makes up 2.5 percent of the Gross National Product, compared with 0.8 for Denmark and 0.17 for the UK, with the Netherlands and France close behind. 80 percent of Denmark's catch is for conversion into fish meal and Denmark's catch went up by one quarter in the decade during and after her negotiations for and entry into the Community. Ireland's catch went up by a half during the same period, whereas the UK catch fell by 20 percent. By 1980 the UK had not only been excluded from more distant fishing grounds by successive Cod Wars with Iceland, starting in previous decades, but also by the 200 mile limit imposed by Canada and Norway. The recent entry of Spain and Portugal has presented the Community with yet further problems. Nearly one quarter of a million people in Spain are connected with fishing, more than in the whole of the EC.

As with historic rights to fishing grounds conservation has also provoked recent controversy. The first real international attempt to allocate these rights and to conserve stocks was made in 1882, when a 3 mile limit was agreed in Western Europe, with Norway and Sweden withdrawing to insist on 4 miles. When in 1951, three quarters of a century later, the International Court of Justice at the Hague upheld Norway's 3 mile limit, Norway extended it to 12 miles and, when the UK accepted this, Iceland followed Norway's lead, which resulted in the first Cod War. When Britain again conceded, the Faroes and Greenland also imposed their 12 mile limits. In 1954 suggestions were mooted to conserve stocks by regulating the size of mesh in nets and ten years later Mr. Heath negotiated the European Fisheries Convention, agreeing exclusive national fishing rights within a 6 mile limit, with a further 6 miles, in which countries with historic rights could continue to fish. Norway, Ireland, Switzerland and Denmark, on behalf of the Faroes and Greenland, refused to sign this agreement and a Commission set up to recommend measures for conservation was therefore given no powers of enforcement. Four years later the EC agreed the Common Fisheries Policy, creating a Community 'Pond', within which member states, who must not make bilateral agreements, would either have to grant equal access to all states, or nothing at all – in which case they would be excluded from the waters of other members. France's disinclination to allow the liberalisation of fish markets and Germany's anxiety about being excluded from fishing grounds were set off against each other to secure agreement – Germany getting her fishing and France the money required to set up Producers' Organisations. Agreement was hurried through to clear the decks for enlargement of the Community.

Britain's inshore fishermen were against her joining the EC, fearing their grounds would be threatened, while distant fishermen who had lost other waters, supported entry. After enlargement arguments about fishing world wide became so vituperous that in 1974 the United Nations held a Conference of the Law of the Sea, which proposed a 200 mile limit, within which countries could exploit their own natural resources, without regard to historic foreign rights. Iceland, Norway, the USA and Mexico immediately legislated to enforce the new rules. 72 percent of EC fishing now fell within the waters of its members and between 50 and 60 percent of fish within these waters were found in the limits running round the UK and Eire, the UK now only deriving 0.3 percent from fishing in the waters of other member states. Holland and France would be by far the greatest gainers if allowed to fish in these UK waters, but West Germans, Danes and other states would all be gainers also. The Commission endeavoured to find a fair answer. Since the UK would now see her newly defined waters exploited by EC fishing and would now be excluded from distant waters by the 200 mile limit, the Community postulated that, following the 'Pond' principle, each country must have a 6 mile limit of its own, in which only nations with historic rights and coming from the same geographical area could fish. This area, it was suggested, could be extended to 12 miles, if there was regional dependence on fishing. Historic rights meanwhile could be steadily withdrawn. The continental states, however, felt that the UK had the best of the bargain and refused to agree, so the Commission backed down. It was becoming apparent that, if EC countries were to be denied distant fishing, except by agreement, it was essential to preserve stocks. Total Allowable Catches (TACs) were therefore proposed, with national quotas for each species and a fisheries control was set up to monitor catches, together with a register of boats and skippers, who would be required to record position and results. Again the continental states refused to co-operate as long as the UK continued to deny them what they saw as their fishing rights. The Dutch, whose inshore fishermen have habitually taken 40 percent of their catch from outside their zone, said that since they had been fishing for 2,000 years and the British had other resources, such as coal, they had as much right to British waters as the British themselves. Labour Members of the British Parliament asked why this did not apply also to Dutch gas and German coal.

The UK, recognising the urgent need for agreement on conservation, then cut her offer to a 100 mile limit and later to 50, insisting at the same time that proper conservation could only be imposed on a national basis. With no agreement secured, the British government became so concerned about the failure of stocks owing to over-fishing that it took unilateral action, banning herring fishing and putting restrictions mainly on industrial species in what became known as a 'Norway pout box' area of the North Sea, in order to protect haddock and whiting stocks. It also announced it was setting percentage limits on by-catches (fish caught by mistake when fishing for other species) and would be preventing boats from carrying nets of various sizes to escape detection. (One of the main problems for conservationists is that of by-catches, which causes over-shooting of quotas or the discarding of valuable breeding stock).The Commission accepted these proposals, but Denmark threw them out in the Council of Ministers. With the European Court refusing to accept any increase in the size of the Norwegian pout box, the UK suggested a compromise 12 mile limit, in order to gain agreement on conservation matters, such as mesh, gear, by-catches, closed seasons and areas. But the Danes then exceeded their herring quota, which led to a closed season, during which imports of fish to the EC doubled, prices increased and consumption fell. Meanwhile the French continued to insist on fishing within 12 miles of British shores, taking a higher level of catch there (6 percent of total) than from any other country. Although they reduced their catch in the equally disputed Irish waters by half, they only reduced their catch in British waters by 10 percent. Britain, who now owned over 50 percent of the fishing grounds within the EC, was then offered 36 percent of the catch, which was still the highest in the Community, but left her with surplus capacity. The British responded by trying to ban larger boats, but that failed too. Unfortunately the dispute came at a time when Britain was claiming substantial financial rebate from the EC and the French and Germans gave her the option of striking a bargain between the two – one or other, but not both. At last came a break through. Britain could have a 6 mile limit and a further 6 miles in which historic rights would be observed. She also secured a box round Orkney and Shetland, from which larger boats would be banned, but only if she allowed this to be administered by the EC. In return for giving away on this point she obtained the concession, vital for conservation, that by-catches must be part of the quota of that particular species, even though caught by mistake and discarded. Lastly it was agreed that an EC Inspectorate should be appointed. The Danes agreed reluctantly, seeing that their catch had suffered less than others. Sometime after these hazards had been overcome the Spaniards and Dutch, with endorsement by the European Court, began buying boats registered in the UK and now used for other purposes, such as the oil industry, and re-registering them in order to fish in British waters.

Meanwhile the EC had been trying to arrange agreements with other countries that permitted fishing within their 200 mile limits in return for reciprocity. They found that the Norwegians, who were entitled to a percentage of TAC in the North Sea, refused to let their percentage fall when the total catch fell. At the same time efforts were made to secure a bilateral agreement with Canada, which had increased her catch 10 times since the new limit was set. Together with the EC and Norway, she had set up the North West Atlantic Fisheries Organisation to promote conservation, but by 1990 the Canadian government, parliament and media were becoming increasingly critical of the EC approach to conservation, claiming that in some nursery areas almost half of EC catches were made up of juvenile fish. They had become concerned about the activities of the Spaniards and Portuguese and to a lesser extent the West Germans, not to mention the East European countries, all of whom were fishing in the 'nose' and 'tail' of the spawning grounds on the Grand Banks of Newfoundland just outside the 200 mile limit. Meanwhile the French were claiming the 200 mile limit round certain islands in the approach to the St. Lawrence, where their fishing boats were busy. Canadian newspapers stated that the EC had played the rules until the entry of the Spaniards and Portuguese, which had destablilised the balance of fisheries, and that the EC was setting quotas 12 times over those proposed by NAFO. Canada is now considering extending her limit unilaterally to include all the Newfoundland spawning grounds and shutting down cod fishing for a period in the hopes stocks will rebuild.

EC arrangements, as agreed by the British government, have been more advantageous to Scotland than to England (the Scottish share of the UK total catch having gone up from 45 percent in 1945 to 63 percent in 1991). In evidence to the European Committee of the House of Lords on December 12 1991, the Scottish Fishermen's Federation pointed out a number of unsatisfactory matters in EC arrangements and contributed suggestions for reform. First, although TACs are essential they have varied so dramatically and mostly in a downward direction (recently coming down by nearly three quarters in the case of haddock and 40 percent in the case of cod) that it has been impossible to plan. Because TACs lead to fishermen catching one type of fish within their quota and discarding others within another quota (a ridiculous waste of fish and thus a temptation to cheat), it would be better to have multi-species quotas. Second, there must be far more consultation between the fishermen and the scientific advisors, who do not listen and do not notify changes in quotas and policy in time for discussion. Surely, say the Federation, they must know in advance of shortage of stock and yet they do not act until too late. Third, there must be proper enforcement of conservation rules. it being admitted by all states that UK enforcement is currently by far the best. The Federation wants one net carried (except in certain circumstances), inspection of boats in port as well as on the high sea and the licensing of salesmen and buyers of fish. Fourth, industrial (fish meal) fishing should be banned except for two suggested types of fish, since it means that young stock of all species are swept into the nets and lost to proper fishing or later breeding. (It was the Russians who blazed the trail by using factory ships in their massive industrial fishing). The Federation expressed concern about the way the Danes want whiting 'fished down' (possibly so that it can be used for industrial purposes) on the grounds that it is predatory, when Scottish fishermen's annual catch of whiting is worth £24 million. Fifth, the Federation asked for proper testing and exper- imentation with mesh sizes leading to rational agreement, instead of one arranged as a bargain – what the fishermen called a 'Predictable political compromise'. Sixth, they would like to see all vessels licensed and not just those over a certain size. Seventh, the method of reducing effort by compul- sory tying up of boats is not one welcome to the fishermen, although to an outsider the government's reluctance to pay for taking boats out of commis- sion is not perhaps altogether surprising.

The fishing industry and the consumer have faced great problems in the last few years. In 1990 the price of white fish rocketed, but, with quotas cut by half in two years, the industry then faced dislocation on a grand scale. As in the wider shipping context the government failed to recognise in time the effect of their grants given for the building of new boats in the 'boom' period and the danger of over capacity. The Community and the British government thus found themselves on a collision course, with Brussels claiming British surplus capacity of 30 percent and the fishermen caught in between. Brussels is now threatening to cut the British share yet further. The government is reluctant to decommission and would prefer to reduce effort rather than to cut the number of boats. The Sea Fish (Conservation) Bill currently going through Parliament extends the licence system to owners of boats under 10 metres. These will now have their own quotas instead of only being part of the UK aggregate. The licence and quota system is a right to fish for what may be 'in the pot' next year, with the amount of each vessel's quota being determined annually by the Producers' Organisation. The British fishermen are resisting what they see as a public right being transformed into a private individual transferable quota, which can be attached to each owner and boat and could then be bought and sold to make aggregates of quotas. This the fishermen say would create monopolies in the industry and totally destroy the traditional nature of the fishing fleet, which dates back to antiquity – and has been throughout history one of the main planks in the defence of the United Kingdom. Despite these domestic disagreements – however fundamental they may be – there is complete accord between the government and the fishermen over the attempt by Brussels to take over the whole licensing system for the fishing industry, which they will then issue on a regional and not a national basis. The British public and parliament should remember the importance of the fishing industry to the defence of the realm.

As well as providing pooled fishing rights and proposing the regionalisation of fishing licences issued by Brussels, the Community is also moving towards the idea of an EC fleet of merchant ships with a European flag. This question was discussed by the House of Lords Select Committee on Shipping in the Parliamentary Session of 1989/1990. There was serious concern voiced at this time at the decline of shipping throughout the EC, by far the most striking being in the UK, which had slipped from first to eighth place. The employment of seafarers in EC countries is governed by Commission regulations, which are based on British requirements on crews and manning. This employment has declined in a decade by 10 percent, while in the same period EC tonnage halved and its share in the world fleet fell to just over a quarter. Whereas flagging out in the Community has reached nearly 50 percent of its total, in the UK 80 percent of ships are flagged out. Both Denmark and Germany run their own off-shore registers and Holland and Denmark give shipowners a tax rebate for the seafarers they employ. The Commission wishes to give shipping preference to ships flying a Community flag and to encourage countries to abandon their own flags and come under EUROS – the initials representing a Community flag. This is strongly opposed by all British shipowners, represented by the British Chamber of Shipping. They argue, among other things, that this is a return to historic protectionism, which Britain, in 1848 at their urgent request, abandoned in their favour. It is, of course, also a threat to all Britain's overseas interests and commitments and to her maritime marine. A number of member countries want to build up a strong EC fleet by giving aid and concessions for a fixed period of years to that end, whereas the UK wants the EC to harmonise its arrangements on aid, tax concessions and shipping restrictions with the rest of the world rather than to give internal protection. The House of Lords Committee stressed that it is essential for the Single Market that cabotage within the Community is free. Brussels has at last heeded this advice and issued phased directives (Spain, Portugal, Italy, Greece and France being the worst offenders). The Committee also called for greater ease of transfer of ships between member countries and greater standardisation of qualifications of seafarers. The attitude of the Community to subsidies and financial aid to shipping and shipbuilding is that, 'This must not be out of proportion to the aim of restoring a competitive community fleet', a phrase which the Committee felt could be interpreted as any country wished.

It was strongly felt by members of the Select Committee that Britain must never agree to being locked into a EC fleet flying a EUROS flag for, 'An island state ultimately dependent on shipping for carriage of imports and exports has a stronger interest than a land locked state like Luxembourg'. If a Community flag were to be accepted, Britain's fleet would be seriously endangered, particularly at the moment, when, owing to lack of government aid, it is small, old and flagged out. A Merchant Navy is more essential to France and the UK because of their overseas interests and places on the Security Council of the United Nations. Some ideas, however, contained within the proposals for EUROS were acceptable to shipowners, including the importance of fluency in other languages and the balance of EC and non EC crews – but the flag was not acceptable, nor was the protection of the carriage of food aid. Looking outwards, the Committee recommended that GATT – whose birth was the product of the European Community 'marriage' – should take up the whole question of financial aid given to shipping and shipbuilding by the countries of the world and consider also the matter of protectionism provided by liner conferences and group consortia. Already UNCTAD had laid down different criteria to those put forward by Brussels, the UN recommendation being that a balance be agreed between the national requirements of emerging nations, liner conference and group consortia needs and the freedom to engage in cross trades. The UN and GATT were the only bodies with the powers to try and monitor what is going on in the rest of the world. Japan's subsidies being covert were difficult to monitor, and the USA – although not building a merchant ship in years – still restricted all cabotage and had bilateral cargo reservation agreements typical of the last century.

It would seem that Churchill's vision of Britain, safe in her maritime 'deep sea' trade, supporting and supported by the Commonwealth and freely trading with a strong, secure Europe, has been transformed into something closely resembling a caricature. She faces instead a picture of herself hedged in by European restrictions and financial responsibilities, with her trident lost and her last ships under threat of removal, with other nations, including her oldest friends, neighbours and allies, hovering round to help themselves to any valuable overseas trade that is still left. A Community flag would remove London's remaining maritime position, trade and status and carry it away to Brussels or Luxembourg or New York. Has she brought this fate upon herself or has she acted too unselfishly in the interests of other nations? At some point in the spiral of decline she must stand up for her own interests and realise that gratitude is not always a common European characteristic. 'This country', said the Committee, 'as an island trading nation does require for strategic reasons a substantial merchant fleet'.

CHAPTER IX

WHO GUARDS THE MOAT AND SUPPLY LINES?
THE ROLE OF THE ROYAL NAVY

While the House of Lords European Committee highlighted the need for a Merchant Navy to provide auxiliary vessels for the defence of Britain in time of war, nothing can detract from the paramount need for an effective Royal Navy, for whose support those auxiliary forces are supplied. An island with a prosperous commercial base, fertile fishing grounds and a Merchant Navy with a valuable carrying trade is a hostage to fortune without sufficient maritime forces for the protection of its shores, coastal waters and merchant vessels. Whereas Amsterdam, at the height of its commercial power, was defended only by forts and dykes, Britain was in Shakespeare's words, 'A fortress built by nature for herself against invasion and the hand of war'. The poet saw in his mind's eye, as all Elizabethans did, an island surrounded by sea and guarded by ships. That picture, imprinted on the nation's inward eye, did not alter during the succeeding centuries. Trade and the flag followed each other, and by the end of the eighteenth century Britain, so it was said, 'In a fit of absence of mind', had acquired overseas possessions, which had grown out of the trading posts and ports established in the face of European competition, and defended by sea power. Prior to the Revolutionary and Napoleonic Wars the Younger Pitt allowed the Army to run down, but his spending on the Navy remained constant, without which Napoleon would have invaded Britain. 'The best economy', said Pitt, 'that any country can practice in time of peace is to keep up such a force and take such measures of defence as would be most likely to render the peace permanent'. After the defeat of Napoleon Britain's sea power was unchallenged and with her Navy and island bases she kept the Pax Britannica. When in the 1880's she allowed her Navy to run down, presuming trade could be internationalised, an officer in the German Imperial Navy said to a dinner guest, 'You have no right to have such an Empire and defend it so lightly. You are tempting the rest of the world'. Although by the turn of the century the Navy's former strength had been restored, this imbalance and correction may have contributed in some part to the clash of Empires of sea and land in 1914, when the British alliance with Japan was a vital component of victory. By then the British Empire was starting to transform itself into the British Commonwealth, a family of nations with a love of liberty and admiration for those who 'play the game' according to rules, enjoying a share of common inheritance, regardless of colour, race or creed. After World War I the naval defence of the Commonwealth should have been uppermost in the public mind, but, having won the war, Britain lost the negotiations after peace, and failed to insist at the Treaty of Washington that the Commonwealth should not be included in her defence allocation, so that she could transfer to it ships assigned to be scrapped. By accepting the Treaty's cuts and arbitrary limitations Britain's Navy was dependent on Allied help in World War II and, with the French Navy lost to her after the fall of France and so many USA ships sunk or damaged at Pearl Harbor, her Navy was hopelessly overstretched in the first years of war.

As in former conflicts World War II brought a great increase in shipbuilding and in the size of the US and Royal Navies. By 1945 (excluding minesweepers and smaller vessels) Britain had 809 naval ships, of which 65 were fleet and auxiliary aircraft carriers, compared with 837 in 1812, showing that an island nation requires approximately the same number of naval vessels for victory, regardless of whether the threat comes from air, submarine or surface privateer. After 1945 the USA continued to develop its Navy, but Britain in a debtor position, sold off a number of aircraft carriers and other ships to Commonwealth and Allied nations, hoping to make them responsible for their own defence. Nevertheless, when the Cold War began in 1947, she maintained a formidable fleet of 450 ships (130 more than in 1939) made up of 23 fleet and light aircraft carriers, 5 battleships, 37 cruisers, 180 destroyers, 182 frigates, 92 submarines, and 30 midget submarines. Even by 1957 the Royal Navy still consisted of 336 ships, including 10 aircraft carriers, 5 battleships, 24 cruisers, 66 destroyers (including 4 guided missile, 4 anti-submarine and 8 large), 163 frigates and 68 submarines (including one nuclear powered). Although the proportion of submarines remained at 20 percent of the fleet between 1947 and 1957, the proportion of aircraft carriers fell from 8 percent in 1945 to just over 5 percent in 1947 and then to under 3 percent in 1957, despite the fact that the Royal Navy had been the first Navy in the world to fly a jet aeroplane from a carrier, recognising the increasing importance of seaborne air defence. In that year, following upon Suez and the creation of the EEC, the building of a new air defence weapon system was abandoned for reasons of economy and Duncan Sandys, Minister of Defence, a committed 'European', questioned for the first time the principles upon which Britain's maritime strategy was based. Acknowledging the need for naval ships and aircraft carriers to play an amphibious role overseas, keeping the peace and protecting colonies and dependencies, he did not give pride of place to the historic role of the Royal Navy in time of war – to protect the island of Britain and her commercial shipping. 'The role of naval forces in total war', said the 1957 Defence Review, 'is somewhat uncertain'. What did Sandys mean? Was he suggesting that in 'all out' nuclear war (or one with nuclear weapons used before the Channel was reached) the role of the Senior Service might not be required? Or was he referring to the forward strategy favoured in 1903 and current in some US quarters, that by forming a protective naval screen, aided by laying mines, the enemy could be prevented from breaking out from his home waters, thus obviating the need to protect Britain from invasion or merchant shipping from predators? Whatever the reasons for his postulations the politicians seized upon them, for, although the Royal Navy did not immediately suffer as badly as the other Services, nevertheless, within a year or two there were swingeing cuts in ships, naval air stations, dockyards and other establishments, together with the disappearance of the RNVR and Mothball Fleet of 276 ships (with 45 sold and the rest scrapped). Not since the reign of Charles I has there been, as now, no Reserve Fleet. Lord Cunningham of Hyndhope observed in 1958,

'Unacceptable risks are being run at sea'.

What did Sandys mean by total – the dictionary definition of which is 'the entire amount'? In this sense wars have been total for two centuries, for the Napoleonic era ushered in the modern concept, involving the whole national armed force of post-revolutionary France, instead of only professional armies, and it was thus that the American Civil War was fought. In opposing Napoleon, General von Clausewitz formulated a German concept. Backed by the entire nation and subordinated to the master plan of the political leader of the day it must involve everyone – women and children too. War, said Clausewitz, is a continuation of foreign policy, used when conquest by peaceful, economic and political means break down – 'An act of violence to compel our opponents to do our will'. Nations seeking to annex another's territory or impose a puppet state should wage limited war only, placing the burden of declaration upon the defenders of smaller states and allowing the aggressor to pretend to its own people that it has been attacked – a blue-print of German policy in the century to follow. War may also be total in the sense that a nation threatened with subjugation may resolve to fight to the death. Overnight, in response to Churchill's first speech to the nation in 1940, 'We will fight them on the beaches, we will fight them on the landing grounds, we will fight them in the air and on the sea, we will never surrender' the whole British nation united behind him to defend their homeland. John Colville noted in his diary in 1940 the realisation by the British of the fate awaiting them in the event of invasion, whereas the Axis forces knew, or should have known, that Western intentions towards them were benign. It has been said that Churchill mobilised the English language and sent it into battle, acting as a mirror himself to reflect the courage and indomitable will of the British people. A war may also be total in that it is global, as the two world wars have been. Again the Napoleonic wars have a similar valid claim, since they also embraced not only Europe, but the Near, Middle and Far East and, after the Americans entered the war on the side of the French, the Atlantic also, with the Royal Navy fighting in all the oceans of the world. Lastly, a war may be total in that it leads to a nuclear holocaust. In this case none of the three Armed Services could operate in its historic role.

According to the first four definitions it is hard to see how the role of the Royal Navy could be different from the one it has fulfilled for centuries – to defend the island of Britain from invasion, to ensure her supplies by protecting her merchant shipping, to blockade the enemy and destroy his fleet, to play whatever part is necessary in relation to land forces, either in landing, supporting or evacuating them, and to protect British interests world wide. Duncan Sandys could hardly have been questioning these requirements; nor could he surely have been unaware of the important functions of the Royal Navy in time of peace, when its ships have a much wider task than perhaps the public realises. As the ice flow of the cold war melts, leaving nationalism once more on the march, what threats does the Royal Navy now have to meet and what are its functions to maintain the peace? Not only does the Navy in alliance with the USA and NATO have to maintain a sufficient presence to deter war, it must also guard waters coming under national jurisdiction, defend overseas interests and dependent UK territories, provide help for Commonwealth and Allied countries with whom Britain has treaty obligations, carry out its functions required by the UN, protect oil and fishing rights and off-shore interests (no civilian body can properly fulfil these tasks) and be a popular ambassador, making and maintaining friendships with other nations (the word friendship itself based upon the mutual assistance ships give to each other in time of need).There must also be participation in disaster relief, in operations for clearing mines and in making surveys for hydrography, for which there are two ocean going ships and three coastal ships left, as well as three smaller craft. Furthermore, the Royal Navy must play its part in preventing drug smuggling – which is undertaken by customs in UK waters – and arms smuggling and other cases of piracy, particularly in such places as the Straits of Malacca, the Gulf of Aden and the China Sea, all of which is currently borne by the US Navy, mostly on its own. Because of the Royal Navy's historic world-wide involvement, naval intelligence – before cuts in personnel – offered great opportunities for accurate and sympathetic reporting, while the strength of friendships forged overseas, both at individual and national level was often remarkable. In the 1920's the links between the British and Chinese peoples were, to a considerable extent, maintained by the Royal Navy's acts of friendship to the Chinese peoples. Against Foreign Office instructions naval commanders twice used gunboats as successful venues to induce northern war lords to sign armistices, while in the south a gunboat rescued Sun Yat Sen from the clutches of the Bolshevist Military Governor of Canton. The Navy did not stand on dignity, but shared its humour and enthusiasm with everyone, including children. Lord Fisher re-organised the Royal Dockyards and built the Dreadnoughts, but he also insisted that his midshipmen learnt to waltz. Since the days of Queen Elizabeth Britain's foreign policy has been to ensure friendly relations with other nations, to maintain stability among them and not to allow a power block to develop on the continent without throwing her weight into the scales in defence of smaller countries. Without her intervention the continent would have succumbed three times to dictatorship in the last two hundred years, but although the defence and liberation of the continent requires military forces working within an alliance, Britain, being an island, is dependent primarily for her own defence on the strength of maritime forces. 'With a navy', warned Churchill, 'all unpreparedness can be redeemed, without a navy no preparation, however careful, will avail'. 'He who commands the sea', said an early Greek commander, 'commands everything'. Although in this century it is necessary to add the air to these dicta people often forget that it takes three years to build a ship.

What is meant by command of the sea? No nation can command the whole sea, it is impossible. All that one nation can do is exercise control in certain areas and limited control in others. It should also by sea denial seek to prevent enemy ships from deploying into oceans in which it has an interest and through which its shipping passes. It is now aided in this task by mines, submarines and long range maritime aircraft. Although twice in this century, British sea power has prevented invasion by controlling the Channel and Britain's coast line – while in 1940 her fighter pilots fought overhead to command air space – it has not been able to prevent large losses of merchant ships bringing supplies to her shores. Once the surface raider had been joined by the submarine, mine and aeroplane, all of which sank merchant shipping indiscriminately, this truth – that no nation can command the whole sea – became increasingly apparent. All that one nation can do is to attempt to exercise control in the area around its base and sea denial or limited control in areas through which convoys are passing. Owing to insufficient resources even the Battle of the Atlantic was not won in this sense until far on in both wars. Command of the sea really means control of the lines of communication, while they are being used for commercial purposes, as in the case of merchant convoys, or for military purposes, as in repelling invasion or landing, supplying or evacuating military forces. It has become fashionable to think that Britain's response to her enemies has grown weaker, but this is not entirely accurate, for during the early years of the Revolutionary and Napoleonic Wars Admiral Jervis withdrew from the Mediterranean in October 1796 for nearly eighteen months, whereas in World War II, because of the vital need to secure Middle East oil supplies and later to prevent the possibility of a linkage between all three Axis forces, the convoys in the Mediterranean were fought through, despite enormous losses, with only a short interruption. Conversely, in the Far East – where once the East India Company had been responsible for defence of its own trade – for a period in 1942 and 1943, after Japan's entry into the war, the writ of the thin blue line hardly ran at all.

How can command be won? First, by destroying the enemy fleet in battle it can be gained almost in hours, as Nelson did in the Victory at Trafalgar, leading the British assault with dauntless courage – steering straight into the French flag ship's fusillade, altering course to pass astern and raking her decks with gunfire. No wonder that in countless actions since Nelson's favourite signal has been used – 'Engage the enemy more closely'. Admiral Cunningham put this into effect at the Battle of Matapan in 1941, where he won a splendid victory, sinking three Italian cruisers and two destroyers for the price of only one aeroplane. To bring a reluctant enemy to action is not easy, for both Navies have freedom of movement and the sea is too large an area in which to, 'Seek, find and destroy'. There are ports, islands, bases, fiords and tracts of ocean in which to hide, although satellite surveillance systems now make it more difficult for surface ships to escape observation. Even when superior in strength in the Mediterranean in World War II the Italian Navy did not have its heart in the fight and Admiral Cunningham failed many times to tempt it to battle. When trying to make contact with the enemy a naval commander's hands are tied in many ways – he must never leave his base undefended or follow the enemy in a, 'Wild goose chase'. In 1588 Queen Elizabeth at first refused to sanction Drake's request to sail for a second time to Spain to destroy the Armada and thus prevent it sailing, realising he might not find the Spanish fleet and could leave England undefended. She was nearly proved right, for, when over-persuaded, she at last gave permission he was constantly blown back by gales and was caught refitting at Plymouth when the Spaniards hove in sight. The belief that genius takes liberty with principle is not founded on fact, for when Nelson left his station in the Western Mediterranean to follow Napoleon's expedition to subdue Alexandria, and there annihilated the French fleet in Aboukir Bay, Britain was not in danger at the time. Likewise, when in 1805 he crossed the Atlantic at speed to save Jamaica from combined Spanish and French fleets, there were sufficient forces in the Channel and off Ferrol to counter Napoleon's threatened invasion. Although in this century there has been a movement away from the opposing fleet strategy to a war of attrition on the trade routes, nevertheless it remains true that command of the sea is won by destroying or damaging sufficient numbers of enemy ships and, unexpected attacks without declaration of war excluded, this is done most quickly in large fleet battles. Anyone doubting this need look no further than the US victories in the Pacific in World War II.

Even without such a decisive victory, there is a second method of winning temporary or limited command: it is to so deter the enemy that he withdraws his fleet to the safety of port. He remains a force to be reckoned with, but he is not at sea. This is what happened to the German High Seas Fleet in the latter years of World War I. At the Battle of Jutland Britain's luck was out. The position of the two fleets was given away by a Danish coaster before the main part of the Grand Fleet had joined Beatty's battlecruisers, whose gunnery was often not as accurate as that of the Germans, and the battle was a draw, both sides claiming victory. Jellicoe was accused of yielding to the fear of a submarine, or mine trap and not pursuing the escaping Germans with sufficient determination, but in reality the balance was in Britain's favour. The Germans retired to lick their wounds and their fleet was largely confined to port by the Kaiser for the rest of the war, which contributed to the mutiny of the German Navy in 1918 and left the RN with a freer hand to conquer the Atlantic U-boats.

Third, command can pass from one fleet to another with the destruction of naval ships in port, a method often used by the British, particularly to deter invasion. When Drake sent in his fire ships to Calais Roads with exploding guns and ammunition on board, Sidonia's Armada fleet was thrown into confusion. The English set upon the 40 ships still at anchor, while others in mounting panic fouled one another and drifted out to sea. This strategy set a tradition for the Navy to follow. Captain Warburton-Lee's daring raid on German destroyer flotillas in Narvik in 1940 reduced Hitler's destroyer strength by more than a third (and with it his chances of successfully invading Britain), for the crippled destroyers, trapped in port, were later sunk by superior RN forces. The British naval air attack on Taranto later that year sank or damaged three out of five Italian capital ships, weakening their presence in the Mediterranean and making them unduly cautious. Such actions involve great bravery, whether it be by surface ships or aeroplanes – as in these exploits – or by midget submarines – as in the British attack on the Tirpitz in a Norwegian fiord – or by human torpedoes – as in the Italian attack on the Valiant and Queen Elizabeth in Alexandria in 1941 – or by a lone submarine – as in the

entry into the Sea of Marmara by Commander Dunbar Nasmith in 1915, challenging dangerous currents and gunfire and sinking and damaging enemy
vessels up to the harbour gates of Constantinople*. The crippling of naval
ships has significant influence on the outcome of the war at sea – damage to the
two British capital ships in Alexandria left the Italians in temporary command
of the Eastern Mediterranean, while that to the Tirpitz meant that convoys for
the beleaguered Russians had a better chance of getting through. Similarly the
sinking of and damage to the French fleet at Oran, a necessary but sad task
undertaken with great regret by Admiral Somerville, prevented its feared hand-
over to the German High Command.

Fourth, more durable command can be won by denying the other fleet
access to all ports and bases, either by occupying or neutralising them. In the
past the latter course has been attempted and effected by long range naval
gunnery, air attack and sealing off the base by submarines and mines.
Aeroplanes, U-boats and mines were all used in the failed attempt to neutralise
Malta. Now there are also missiles, which can be fired from air, surface or
submarines. In 1940 the Royal Navy was denied all ports on the western coasts
of continental Europe except Gibraltar and in 1942 Japanese naval and air
power temporarily made Mombasa the only safe port for the Eastern Fleet.

Fifth, command can be won by a blockade of naval forces in enemy ports.
The enemy can be prevented from leaving port by a close blockade, strengthened by mines, or be brought to action when he tries to escape by ships and
submarines lying in wait in open blockade. Fear of the latter, although in part
bluff, was the cause of Captain Langsdorff's scuttling of the Graf Spee in
Montevideo in 1939, when the Royal Navy lay in wait for him at the mouth of
the River Plate, after an action, in which the Achilles and Exeter both received
damage. Requiring more ships for the watcher than the watched, the close
blockade was an extravagant form of naval warfare. It also arrested offensive
action, placing blockading forces in a defensive position, with the element of
surprise passing to those attempting to escape. Hawke and Nelson employed
both open and close blockades and just before Trafalgar the octogenarian First
Lord, Lord Barham, brilliantly masterminded the French into a blockade in
Ferrol and Brest. In this century dangers from mines, shore based aircraft, long
range guns, missiles, submarines and small craft armed with torpedoes have
necessitated a more open approach and even this has been difficult to enforce.
The German occupied ports in World War II, stretching from Norway to the
South of France, covered too great an area for watching ships to prevent
escape. It is one thing to blockade a fleet of surface ships into port, another to
prevent U-boats or single surface raiders from slipping out in fog or cloudy
weather, or emerging through the waters of the Skageraak. Some modern
strategists again place faith in recent technology and predict that a forward
screen can prevent enemy ships escaping from home waters, while arguing that
the convoy system is out of date because of the speed of nuclear powered
submarines. The same predictions, albeit on a slightly different premise, were

* Later Admiral Sir Martin Dunbar-Nasmith VC, KCB, KCMG.

made in 1903 and had been abandoned by 1917. In a blockade of naval forces battle squadrons were traditionally deployed, whereas in a blockade of merchant shipping cruisers and destroyers were more usual. A blockade of merchant shipping, imposing economic sanctions and forcing naval ships to put to sea in defence of convoys, should be imposed by commerce prevention and not by its destruction. Commerce prevention is within the Humanitarian Rules of the Sea and has been likened to the legal sanction of 'distress' whereas commerce destruction is a return to the methods of the privateer or pirate, disregarding agreed principles of International Humanitarian Law, that ships must be challenged, searched and not sunk, without making provision for the safety of crews. British submarines on the morning of April 9th 1940 were even under orders to give a warning to German ships engaged in carrying invasion forces and military supplies to Norway, but, since in the restricted waters of the Baltic this almost neutralised their actions, the orders were lifted by the afternoon.

Sixth, command or limited command can be won by merging defensive and offensive operations, as in countering attempted invasion or preventing attacks upon lines of communication. Indeed, the greatest British naval victories have been won in defence of homeland – as in the defeat of the Armada or Nelson's victory at Trafalgar, which destroyed Napoleon's future invasion plans. On the trade routes of the world, criss-crossing at focal points, offensive and defensive naval operations are sometimes hard to distinguish and a nation seeking control of communications must keep a balance between occupying the enemy's trade routes and safeguarding his own. Traditionally the Royal Navy's method of dealing with the merchant raider has been to let the enemy come 'to the honey' and destroy him there. Victories in World War II were won within the convoy system, picking off U-boats as they came in to attack, either singly or in wolf packs, and later in the war, as ships became more plentiful, temporarily detaching support escort vessels from the convoy to destroy enemy raiders. The calm courage, concentration and expertise of those who wait to be attacked day in, day out, year in year out, without flinching or complaining is in the highest traditions of the Royal and Merchant Navies. Whereas the Italian and Japanese Navies in World War II fought principally in fleets or squadrons – the Japanese also using single raiders for commerce destruction – the Germans shifted from the opposing fleets policy of the First World War to one of powerfully armed and armoured surface raiders and U-boats, acting singly or with support. The exception was their invasion of Norway, mounted in six units of naval forces. By the end of that campaign, despite not presenting an ultimatum until after the invasion had begun, the Germans had lost one heavy and two light cruisers, ten destroyers and one pocket battleship out of action for a year – a heavy toll which increased Hitler's dependence on surface raiders and U-boats as well as decreasing his chances of invading Britain.

Seventh, command of the sea can be won by land or sea based aircraft destroying ships insufficiently protected from air attack. Whereas the horrors of U-boat warfare were fully comprehended by World War I, it was not until

1940 that the aeroplane also took its terrible toll of the Navies and Merchant Navies of the world in a war of attrition. It takes years to build a naval ship, but aeroplanes and trained pilots cannot be swiftly replaced either and if sufficient numbers are shot down command of sea and air will pass again. Air power gave ships an added range – reconnaissance aeroplanes became the eyes and ears of the fleet, fighter aircraft its protectors and bombers and dive bombers its long and short range gunnery. Although in World War II command of the sea area close to the enemy shore could not be secured until airfields were destroyed, nevertheless, so long as an aircraft carrier supported the fleet, command was in dispute. Convoys without air escort from shore or ship or without a catapult aeroplane were, if faced with determined air attack, doomed to destruction. Enormous casualties were inflicted on convoys to Russia by German aircraft flying from bases only 50 miles from Murmansk, as they were on Malta convoys sailing from Gibraltar through the Skerki Channel and from Alexandria through what became known as Bomb Alley.

In most wars command goes back and forth, one way and then the other, until one side is victorious. This pattern is illustrated by the Battle for the Mediterranean in World War II. It is a microcosm of the war at sea and shows the rapidity with which control can be won and lost. First, Allied navies were in command, then with Italy's entrance into the war, both sides were evenly balanced until, with the fall of France, the British were heavily out-numbered. The Italian Navy was reluctant to engage battle. Without radar, it did not like fighting at night and was deterred by the British tactic of 'making smoke'. So, after the loss of capital ships at Taranto in a harbour attack by the Fleet Air Arm, command was reversed in Britain's favour. Neither side had sufficient sea-trained air crews, but the modern carrier Ark Royal at Gibraltar gave Britain the 'edge'. Hitler therefore sent the Luftwaffe to Sicily, with pilots specially trained in ship attack. The aircraft carrier Illustrious was damaged from the air and thereafter no Royal Navy carriers could be deployed safely in the central basin of the Mediterranean. Nevertheless, German promises of air support to their allies were not always fulfilled and seaborne aeroplanes flying from the Formidable and a crescendo of gunfire gave the Royal Navy victory at Matapan, inflicting great damage on the Italian fleet. Then the Luftwaffe arrived in force to aid the Axis armies in Greece, and, after the Germans had compelled the British to evacuate, they took Crete in an airborne invasion – which nearly failed. In preventing enemy reinforcement of the island by sea and then in evacuating British troops, the Royal Navy, with no air cover after the crippling of its only aircraft carrier, suffered a heavy toll. 3 cruisers and 6 destroyers were sunk, 2 battleships, 2 cruisers and 2 destroyers were badly damaged, with 3 cruisers and 6 destroyers less severely damaged – a very large part of the Eastern Mediterranean fleet. Back went the British on to the defensive, suspending convoys to Malta, until, with the German invasion of Russia in June 1941, many Axis aircraft were withdrawn, leaving only 200 operational in the Mediterranean (out of total of 351) to cover the bombing of Egypt and supply lines to Tobruk. The Axis air assault on Malta had to be halted and British submarines and aeroplanes could again operate from the island, sinking

63 percent of Rommel's transports in November 1941. Neither side could claim command, however, for, with no aircraft carrier in the Eastern Mediterranean and, outnumbered by the Italian Fleet and surrounded by hostile land-based aircraft, British ships could not safely operate in the central basin of the Mediterranean, while supplies to Malta, which was critically short of food, could only get through by submarine.

Malta's air defences were now strengthened by aircraft flown from Gibraltar-based carriers. Two relief convoys got through, a surface force K arrived on the island and Rommel, his supplies threatened, retreated to the borders of Tripolitania. But Hitler, concerned at the deteriorating situation, ordered the Luftwaffe back to Sicily and more U-boats to the Mediterranean, so that the balance of command altered again. Rear Admiral Vian successfully escorted single fast auxiliary supply vessels to Malta, to protect one of which he fought the First Battle of Sirte; but the Ark Royal and the battleship Barham were sunk by U-boats off Gibraltar and Alexandria; the Malta-based surface force K ran into an unknown minefield and was reduced to a cruiser and three destroyers and in December 1941 – the month the Japanese entered the war – the battleships Valiant and Queen Elizabeth were damaged in Alexandria. Admiral Cunningham's fleet was now down to 3 light cruisers, 1 anti-aircraft cruiser and a handful of destroyers, while in Gibraltar Somerville's Force H was reduced to one battleship, one light cruiser and destroyers – facing an Italian Navy three times that strength. In December 1941 Rommel reported that his 'peril (was) considerably eased'. Nevertheless, with the Cyrenaican airfields now in British hands the Royal Navy could run some convoys from Alexandria to Malta under cover of shore, until Rommel rolled back victorious towards Tobruk. This made Hitler sufficiently confident to decide the time had come to neutralise Malta from the air and so reduce the risk to Rommel's convoys. Now began the island's terrible trial – with odds of 10 to 1 and with 262 air raids in January only 15 Hurricanes were left. C-in-C's were told, 'Malta is vital. No risk to ships need deter you'. But convoys were either being sunk or were so badly damaged that there was no alternative to turning back. Then the first Spitfires were flown to Malta from Force H carriers (one lent by the USA) and Rear Admiral Vian set out again with a convoy from Alexandria. Defended on the first day by the new RAF Special Naval Protection Group and afterwards dodging in and out of his smoke screens, he fought off the Italian Navy in an action named the Second Battle of Sirte and two freighters reached Malta to a delirious welcome. Air attacks then rained down on the docks and only one fifth of the supplies were safely unloaded.

In April 1942 the Luftwaffe flew 9,599 sorties to Malta, with a daily average of 170 bombers. No dockyard workshop was in action, all docks were damaged, there was no electricity; arriving Spitfires were destroyed before becoming airborne; the harbour was sealed in by mines and there was no fighter protection for minesweepers to clear them. With the last members of the surface fleet escaped to Gibraltar, the submarines left also. The end seemed nigh. Yet still Malta hung on. With Hitler requiring more aeroplanes in Russia, Rommel judged Malta to be suppressed and wanted to recapture Tobruk, but in

May the balance of air power shifted. More Spitfires arrived on the island and were airborne within 35 minutes. Axis losses were now greater than British and daylight raids on the dockyards ceased. Hitler, remembering the near-failure of the airborne drop on Crete, postponed the proposed capture of Malta from the air until July, meanwhile giving Rommel the go-ahead for his offensive, but ordering him not to go beyond the Egyptian border. While Auchinleck, who was losing air strength to the Indian Ocean, kept postponing his advance, Rommel struck first, capturing Tobruk and its supplies. Elated by success he was convinced he could drive the British from Egypt, but he failed to break the British line at El Alamein. A convoy now set out for Malta from Alexandria, under orders from its new Combined Operations Room, but it failed to get through – with Rommel's airfields now only 160 miles from Alexandria, all RN ships were dispersed from the port down the East Mediterranean coast. Another convoy from Gibraltar, however, survived all attacks and arrived safely.

The Battle of the Mediterranean had reached its crucial stage. In August Generals Alexander and Montgomery arrived in command of the Middle East and 8th Army respectively and new US battle tanks were delivered. In Malta the Spitfires were inflicting twice the losses they were suffering. With the submarines returning in July, Rommel's supply losses had risen again and now stood at 34 percent. Hope was renewed, but Malta's food, fuel and supplies were fast running out. The story of Malta's famous relief convoy – Operation Pedestal, when, 'The fate of Malta and, it may well be, of British fortunes in the Middle East hung by a thread' – should belong, as indeed do those of the other Mediterranean convoys, to the chapter on the convoy war, but so crucial was its success to the outcome of the war and so interwoven was it with the story of the Battle for the Mediterranean that the author may be excused for recounting it here instead. An American tanker, the fastest afloat, with a British crew, and 13 freighters set out from Gibraltar, with a huge naval close escort and supporting force. Lying in wait were 1,000 Axis aircraft, mines, submarines and the Italian fleet. The Royal Navy escort and support forces consisted of 72 aircraft aboard 3 carriers, 2 battleships, 3 anti-aircraft cruisers, 3 cruisers, 24 destroyers and minesweepers, nearly the present strength of the Royal Navy – to fight through one convoy. All ships were to accompany the convoy to the narrow waters of the Skerki Channel, where the main fleet would turn back leaving 3 cruisers, one anti-aircraft cruiser and 12 destroyers as 'through' escorts. The first casualty was an aircraft carrier, sunk by a U-boat. Then came an air attack, in which new aerial torpedoes circled on parachutes above the convoy. Convoy drill was so perfect that ships turned 90 degrees to starboard, regardless of the attack. One freighter was hit, and later sunk following the shore route with an escort. In the evening an air attack put the second aircraft carrier's flight deck out of action. Then a destroyer was sunk. At the Narrows the supporting force turned back, leaving an additional cruiser and 2 destroyers to join the close escort continuing to Malta.

Now came an onslaught by Italian submarines, hitting a cruiser, which had later to be sunk, an anti-aircraft cruiser and the tanker, Ohio. Order was lost as ships went to each other's rescue. Then aeroplanes dived out of the sky and, although intercepted by Beaufighters from Malta, another merchant ship was set on fire and abandoned. Two more were hit. One got under way, followed the shore route and arrived safely in Malta. The other was sunk. Destroyers sped up and down restoring order. Fires on the tanker were put out and she limped after the convoy. But German and Italian E-boats were lying in wait with torpedoes. Another cruiser was hit and scuttled; 4 more merchant ships were sunk and one damaged, leaving 6 in the convoy; further air attacks followed. Then came word that 6 enemy cruisers and 11 destroyers were steering straight for the convoy. 'The future of the convoy and, it may well be, of the Middle East' and therefore of the war was in the balance, but Axis orders were that every aircraft should be thrown into bombardment of the convoy and, since this left the Italian fleet without air cover, it returned to port.

Massed dive bombers came in to attack. A merchant ship exploded and its burning debris fell on another, causing such damage that 36 unseasoned crew members jumped into the sea and had to be rescued. The Ohio, also hit by burning debris, was again on fire. A further air attack immobilised another freighter, which, with a destroyer standing by, was hit again and sunk. Meanwhile the 3 surviving freighters and their escort and minesweepers reached Malta to a delirious welcome. Immediately a destroyer and three minesweepers returned to help the Ohio, whose crew, after successfully fighting the fire, had been taken off by a destroyer to return at night and get her in tow. With a minesweeper towing in front, one destroyer lashed alongside and another secured to the stern to provide direction and a third destroyer and 3 minesweepers providing an escort, she made progress, but a bomb from another air attack hit her hull, the towing wire parted and had to be rejoined. The escorting destroyer was lashed to her other side and thus, with a destroyer lashed on either side, one attached behind and a minesweeper towing in front they sailed into Malta, carrying 10,000 tons of oil. Malta was saved. Every enemy effort had been thrown into the battle, but to no avail. The sea lanes had been kept open and 32,000 tons of cargo were unloaded.'Thus ended what was to prove the last of the many major operations undertaken to save Malta.'* The Royal Navy gave pride of place to the 'conduct, courage and determination' of the crews of the merchant vessels. With the relief of Malta the Battle of the Mediterranean was virtually won. Command of the sea had passed to the British and now it was Rommel who was short of supplies, including petrol and food. The Panzer Army was consuming twice the supplies crossing the Mediterranean. In October the Battle of El Alamein was a decisive victory for the British. Suffering heavy casualties, Rommel streamed westwards. This story of the struggle for command of the Mediterranean Sea shows clearly how it goes back and forth; how dependent it is upon command of the air, how it affects the military situation on the ground, enabling and preventing amphibious operations to take place, reinforcing, supplying and, if need be, evacuating

* In the final convoy to Malta – Operation Stoneage in November – only one naval ship was damaged.

ground forces and preventing the enemy from doing the same; lastly, how in turn the situation on land affects command of the sea by the capture, holding or loss of airfields.

The story of the Mediterranean demonstrates a number of the principles lying behind such strategies and tactics. Because the sea is a continuing potential enemy or friend, many of principles of naval warfare have remained the same for centuries, despite the invention of new weapons and technology. What are these principles? First, there must be a flexible balance of concentration and dispersal in naval forces. Squadrons concentrated in a fleet have been likened by naval strategists to a fan that opens and shuts, sufficiently concentrated to achieve cohesion, sufficiently distributed to maximise the reach of individual ships or squadrons. The secret of success is to disperse and rejoin at will. In the Napoleonic Wars the eye of the fan was, as always in British history, the entrance to the Channel. Just before Trafalgar, one concentration of ships guarded the French ports and North Sea, another the Western Approaches and the Atlantic, while a third, based on Gibraltar and operating within and without the Straits, blockaded Brest and Toulon. In World War II Admiral Somerville's Force H based on Gibraltar operated in this dual role. While also having an important presence in the Mediterranean, the carrier Ark Royal flew off the aircraft which blocked the Bismark's escape into Brest and, by damaging her with an aerial torpedo, enabled the battleships King George V and Rodney, the cruiser Dorsetshire and Vian's destroyers to surround and sink her. Although in fan formation a fleet is ready to deter invasion and protect the main trade terminals, it must disperse to protect commerce at sea or effect a blockade. This means there must be sufficient forces to concentrate at the base to prevent invasion and to disperse for the protection of lines of communication. Shortage of ships and aircraft carriers bedevilled this strategy in World War II, yet in 1939 the Fleet consisted of 367 ships (not including minesweepers and 19 Commonwealth ships). If a Navy of that size was stretched to defend Britain's shores, merchant shipping and vital interests overseas, Britain's present Navy – one fifth of the size – must seem to any reader woefully inadequate.

A corollary of this principle, which the Japanese twice disregarded with fatal results, is that to arbitrarily divide a fleet going into action into different units is to weaken it and risk defeat. Admittedly the technique has been used successfully by the Royal Navy on specific occasions – to prevent invasion or set a trap or in certain special circumstances arising in amphibious operations – but again the two fleets must remain in close contact, acting in concert with one another and able to rejoin quickly at will. The British fleet was divided when the Armada hove in sight, Seymour was on blockade duty in the Channel, Drake was to windward, coming up from the west country, but Drake sent Seymour orders to join him and the two fleet acted in unison and the enemy found themselves with little room to manoeuvre within the fan. If the fleet is distributed the fan must be able to snap shut before the main battle is commenced. The risk is that, owing to bad weather, lack of communications, or precipitate enemy action, the two parts of a fleet will not be able to rejoin in time – as at Jutland, when battle was engaged before the Grand Fleet met the battlecruisers. In theory modern communications should cut down the risk of losing contact. Yet, without these, Nelson relied successfully on his frigates to relay accurate messages, whereas at Jutland Jellicoe's cruisers failed to pass on vital information, so that he sometimes did not know the position of parts of his fleet, even after battle was engaged. It was this lack of cohesion, caused by dividing their fleet into three or four units, that helped to destroy Japanese chances of victory at the Battles of Coral Sea and Midway, while in the subsequent sea battles fought around the island of Guadalcanal, the US Navy also lacked cohesion and proper communications, so that in night battles ships were in real danger of firing at each other.

Since the sea is always in perpetual motion, sometimes friend, sometimes foe, its moods if correctly interpreted and utilised can offer opportunities for victory or escape. This knowledge of the sea and seamanship constitutes a second principle. Again and again in sea battles and convoy protection, fog, mist or snow in the Atlantic or Barents Sea offered protection from aeroplanes or surface raiders far more effectively than the smoke screens on which Vian had to rely to hide his convoys in the Mediterranean. In the days of sail, when wind was a key element in a battle the enemy could be deprived of it and driven on to shoals, cliffs or into races by a fleet with superior knowledge, seamanship and advantage of wind. As the Armada proceeded eastwards after the first engagement off the Isle of Wight to rendezvous with Palma's transports at Dunkirk, Drake and Howard tried to harry the galleons on to the dangerous banks known as the Owers and again as they fled northwards from the fireships, with the gale behind them, the English tried to drive them on to the Zealand Banks. 'God blew with his wind and they were scattered', said Elizabeth, but she was aware that her seamen understood the nature of that wind. In the nineteenth century English superiority in seamanship made them reluctant to turn to iron and steam, but despite modern engine power and steel ships the elements of nature – wind, weather, swell, the movement of the ocean, the presence of its rocks and tides and races, the fall of dusk and the onset of night – all these remain a vital part of sea craft and high standards of training in seamanship continue to be a key to superiority and survival.

The third principle governing the way command can be won is to achieve a high degree of mobility and speed. This has always been the tradition of the Royal Navy. It was Nelson's greatest genius – a strategy and tactic on which he constantly relied – and a principle on which the Royal Navy, with one or two exceptions, has refused to compromise (although it is curious how slow they were to introduce refuelling at sea). When there has been a conflict between increased armour and speed the British have always courageously chosen speed. Because of that the British could get round the enemy ships, cut them off, escape from them, spring surprises, lead them away in a ruse from their main object or overhaul them in a chase. In the American War of Independence Howe with 22 ships defended British shores from a combined French and Allied force of 36 vessels. He swiftly and secretly got to westward of them at night, knowing they could not enter the Channel without discovering his position. They beat up and down looking for him, and, failing to find him, lost the initiative. His campaign ended with his famous relief of Gibraltar. At the Battle of the Falklands in World War I the German Pacific Fleet consisted of two heavy cruisers and a few light cruisers, which had been ordered to do what damage they could to British merchant shipping. Operating in the South Atlantic they were unaware that British ships were in Port Stanley until they saw smoke rising from their funnels. They set off at once in escape, but in spite of unavoidable delays in finishing coaling and putting to sea, it was not long before the British battlecruisers and cruisers – not younger in years, but more modern in design – had overtaken them and sent them to the bottom. Some types of naval ships are built for greater speed than others. With her sister ships still building in 1939, the Duke of York was in the fastest class of British battleship afloat, but, even if the Germans had observed the treaty by which they were bound, she could never have had the speed of the Scharnhorst, which was a battlecruiser. In December 1943 the Scharnhorst, under orders to annihilate an Allied convoy to Murmansk, was damaged by the guns of the Duke of York, who could not, however, then catch up with the fleeing battlecruiser. Four escort destroyers followed her, 'Their bows buried, their sterns riding a-top the waves, going at such a speed in relation to their size that they were in danger of swinging broadside on and capsizing'. The damage inflicted by the Duke of York suddenly slowed the Scharnhorst's speed and two destroyers on one side, two on the other, sank her by torpedoes and gunfire.

Superiority in speed, manoeuvrability, marksmanship, or any other naval expertise cannot be achieved without keeping ahead in technology, particularly true today, when invention is so rapid. This constitutes the fourth principle – that command of the sea can be won or lost according to the superiority of weaponry and equipment of either side. The Germans entered World War II with a fault in their torpedoes, not corrected until 1940, whereas in the Far East it was the US Navy, which had faults in their pistols and depth gear, so that their torpedoes were not properly effective against the deadly Japanese Long Lance torpedoes during the battles round Guadalcanal in 1942. By 1941 British technology could detect a surfaced as well as a submerged U-boat and likewise in battles between surface ships in the Pacific blips appeared on radar at distances far greater than the huge Japanese binoculars could pick up, while the position of the Scharnhorst on her last voyage was known to the British long before the presence of RN ships was known to the Germans. Yet, although British naval radar was superior and improved intelligence and high frequency direction finding equipment were later to reveal the presence of assembling wolf packs, had the war continued longer the development of the schnorkel would again have given the German U-boat the 'edge'. As always, a balance must be kept. Although in the earliest days of war asdic sometimes detected the U-boats long before the eye could spot the white track of the torpedoes, nothing could ever detract from the need for look-outs, watching with the naked eye and binoculars. In Russian winter convoys the need for captains of ships to remain alert throughout the tediously long hours of darkness was so great that well-wishers on the distaff side encouraged them to take up knitting to keep themselves awake! Although the Falklands and Gulf War showed that electronic warfare technology had increased at a speed undreamed of only a few years ago, it is extraordinary to what extent the Falklands War was fought along lines similar to those of World War II, because the Royal Navy had lost its air early warning capability, removed by men in Whitehall who believed that shore based aircraft would always be available.

The fifth principle, which had to be relearnt at the Falklands by the British government, parliament and public, although not by the Royal Navy, is the twin concept that surface ships are still the main spring of all maritime operations – without them large numbers of men, vehicles, equipment and other supplies, including food and fuel cannot be moved across the oceans and neither can an island be defended from invasion – but they must be protected by air cover from either land or carrier. It was the disaster of the Norwegian campaign, during which sleepless sailors withstood days of dive bombing of their ships without respite, that first brought home to everyone that without adequate air defences command of the sea is lost. Here in the fiords, with the short visibility of the steep mountain peaks making the task of the defenders yet more difficult, the lesson was learnt that the gun alone was no longer master at sea. Had the training of the German pilots been of the same standard as later in the Mediterranean few ships would have survived. Royal Navy carriers were few, most were antiquated, and Fleet Air Arm fighters were obsolete. With Stavanger airfield in the hands of the Germans, desperate, improbable measures were taken to provide airfields, and all failed. Too late it was understood that aeroplanes operating at sea are a specialised form of air command and require specialist aircraft and training. If they are sea-borne and are part of the RN they are specially trained, but if they come from land bases and are provided by the RAF then a special Naval Protection Group is required (as set up in the Mediterranean in 1942), not only to train pilots at sea, but to act as a link between Navy and Air Force and to promote the specialist designs of aeroplanes required. The fact that young naval pilots flying aircraft designed for high level bombing in almost suicide missions at mast height against enemy warships gave their lives willingly, gallantly, and with lightness of spirit does nothing to lift the burdens of pre-war failures in proper strategic planning. The lessons repeatedly demonstrated in the battle for the Mediterranean were: that it is sea and air power together which hold the key to victory; that the best aircraft base is an island inhabited like Malta by courageous and determined people; that air power alone cannot move men or supplies in sufficient volume; that naval guns and missiles are still required to back up the bombs of the Air Force or the shells of artillery; that ships need adequate and highly mobile seaborne air defences and that without air cover they are sitting ducks on the oceans of the world. The truth was that the Royal Navy in the inter-war period had lost control of the Royal Naval Air Service to the RAF until 1937, too little money had been available and what funds that there were had been channelled into gunnery. Nevertheless, even gunnery control systems were also antiquated at the start of World War II, the moral being that it is not possible to have an adequate defence policy without proper funding.

This introduces the sixth principle of naval warfare, dating from the seventeenth century. Sometimes, if hopelessly outnumbered by ships, aeroplanes or weaponry, it may be that escape is – for the moment – the only answer. This need to survive constitutes the sixth principle, that of keeping 'a fleet in being'. If naval forces are not adequate to join battle with the enemy then the commander has no option but to maintain a 'fleet in being', as Tennyson, whose detailed knowledge of the Navy came from his naval shipbuilding cousin, set out in his poem, THE REVENGE.

> At Flores in the Azores Sir Richard Grenville lay,
> And a pinnace like a fluttered bird came flying from far away.
> 'Spanish ships of war at sea! We have sighted fifty-three!'
> Then sware Lord Thomas Howard: ''Fore God I am no coward;
> But I cannot meet them here, for my ships are out of gear,
> And the half my men are sick, I must fly, but follow quick.
> We are six ships of the line; can we fight with fifty-three?'

Lord Thomas Howard – the Admiral of Elizabeth's fleet – withdrew five ships, all requiring refitting, not through cowardice, but in order to maintain a 'fleet in being', his country not being able to sacrifice five ships of the line to certain loss. Although a weaker 'fleet in being' cannot engage the enemy, it can hover around and keep his attention – it can prevent him from behaving as if it did not exist and it remains a force to be reckoned with when he draws up his plans. In the Napoleonic Wars the French maintained a 'fleet in being' against superior British naval forces and Napoleon postponed the risk of losing command until he controlled enough of the continent to feel (wrongly) that he did not need the sea. In World War II Admiral Somerville had the experience of being outnumbered in the Western Mediterranean, but it was not until he was appointed C-in-C Far East in February 1942 that he received explicit instructions to remain a 'fleet in being'. 'You quite realise', wrote Winston Churchill to him, 'that you enjoy the fullest confidence not only of the Admiralty, but of the Government'. Somerville, however, confided to his diary his misgivings about his unenviable task, 'This damned appointment gives me no kick at all, and I keep asking myself why the hell am I here at my age'. He was the ideal replacement for Admiral Phillips, under whose command the Prince of Wales and Repulse were lost, for Phillips had the reputation of pushing on regardless of cost, posing great hazards in the circumstances appertaining then in the Far East. Somerville, who was past the normal age for retirement, was chosen for both tasks, partly because of his unique experience in radar, but also because of his individual style of leadership – 'cool courage and earthy humour', enabling him to face impossible odds with equanimity and a reputation for not leaving his 'boys' in trouble, so that they never lost their trust in him. A 'fleet in being' must either be kept on the move or in a safe port – and even this is a questionable proposition in the days of cruise missiles.

Although the Japanese did not know of the existence of the Addu Atoll fuelling station in the Indian Ocean (which the Navy with typical humour nicknamed Scapa Flow with palm trees), nevertheless this could hardly be regarded as a safe port. Once, therefore, Colombo and Trincomalee had been bombed and the main part of his small fleet had only been saved from elimination in their harbours by luck, good communications and wise judgement, Somerville had no alternative but to retire to Mombasa, having first secured the Vichy French naval base in the island of Madagascar, around which Axis submarines had been operating. The essential requirement for Britain and the Allies at that time was to keep open the supply route across the Indian Ocean and for this the maintenance of a 'fleet in being' was a vital necessity.

One final principle stands supreme – the upholding of a great tradition. Sometimes, in pursuit of duty and of a great and worthwhile object, it may be necessary to risk a 'fleet in being' or sacrifice a single ship or ships. When the advisability was questioned of a return to Crete to evacuate further British forces Admiral Cunningham, in spite of having no protection from the Luftwaffe after the damage inflicted on his aircraft carrier and the loss of so many ships, replied, 'It takes three years to build a ship, it takes three hundred to build a tradition'. Thus the soldiers on the beaches heard again the terse and welcome words, familiar from the first dark days of war, when British prisoners were freed from the German prison ship Altmark – 'The Navy's here'. Sometimes also a ship or a few ships may be caught alone or in a trap and, when faced with the choice of attempting to escape or fighting it out against overwhelming odds, may courageously choose the latter. Caught in this predicament their captains have weighed in the balance against the loss of their own ship and lives the damage that can be inflicted on the enemy, for such damage can affect not only battles, but the whole war. When Lord Thomas Howard sailed away that day in the Azores with his five ships of the line the REVENGE was left to take her wounded off from shore, rather than let them fall into the enemy hands. On the way back to the open sea they were trapped – 'Shall we fight or shall we fly?' asked their captain, ' For to fight is but to die'. At first, recounts Tennyson, the fifty three ships of the Spanish line laughed derisively at their tiny prey, as she sailed between their lines, emptying her guns at them, but soon they found that they were handicapped in their own bombardment by the fear of sinking one another.

> And the sun went down and the stars came out far over the summer sea
> But never a moment ceased the fight of the one and the fifty three.
> Ship after ship the whole night long, with her thunder battle and flame;
> Ship after ship the whole night long, drew back with her dead and her shame;
> For some were sunk and many were shattered, and so could fight us no more.

With their captain wounded, the crew finally surrendered, but,

> The little Revenge herself went down by the island crags
> To be lost evermore in the main.

There is something strangely similar between this story from the Spanish Main and one from the Far East recounted by Captain Donald Macintyre in his book FIGHTING SHIPS AND SEAMEN. In February 1942 a combined Dutch, British, US and Australian fleet sailed under the command of a Dutch Admiral from Australia to try to prevent or delay the planned Japanese invasion of Java. This assorted force failed to get past the superior Japanese fleet and to get at the convoy and at the last battle almost every ship was sunk, with virtually no damage inflicted. After it was over two escaping cruisers – the Perth and Houston – ran by chance into the invasion fleet at Bantem Bay. Transports lay everywhere around them. Like the Revenge they steamed up and down the lines, sinking and damaging as many Japanese ships as they could, knowing that the Japanese could not properly hit back without risking their own convoy. After 45 minutes, with their ammunition expended, both ships were sunk. The Japanese Admiral saluted their courage with courtesy from his ships rail and saw to it that the crew were rescued and well treated. Tragically two thirds of them died in POW camps, such now in the days of bureaucratic tyranny is the reward for courage. Admiral Cunningham described Captain Waller of the Perth as, 'One of the greatest Captains who ever sailed the seas'.

This same fighting spirit was displayed by the destroyer Acasta, which, with the Ardent, was accompanying the aircraft carrier Glorious on her return from Norway in May 1940, with the latter carrying so many evacuated RAF aircraft that she was not properly able to fly her own. The Acasta saw both ships sunk by the Scharnhorst and Gneisenau and fled into her own enveloping smoke screen. 'Don't think we're escaping', said her Captain, Commander Charles Glasfurd, and, turning one hundred and eighty degrees, the Acasta re-emerged from the smoke to fire four torpedoes, one of which hit the Scharnhorst, inflicting damage which put her out of action for many months. The Acasta was sunk, but the result of the action was that other British ships returning from Norway were not harassed by the two German battlecruisers, which were forced to return to Trondheim. Even that was not the end of the story, for when the Scharnhorst, after being temporarily patched up, limped home for repair, the Gneisenau, making a ruse sailing to distract attention from the movements of her crippled sister ship, was also hit by a torpedo. Thus far reaching are the ripples which go out from the heroism of these lone acts. The crews of the Glorious and her two destroyers were not picked up by the Germans and only one survivor from the Acasta, two from the Ardent, and forty three from the Glorious were rescued after a long ordeal in an open boat. To the British public it seemed at the time that fifteen hundred men had tragically been swallowed up, as the crew of the Hood was later to be, into the mists and trackless wastes of the North Sea, but, as with Captain Warburton Lee's heroism at Narvik, it is these great acts of gallantry and sacrifice, which not only inflict damage upon the enemy, but lift the morale of a nation in perilous days and inspire others to treat with total disdain the possibilities of defeat.

CHAPTER X

'FOR THE SAKE OF A HANDFUL OF AIRCRAFT AND ONE OR TWO DECENT SHIPS'
DETERRING INVASION

'Decisive naval superiority', said George Washington, 'is to be considered a fundamental principle and the basis upon which every hope of success must ultimately depend'. If George Washington had lived in the twentieth century he would have added 'air' to his dictum. Yet from 1957 onwards the Royal Navy, for reasons of financial stringency, was increasingly cut down and its strike aircraft cut out, while on the other side of Europe the Russian bear was learning to swim. Exactly one decade after Sandys' Defence Review, Soviet warships sailed through the Dardanelles into the Mediterranean Sea during the Second Israeli War. By 1968 the Soviet Navy had increased from its low profile in World War II to 505 ships, including 380 submarines (55 of which were nuclear powered), with 750 additional coastal escorts and minesweepers. Since the submarine is primarily a vehicle of attack, these figures alarmed the West. Moreover, while the British public unwittingly repeated views expressed in the White Paper about there being no need in the modern world for sea-borne air cover, the Soviets began to build helicopter and then aircraft carriers. By that year the British had decided to withdraw East of Suez and the Royal Navy had been more than halved in a decade to 147 ships, consisting now of 4 aircraft carriers, 3 cruisers, 26 destroyers, 70 frigates, 44 submarines, of which 4 were Polaris and 3 others were nuclear powered, and minesweepers. The 4 carriers, with fixed wing aircraft, were then phased out by the Labour government, despite the resignation of the First Sea Lord and Minister of the Navy. The elimination of the battleship in the 1968 Royal Navy list and the reduction of the cruiser strength to 8 percent of the 1947 figure left gunnery bombardment dependent on the remaining 3 cruisers (themselves soon to go) and on the small 4.5 inch guns of the destroyers – which had also been cut down to 14 percent of their 1947 figure. A solemn promise was given by the government in the debates leading to the decision to develop Polaris that funding for any nuclear deterrent would come from the total defence budget and not from Navy Estimates, a promise which won support for the change from Members with naval backgrounds and which was initially honoured by a separate 'strategic' account. At present, however, the Navy pays for the lion's share of Trident, which reduces amounts available for other vessels and equipment. Fortunately for the freedom of the Western world the USA continued to provide a balanced fleet – with the exception of their omission of minesweepers – of 536 ships, consisting of 25 carriers, 10 cruisers, 227 destroyers, 105 frigates and escorts, 128 submarines and 41 Polaris submarines.

During the next two decades the Soviets expanded the numbers of nuclear submarines and of cruisers, launched 4 aircraft carriers and 2 battlecruisers, and decreased the strength of their destroyers and frigates. During the same period the US Navy increased its capacity for heavy gunnery bombardment by reintroducing 2 battleships and adding 3 cruisers to the fleet, while at the same time cutting the carrier and destroyer strength by half and two thirds, with the number of frigates and escorts remaining approximately the same. The British, on the other hand, during the same period, continued to make cuts right across the board. In Captain Donald Macintyre's words, 'Since 1960 the only decision taken has been one of indecision'. The figures for the Royal Navy, set out in Options for Change in July 1990, bear no relation to its former strength, proposing approximately 40 destroyers and frigates, a figure already looking optimistic, 16 submarines (plus 4 ballistic), 3 small aircraft carriers and an amphibious capability. These aircraft carriers, developed by the Royal Navy under the name of 'Through deck cruisers' carry the Harrier jump jets, which showed their worth at the Falklands. Currently the Royal Navy's surface fleet is smaller than that of the Japanese, who have 63 destroyers and frigates – called by Treaty a Naval Defence Force. It is impossible to believe that a fleet of this size can properly fulfil its peacetime role, much less fulfil the tasks that would be assigned to it in war.

What then are the tasks of the Royal Navy with regard to its most important role – the defence of homeland? Since 1066 there have been no major invasions of England and it is difficult for the British people to picture that peril, until – as in 1940 – transports face them across the Channel. In the defence against invasion the objective of the Royal Navy has always been the destruction of the enemy's army, whether sailing on warships, landing craft or transports. Sometimes an enemy will plan to let his main fleet sail with the transports, in which case the cumbersome convoy can easily be set upon by naval forces; sometimes he gives his transports a light escort and lets his main supporting fleet sail separately. If Britain has command of the Channel and the coast line the invasion will not be attempted. If it is in dispute, it may be. Since the sixteenth century British strategy has been threefold. First, the Royal Navy has used the narrowness of the Channel as the best weapon in its armoury. 'We'll drum them up the Channel', wrote Henry Newbolt, 'as we drummed them long ago', and this the English did at the Armada, where victory was won by superior seamanship and strategy, using wind, narrow waters, dangerous banks and coastline. As the Spaniards fled northwards from Calais Roads few shots were fired, the English were short of ammunition – but with sails and rigging cut the ships became the victims of the elements. During the American War of Independence, a later attempted invasion by combined French and Spanish forces was met by similar strategy. 'I shall do my utmost', wrote Sir Charles Hardy, 'to drive them up the Channel, forcing the covering fleet and transports together into the narrow waters'. In this instance also the elements again intervened and the French, delayed in sailing, arrived to be swept out of the Channel by a rising gale, so that, despite outnumbering the British by almost 2 to 1, they subsequently avoided battle and cancelled the invasion. The Channel moat has stood Britain and the cause of freedom in good stead for nearly a thousand years. 'Let us be master of the Straits for six hours', said Napoleon, 'and we shall be masters of the world'.

Second, the Navy has closely watched the embarkation ports by means of blockade, forcing the enemy to detach increasing strength from his fleet to match that of the watching flotillas. During the French Revolutionary Wars in the last decade of the eighteenth century, Napoleon's attempted invasion of Britain failed for these reasons. The Royal Navy stuck to its watching brief and Napoleon was forced to bring his battlefleet up to defend his transports, thus rendering the whole armada too cumbersome to manoeuvre across the Channel. Third, the RN battlefleet has never allowed itself to be enticed away from this watching brief in order to fight the enemy in other spheres of operation. The enemy may attempt various ruses to divide and disperse the Navy, but, provided its aim remains constant, he will ultimately be faced with three choices. He can either force his transports through, closely protected by his fleet in an unwieldy mass, or first defeat the British battlefleet before his transports sail, or divide his fleet into two, one part in close escort, another to cover the opposing fleet, so that both units are then too weak to withstand attack. Poised again to invade before Trafalgar, Napoleon thought Villeneuve had successfully enticed Nelson away from British shores in a ruse, but the speed of Nelson's dash across the Atlantic and back foiled his plan, as did the strength of British forces left in the mouth of the Channel. Seeking to disperse the Royal Navy, Napoleon succeeded only in consolidating it.

Although England has suffered no invasions for a thousand years some have arrived on the shores of Ireland. In the reign of Louis XIV the French landed 5,000 men to restore the Roman Catholic branch of the Stuart dynasty to the throne of Britain. Their military failure meant that the subsequent landings of the two Stuart Pretenders in Scotland were almost solo affairs. During the Irish campaign, which opened with James II marching north to besiege Derry and Enniskillen and terminated with the relief of Derry from the sea and victory on the Boyne, Britain's peril was compounded by the Queen's insistence that her outnumbered Navy give battle. The French, however, being over-committed on the continent, made little of their victory and command of the sea passed again at the naval Battle of Barfleur, after which French supply lines were cut. In the next century, with the Protestant succession seemingly secure, British sea power was established in the Mediterranean, and Admiral Rooke's capture of Gibraltar with 2000 marines, ratified by the Treaty of Utrecht, safeguarded Britain's supply route to the Levant and South Atlantic. Nevertheless, in 1715 and 1745 the risings and landings of the Old and Young Stuart Pretenders were serious incursions and the latter, reaching Derby, rocked the British throne. When during the Seven Years War, little more than a decade later further invasion forces were drawn up in Channel ports, the Elder Pitt diverted the first by diplomacy and deterred the second with, 'Preparations as have never been made since the Armada'. He stationed regular soldiers in the Isle of Wight, off which the Armada had first arrived, called out the militia and added 37 ships to the Royal Navy to guard the Channel and blockade the French coast, keeping his nerve to such an extent that he sent forces to the help of Britain's ally Frederick of Prussia. 'Of all the public services', said Edmund Burke five years later, 'that of the Navy is the one which tampering with may be of the greatest danger, which can worst be supplied in an emergency and of which

any failure draws after it the largest and heaviest train of consequences'.*
When the Younger Pitt inherited his father's mantle he never saved money on
the Navy and, during the invasion scare in the Revolutionary War, he raised
the Sea Fencibles, forerunners of the RNVR, so that, once the dangers of Napoleon's attempted invasion had passed and victory had been won at Trafalgar,
British sea power was sufficiently strengthened for the dangers of invasion to
recede until 1940. Although in the First World War the German Navy on a
number of occasions bombarded British ports and coastal towns this was more
by way of a ruse to lay minefields than as a prelude to an attempted invasion.
Thus, although 70,000 troops were ear-marked for an assault on Britain –
increasing temporarily to 130,000 – and a number of barges were assembled
across the Channel, numbers were soon reduced back to 70,000 and finally the
idea was abandoned. Despite crippling casualties, the Allied lines were holding in France and Germany did not have command of the sea.

In 1940, however, the peril was real and the British people thanked
Providence for their moat. They had seen Poland, Denmark, Norway, Holland,
Belgium and France collapse within days or weeks under the scourge of the
blitzkrieg – swift mobile armoured forces, inflicting heavy casualties and
suffering few. They had seen the Polish Air Force, approximately the same
size as that of the French, being overwhelmed almost in hours. They had
watched with growing anxiety as General Alan Brooke, with a quarter of a
million men of the BEF, fought back towards Dunkirk, extricating them with
'Great dexterity from the closing defile of its enemies'. They had faced
France's imminent surrender, and the hopelessness of Brooke's second
mission to France with a fresh division to bolster her resistance and try and
snatch some territory from the jaws of the conqueror. Returning home, this
time from Brittany with 140,000 men, Brooke was put in command of Home
Forces to meet Hitler's impending Operation Sea Lion, which had to sail
before the September equinox gales. The soldiers under his command
consisted either of the exhausted troops who had returned from Dunkirk and
whom the British public had seen grey faced, dead asleep on railway plat-
forms, or fresh, untrained and under-equipped divisions. All were desperately
short of equipment and ammunition, for left on the continent were 2,500 field,
anti-aircraft and anti-tank guns, 6,400 anti-tank rifles, 11,000 machine guns,
675 tanks, 75,000 motor vehicles and supplies of ammunition. But the
Germans also needed time to reorganise and re-equip, Hitler had not got
command of the sea, nor of the air and soon supplies were beginning to arrive
from the USA under Lease Lend. Hitler intended landing 40 divisions, realising that, as his near failure in Crete was later to prove, reinforcing and supplying them without command of the sea would be the most difficult part of the
operation. He knew that the Home Fleet was watching his preparations from its
northern base at Scapa Flow. Although after the evacuation from Norway and
Dunkirk, British destroyer strength had been cut by half, a destroyer screen in
the Channel was formed at the sacrifice of vital escort duty in the Atlantic,

* P98 The works of Edmund Burke [Vol. II] Rivington & Hatchard. London 1801

while smaller craft, aided by fleets of fishing vessels, kept watch over the East Anglia coast.

Without command of the sea Hitler and Admiral Raeder knew that the Germans must first master the air. In June German fighters outnumbered the RAF by 3 to 1, but, with 500 aircraft emerging from British factories in July overtaking German production, it was estimated that by August the gap would close to 2 to 1. Hitler planned to mine a corridor across the Dover Straits to deter the British fleet, down which would pass his barges, escorted by pocket battleships and other warships, which in turn would be protected by the Luftwaffe. When the Royal Navy intervened it would be destroyed from the air and by his long range super guns stationed in France. Able to launch his invasion fleet anywhere from Norway to the Spanish border, he had the advantage of surprise, but soon the intended target narrowed to the area between Dover and Worthing. To oppose any forces able to land, Brooke's strategy was one of swift mobile strikes by reorganised defence forces operating within a coastal defence system of concrete pill boxes, tank obstructions and barbed wire – relying on the RAF to bomb the beachheads and on the RN to prevent the landing of reinforcements and supplies. 'What is our aim?' asked Churchill, 'It is victory at all costs' and to remind the nation of this he mobilised – as Pitt had done 200 years earlier – a militia or Home Guard, armed with shot guns and pikes, inventing a slogan which rang in the nation's ears, 'Take one with you'. The message was clear – 'With a thrill', says Arthur Bryant, 'the world realised that Britain was going to fight'. Again, like Pitt had done before him, Churchill kept his nerve to such an extent that he sent out of the country 3 armoured regiments to the Nile Valley, where the British Army was hopelessly outnumbered by the Italians. The main air battle began on August 8th with the bombing of ports, coastal towns and incoming convoys. Then it was the turn of the radar stations, airfields and aircraft factories. On August 15th 1,800 aircraft – 500 bombers protected by 1,300 fighters – crossed the Channel to attack in waves. They were met by the valiant hearts of the young fighter pilots in their Spitfires and Hurricanes, whose gallantry was only matched by their mastery of their machines and gunnery. In every attack Hitler lost more than twice the number of aircraft lost by the RAF.

By September 1st slow silent columns of barges were reported by RAF reconnaissance planes to be moving down the Scheldt towards the sea. The invasion was expected imminently. At Ostend alone 18 barges on the 18th of August had increased by September 6th to 205. While the RAF bombed the assembling barges and fought off German attacks from the air over the Home Counties, destroyers and smaller craft cruised incessantly on watch in the Channel and North Sea and the Home Fleet maintained its watching brief. The world held its breath, while daily dog fights took their toll of men and machines. Then Churchill, in retaliation for the bombing of London on August 24th, sent bombers to Berlin and Hitler, enraged by their effrontery, diverted his attacks from strategic targets to the capital, saying on September 4th that he would, 'Wipe out London'. Day and night the raids continued and with the main anti-aircraft defences guarding the strategic sites, damage was extensive,

with 60 bombs dropped in one hour. On September 6th, by which time shipping was concentrated along the French and Flemish coast, a preliminary
Invasion Alert was issued. But the conditions insisted upon by Hitler and
Admiral Raeder had not been fulfilled – command of the air had not been
established and the armada did not sail. On September 11th, with the invasion
still impending, Churchill broadcast to the nation, saying it might be launched
at any minute, at any place or in a number of places. The days, he said ranked
in importance with those of the Armada, 'Or when Nelson stood between us
and Napoleon's Grand Army at Boulogne'. But the invasion did not come.
Instead it was again postponed and still Admiral Raeder insisted the conditions
for the attempt were not fulfilled – air superiority had not been established and
without it Britain had command of the sea. With US help after Lease Lend
Britain's destroyer screen was daily becoming stronger and there were more
frigates and small craft in the Channel and North Sea. On the night of
September 13th, while the Home Fleet moved from Scapa Flow to the Firth of
Forth, the RAF sank 80 barges But losses in the air were mounting on both
sides. In ten days 367 German aircraft had been shot down to the RAF's 213
but by September 3rd British fighter pilot strength had fallen from 1,438 to
840. On September 15th the date of the start of the equinox gales, the most
concentrated attack of all was launched on London and the last RAF reserves
were thrown into the battle. On that day Hitler, watching his losses in the air
mounting to unsustainable levels, called off the invasion for the moment and
announced he would continue with his nightly raids on London, which Britain
was ill-equipped to meet. 'Having', in Arthur Bryant's words, 'failed to
capture Britain's army in France, to penetrate her Navy's guard and to destroy
her Air Force, the only way to end the war seemed to be to break the spirit of
her people'. In the south of England, with the Home Fleet out of sight in Scapa
Flow, and daily dog fights going on in the air space above, people understood
the meaning of air power and their debt to the fighter pilots who maintained it.
In Scotland, although they followed with equal anxiety and admiration the
exploits of Fighter Command, naval presence was closer and more obvious.
Thus it was that Colonel Toogood, RE Senior Staff Officer, Scottish
Command, afterwards wrote these words, 'By early October we in the army
breathed again for by that time we had the ammunition and equipment to
defeat any invasion. Defeat was only then possible in the long term if we lost
command of the sea, not forgetting air power in this context'. Hitler also knew
that the moment his barges sailed the Royal Navy would have descended upon
them and upon the beachheads from their eagle's nest in the North Sea with all
the ferocity for which Drake and Nelson were erstwhile famous. On October
13th Operation Sea Lion was officially postponed until 1941.

When 1941 came, however, it brought a different invasion and one in which
Allied Naval Forces were inadequate and outnumbered. It was, of course, the
invasion by the Japanese of the Philippines, Hong Kong, Singapore, Burma,
the Dutch East Indies and islands in the Pacific. On December 8th, the day
after the Japanese attack on Pearl Harbor – where, like the German invasions
of neutral European states, the declaration of war was announced after the fait

accompli – Japanese amphibious landings were made on the Malay peninsula, at Singora in Thailand, whose neutrality the British refused to break, and at Kota Bharu in Malaya – the target being Singapore. The signs of Japanese hostile intent had been noted by the British in 1940, when the Japanese stationed troops and took over airfields in French Indo China, and in July 1941 Japan forced the Vichy French to declare a Mutual Defence Zone over the area, from which she now controlled the China Sea with ships and aircraft. Watching this build up with alarm the British government in October 1941 sent out as a deterrent the battleship Prince of Wales, the battlecruiser Repulse and four destroyers to join the China squadron, which, because of the demand for ships in the Atlantic and Mediterranean, consisted of only three veteran light cruisers and some First World War destroyers. It was intended also to send the carrier Indomitable, but she was damaged running aground in Jamaica. Britain knew that, without the French fleet, she was dependent on the strength of the US Pacific fleet with its 3 aircraft carriers based at Pearl Harbor in Hawaii and on the small Dutch presence in the Dutch East Indies. 'The Japanese', wrote Churchill in November, 'would never attempt a siege of Singapore with a hostile superior American fleet in the Pacific'. The loss of this US fleet, excluding the carriers (and the new capital ships which had not yet left the slips), but including 4 battleships sunk, one beached and 3 severely damaged, as well as 3 cruisers and 3 destroyers badly damaged and 183 aeroplanes lost and 31 damaged, cut the defending string of sea power and allowed the Japanese to rampage unchecked over the Far East, throwing into the melting pot the future of the Free World.

Why had the military effectiveness and political intentions of the Japanese been so undervalued? They had established themselves as a modern naval power in 1904 and shown considerable political dexterity over the controversial Western inspired loan to China in 1911. They had kept open the China Sea for the Allies during the 1914-18 War, but in 1915 they had forced upon the Chinese – weakened by internal strife – the nefarious 21 Demands, which Britain was able to curtail but failed to prevent. After the War the Americans feared Japanese expansionism both in the Pacific and on the Chinese mainland and in the 1920's Foreign Office reports, warning that Japan's consequent feelings of isolation, if unchecked, would turn to something more sinister, were ignored. Industrialising at speed, Japan was weaving plots within Manchuria, which she saw as the answer to Western emigration curbs and her need for increased agriculture to feed her growing population. In 1931, taking advantage of China's civil war, she entered South Manchuria, resigning from and treating with contempt protests by the League of Nations. Two years later her troops entered North China and set up a puppet regime. Then, with the Kuomintang and Chinese Communists uniting against her she launched undeclared war and entered Nanking in South China, carrying out appalling atrocities and setting up a puppet government. Accelerating her naval programme and developing her maritime aircraft she announced her intention to create a new order in the Far East, called the East Asia Company Prosperity Sphere, and, when in 1939 she occupied the island of Hainan dominating the Gulf of

Tonkin and French Indo China, the USA became alarmed and gave 6 months notice of her intention to discontinue the sale to her of petrol, iron ore and scrap. The Japanese answer was one of defiance, seeking alternative supplies of oil, rubber and tin in the Dutch East Indies and British and French Empires, and putting pressure on the USA, Britain and France to try and force them to discontinue their Open Door policy of trade with China and accept the status quo of her occupation. When on July 25th the USA finally stopped the export of these key materials the Japanese moved troops and aircraft into French Indo China, signed the Tripartite Pact with Germany and Italy and turned Thailand into a satellite. Then, with the USA continuing to insist that she disgorge her ill gotten gains in China and South East Asia, the Japanese extended their empire by forming a Defence Zone in French Indo China. In October, the month the RN warships left for the Far East, the militarists took over in Japan, so that war was now only a bamboo curtain away. The two Western bases in the Far East, Singapore and Pearl Harbor were in mortal danger.

Discounting the reinforcements of Singapore, which continued almost up until surrender, the balance of personnel was 19,000 British troops, 12,000 Chinese and Malay, 15,000 Australians and 37,000 Indian. Why was the base not tenable and why was it not evacuated before surrender? According to Professor Morison, the US Official Naval Historian, at the Washington Conference in 1921, when the USA, British, French and Japanese interests in the area were mutually agreed and a collective guarantee was given of Chinese independence, Japanese co-operation had been secured by Britain and the USA agreeing not to defend bases east of Singapore or west of Pearl Harbor. This resulted in the Australians seeing Singapore as the last Commonwealth bastion before Australia, which had to be held at all costs, and in the USA having to defend the area from a base tens of thousands of miles away in Hawaii. Instead of building up a modern Eastern Fleet with adequate airborne strength, Britain between the wars had spent the money available in modernising and strengthening the sea defences of Singapore, where 335 first line aircraft and over 80,000 troops were expected to defend the fortress. Whereas it was known that Hong Kong was untenable in the face of attack it was thought Singapore was impregnable and this belief produced a false sense of security. In the event Hong Kong – owing to the outstanding courage of both the professional army and the volunteers – surrendered after 17 days, Singapore after 69. In judging the situation with hindsight it must be remembered that there never was an intention to hold Singapore without sea power. There was no reason why the British should not have believed in the strength of their Allies and in their naval presence. They could no more have envisaged that the French would make a separate peace, which removed their large Navy from Allied control, than they could that the USA would lose much of their Pacific fleet at Pearl Harbor. Yet both these events occurred. Faced with a Japanese attack, the British were now left reliant on their own inadequate naval forces to defend the base and they knew as well as any critic today that a naval base without an effective fleet is as valueless as an effective fleet without a secure base. All that posterity can do in these matters is to grasp at the loose ends of a tangled skein and try to unravel them as comprehensively as the complexity of events permit.

Now, in order to reach vital war supplies of oil, rubber and tin the Japanese drove south, east and west towards islands and peninsulas with the required mineral wealth – ever onwards towards India, Australia and Hawaii. Also on December 8th they attacked Hong Kong, various other Pacific Islands and the Philippines, where, flying further than judged possible, they surprised General MacArthur, destroying the naval base and 100 aeroplanes on the ground. The Japanese came down in a four pronged assault. If they met stiff resistance, as from the US Marines in Corregidor, where General MacArthur had 125,000 men, they simply neutralised it by circumventing the area and accepting surrender five months later. On February 15th, after advancing down both sides of the peninsula, fighting through jungle hitherto deemed impenetrable – using bicycles and circumventing the densest parts by amphibious landings and seaborne transport of tanks and armour – they entered Singapore, where the 130,000 reinforced defenders, driven back from every natural defence line and in the final stages deprived of water supplies, laid down their arms. In the same month the Japanese made landings in Sumatra, Java and Timor, only 300 miles from Port Darwin, which was heavily bombed. By the end of January they had captured Borneo, Celebes and Amboina, moving relentlessly on towards Australia. In March further landings were made on New Guinea and Java surrendered. The Japanese now controlled most of the straits leading to India and Australia. There seemed nothing between them and the conquest of half the globe. That was what undisputed sea and air power had accomplished in weeks.

What action did the Royal Navy take to prevent these disasters? When word was received in Singapore of landings in Malaya, Admiral Phillips, who succeeded Admiral Layton as C-in-C Eastern Fleet, sailed north with the Prince of Wales, the Repulse and a destroyer escort. He thought that, given fighter support and surprise, he could successfully oppose the landings and although he received a signal warning of hostile bombers in Indo China and saying that, with local airfields already captured by the Japanese, he could not have fighter protection, he pressed on until he was sighted by enemy aircraft, when he reversed course. Receiving a further signal warning of unconfirmed reported landings at Kuantan he decided to go there, mistakenly thinking he was by now out of range of Japanese aeroplanes. The first report received by the RAF was from the Repulse – that both ships were being attacked. Fighters were sent who witnessed rescue operations, 'I have seen many men', wrote a young airman, flying over the scene,' in dire danger, waving, cheering and joking as if they were holiday makers at Brighton. It shook me, for here was something above human nature. I take my hat off to them for in them I saw the spirit which wins wars'. It was the same sang froid described in the early days of soldiers retreating from Le Cateau in World War I, 'More like men returning from a cricket match, chatting and smoking pipes'. But the loss of these two capital ships, played its part in the decline of morale in Singapore and the vulnerability of the whole area.

It seemed that nothing could stem the tide of the Japanese advance. The Allies had immediately set up twc commands: ANZAC, a sea command only, covering the area to the north-east and east of Australia and ABDA (American, British, Dutch, Australian) covering the island barrier stretching for thousands of miles to the north and north west of Australia and for a short time part of Western Australia also, under the overall authority of General Wavell in Java. Both naval commands were under US Admirals, ANZAC consisting of 6 Australian, New Zealand and US cruisers with destroyer support; ABDA of nine Dutch, British and US cruisers, 25 British and Dutch destroyers and 32 Dutch and US submarines – the British submarines remaining independent. This ABDA force, under the flag command of a Dutch Admiral Doorman, was stronger on paper than in reality. The ships were old, there had been no combined training, and each country wanted to fulfil its own commitments. In Malaya, as the Commonwealth Army fell back, abandoning each natural line of defence, reinforcements were repeatedly requested and the forces of ABDA were called upon to transport them. Between January 1st and February 8th ABDA conveyed 45,000 men of all services to Singapore, while 150 Hurricanes were crated or flown from carriers in the Indian Ocean. Then, as the Japanese moved southwards to Sumatra and Java, cutting off retreat at the coast, Admiral Doorman's force made three unsuccessful attempts to prevent the invasion of these islands at none of which was any damage inflicted on the enemy. At the last – the Battle of the Java Sea – almost every Allied ship was sunk, except for the damaged cruiser Exeter and destroyer Encounter (both of which were sunk two days later), 4 US destroyers, which had broken off to refuel, and the Perth and Houston, whose last courageous exploits were recounted in the previous chapter. The reason for this disastrous defeat was not hard to find – the ships had no air cover, they were subjected to attack by deadly superior Japanese torpedoes, and their poor ship communication and consequent uncertainty of command led to loss of fighting formation. Faced with the decision as to whether to withdraw their ships or leave them to fight it out against hopeless odds, the Allied governments had come to the conclusion that there was no alternative but to leave them to their fate. Tribute was paid to the courage of their captains and crews, for their stories read more like inevitable Greek tragedy than the naval battles of recent times.

Meanwhile the cruiser Durban and two destroyers had been recalled from ABDA to transport key personnel from Singapore to Colombo, where Admiral Layton had temporarily re-assumed command of the Eastern Fleet. These warships left, escorting two liners with civilians on board and followed by smaller ships, just before the Straits were closed by Japanese warships. Of the gunboats, MTBs and other small craft that followed between then and Black Friday, February 13th, two days before Singapore fell, less than a handful got through, only one person in four surviving. Their stories rank among those too terrible to tell. Civilians – men, women and children – were machine gunned and bombed from the air as they swam from wrecked and burning boats and the descriptions of the wounds and suffering endured in the sea and on the myriad of islands, where some gained temporary refuge, numb the mind with horror, except for the shining examples of selfless courage which are also recounted. It was the same ruthless sadism seen in the German invasions in Europe, directed towards the breaking of resistance and the human spirit, with a further lurch into the worst atrocities of the Middle Ages.

Undoubtedly to use the word ineptitude to describe the leadership in Singapore is a gross under-statement. There were difficulties with morale among some units, faced for the first time by Japanese jungle warfare. But never before in history had a British army fought back towards the sea with no naval defence of its flanks, no naval gunnery bombardments and prevention of amphibious landings and no means of escape, into the arms of a civilian population of all colours and creeds, unnerved by the knowledge of Japanese atrocities in Nanjing and Hong Kong and fearful of the fate that awaited them on surrender. Here, as never before, there was virtually no Navy, no support from the sea, no ships to take them off. In the evacuation from Crete 18,000 troops were taken off from the 32,000 originally landed, but just prior to the decision to evacuate Crete Admiral Cunningham twice countermanded government orders that more men be landed, and twice returned one shipload to Alexandria. It was fortunately what Admiral Layton was to do with the last too-late consignment of Hurricanes from Ceylon. At Singapore, there being no further secure base upon which to fall back for the defence of Australia, no thought was given to the possibility of defeat or evacuation and no one on the spot countermanded the orders for reinforcement. The Australian Prime Minister was adamant that Singapore must be held and this was the decision that had been taken at the Washington Conference in January 1942 by the two leaders and by the newly formed Combined Chiefs of Staff. Since then myths have been woven round the story to hide the hurt, such as that the guns only pointed towards the sea. Certainly the shells were armour piercing and would only explode upon heavy impact, rendering them useless against the advancing Japanese, but the only thing that pointed towards the sea was Nelson's legendary telescope, searching the horizon for Allied vessels that were not anywhere to be seen.

In the face of such a rout, with the Japanese careering across one third of the globe, people ask why did they not continue with their successful invasions west and south and east. It seemed to Churchill that the Japanese were sailing to India with that in mind when, in the first week of April, they rounded Sumatra with 5 fleet carriers, 4 fast battleships, 3 cruisers and 8 destroyers and, as always, a second force of one light carrier, 6 cruisers and 4 destroyers, heading across the Bay of Bengal to attack shipping on the east coast of India. Churchill described it as the most dangerous moment of the war. Opposing them was only a scraped together Eastern Fleet, comprising 5 veteran battleships from World War I, only one of which had been modernised, 2 carriers, one small light carrier, 7 cruisers, (later joined by 8 veterans), 16 destroyers, mostly old and in urgent need of repair and 7 submarines now under the command of Admiral Sir James Somerville, C-in-C, Eastern Fleet, with Admiral Layton appointed C-in-C, Ceylon. The naval air element also was no match for the Japanese for, between them, Somerville's three carriers carried only a hundred strike aircraft and fighters. Nevertheless, in Ceylon were the three squadrons of Hurricanes, whicn had arrived there too late to be of use in Singapore. 'It seems amazing,' commented Somerville, 'but I suppose 'so very English you know' that we should have got ourselves into this dismal mess'. But his attitude was always pragmatic, 'Things are pretty sticky. But that's no reason to wring our hands. What we've got to do is to buckle to and see how to get out of this mess'. Churchill pleaded with Roosevelt, to 'Let us have some modern ships for the Indian Ocean', but Roosevelt, mindful of what lay ahead for the USA in the Pacific, could only lend one or two ships for the Home Fleet to free the same number of RN ships for the East, although by the end of 1943 the Saratoga operated from Trincomalee with the Royal Navy.

The air defences of Colombo were, however, stronger than the Japanese expected – 42 Hurricanes and 2 Fulmars met 130 dive bombers and fighters, Somerville's fleet was not there, the harbour had been cleared of ships and the port was not put out of action. At Trincomalee Japanese bombers were met by only 22 fighters and, although the harbour was cleared, more damage was done to installations. 17 Japanese aircraft were lost in both attacks. After the first air raid, 2 RN cruisers, one awaiting a refit, and after the second, 1 light carrier and 2 destroyers were found and sunk by the Japanese 24 hours after they had sailed. As darkness fell, Somerville, who had a reputation for never leaving 'his boys' in trouble returned to pick up survivors from the 2 cruisers with help from the USS Enterprise. Meanwhile the other Japanese surface naval force, aided by submarines, was sinking 28 merchant ships in the Indian Ocean. It was then that the Admiralty advised Somerville to draw back his slower ships to guard the East African coast and slower troop convoys and keep his few fast ships at sea to guard the convoys in the Indian Ocean and act as a 'fleet in being' – but at all costs to keep clear of Ceylon. Until a modern Eastern fleet could be built up all that stood between Ceylon and a Japanese invasion was, in the Prime Minister's words 'hope and faith'. 'It looks as if we might lose India', commented Somerville, 'just for the sake of a handful of aircraft and one or two decent ships'. He saw that if Ceylon was lost it would be extremely difficult, but not impossible, to maintain communications between the Middle and Far East, 'But if they get Ceylon and destroy the British Eastern Fleet then the situation will be desperate'. Unknown, however, to the British the Japanese planned to concentrate on the invasion of Australia, and to attempt both was beyond their stretched resources. The invasion of India from the sea was therefore not attempted and the only course now open to Somerville was to reduce pressure on the Pacific Fleet, which was guarding the islands north of Australia, by creating diversions in the Indian Ocean to attract Japanese attention – the traditional function of a 'fleet in being' – and to endeavour by all means available to keep open the trade route across the Indian Ocean. The problem was that the British were fighting a five ocean war with a two ocean navy.

No hindsight judgement can recreate the atmosphere of anxiety and tension at the news of further disasters and the swift decisions that had to be made, choosing the least dangerous course between a very limited number of options.

With so many soldiers captured in Singapore and so many ships and aeroplanes lost or damaged and sailors and airmen killed, captured or wounded, three things only now stood between the Japanese and Australia: first, the sea and air power of the USA, aided by a very small Australian contingent, the latter under the command of two successive RN Admirals; second, the stout Australian resistance, which met the Japanese advancing overland towards Port Moresby in New Guinea; third the swift transport by large British liners, which brought Australian troops back from Colombo and thousands of US troops from America to Australia. Later the courage of the US Marines allowed the Allies to break out of the Japanese defensive ring and to start pushing them back towards their own borders.

In May the Japanese launched an invasion fleet to Port Moresby, an excellent jumping off point for Australia. In true Japanese style they divided their fleet into three parts: an eastern force to establish a seaplane base in the Lower Solomons from whence they would come down to New Caledonia, to the east of Australia; a second force of 1 light carrier, the Shoho, heavy cruisers and destroyer escorts to cover the Port Moresby transports and a main fleet of 2 carriers, 2 heavy cruisers and 6 destroyers, which would enter the Coral Sea from the east passing the Louisades. The Americans had a weaker fleet, but the gifts of judgement, courage and good fortune, combined with first class intelligence, were bestowed on them that day. The 2 US carriers with escorts duly met and were joined by the combined US and Australian squadron of three cruisers, under the command of British Admiral J.G. Crace, (an Australian by birth who was later Admiral Superintendent, Chatham, during the Normandy landings). The US Admiral was not diverted by the Japanese expedition to the Lower Solomons and his aeroplanes sank the light carrier, the Shoho – claimed as mistaken identity for a fleet carrier. Although apparently an error it was according to the classic British tradition for repelling invasion – namely to concentrate always on the invasion fleet itself. Admiral Fletcher then gallantly sacrificed three screening destroyers to accompany Admiral Crace's squadron on its surface bombardment of the Japanese transports – an action known as Crace's Chase. These ships, although attacked by Japanese dive bombers, fought off their attackers without receiving a scratch. With his light carrier sunk and under threat from surface ships, the Japanese Admiral then called off his transports, ordering them to 'steam around' in the direction of the Louisades, from which the main Japanese fleet was expected to arrive. Meanwhile the two carrier fleets were reconnoitring each other's position and the action that followed was the first naval engagement fought only by seaborne aircraft, in which neither fleet was in sight of the other. The number of ships in both fleets was evenly balanced, but the Japanese had the advantage of mist, the US the disadvantage of sunshine. Although the US lost more ships – with one fleet carrier sunk and another, the Yorktown damaged – to only one Japanese light carrier sunk and another two damaged, nevertheless it was a great US victory. The invasion was called off, the Japanese lost 40 aircraft, (US 33) to add to the 540 already lost operationally, and the Japanese fleet carriers were too badly damaged and deprived of air strength to take part in the

Battle of Midway less than a month later, a battle which stemmed their advance eastwards towards the USA, as the Battle of the Coral Sea prevented their thrust to the south.

The Battle of Midway, fought to defend from invasion this easternmost island of the Hawaii chain, half way between Japan and the USA, belongs to that grey area between an offensive and defensive action, for the USA had broken the Japanese code, had precise knowledge of their plans and was able, therefore, to turn the tables upon the aggressors. How crucial was the decision, is, however, reflected in the orders to Admiral Fletcher – 'Avoid exposure of your force without good prospects of inflicting greater damage upon the enemy' – in other words, 'Sink the enemy, but don't on any account let him sink you'. No Admiral ever received more daunting orders or achieved a more overwhelming victory over an enemy whose combined fleet numbered twice his own. The Japanese, who had already captured the tiny island of Wake, half way between Japan and Hawaii, again divided their fleet and employed complicated tactics. With a two pronged northern force acting as decoy they bombed the Eastern Aleutians, while occupying islands in the Western, a diversion within a diversion, which, although deceiving the US Admiral in the North Pacific Force, failed to lure the Pacific Fleet away from the main battle area. Meanwhile, the Japanese Midway force was divided into three, its submarines acting separately. There was a transport unit, escorted by destroyers with battleships and cruisers in support; a strike force to neutralise Midway from the air, composed of 4 carriers, 2 battleships, 3 cruisers and destroyers and lastly the main body of their fleet composed of 7 battleships, 3 cruisers, a light carrier and destroyers to bombard Midway from the sea. Japanese tactics had changed since the Coral Sea, for their transports did not have their own air support and the fleet carriers were separated from the main fleet. In these new arrangements, 'They abandoned two important principles, maintenance of objective and concentration of force'. They were soon to pay the price.

Dockyard workers at Pearl Harbor had, meanwhile, been working round the clock to repair the Yorktown, so that the opposing carrier fleets were more evenly matched – the Japanese had four carriers, the US three, to which must be added the tiny island of Midway itself, which, like Malta, was an unsinkable aircraft carrier. The two carrier fleets were soon approaching one another, with the task of finding the Japanese carriers undertaken by Midway reconnaissance planes. The first air attack on the island cost the Japanese one third of their aircraft and, while survivors were still returning, the Midway planes came in to attack. The Japanese Admiral was thrown into indecision as to whether to order an assault on Midway with bombs or a search, find and attack mission against the US carriers with torpedoes. At that very moment the torpedo planes from the US carriers arrived, but, without fighter support (the latter having lost their way), they sustained huge losses. No sooner was their attack called off than the US carrier-borne dive bombers swooped out of the sky and sank three of the Japanese carriers in six minutes and all their surviving aircraft. The Japanese Admiral did not, however, give up and planes from his surviving carrier found and caused such damage to the Yorktown that the order was given to abandon ship.* Dive bombers from the Enterprise then avenged her, so that all four Japanese fleet carriers were lost. The Japanese bombardment of Midway by the surface fleet was cancelled but not before two heavy cruisers were damaged by air attack as they retired. Because the US had broken the Japanese code and knew their plans it is not right to judge the strategy of the battle and apply it to other circumstances, as the later Battle of Leyte showed, but what can never be in doubt is that the Battle of Midway forced the Japanese back on the defensive with over-extended lines of communication and insufficient merchant ships to form proper lines of supply. A few US Navy pilots altered the course of history and the Pacific War, their courage, daring and precision straight out of the US Navy Handbook and in the tradition of its privateer founder John Paul Jones, who, when asked to surrender his damaged ship, replied, 'Surrender! I have only just begun to fight!'.

Describing these battles, Captain Roskill in THE WAR AT SEA asks how his readers would feel if one of these islands had been – as at the Armada – the Isle of Wight, and the battles had been raging round Sandwich and Ryde instead of thousands of miles away in a southern sea. Because the US Navy was fighting many miles from home they had to depend on carriers as well as on shore-based aircraft, operating from Midway. Although in the summer of 1940 the Royal Navy had command of the sea and the RAF were operating from a home base, nevertheless they had only just sufficient fighters to prevent Germany winning command of the air. No one who did not have the privilege of living through that extraordinary summer of 1940, when the beauty of its sunny days shone in sharp contrast to the dangers, of which the hastily contrived defences were a constant reminder, should ever under-estimate the steady courage or deep underlying anxiety of the nation or the reality of their peril. Although in this century the apparatus of defence has been strengthened by concrete ramparts, booms, mines and nets, and invasion forces can now be watched with flotillas of light ships armed with deadly weapons and aided by satellite, radar, aeroplanes and submarines, nevertheless, the key to deterrence remains mastery of sea and air. As at Dunkirk the British saw their escape as a miracle, knowing that, in Churchill's words, 'The odds were great, our margin small, the stakes infinite'. Yet Britain had command of the sea in 1940, a fact now too often forgotten and owed her escape to that as well as to the battle in the air. The disturbing current position is that the Royal Navy has been so reduced in strength that in war it could not function without help from its Allies even for defence of its homeland, an unsustainable predicament and one which the British people allow to continue at their peril. They should be mindful of Captain Donald Macintyre's warning, 'We are maintaining a fleet which is too weak to fulfil its functions in an orthodox war'.

* The Yorktown was sunk 3 days later by a submarine

CHAPTER XI

SO GREAT A DELIVERANCE
THE WORK OF THE CONVOY ESCORTS

The last chapter highlighted the number of ships and aircraft required to defend an island's shores, this chapter demonstrates the extensive maritime forces needed to defend its merchant shipping. 'We must regard the Battle of the Atlantic as one of the most momentous ever fought in all the annals of war', said Churchill in March 1941. Because only half of one per cent of the volume of Britain's trade goes by air no blockade of the vast resources of the continent can compare in severity with a blockade of the island of Britain, dependent as she is on the import of raw materials, food, steel and military supplies. With predators drawn to convoys like birds of prey to their victims, modern underwater methods of destruction have given the side with the weaker surface fleet an advantage. Even in earlier centuries it took larger forces to protect sea communications than to attack them, but now a ruthless enemy, intent upon starving Britain out, can sink 'soft' targets without warning along her lines of communication with an ease of attack out of all proportion to the difficulties of defence. Surface raiders, submarines and aeroplanes can be moved to places where defence is weakest and the enemy can sink shipping out in the depths of the ocean or at focal points, where trade routes converge, or where they come within range of his airfields or enter their own home waters or overseas ports.This range of opportunities places an island people in peril and without preparation demands defence out of proportion to the national purse.

Convoy protection in war goes back to medieval days. Merchant ships sailed in convoy in Tudor times and a number of Convoy Acts were passed in the seventeenth, eighteenth and nineteenth centuries, imposing upon a master the requirement to sail in convoy. The reader will remember that in early history there was little difference in design between merchant ships and men of war. In the sixteenth century merchant ships were armed and in the reign of Charles II they were still expected to defend themselves. In 1707, however, a Convoy Act delegated 43 'cruisers' to special convoy protection, with ships of the line to be added as required. The strategy of the Royal Navy was to hold the terminals and their surrounding water in strength and to escort merchant convoys across the sea lanes of the world with smaller naval ships. Many thousands of British merchant ships were engaged in carrying supplies during the eighteenth century French wars and fleet battles were fought to protect convoys which often comprised hundreds of vessels. In those days the aim of the enemy was seizure and large numbers of British merchant vessels were captured in the American War of Independence, when convoys were smaller and escorts consequently weaker. In the Napoleonic Wars convoys of over 500 vessels sometimes sailed together and insurance premiums were fixed at half price for ships sailing in convoy. In Nelson's day cruisers and battle squadrons went out from defended ports in support of outgoing and incoming convoys, while sometimes focal trade points in mid ocean were also held in strength.

Britain's little ships on night patrol. Motor Gunboats at high speed returning to base at dawn. World War II

Convoy at sea between sunset and darkness, August 1941, seen from the AA platform of a corvette, Canadian steamer in the foreground

Malta Convoy under attack, September 1941. HMS Prince of Wales in the foreground

The Second Sea Lord presenting awards to Allied Naval Officers, World War II

Otherwise communication lines were not defended and frigates and smaller ships acted as escorts, strengthened if need be by battle squadrons. Terminals on the North Sea were defended by an Eastern Squadron, responsible also for blockading enemy ports to the north and east; while a Western Squadron, in the mouth of the Channel, defended home ports to the south and west and blockaded enemy ports in the Bay of Biscay. Another cruiser squadron based at Cork guarded the Western Approaches, and at the scattered ports in between smaller squadrons and flotillas protected coastal traffic and the herring fleet. (For centuries western bound ocean traders sheltered in Irish ports, but these rights were renounced to Eire in 1938 under treaty obligations, creating great dangers in 1940, and in World War II most convoys assembled on the Clyde and at Liverpool, with 'joiners' collecting off Northern Ireland, while many eastern bound gathered on the Tyne and at Methil in Fife.) In Nelson's time a similar system of defended bases operated overseas, where forces consisted of cruisers and smaller ships,strengthened by battleships if need arose. In the Mediterranean escort squadrons were stationed at four points, including Gibraltar, which covered the area inside and outside the Straits. Deployment after Trafalgar did not present the agonising decisions of 1939–1943, when shortages of ships meant that requirements could not be met, for in 1812 there were 837 ships of war in the Royal Navy, albeit a number of them small. Although by the end of World War II ships in the Royal Navy had nearly reached the 1812 figure, in 1939 the total number of ships stood at 367, made up of 12 battleships (and 5 building), 3 battle cruisers, 23 heavy cruisers (9 building), 29 light cruisers (10 building), 6 anti-aircraft cruisers, 6 aircraft carriers (6 building), 172 destroyers (28 building), 47 escort vessels (4 building), and 69 submarines. There were also 42 minesweepers, 2 monitors, 1 minelayer (4 building) and 19 Commonwealth cruisers, destroyers and sloops.

What was it that interrupted this successful strategy for protecting British trade? During the debate on the Repeal of the Navigation Laws it was hoped in sanguine faith that shipping would take on an, 'Increasingly neutral and international aspect'. Despite the proved ineffectiveness of the patrol system in defence of merchant shipping and of a submarine attack on a warship in the American Civil War, followed by the Austrian invention of the torpedo (which Britain herself developed and mounted first in torpedo boats), both of which increased the risk to surface ships, the last piece of legislation imposing convoys was contained in the 1864 Naval Prize Act. After that the invention of steam and the iron ship began to change attitudes and in 1903 the Royal Commission on the Supply of Food and Raw Materials in time of war stated that the possibility of varying trade routes afforded by steam and the constant and steady flow of ships crossing the oceans, 'Make the conditions of the chief trade routes an extremely favourable one for successful defence'. The Royal Navy thus changed its policy to keeping safe the sea lanes of the world by a system of patrol. The unhappy results of this change in naval policy prior to World War I has been already been recounted, as have the catastrophic losses suffered before it was reversed in 1917. Although convoys were introduced some days before war began in 1939, nevertheless trust in the efficacy of patrol and hunt,ng groups was not finally laid to rest until it had ended in almost total failure and accounted for many losses. In the early days of war the aircraft carrier Courageous was sunk pursuing this policy of 'search and destroy', and the Ark Royal nearly suffered a similar fate.

Why was it that in the inter-war period the British were again less concerned about underwater attack than about the dangers of surface raiders, which in the event sank only one twentieth of merchant shipping lost? First, it was hoped that the need to refuel would inhibit U-boat activity in mid ocean (in 1934 U-boats were short range). Second, it was forgotten that by 1918 many U-boats attacked by surfacing at night, nor was it fully realised that Dönitz was already advocating night attacks. Too much confidence was therefore placed in asdic, a transmitter receiver sending signals, which reflect back when striking underwater objects – the performance of which was reduced in rough weather. It was not until March 1941 that radar could spot a surfaced submarine. While new and improved versions of asdic had been fitted to warships since 1922, time was also spent fitting asdic into trawlers, drifters and yachts – used in World War I – but no match in mid ocean for modern submarines.Initially, owing to the shortage of escorts, these trawlers sailed at the front of convoys and later at the rear to rescue survivors, but they only sank 6 U-boats during the whole war. Third, there was less attention paid to the destruction of U-boats, once detected. Thus, improvements were not made in the patterns and range of depth charges, nor were new weapons developed until well on in the war. Fourth, the British again refused to believe that the Germans would once more violate the Rules of War at Sea and International Humanitarian Law laid down by the Hague Conventions and by the Treaties of Washington and London, the latter of which they signed and ratified in 1937. This was a crucial miscalulation, for – leaving aside the humanitarian aspects – searching for contraband, giving warnings to ships and arranging for the safety of crews put a top limit on the number of sinkings per day. With the exception of the sinking of the Athenia and other incidents, Germany held her hand until after the fall of Poland when Hitler realised that Britain and France intended to continue the war. On the 23rd of September he issued an edict saying that any ship using radio would be sunk immediately. On the 17th of October the German Navy was told it could sink British merchant ships without warning. In November 1939 the order was extended to liners and by August 1940 to neutral shipping as well.

In 1939 only a very few of the destroyers, escorts and sloops did not have asdic, but the corvettes laid down the previous April had not the speed of a surfaced U-boat and it was not until 1942 that the first River class frigates, specially designed as ocean escorts, put to sea. RN manpower was also insufficiently trained to counter the U-boat menace, and, although the RN had re-assumed responsibility for the small Fleet Air Arm in 1937, it consisted of only 232 first line aircraft (over half of which were Swordfish). Meanwhile Coastal Command had been told its primary role would be North Sea reconnaissance and trade protection in co-operation with the RN, but the RAF had no aircrews or aeroplanes specially trained and designed for anti-submarine work. Indeed for the first year of war Coastal Command was only supplied with inadequate anti-submarine bombs and no depth charges or searchlights with which to spot surfaced U-boats. The few available escorts took convoys out from Britain 150 to 200 miles into the Atlantic, where they met incoming convoys and left those outgoing either to sail together without escort or independently. Incoming convoys were escorted in mid Atlantic by one sloop or armed merchant cruiser and in these circumstances the only course if attacked was for the convoy to scatter, while the escort took on the enemy. As time went on these distances increased. The Royal Canadian Navy had its own corvettes built in Canada and provided trained crews who came out to escort convoys to Newfoundland and Nova Scotia – by 1942 they were almost taking an equal share – but in the first year of war the number of ships and men and the standard of Canadian equipment, training and asdic were not up to that of the Royal Navy, and Canada could only give generously within her limits.

How were the convoys formed and how did they sail? After moving out from home waters in long lines ships were drawn up in columns of five and four, the longer columns in the centre. In the early days of war convoys were mostly composed of 30 to 40 ships, covering a distance of approximately 5 square miles, but, when it was realised that losses were fewer in larger convoys with stronger escort protection, their size was increased to sometimes as many as 80 ships, the number of columns and the area covered increasing in proportion. The escort destroyers were, 'Flung in a ring round the convoy, sometimes as far as three to five miles outside it. Each had a patrol area and moved back and forth within it.' The outside ships were a number of miles apart, and even after radio telephone on short wave was fitted, it could be intercepted and required coding. Signals therefore were sent by flags, and coloured searchlights – or in the case of the commodore's orders by siren – until the fitting of very high frequency (VHF) short range transmission enabled commanders to communicate freely with one another. The escort commander was responsible for the convoys' defence; the commodore, often a retired admiral who flew his flag from the leading ship in the centre column, was responsible for passing on his orders and seeing they were carried out. The presence of these commodores, many past retiring age, was responsible for the excellent discipline of the convoys upon which their survival depended. The courses open to ships under attack required precision and seamanship. If torpedoes were sighted in time, vessels could repeatedly alter course (zig zag) to avoid them, but they had to take care to avoid collisions, particularly difficult if altering course for any reason at night. Secondly, the convoy could wheel and alter course to avoid a U-boat ambush or, in a sudden emergency, it could turn in a line of bearing at forty five degrees to the leading ship and proceed for a short time in echelon, but unless ships were able to turn back on course quickly their escorts were not well placed and had to alter station. Lastly, the convoy could make smoke to provide a covering screen. The need to maintain formation in the face of attack was important because, as more effective anti-aircraft guns were fitted, the mass effect of their fusillade acted as a deterrent to dive bombers, while loss of formation, caused by ships stopping to rescue survivors from sinking, exploding and burning ships, allowed U-boats more easily to penetrate the lines of the convoy. This problem was eased but never eradicated, first by using asdic-fitted trawlers as rescue ships, so that stricken ships did not take others out of convoy, and later by introducing specially fitted rescue ships with nets to clamber up and medical facilities.

Courtesy usually prevented arguments between escort commanders and commodores, but if problems arose the naval commander was senior, despite differences in rank. Each commodore had his own style of leadership. Admiral Sir Charles Ramsey, nicknamed the Ocean Swell and previously C-in-C, Rosyth, was Commodore of HX231, which came across the Atlantic in March/April 1943 with British, American, Norwegian, Dutch, Swedish and Panamanian ships, under the expert escort of Commander Peter Gretton.* In spite of being attacked by 28 U-boats, it only lost 3 stragglers, whose fate was not known for several days. It was a dramatic turn of events and on the 7th of April there was a statement on this achievement by Admiral Sir Max Horton to the Cabinet Committee. A more gentle style of leadership was adopted by Rear Admiral C.G.Brodie, known to everyone as Brodles, who had been Captain-in-Charge, Rosyth Dockyard in the early days of war and was the twin brother of T.S., the submarine commander who first volunteered and navigated his submarine through the dangerous Straits which lead to the Sea of Marmara, being killed on that exploit. A few hours out from Alexandria with a Malta convoy, an extensive fire broke out on board and the Egyptian crew threatened to abandon ship if they did not return to Alexandria. While Brodie was persuading the Dutch captain to make one last effort to control the fire, the escort commander sent repeated signals, 'Air attack imminent. Make smoke! Make smoke!' Almost suffocating from the smoke from his own fire Brodie eventually signalled back, 'Would welcome air attack as a diversion', his wry humour not shared by the escort commander, a keen polo player without much time for wit.Mercifully the fire was put out and the convoy arrived safely in Malta.

The Battle of the Atlantic was a war of attrition, directed as much against the merchant seamen in whose hearts it was intended to strike terror, as against the ships in which they sailed. It began in earnest in the summer of 1940, by which time the Germans had corrected the fault in the detonators of their torpedo warheads, and with many Royal Navy destroyers sunk or damaged at the Norwegian and Dunkirk evacuations, British merchant ship losses doubled. All west European ports were now home to U-boats and the Focke Wulfs, converted from civil aircraft in double quick time, had a longer range than Coastal Command aeroplanes. The further UK escorts went out with the convoys into the Atlantic, the further the U-boats followed to strike when the convoy was either not protected, or sailing with only light escort. In an October Cape Breton convoy 20 merchant ships were sunk out of 34, and the government knew it must find more destroyers or lose the war. US destroyers, handed over to the British after the exchange of letters leading to Lend Lease, were

* Vice Admiral Sir Peter Gretton KCB, DSO**, DSC, OBE

delivered in batches to Halifax and manned by 'hostilities only' crews with a few regular service ratings. They were immediately put on convoy duty – 7 going to the Canadians – and other RN destroyers, previously held against invasion, were sent to the Atlantic. Sinkings decreased in January 1941 to the lowest number since May and Hitler turned for success to his surface raiders, which he ordered to hunt in pairs. The Scharnhorst and Gneisenau sank 20 merchantmen on their first voyage, but were then blockaded in and damaged by RAF bombs on return to Brest. The Bismarck, after a foray in company with the Prinz Eugen, was sunk by the Royal Navy after a touch-and-go chase, but the Admiral Hipper, sailing alone, returned safely to port with a score of 8 merchant ships. These powerful warships exceeded tonnage limits laid down by treaty and outclassed their RN equivalents in speed, armaments, size and protection, making them formidable foes and very difficult to sink.

Improvements in naval radar, which had been developed separately from that of the RAF, were making easier the detection of all surface contacts, including U-boats. This, together with the provision of stronger escorts, averaging 2 destroyers and 4 corvettes for each convoy, and more Canadian escorts – now totalling 28 – which came out to rendezvous on the far shore, resulted in the loss of 5 U-boats in one week in March 1941. Three of these had ace commanders and two were in U-boats attacking the same convoy, under the escort of Commander Donald Macintyre, whose expertise, determination and courage brought him the title of the Bulldog Drummond of the Atlantic. Naval staffs would not believe that U-boats could dive as deep as escort commanders knew they could. At this stage of the war a U-boat could only be destroyed by a depth charge dropped within 30 feet, because the pattern of the charges and the depth at which they exploded were both limited, or, after patiently waiting for it to surface, by sinking it with gunfire or ramming it with the bow of a destroyer (also inflicting self-damage). Aeroplanes were of maximum value, both in the detection of U-boats – spotting and guiding warships to them – and in protecting convoys from dive bombers – a hazard mostly encountered in the Mediterranean and Russian convoys. In April, in order to try and close the gap in mid ocean which no shore based aircraft could reach, the first catapult aircraft were fitted to warships. Fifty more were ordered for merchantmen (to be known as CAMS), the first of which was operational by August. Although experiments were made in peacetime in winching planes back on board, this was not practicable in heavy seas or under attack in war. After an action,therefore, the only option for these gallant pilots was to bale out or ditch in the sea, unless they had sufficient fuel to fly to a friendly airfield. In June the first auxiliary escort carrier entered service. A captured German merchantman, which the RN converted to take a flight deck, Audacity carried Martlets, and, after successful trials, orders were made for eleven more vessels to be converted – six in US yards. In April ships and aircraft were stationed in Iceland, whither Britain had sent troops in 1940, and these now began to rendezvous in mid Atlantic with convoys, which they escorted until meeting shore based ships. The bases at Reykjavik and Hvalfjiord were also used for refuelling. Meanwhile the Americans extended their defence zone half way across the Atlantic and in July announced their intention to escort US ships going in the direction of Iceland, to which they sent troops in August.

The difference made by these improvements was dramatic. Losses went right down in July and early August 1941, although the 300 mile Black Gap still yawned in mid ocean. Hitler now realised that his U-boats were coming dangerously close to the US defence zone and he therefore moved a number to the Western Approaches, the Mediterranean and the Freetown/Gibraltar route. In this eastern area of the Atlantic they sank 81 merchant ships in a short space of time, the U-boats being refuelled in the Canary Islands, until diplomatic pressure was put on the Spaniards to stop the practice in September 1941. Britain was now faced with the need to divide her escorts between different spheres of ocean and, since by September Hitler had 180 U-boats in commission (compared with only 57 in 1939 of which 30 were short range), he could keep up the pressure in a number of places at once. Submarines were being built faster than they were sunk, a trend which, unless reversed, meant the war was lost. The US immediately helped by escorting all vessels, including British, going in the direction of Iceland and by opening air bases in Greenland and Bermuda and refitting British ships in US yards. This reduced pressure on escorts in the West Atlantic and in September the Audacity was sent to the East Atlantic to stop the unsustainable losses there. The Germans regarded her presence as the greatest possible danger to U-boats and Dönitz ordered her destruction. She was sunk in December, after moving out at dusk from the convoy, there still being insufficient warships to provide her with her own escort.

Meanwhile Admiral Sir Percy Noble had become C-in-C, Western Approaches in February 1942. He was a man who believed in experiencing for himself the problems of commanders and pilots and he quickly saw what needed to be done. Escort groups were formed, so that instead of assembling independently for convoy work they trained at a school in Tobermory as teams which were kept together, with members able to evaluate each other's expertise and intuition. The strain on escort commanders was considerable, 'Day after day, night after night, they had to watch their helpless charges sunk one by one or blown up in a sheet of flame'. As soon as the convoy was attacked they were faced with too many tasks – to locate and destroy the attacker, to rescue survivors and round up stragglers, to give assistance to and protect damaged ships, while all the time their first priority was to escort the remaining members of the convoy and keep them in formation. Realising their dilemma Sir Percy Noble managed to secure faster destroyers fitted with radar for convoy work and at the same time ordered escorts to stay with the convoy and not go so far out in search of a foe that they could not get back on station. He recognised the ability of a certain retired Commander Walker, to whom he gave command of an Escort Group, asking him to introduce the system he had invented of escorts sweeping the sea with asdic in a buttercup formation round a convoy to winkle out the U-boats and to ensure all areas were covered. Meanwhile proper quantities of depth charges for Coastal Command were coming on stream, together with better aircraft radar and new searchlights for seeking out U-boats. This increased the capability of their pilots, for during the first 2 years of war Coastal Command had only been responsible for one U-boat sunk, another captured and 3 shared with the RN. Merchantmen were given more opportunity to take part in their own defence. Snowflake rockets were provided to light up the convoy at will and larger,more effective anti-aircraft guns were transferred from shore batteries to merchant ships manned by trained crews, of which there were 38,000 by 1944.

The Atlantic in November was, 'Poised for a decisive clash' and, with Hitler sending large numbers of U-boats to the Mediterranean, it looked as though the initiative, in one area, had been wrested from the Germans. It was not to be. Within a month Pearl Harbor had happened. Naval ships were again in desperately short supply. Not only were they now needed in the Far East, but also in the Arctic, where Britain had, since August 1941, been sending supplies to the beleaguered Russians, including food, aeroplanes and tanks, of which she herself was critically short. In the summer of 1941 Rear Admiral Vian went to Spitzbergen to inspect the area and in August he made another expedition to the island to intercept, destroy or seize German mines, supplies and facilities, to evacuate Russians and Norwegians and to reconnoitre bases from which to mount a defence of British convoys. In spite, however, of a successful encounter with enemy ships which reads like the buccaneering exploits of Francis Drake, Spitzbergen was not secured until the following year by the Norwegians, who were supplied by a Catalina of Coastal Command. Not only had the Russian convoys to pass within reach of German held Norwegian air bases, but they had to go so far into hostile seas that there were real dangers of fleet entrapment. In winter they headed into almost perpetual darkness – storms, icy fog and snow and in summer into seas totally calm under a midnight sun, with dense fog alternating with such extreme visibility that the sky gave mirror images of ship action on the sea. It was a nightmare world like that of Coleridge's poem, The Rime of the Ancient Mariner, 'And now there came both mist and snow, And it grew wondrous cold'; and, in antithesis, during the summer, 'All in a hot and copper sky, The bloody sun at noon, Right up above the mast did stand, No bigger than the moon'.

Aid for Russia was motivated by self-interest and the altruism of a shared goal. If Russia stayed in the war, the expansionism of Nazi Germany would be defeated; but, without such aid, the splendidly equipped and trained Panzer Divisions of the 3rd Reich would, it was feared, sweep the Russians back, as the Kaiser's troops had done in 1917. Was this to be Moscow's stand before Napoleon or Lenin's ignominious terms of peace? These thoughts were foremost in the mind of the British public and upon the overstretched Royal and Merchant Navies – the latter joined in this task by a small number of Russian, Norwegian, Polish and Free French ships – was laid a new and fearsome burden. At first, the Germans did not realise the value of the supplies – 48 Hurricanes went in one convoy alone – and thus the first seven convoys sustained only one loss. Initially the Russian convoys assembled in Iceland and, depending on the position of the ice barrier, sailed either north or south of Bear Island, which lies on the southernmost edge of the Barents Sea with the

Arctic beyond. The journey to Archangel took just under three weeks, that to Murmansk shorter, and convoys were under constant air and U-boat attack and under threat from surface raiders lurking in Norwegian fiords. Tankers accompanied convoys for ships to refuel and others were stationed at Spitzbergen, which the Allies used precariously as a base in the face of German opposition. In the perpetual daylight of summer, convoys sailed further north to avoid air attacks but, once they had turned south towards the Kola Straits and the White Sea, German forces were only a short distance away. In the spring of 1942 German torpedo planes joined the bombers and by the summer enemy airforces totalled 250 aircraft. At the same time the German surface fleet sailed north. Spotted by the RN, the Scharnhorst, Gneisenau and Prinz Eugen were damaged en route by mines or torpedoes, but the battleship Tirpitz, surviving aerial torpedoes and RAF bombs, the heavy cruiser Hipper and the pocket battleships Admiral Scheer and Lutzow lay in wait in the fiords with 10 destroyers and 10 U-boats. The Home Fleet with its single aircraft carrier, Victorious, was now faced with the tasks of not only guarding British shores and maintaining a blockade to prevent the escape of these ships to the Atlantic, but also of providing both close escort and support forces for the convoys in circumstances which must be described as perilous.

During the summer of 1942 the casualties to naval and merchant ships on the Russian convoys increased so dramatically that the First Sea Lord, after the loss of 2 cruisers in 2 weeks, wrote to his American counterpart, describing the assignment as, 'A most unsound operation with the dice loaded against us'. The Navy saw the large number of ships arriving and returning as nothing short of miraculous and this, combined with the splendid discipline of the convoys, which, like the PQ16, maintained position and delivered concentrated anti-aircraft fire, lulled the British government into a false sense of security. In vain did the Navy plead for the convoys to be stopped during the summer when there was no night shield of darkness against air attacks, but, apart from one convoy cancelled in early June, when escorts were needed for the relief of Malta, the answer from the government was always that Russian needs were paramount. In these circumstances it seemed inevitable that disaster would strike.

In June the PQ17 convoy assembled – 36 freighters, 22 of which were American. Because of the danger of the fleet being trapped in the Barents Sea there was to be a new deployment. A covering force of 2 battleships – one American, the carrier Victorious, 2 cruisers and supporting destroyers would enter the Barents Sea only if they had definite information that the German ships were there. In this way they could not be surprised from the rear and unable to escape. A support force of 4 cruisers, including 2 American, would enter the Barents Sea, but because they were too light successfully to engage a German force including the Tirpitz – they would turn back before reaching 25 degrees (25E) the longitude of North Cape. Lastly, a close escort force of 6 old or small destroyers, 4 corvettes, 2 submarines, 2 AA ships, 3 minesweepers, 4 anti-submarine trawlers and 3 rescue ships would accompany the convoy to Archangel.

Morale in the convoy was high, the Americans celebrating Independence Day south east of Bear Island with coloured flags, but the Admiralty and Admiral Sir John Tovey, C-in-C, Home Fleet knew the danger. When reports came that the German ships had escaped undetected from the fiords in foggy weather, their whereabouts unknown, the Navy knew at once that it was witnessing the worst possible scenario. The Admiralty now wanted the cruisers to carry on further east, but Admiral Tovey, seeing the danger of their being annihilated by a superior force or of being damaged without hope of extraction, ordered them to return as planned if there was any chance of their meeting the Tirpitz. It was the month of July, and August was the crucial date in the Battle for the Mediterranean, a turning point of the war. Every naval ship would be required and the loss of these four cruisers would have been disastrous. So far only 3 freighters in the convoy had been sunk, since dive bombing had been erratic. Then on the evening of July 4th came a signal from the Admiralty telling of the reported whereabouts of the Tirpitz. She had sailed with the Scheer and could be with the convoy by 2 am. The cruisers were ordered westwards at high speed by the Admiralty – they presumed into action – and the destroyers, believing they were about to join battle, followed them. The convoy was ordered first to disperse and then to scatter – the lighter escort vessels continuing to Archangel independently with the scattered convoy.

The order was received with consternation for, whereas it was normal for an Atlantic convoy, set on by superior surface forces, to scatter while the escorts held them at bay,it was different in the Arctic with ice on one side and hostile aircraft on the other, with U-boats in front and behind – particularly when the best defence against air attack was to maintain rank and give concentrated fire. Some of the tragic and heroic stories of the scattered convoy have already been recounted – a number of ships sailed alone, others in groups with escort vessels, while some crews of damaged ships took to the boats. The weather was crystal clear, the sky mirroring back pictures of the ships being bombed on the sea, which, although eerie, facilitated rescue. When, days later the stragglers had been rounded up only eleven had survived out of 36, 4 percent less than in the famous convoy to Malta five weeks later, but in the PQ17 the merchant ships had not been defended, and, although it was providential to the outcome of the war that no naval ships had been lost, a great tradition had been broken – that it is the duty of the Royal Navy to protect at all times the convoy which it is escorting. The Tirpitz was, in fact, 300 miles away, and, had the C-in-C been told that the destroyers had followed the cruisers, he would have ordered them back when her correct whereabouts was known. It was a tragedy with wider recriminations than those concerning only naval decisions. Admiral Tovey had repeatedly criticised the way in which U-boats were allowed to lurk within the Kola Straits and Russian aircraft and ships had failed to come out to escort incoming convoys.

As often happens good springs from disaster. If the convoys were to continue ships and aircraft had to be made available, whatever the shortages. The Russians now agreed to grant permission for British aircraft to be based on their northern soil and Russian warships came out to escort the later convoys.

The PQ18 sailing from west Scotland was not only accompanied by a merchantman with a catapult Hurricane, but also by an auxiliary aircraft carrier with 12 Hurricanes and 3 Swordfish, supported by 2 destroyers. There was maximum RN presence. A support group of one cruiser and 16 fighting destroyers would go nearly the whole journey and rendezvous with the incoming convoy, thus providing the attacking arm for the close escort of 2 destroyers, 2 submarines, 2 AA ships and 11 other smaller vessels. There was also a covering force of 3 cruisers and a distant covering force of 2 battleships, one cruiser and five destroyers. In the event the support group turned back when Russian destroyers came out to meet the convoy and, despite repeated air and underwater attacks, the number of surviving ships was almost identical to those lost in the PQ17, with 3 U-boats sunk and a number of aircraft destroyed.

If the great tradition of convoy protection had thus been restored, the sacrificial loss of the little destroyer Achates, sailing with a December convoy to Russia, must have expiated any further feelings of self-reproach that may have lingered in the minds of the Royal Navy. The Achates was the only veteran in a close escort of 6 destroyers, 2 corvettes and smaller ships, supported by two cruisers sailing from Kola, which, once the main part of the journey had been accomplished, were to rendezvous with and escort an inward sailing convoy. It was winter, rendering unnecessary the presence of an aircraft carrier,but in the atrocious weather the cruisers got too far ahead and temporarily lost touch. If sighted by surface ships the convoy, escorted by the Achates and smaller naval vessels, was to turn away and make smoke, while the other destroyers intercepted the German ships. With a U-boat spotting the prey, the Hipper and 3 destroyers attacked at the rear, while the Lutzow with 3 more destroyers moved to block the convoy's line of escape. In the unequal battle with the Hipper, during which the destroyers refused to be lured away from the convoy and took it in turn in pairs to either attack or guard its rear, the Onslow received a crippling hit, disengaged and moved to the front of the convoy, just as it ran, mercifully shielded by a fall of snow, straight into the arms of the waiting Lutzow. The Achates, which had also been damaged by the Hipper's gunfire, was now ordered to the front to support the Onslow but, as she cleared smoke, she received another devastating hit, mortally wounding the little ship and killing those on the bridge. Her second-in-command, realising she could not comply, ordered that, in spite of her incredible list, she continue to steam precariously up and down making smoke to shield the convoy. Only after the cruisers had arrived to the rescue and the Hipper and Lutzow had fled, leaving one destroyer sunk and all danger past, did she at last signal for help. A trawler went immediately to her rescue, but it was too late. Before it reached her she capsized. She had protected the convoy to the end; Captain Sherbroke of the Onslow, in command of the operation, received a VC and the action of the Achates was described by the C-in-C as 'magnificent'.

In the spring of 1943 the Arctic convoys were suspended because of the critical stage of the Atlantic war (there had also been a brief suspension during November because of the North African landings). Then in April 1943, under the direction of Rear Admiral C.B. Barry – who, as captain of the Queen Elizabeth, had seen his ship damaged by frogmen in Alexandria – training began for a September attack on the Tirpitz in Kaa Fiord, which was carried out by midget submarines, towed across the North Sea by 'parent vessels'. The Tirpitz was put out of action and was later again incapacitated and then sunk by Fleet Air Arm and RAF bombers, while the Scharnhorst was destroyed in the dramatic chase described in Chapter VIII. Although air and underwater attacks continued after this date, with U-boats now armed with acoustic homing torpedoes, and more minefields were laid north of Murmansk, a considerable degree of safety came to these Arctic waters by 1944, due to the presence of stronger surface escorts and two escort aircraft carriers for each convoy. To the memory of these final victories – during which Admiral Bruce Fraser was C-in-C Home Fleet – and to all the Arctic convoys, fought through 'In the most arduous physical conditions that nature could produce against the most relentless onslaughts that man could devise', a memorial stone was erected at North Cape.

Meanwhile, on the other side of the globe in the distressing heat of Far Eastern waters, escorts in 1942 were so few that merchant ships began by sailing independently, leaving – as in World War I – little trace of their loss. Only bare statistics and a few personal stories survive to give any picture of the perils surrounding this part of the convoy war, which is in danger of dropping out of recorded history. Fortunately, at the start, the Japanese only used their submarines against naval targets, as the British did for the first 18 months of the European war, and, even when submarines were used against merchant ships, they were less effective than expected. This was also true of the armed surface raiders when operating alone. However, when both naval arms were used together, the results were devastating and 1½ million gross tons of shipping were lost between January 1942 and May 1943. Although RN escorts could only be provided singly if at all, orders were given for convoy sailing. Axis submarines, both German and Japanese, working on the East African coast, used supply ships to refuel. Losses in the Mozambique Channel, to which anti-submarine trawlers sent from the UK did little to stem, became so numerous and risks to shipping so great, that the decision was taken to secure the Vichy French base at Madagascar. Because of the earlier failure of the combined Free French and British amphibious attack, launched for the same reason against Dakar, British troops were used alone and success was achieved. This rendered safer the inshore waters of Africa,while at the other side of the Indian Ocean Royal Indian Navy vessels came out to escort convoys, both in their own waters and in the Persian Gulf. Out on the sea lanes, however, both here and on the longer haul to Australia and New Zealand, the position was perilous. Like the escort ships, aircraft were few and far between and flying boats, operating from a common pool, were used to supplement them.

As 1942 drew to its close demand for ships for the amphibious operations in the Mediterranean became paramount and by the middle of 1943 48 ships had been removed from Admiral Somerville's Eastern fleet to take part in the invasion of Sicily. In their place some escort vessels came up from South

African waters, but shortages of ships meant that convoys were so underprotected and losses so heavy that by the end of the year independent sailings were briefly resorted to – even with the willing approval of Admiral Somerville. It was a policy of unrelieved desperation, Somerville realising that if he used fast destroyers as escorts the fleet was immobilised and if he used slow escorts they were too weak to destroy enemy vessels, robbing the strategy of half its purpose. His command covered so large an area that it was impossible for those engaged in the western conflict to comprehend the distances. The east-west route stretching from Australia to the Persian Gulf made the north-south Atlantic route seem like an inland lake. It was a 'no win' alternative and losses at once shot up. In January 1944 some warships returned and convoys were resumed the following month. It seemed that in the face of danger any company was better than none at all. Certainly this was so in the case of the Ondina, a Royal Dutch Shell tanker with a 4 inch gun, which sailed from Fremantle to Diego Garcia in November 1942 escorted by the Bengal, a little minesweeper of the Royal Indian Navy with only a small 12 pounder gun. Sighted by 2 Japanese merchant raiders, the Bengal signalled to the Ondina to act independently and took on one raider fifteen times her size, armed with 5.5 inch guns. The Ondina, seeing her plight, came to her rescue, a lucky hit from one of their guns setting on fire the raiders' ammunition store. Leaving the Bengal engaging the other raider, she then set off in escape, but minutes later, with the Bengal hit, out of ammunition and also turning to flee, this second raider caught up with the Ondina, hitting her bridge and killing her captain. With her ammunition also expended, the order was given to abandon ship, but, although she was hit by two more torpedoes, the Ondina refused to sink. After machine gunning the crew in the lifeboats, the Japanese departed to the rescue of the survivors of the sinking raider but, as recounted by Captain Macintyre, on their return, after firing one more torpedo, they sailed away, apparently losing appetite for further carnage – sometimes the case with the Japanese. At night the crew returned and got the Ondina safely under way back to Fremantle, while the Bengal reached Colombo. Thus two ships, one unwieldy, the other small, successfully supported each other in the face of danger.

So intertwined were the events taking place in the various oceans of the world that the loss of much of the US Pacific Fleet at Pearl Harbor contributed in no small measure to the troubles in the Atlantic, whither fortunately the majority of U-boats did not return from the Mediterranean until August 1942. In that year losses of merchant ships in the North Atlantic totalled 5½ million gross tons. The reasons were two fold. Early in the New Year Dönitz sent 5 U-boats to US inshore waters, which he later increased to 12, and these created a U-boat paradise, because the Americans, in spite of years of warning, did not order convoy sailing until May – 23 ships were sunk in January, 64 in February, 48 in March, while US vessels, navigation marks, shore installations and civilian houses, hotels and sky-signs continued to show lights and use wireless freely. Ships sailed independently and the Americans would not listen to British advice. The few available US escorts and the anti-submarine trawlers lent by the British, went on unsuccessful 'search and destroy' patrols, which achieved nothing. The USA regarded convoys as purely defensive and therefore 'cowardly', believing that introducing them would inhibit the positive approach of the US Navy. Admiral Pound suggested sending them 10 corvettes immediately after Pearl Harbor – and, in answer to US Admiral King's urgent requests for help, two escort groups of anti-submarine trawlers were sent from Halifax naval forces in April 1942 and two weeks later a further escort group from mid Atlantic, making a total of 24. It was extremely irksome to the British, who could not really spare them, that these were not used for convoys, but were sent out on useless patrols. The excuse the USA offered was that they did not have sufficient escorts to convoy, but figures belied this claim, for in 1939 the British had 112 surface escort vessels in the Atlantic and 45 aircraft, compared with the 1942 US figure of 173 surface craft and 268 aircraft. The refusal to escort stemmed from ideological and strategic beliefs (and a disinclination to be taught by the British) rather than from shortage of ships. At last, Admiral King – not a man easily persuaded – began to bow to the arguments of the Royal Navy, who saw British controlled merchant vessels – which had survived the long haul across the Atlantic – being sunk in unprecedented numbers in waters where their writ did not run. In April rudimentary escorts were provided and in May the first convoys were introduced in US in-shore waters.In July, when they became universal, losses immediately fell.

It was not before time, for in August 1942 the U-boats returned in strength to the Atlantic. By this time the dangers from U-boats far exceeded any other threat. In the year 1942 1,160 merchant ships were lost in all waters, 1006 to submarines (86% of the total) and the number of U-boats in commission rose from 249 to 393, with only 87 lost. Even British and US shipbuilding combined could not stem the tide of losses. Although US generosity to Britain knew no bounds, nevertheless demands in the Pacific reduced their commitment in the Atlantic so that escorts were now 50 percent British, 46 percent Canadian and 4 percent US. The British percentage included a number of Allied ships and crews.These, both naval and merchant, were beginning to give the operation a more international complexion, with Norwegian, Polish, French, Dutch, Greek and other nationalities playing a part – the Norwegians 'pouncing like terriers upon the U-boats'. As the year went by there were many improvements in organisation: a tactical unit was opened in Liverpool; eight auxiliary escort aircraft carriers were commissioned into the Atlantic and long range aircraft gave improved cover in mid ocean, where the Black Gap yawned; although, after the loss of their ace commanders, U-boats were now attacking in 3 or 4 patrol lines, making combined groups of 60 to 70, high frequency direction finding revealed their position the moment they gave orders to assemble; up to ten depth charges could now be dropped over them at once,set to explode at variable levels, and a new weapon – the hedgehog – could also fire a number of bombs simultaneously 250 yards ahead of the attacking ship; with more tankers, refuelling at sea had at last become the norm, enabling the same escorts to cover the whole voyage, while the provision of more rescue ships lessened their responsibility for survivors. On the other hand the long strain was beginning to tell and many merchant seamen had been sunk two or three times. On an August convoy, escorted almost entirely by corvettes, 11 merchant ships were sunk to only 2 U-boats destroyed. With 5 ships going down simultaneously – 3 of which, including the Commodore's ship, disappeared within seconds – the crews of 3 other ships, including one trained British gun crew, took to the boats in panic, thinking they too had been torpedoed. Escorts cajoled them back on board, with the exception of one coloured crew, whose nerve had failed, The Admiralty knew that success or failure depended upon the strength of the escort, but because of the demands for ships and aircraft in the Mediterranean, both for the relief of Malta – the story of which has been told in Chapter VIII – and the invasion of North Africa, it could do nothing to rectify matters. In one September convoy 7 ships were lost to no U-boats sunk, while, at the other end of the spectrum, in another convoy no ships were lost to 2 U-boats destroyed. 125 flotilla vessels had to be withdrawn from other areas for service in the Mediterranean, together with minesweepers and smaller vessels and, more importantly, the 8 newly introduced escort aircraft carriers.* 10 Very Long Range Liberators were sent to the Atlantic in their place, but fewer naval ships meant convoys had to be made larger and re-routed with longer sailing times and more strain. Thus problems by the autumn had multiplied almost beyond endurance and it was merciful that Hitler withdrew his U-boats to the Mediterranean in November, so that, as winter settled in on the Atlantic, the battle began to flag.

Meanwhile in the Mediterranean in January 1943 British ships, aircraft carriers, aeroplanes and submarines were joined by US forces to cut Rommel's supply lines to North Africa, first by 55 percent, then by 60 percent, Hitler insisting until too late that his army fight to the last man. 'Sink, burn and destroy!', ran Cunningham's signal to his ships, 'Let nothing pass'. In May a quarter of a million men surrendered and the first 'through' convoy for two years was run from Gibraltar to Alexandria. With the invasion of Sicily planned for July, the turning point of the war had passed, but it did not mean the war was won or that it could not still be lost. Unfortunately, this success in the Mediterranean did nothing to alleviate the critical situation in the Atlantic, whither the U-boats returned in February, Dönitz believing that Britain could still be defeated by lack of vital supplies. March was a terrible month, both for weather and losses of merchant ships and – as in the Far East – the Admiralty began to doubt its own faith in the convoy system, although losses for independent sailings were twice as high. No fewer than 97 ships were sunk in the first 20 days of March, 34 in 3 convoys alone. Then, in the last days of the month, hurricane force winds battered Allied and Axis vessels alike, so that they were as much absorbed with their own survival as with the enemy. 'Incoming merchant vessels were so deeply laden as to be sometimes almost awash, while those outgoing and in ballast were riding so high that in the fierce seas they were in danger of capsizing.' The Commodore's ship in one convoy

* P215, The War at Sea [Vol II] S.W. Roskill. HMSO. London. 1956

did capsize and was lost with all hands. 'The little ships of the escort force climbed the steep sides of the monstrous waves and hung momentarily poised on their crests with bow and stern out of water, before plunging dizzily down the farthest slopes'. It was as if the gods were saying, 'We will give victory to the side which endures the greatest hardships, for they will have the firmest belief in the justice of their cause'. The critical stage of the U-boat war in the Atlantic had arrived.

It seems that only now, 50 years later, British people may be prepared to try to comprehend the ferocity of the battle, the extent of the sacrifice and to 'Thank whatever Gods there be' and their forefathers for granting them so great a deliverance. What was needed was more ships and more aircraft. Yet in March 1943, the month the first convoy crossed the Atlantic without loss, the battle had, in fact, been won, for in the month's last days surface vessels and auxiliary aircraft carriers began to return from the Mediterranean and more long range Liberators arrived to be based in Northern Ireland and Iceland and to shrink the Black Gap further; Coastal Command was given new radar and sank more U-boats, while surface vessels were given radar screens – plan position indicators (PPI),which gave an all round radar picture. Now, with an average of 7½ escorts for each convoy – out of which 2, supported by spotting aeroplanes, were engaged in hunting down attacking U-boats – kills began to exceed losses. Captain Walker's Support Groups, the introduction of which had been held back because of shortage of ships at the time of the North African landings, were put on stand-by duty to aid convoys under pressure and a practical training school was opened in Larne, using Tommy Sopwith's steam yacht to represent a convoy under attack from submarines and defended by the Escort Group under training. A new research unit showed that with air escort for 8 hours a day losses were reduced by 64 percent and that increasing surface escorts by one half produced an improvement of 25 percent. All that was required were sufficient numbers of trained air and sea escorts working together, for research demonstrated that in convoys where both air and sea escort were continuous losses were minimal. There had been close co-operation since 1939 between the Admiralty and Coastal Command and in February 1941 the Admiralty had taken over operational control, thus fully integrating naval and air convoy protection.

At the end of March 1943 Dönitz recalled his U-boats to rearm and refuel after a period of hectic activity, giving the Allies a pause. At the beginning of April the convoy HX231, which had sailed from Canada, accompanied by Liberators and under Commander Peter Gretton's escort, accounted for 2 U-boats lost and a number of others damaged with only 3 ships sunk – all of which had become stragglers, (one with engine trouble and two foreign ships which left the convoy by choice). As already recounted, tribute was paid in Cabinet Committee by Admiral Sir Max Horton. Very Long Range aircraft came down to meet the convoy and it was joined by 4 destroyers in support, which later were part of Captain Walker's 2nd Escort Group. Then on the 22nd of April the slow convoy ONS5 set out for Canada again under the escort of Commander Gretton, and, although this time 12 ships were lost, 7 U-boats were sunk out of the 60 attacking. Dönitz reacted at once. Because the new U-boats could dive deeper and, because he feared the increasing superiority of British radar, which was wresting the initiative from him, he ordered his U-boats to dive by night and surface by day, having first fitted them with anti-aircraft guns. It was one of his few tactical and strategic mistakes of the war and only increased the score against him. At the beginning of May a fast and a slow convoy were both accompanied for part of the voyage by the carrier Biter, the fast convoy losing 3 merchant ships for 3 U-boats sunk, the slow convoy 2 ships for 2 U-boats lost, with more damaged. Later in the month Commander Gretton again set out with a slow convoy, SC 130, and so confident was he this time of success that he sent a signal asking for increased speed because he was getting married. The convoy delivered – no merchant ships were sunk, yet 5 U-boats were destroyed, one of which contained Dönitz's son. Admiral Sir Max Horton, C-in-C, Western Approaches, without whose, 'Determination, drive and knowledge of submarine warfare, the battle of the Atlantic could not have been won', paid tribute to Gretton's 'outstanding ability'.On the 23rd of May, during which month 41 U-boats were lost, there was a sudden cessation of hostilities. The remainder had been withdrawn and when they returned it would never be with the same intensity.

Although in a sense the Support Groups were 'an offensive arm of anti-submarine warfare', nevertheless most of their successes were when engaged in convoy escort or when coming to the assistance of a convoy under attack. By March 1943 there were five such groups, of which Captain Walker's Second Escort Group was the most successful, sinking 14 U-boats in 14 months. The escort carrier Biter joined the Fifth Support Group – this was a major turning point – and escort carriers were then attached in increasing numbers to the Support Groups, which in 1944 were extended to the Arctic. Meanwhile co-operation between them and Coastal Command had been continuing under a centralised inter-service administration and in August 1943 the Portuguese allowed the Azores to be used as an Allied air base, which provided better air cover in the Eastern Atlantic. Although the increasing superiority of Allied intelligence (valuable in tracking U-boats) was enabling US auxiliary aircraft carriers to operate successfully on patrol, supported by 3 destroyers, nevertheless it remained true that Allied aircraft achieved their greatest success as convoy escorts – the average number of flying hours for each U-boat sunk being half of those on patrol. In the Bay of Biscay, after 80,000 flying hours on patrol, Coastal Command only sank 10 U-boats for 170 planes lost. In May the Germans introduced the schnorkel to the Mediterranean, which enabled U-boats to re-charge batteries at periscope depth, but by then the Americans had developed an instrument to enable low flying aircraft to track submerged submarines within its calmer waters. Although in the rougher waters of the Barents Sea this equipment gave the U-boats a new 'edge', nevertheless U-boats were now being sunk in increasing numbers and attention was being given to sinking their support ships as well. Modern sloops, armed with sufficient weaponry, commanded by expertly trained men and present in sufficient numbers were, in Lieutenant Commander

D.E.G. Wemyss' words, 'Like a well drilled three quarter line, passing and interpassing'. This team play was part of Walker's method of 'creeping' attack. With ships stationed at vantage points on the perimeter, a directing ship, using asdic, moved behind the U-boat, while an attacking ship went silently and slowly up its track, until it reached a point where the directing ship, assessing the relative positions of both vessels, signalled to it to drop its depth charges. On the 22nd of March 1944 the U-boats were finally withdrawn from the central Atlantic and all operations against convoys in that area were cancelled. By the end of May this cessation affected all areas and there were very few U-boats left now in distant waters.

An island people had been placed in long drawn out peril by lack of ships in sufficient numbers to give protection and carry supplies and by lack of sufficient aircraft to keep the skies above clear and co-operate in spotting and sinking U-boats. Moreover the point had again been proved that if supplies of both are limited, it is essential first to attack only within the context of defence and that, even when ships and aircraft are available, they are still more effective as support groups for convoys rather than on patrol. In Captain Roskill's words, 'The superiority of convoy over patrolling as an offensive strategy was strikingly demonstrated... After 45 months of unceasing battle of a more exacting and arduous nature than posterity may easily realize our convoy escorts had won the triumph they so richly merited'.

CHAPTER XII

OF SHIPS AND MEN
BATTLE AND BLOCKADE

It is claimed that Henry VIII first developed the link between offensive and defensive naval operations, and throughout history this link has repeatedly been demonstrated, as has been seen again in the story of the Battle of the Atlantic. The strategy remains as true today, for in order to protect the home base the enemy fleet must be destroyed; to defend merchant shipping enemy raiders must be sunk and blockades mounted around hostile ports, while to win victory against an implacable foe it may be necessary to undertake amphibious operations, in the form of harassment raids or the landing of large armies. The former require to be evacuated – and indeed sometimes, if plans go awry, the latter also, as happened in World War II at Norway, Dunkirk, Greece and Crete, and these tasks are among the most difficult the Navy has to perform. Although in sea battles victory normally goes to the side superior in ships, aircraft and weaponry, nevertheless inequalities can be off-set by good seamanship, training, intelligence of enemy movements, good communications and mastery of co-ordinated operations. Thus numbers of up-to-date ships, advance in techniques and the training of seamen intertwine to provide a resolute effective fighting force. Excluding the nuclear dimension, the greatest changes over the centuries have been: the abandonment of hand to hand fighting in favour of gunnery, the change from wood and sail to iron and steam, the challenge of long range gunnery, the invention of the mine, torpedo, submarine, ship-borne aircraft and most recently the guided missile.

Of these changes the most fundamental was the first and thus the modern era of seamanship and fighting ships began with Francis Drake. Prior to that, since the function of naval ships was the carriage of fighting troops, merchant and naval fleets were interchangeable. This was true not only of the later medieval English fleets, but of the earliest fighting ships in the Mediterranean, which were also trading vessels. In battle they were drawn up in lines abreast and carried archers, soldiers and planks for boarding. As ships moved out into the wilder waters of the Atlantic and came under sail they became broader, larger and deeper and, with the invention of gunpowder, gunports were pierced in the ships' sides and cannons were carried at different levels on fore and aft castles in Spanish style. Perhaps influenced by Venetian galleasses, which were sailing ships propelled by oars and carrying guns on the broadside, the English began to bring guns down from the castles to the main deck of their great sailing ships, displacing soldiers and turning sailors into fighting seamen. Initially they only cut gunports in the ships' sides, but later they made openings in the sterns, which became squarer to carry more armament. Then in 1509 the brass muzzle loaded gun was used for the first time. outmoding the iron breech loading equivalent and thereafter enemy ships could be destroyed by broadside fire alone. Wind now took on a more important role and fleets had to manoeuvre into fighting positions with care. If the wind heeled them over too far much of their fire power was submerged in salt water and they had to choose the right moment to attack, when the wind provided them with the greatest impetus and direction. Henry VIII, who still followed the Spanish pattern for the formation of his battlefleet, (with a vanguard of merchant vessels, a main body of galleons and two wings of Venetian-type galleasses),was the first English King to issue proper Fighting Instructions. Although in a battle in 1217 the English recognised the importance of wind, passing through the French fleet to turn and get the weather gage, only now was this tactic formalised into an order. If the fleet was to leeward the Admiral was instructed to flee, followed by the fleet, 'And make smoke all he can' (which had to come from the firing of cannon) to hide his ships while they tacked, 'To have wind of the enemy'.

At the Armada the strategy and tactics of the two sides were thus fundamentally different, for the aim of the Spaniards was still to grapple and board. The Spaniards fought as an army, with their ships, 'Like warhorses... not very nimble at turning' formed into lines of battle rigidly drawn, their strongest galleons in the main body, defended by two wings. They did not appreciate the opportunities provided by the elements and saw the wind in limited perspective. Because of the danger of being enveloped by fire and smoke, the Spaniards were ordered not to penetrate too deep into English squadrons, beyond the point of rescue and to, 'Keep the weather gage. For if no other advantage the fleet will avoid being blinded.' Although customarily sailing in line abreast, Spanish naval writers refer to the fleet altering its formation to counter enemy arrangements, which, according to references in J.S. Corbett's history of Fighting Instructions, might include line ahead or 'lance head or triangle' – a pattern still sometimes adopted by the Japanese in World War II. If the latter formation was chosen, then the Spaniards were ordered to form 2 lines – wide at the front and narrow at the rear – and engage the enemy from both sides. The English ships were faster and more nimble than those of Spain; they changed direction easily, going about quickly on to the other tack and forcing their opponents to do likewise by depriving them of the weather gage. The Spaniards spoke of the 'worthy quality' of these 'excellent fast' sailing vessels and 'the sagacity and technical grasp of naval art' of their English officers. Elizabeth issued no Fighting Instructions and her Admirals' despatches concern themselves more with strategy than tactics, but the Elizabethans under Drake valued individual mobility and fought in groups, each of them in de facto line ahead. Until the Armada, the English fleet was divided into three: the Downs, Isle of Wight and Scilly, but Drake showed the advantage of fighting as one fleet, with individual squadrons dispersing and consolidating at speed. The English history of the Armada is currently seen through Spanish eyes (like writing a British version of El Alamein through the eyes of Rommel), whereas naval historian J.S. Corbett relied on the Italian Petruccio Ubaldino, who based his history on Drake's version of the battle. This was that, fighting in line ahead, he sailed parallel to the Spanish ships, raking their decks with broadsides, breaking their masts and cutting and burning their rigging with incendiary and other projectiles, killing their soldiers and seamen. The English had more long range guns than the Spaniards, but found that to inflict damage they had to close and fire at short range. In this way they set the pattern of, 'The enduring love of all our greatest Admirals for close action', a pattern not challenged until the Japanese naval victory over the Russians in 1904. Drake's tactics were for swift action, spreading confusion and this highlighted the inadequacy of merchant ships employed as men of war (with the exception of the East Indiamen), a lesson re-learnt in every later conflict, including both World Wars, when the performance of the AMCs did not fulfil expectations. The vital contribution of the Merchant Navy has always lain in the provision of trained personnel and auxiliary ships.

Drake's style of fighting was incorporated into the written instructions of Sir Edward Cecil, who led the 1625 West Indies Expedition. The fleet, divided and sub-divided into squadrons, was ordered, 'Into action in succession after the leading ship', sailing to windward with the best ships in front. By the Dutch Wars of the seventeenth century these tactics were standard. Men of war fought in line ahead with a hundred yards between them. 'All gave their broadsides.. and then bore away with the ships before the wind till they were ready again'. It was the task of the leading ship to endeavour to 'double-cross'- to sail round the enemy line and back down the other side, subjecting it to simultaneous cross fire, a manoeuvre very difficult to accomplish by any but the best ships and men. Commonwealth orders were more explicit and by 1653 the line ahead was to be, 'Formed upon severest punishment'. Although on June 4th in the Four Days' Battle in 1666, by which time the Restoration had ameliorated some of the fiercest rigours of the Commonwealth Navy, Prince Rupert, having the advantage of wind, led the English line right through the middle of the enemy fleet, this tactic was still seen as a way of getting to windward rather than of setting out to break the enemy line. Indeed the Duke of York's Instructions, differentiating for the first time between attacks from leeward and windward, stated that any division of enemy fleets must only be undertaken from a leeward position. Nevertheless by 1691 it would appear that an Admiral could initiate a division of the enemy fleet by his own signal, being no longer tied to only doing so from a leeward position.

Thus the stage was set for the more imaginative tactics of the eighteenth century and during the early French wars, Anson introduced two new concepts: first 'to equalise', if outnumbering the enemy, by forming a reserve and then to use it in the manner of his successful tactic at Finisterre to cross the enemy's T at right angles. In mid century Hawke introduced another radical idea, that of ships with the wind and in line ahead, turning individually and steering for their opposite number in the enemy line, rather than turning in the wake of the leading ship. Three years later Boscawen varied the traditional line ahead with the signal to form two lines instead of one, both of which, sailing abreast, would come up on either side of the enemy fleet. By 1779 the strategy of concentration, rather than the Elizabethan idea of causing confusion, was beginning to predominate and in that year the 1691 instruction not to fire until at point blank range became a practical reality with the invention of the carronade, deriving its name from the Scottish town of Carron. This smaller traversible weapon was at its most effective at point blank range, outmoding the Elizabethan brass gun, as brass had previously outmoded iron. Then, during the American War of Independence, Rodney at the Battle of Les Saintes in the West Indies in 1782 took his fleet right through the enemy line in three places, sailing himself down the other side to pour devastating horizontal fire on to the enemy's decks. This victory at last changed the Admiralty's attitude and breaking the enemy line now became the prime target of the Royal Navy.

Rodney's signal book of that year may give the modern reader an idea of the discipline required for fighting in formation under sail – a tradition responsible for the precise convoy manoeuvres in World War II. It includes instructions for tacking, keeping station, altering course together, closing distance, changing stations, making 2 lines, engaging more closely, giving chase, forming quarter lines on the points of the compass, and the following year the signal for Rodney's own tactic of cutting through the enemy's line of battle. As the American War of Independence drew to its close Howe developed this idea further, giving the signal for cutting off completely either the van or rear of the enemy fleet – the Duke of York a century earlier had given much criticised instructions to concentrate attack upon the van – and Howe's signal was soon amended, so that it could be carried out not only by the leader but by any specified ship. At the Glorious First of June he put this into practice, engaging and passing through the enemy line – going so close to the enemy flag ship as to 'singe our whiskers' – while all other ships simultaneously engaged their opposite numbers, although most did not pass through. After this victory – of which it was said that 'Howe's attack might be stopped by gunnery, but could not be avoided except by flight' – Admirals were given full tactical control of fleets. Generally speaking, when the attack was to windward, Howe's method was used, when to leeward, it was Rodney's, and there always remained the traditional alternative of sailing in line parallel with the enemy. At the end of the eighteenth century a Frenchman wrote of the Royal Navy that, 'The English do not look for signals, but are bound by the principle of mutual support.' This mutual support was an age old tradition in the English Navy – ships 'seconded' each other and went to the rescue of others. Henry VIII's Instructions ordered pinnaces to go to the relief of stricken ships and in the Commonwealth Instructions the need for succour was explicitly stated and stricken ships were told to signal distress. 'Being thus certain they will not be deserted,' continued the French commentator, ' they use their zeal and judgement to act on the spur of the moment in order to get at the enemy'. The stage was now set for the radical imaginative genius of Nelson.

At the end of the eighteenth century the officer corps that Nelson was soon to command was unequalled by any other European country. Cromwell had made the Navy a professional force, with father to son tradition, building upon the tradition of Drake and the yeomen and small west country landowners, many of whom were expert seamen. It was not until the Restoration that the aristocrats, whose forebears had served in the Elizabethan Navy, returned to command and these two types of men were successfully blended together into the trained highly professional gentleman officer of Jane Austen's time. It was said of Anson that he promoted men on merit and of Hawke that he made gentlemen of them. Pepys had brought in promotional examinations and took boys into the Navy as midshipmen, who lived in the confined quarters of their 'gun room', where they cooked and washed for themselves, learning seamanship from practical experience, emergencies and exposure to sea, wind and weather. Leadership in the Navy was built on example as well as command. As likely as not a young man, momentarily hesitating to climb the mast in a high wind to repair the rigging, would hear the captain of the frigate – there before him – giving his instructions from the cross piece. Reared in such a tradition, Nelson developed his famous characteristics of, 'Tenacity, instant decision, unfailing resource, insight and swift and audacious action', and this was the legacy he handed on to others at his death.

By 1800 the Navy had increased dramatically in size. Nevertheless, at the Battle of Cape St. Vincent Admiral Jervis was outnumbered by two to one, 'Enough… the die is cast. If there are 50 sail I will go through them'. Jervis tore a huge hole in the enemy line and swept on through it, but the Spaniards regrouped to rejoin the rest of the fleet. Commodore Nelson, seeing the danger, made his famous independent move. He disregarded Jervis' signal to follow in succession and instead he broke formation and prevented the Spanish manoeuvre by crossing their T, thus giving the Royal Navy a resounding victory. Nelson's genius combined both concentration of force and Drake's tactic of throwing the enemy into confusion. Favouring close action, his last signal before a battle was always, 'Engage the enemy more closely'. At the Battle of the Nile, the British in single file came between the French at anchor and the shoals on the landward side and pounded them at short range into wrecks so that only two ships survived. He believed in self-reliance and not in over-rigid battle tactics, giving authority to his flag officers to control their own divisions. He saw the vulnerability of the enemy's rear and conceived the principle of attacking with one squadron, while using another for support and the containment of the enemy, with a further reserve squadron to be thrown into the battle at any chosen point. Lastly, he believed in concealment, hiding his true intentions from the enemy for so long that they could not plan retaliation. At the last minute at Trafalgar, Nelson abandoned the plan he had written in a memorandum and spoken of to his colleagues. He reduced his reserve to one ship, put Collingwood in command of the larger portion to attack the rear, while he covered the attack and contained the centre and the van. Collingwood therefore signalled to his squadron a Howe attack, each ship breaking the enemy line by the shortest route, while Nelson held on in line ahead without signalling his intentions. The British thus approached in two lines of 15 and 12 ships and sailed through the combined French and Spanish fleets, the Victory engaging the French flag ship in the centre before sailing down the other side of the enemy.

With their seamanship thus unmatched, it will be understood why the British held their sailing ships in such affection and were reluctant until the Crimean War to recognise the dominance of iron and steel ships driven by combustion engines and screw propellers. The Admiralty feared that, without overseas coaling stations – later provided – steam ships would have shorter range and less room for guns and men. At last they saw that, even when only used as auxiliary propulsion, sails going up and taking the wind heeled iron ships over so far that they were de-stabilised by their own weight, recognising also that, in tests with explosive shells, wood did not stand up well to modern shot. Nevertheless, the British were late to enter the game and to understand that iron ships demanded new gunnery techniques. They had few 'soft' spots in almost impenetrable armour and could shut off damaged areas with water tight compartments, so that, even against armour piercing shells, they were more difficult to sink. Also new technology, coupled with the increased size and strength of hulls, which tolerated greater vibration, meant that guns could be more powerful and could fire at longer range. With salvoes directed by central control, fast loading and accurate marksmanship depended on a team of highly trained human operators, but, while other navies were firing at moving targets, British gunnery training concentrated predominantly on stationary short range targets. Unchallenged at sea after Trafalgar, with twice as many ships as other rivals, Britain, by the third quarter of the nineteenth century, allowed her Navy to decline and was in danger of being left behind. Bismark's bid for European domination did not waken her from complacency, but when in 1883 Germany formed her first industrial, chemical and military cartel – AEG – Britain saw her interests and independence threatened and knew she must build ships to replenish her dwindling fleet. Soon after, with the 'pilot' dropped, Germany was governed by a formidable ruler with ambitions – as his grandfather had in 1870 – to make his country a sea power. Thus, as the twentieth century dawned, Britain was again forced into action to retain her place and, in answer to the Kaiser's challenge, she built Lord Fisher's Dreadnoughts, which at a stroke, with their fast steam turbine engines and centrally mounted revolving gun turrets, made all other navies obsolete. Britain had again regained the lead.

With the Dreadnought's design and construction shrouded in secrecy the Germans, taken by surprise, had to deepen the Kiel Canal before they could get similarly draughted ships from dry dock to the sea. As in earlier days Britain put first in importance speed and size of guns. The Germans, who rebuilt their dry docks to allow increased beam, put their faith in armour and water tight compartments and economised on space for living quarters and fuel, since their ships normally operated in home waters. Yet in spite of their awesome potential these two magnificent fleets produced stalemate at the Battle of Jutland. Why was this? Not only was the British advantage of speed inhibited by dangers from submarines and mines, so that Anson's famous chase at Finisterre could not be repeated by Jellicoe, but British superiority in fire power was counter-balanced by German superiority in long range gunnery training. Moreover, ability to concentrate decisive force was neutralised by large numbers of ships, volume of fire power and the rudimentary nature of communications, so that the battle contained an element of 'hide and seek', with vessels lacking direction and getting out of place. At that time, if all guns were brought into action, 24 ships in single line ahead covered 6½ miles, and, since in order to avoid submarine attack they steamed between engagements in a rectangle 'disposed abeam', they took twenty minutes to change into battle formation. 'Over such a huge force and wide battlefield a C-in-C can only wield limited control'. With no radar and primitive communication, 'The forces were too large to be brought effectively into action in the concentration necessary for a decision'. Although the world did not know it at the time the days of the large battleship were drawing to a close.

Perhaps it was not altogether surprising therefore that after World War I the leading naval powers, the USA, the British Empire, Japan, France and Italy (in a move initiated by the USA) proposed the setting of internationally agreed limits upon the size of fleets and types of ships and these were negotiated and formulated into the Treaty of Washington, which was signed in 1922. Professor Morison records how in 1916, on the eve of war, Congress passed an Act, which, put into effect, would have given the USA a Navy equal to twice the size of the other two largest navies. This, he claims, is what brought Britain to the negotiating table, while, as previously stated, Japan's co-operation was secured by the USA and Britain promising not to strengthen defences west of Pearl Harbor and east of Singapore – a high price to pay. Although Britain and the USA were each to have a ratio of 5, compared with Japan's 3 and France and Italy's one and three quarters, nevertheless these figures looked more generous to Britain that they were. The US fleet was on a rising curve, whereas to date, although the Royal Navy had hardly ever achieved the target of equalling the two largest navies of the world except in war, nevertheless this high ceiling provided a flexibility in shipbuilding, enabling her to maintain the potential, should she so wish. Now, under the limitations imposed, many leading RN warships had to be scrapped, including the majority of Dreadnoughts (Professor Morison gives the number of 20, including 6 battlecruisers),which were caught within the twenty year age limit allowed by the Treaty, and other ships were stopped at construction or design stage (including 4 super Hood battlecruisers) – a costly business with disastrous long term consequences. Veteran ships apart, the USA scrapped only 4 Dreadnoughts and halted the building of 7 battleships and 4 battlecruisers. Moreover the British, far ahead with successful trials of aircraft flying on and off ships and with the construction of fleet aircraft carriers – 2 built and 2 under construction – could not avail themselves of the 'let out' clause to convert battleships or battlecruisers due to be scrapped into aircraft carriers. The USA and Japanese, on the other hand, who each had only one carrier under construction, took advantage of this opportunity. The Americans chose two battlecruisers, the Lexington and Saratoga, which actually made a total over the allowed limit. and the Japanese chose one battleship and one battlecruiser. The British, with their available tonnage already almost absorbed by their existing carriers, could only convert 2 cruisers armoured on light cruiser lines, the Glorious and the Courageous, which left them 20,000 tons under the limit. These two carriers both met the same sad end in the first nine months of war.

The Treaty of Washington was modified in 1930 by that of London – ratified by Britain, the Commonwealth, USA and Japan – and for the next twelve years the British juggled with numbers and tonnage to achieve the best balance within Treaty limitations and financial restraints for each ship and class.

France and Italy stood aside from the 1930 Treaty, although – followed later by Germany – they ratified the Part IV Humanitarian provisions. For effective battle performance the Royal Navy wanted speed, manoeuvrability, powerful gunnery and strong armour and it is claimed that this was best achieved in the design and construction of the Hood, one of three battlecruisers, a magnificent ship with 15 inch guns, 12 inch armour and a speed of 31 knots. However, she lacked sufficient flash barriers between gun turrets and magazines to withstand the one lucky shell from the Bismark, which penetrated a magazine, causing her to blow up and sink in three or four minutes with only three survivors, although the precise details of her end were never exactly established. It was for this reason, and because Beatty's battlecruisers at Jutland had been unable to defeat an inferior force, that Churchill preferred fast battleships to more battlecruisers. The Treaty, however, limited battleships to 35,000 tons, and therefore the Nelson and Rodney, built at this time and carrying 16 inch guns, with powerful 'all or nothing' armour in US style, had many economies made aft and had to cut down on boilers to save weight. Thus, with a speed of only 23 knots, they were far too slow to meet the Japanese equivalent on equal terms in World War II. While the Japanese evaded the Treaty in the construction of their light cruisers, British cruisers built at this time were so lightly armoured as to be nicknamed 'Tin-clad'. The Treaty of London did not restrict fleet tonnage, but defined limitations within class, including cruisers. When the Treaties expired, the British, whose shipbuilding programme was tailored to them, tried in 1936 to gain agreement for a further Treaty of London, but the Japanese refused to sign and denounced the previous Treaties, building ships at speed, taking the tonnage of some battleships to 64,000 tons. Although the UK, Commonwealth, USA and France ratified this 1936 Treaty, with Italy acceding in 1938, by 1939 Britain was also increasing armour and engine power and building more heavily armoured cruisers. A disturbing provision in the London Treaty was the restriction of guns to 14-inch, which meant the battleship King George V was outgunned by the Bismark in 1940. German ships were theoretically still limited by the Treaty of Versailles, which they repudiated in 1935, negotiating an Anglo-German agreement and then exceeding all restrictions on tonnage by 35 percent on battleships and 50 percent on heavy cruisers. Their naval time scale, however, was for war in 1944.

As well as limiting the fire power of surface ships, which – aided by radar and spotter vehicles – could be used in naval battles, to pound shore installations and defend beachheads, the Treaties of Washington and London addressed the problem of underwater weapons and vessels. Mines had first been used in the Crimea, but it was not until World War I, when they prevented British ships from penetrating the Dardanelles Strait and caused landings to be re-located on the Gallipoli peninsula, that their deadly effect was fully realised. By World War II they were making an increasingly dangerous contribution to all sea operations. Activated by contact or by magnetic and acoustic ship signatures, their distribution over the waters of the world brought peril to merchant and naval ships alike. All attempts to outlaw their use against civilian targets were abortive, because of the indiscriminate nature of the weapon.

'It goes without saying', said the Germans in 1939, 'that effective... fighting methods will never fail to be employed merely because some international regulations are opposed to them'. In World War II the Germans laid defensive fields in the Heligoland Bight, the Baltic and later round all West European shores and ports. They mined British coastal waters and approaches to ports, using aircraft, submarines and surface ships (the latter sometimes disguised as neutrals). They also mined the Suez Canal, the strategic channels and harbour entrances of the Mediterranean, New Zealand and Australian waters, the Cape of Good Hope, the Barents Sea and other areas. To act as minesweepers the British formed a fleet of fishing vessels, numbering 1057 by September 1943. Manned by RNR and RN patrol services, these trawlers and drifters swept coastal waters, accompanied convoys and cleared shipping channels for amphibious forces. Having accounted for 1000 mines for the loss of 173 vessels, they were joined and slowly replaced by purpose built motor minesweepers. For their part the British created a defensive barrage at Dover and one running up the east coast to Scapa Flow, as well as mining the Narrows, the entrance to the Irish Sea and setting a line across from Cornwall to the border of France and Spain. Further afield they mined such strategic areas as the approaches to Aden and laid an offensive barrier in the Heligoland Bight and mine fields in the Baltic. The World War I defensive line across the North Sea was not thought cost effective and, although mines were laid from Iceland through the Faroes to the Western Isles, this was no more successful. Depending in 1939 mainly on converted warships and ferries, manned by RN, RNR and RNVR personnel, by 1943 British minelaying was mostly under-taken by aircraft, operating at increasingly high levels and using radar. Mines took a much larger share of Allied shipping to the bottom than lay people realise, while losses to German shipping from mines laid by British aeroplanes were double those lost from bombing at less cost to aircraft. The US naval historian points out that in Normandy the Germans far exceeded the Japanese in laying devices unimaginable in their horror, scattered on the beaches and the shore line, although this does not evaluate the devices which might have met the Americans on the Japanese mainland.

The greatest underwater threat came, however, from the submarine and torpedo. The latter, now launched from the air as well as from the surface and underwater, was developed for the British by Whitehead's Torpedo Company from the Austrian prototype of 1864. It was originally fired from the torpedo boat, which little craft were built everywhere in large numbers before World War I and at Jutland instilled awe out of proportion to their size. To cope with their threat the torpedo boat destroyer was designed and built, which, growing in size and sophistication, became the modern destroyer of today. Whereas by World War II the MTB and torpedo-firing German E boat, while successful in sinking certain targets, could not be said to have influenced the outcome of fleet battles, torpedoes fired from destroyers were, on a number of occasions extremely effective. Particularly formidable was the 'submerged torpedo boat' or submarine. This instrument of death had been first invented by Robert Fulton in 1800, when the First Sea Lord, Lord St. Vincent prophesied that the

Younger Pitt would be, 'The greatest fool that ever existed to encourage a mode of warfare which those who commanded the sea did not want, and which, if successful, would deprive them of it'. The submarine ran counter to the development of Humanitarian Law at Sea, started by the Declaration of Paris in 1856 – a Treaty signed by 26 nations and the German and Italian states – outlawing privateering and defining contraband. Like Pitt the French originally thought the idea of a submarine barbarous. After the Prussians tried it and were wrecked, the Americans sank a warship with it in the Civil War, the submarine blowing up also. Later Turkish and Russian experiments ended also in loss. Then the French carried out successful tests at the turn of the century and, with the Americans again in the van, owing to the lack of support for a British inventor, by 1914 the British had 23 of these underwater craft, compared with Germany's 21. Once the submarine was accepted as an additional arm of naval warfare, attempts to restrict its activities against merchant shipping were continuous. The world reacted with surprise and horror to the German U-boat campaign in World War I – feelings afterwards reflected in the language of the relevant part of the Treaty of Washington in 1922. 'The signatory powers recognize the impossibility of using submarines as commerce destroyers without violating, as they were violated in the recent war of 1914-1918, the requirements universally accepted by civilized nations for the protection of the lives of neutrals and non-combatants, and to the end that the prohibition of the use of submarines as commerce destroyers shall be universally accepted as a part of the law of nations, they now accept that prohibition as henceforth binding as between themselves and they invite all other nations to adhere thereto'. A submarine commander, who did not order a merchant vessel to submit to search and who destroyed it without placing crew and passengers in safety would be liable to trial and punishment. The Japanese signed and ratified this Convention, while the Germans signed and ratified Part IV of the 1930 Convention of London in 1937, which added the phrase, 'Except in cases of persistent refusal to stop on being duly summoned or of active resistance'. In that year the British Naval Staff therefore reported to the Shipping Defence Advisory Committee, 'The submarine should never again be able to present us with the problems we were faced with in 1917'.

Thus, although in 1939 Britain's submarine fleet numbered 56, this reliance on German promises, combined with complacency and shortage of funds led to the Germans having the most effective anti-submarine airborne depth charges and wireless interception, which, together with the reading of British cyphers, forced RN submarines to withdraw from the Heligoland Bight in 1939. When Norway was invaded they returned in company with the French, but high losses continued in the North Sea and Bay of Biscay, demonstrating submarine vulnerability when operating against a well armed and trained enemy. The British, upholding the terms of the treaties, used their fleet mainly against warships, where vulnerability was at its highest, and the Japanese, British trained, mostly did likewise, although their barbarities exceeded those of their Axis Allies, when operating with or without U-boats against merchant shipping in the East. While on blockade RN submarines were restricted in the same way as surface ships by 'Stop and search' regulations and it was not until the afternoon of the day the Germans invaded Norway that these were removed in certain areas in the Atlantic and North Sea. Again, when Italy entered the war, the same regulations came into force and Admiral Cunningham lost one third of his submarines in 10 days, although it is only fair to add that some were to mines and Italian losses were higher. It was not until September 1940 that aircraft were allowed to sink merchant ships with torpedoes and not until February 1941 that the British issued 'Sink on Sight' orders even against Axis military ships bound for North Africa. Within months Rommel's supplies were drastically cut and escape finally denied to Axis forces. In convoy defence the performance of the submarines was disappointing. As well as interfering with the work of surface escorts the number of U-boats sunk by them was below expectations, so that, although employed in support groups in the Barents Sea and as a distant screen in the restricted waters of the Mediterranean, they did not make a significant contribution in the Atlantic. It was therefore decided that, reconnaissance aside, submarines should be used mainly for offensive patrols, blockade, the cutting of enemy supply lines and support of amphibious landings. Submarines were used, for instance, off Brest to blockade into port the German battlecruisers. Employed on reconnaissance before all amphibious landings – both far out to intercept enemy naval forces and inshore to place markers on assault beaches and identify lowering positions – their stealth and freedom of movement made them excellent vehicles for intelligence and communication. In Anson's day it had been special frigates of the 4th rate used for 'cruising', who performed this task and now satellites play an important role. These will not, however, be able to perform the submarine's other functions – liaising with, landing or taking off friendly forces on alien shores, a task undertaken by British submarines in North Africa in 1942. The value and vulnerability of the submarine during naval actions is illustrated by the Battle of the Philippine Sea, during US landings on the Marianas in 1943. American submarines conveyed intelligence on the direction of the Japanese fleet, sank three destroyers and two oilers in preliminary engagements, while in the battle itself they destroyed two Japanese aircraft carriers. Nevertheless in the same period 17 Japanese submarines were destroyed by properly equipped and trained US escort destroyers.

Meanwhile in the inter-war period the ship-borne aircraft was giving back to fleets the mobility and strike power lost in the naval battles of World War I, with the carrier destined to become the 'majestic flagship' of modern navies and the auxiliary carrier playing an understudy role. As so often the British were the leaders, but unfortunately, while the USA and Japan forged ahead, development of aviation in the Royal Navy came almost to a halt between the World Wars because of shortage of funds and the government's decision to transfer control and training of the Fleet Air Arm to the new Air Ministry. The Royal Navy's international lead in naval aviation was therefore lost and by the time command was returned to the Admiralty in 1937 it was too late to develop the required specialist maritime aircraft. 'It is heartbreaking to count the losses that might have been avoided if the navy had entered (World War II) with a sufficiency of aircraft carriers and the aircraft and crews to put in them'. Thus the USA and Japan, whose carriers in 1921 were only under construction, caught up and then surpassed the British, developing maritime aircraft under naval control, while RAF Bomber Command remained convinced that they could protect naval and merchant ships and that there would be no need for aircraft carriers to perform this role. In the event, air support for coastal convoys came under Fighter Command and further out shipping lanes under Coastal Command, which – unable anyway to reach across the Atlantic – was so short of aeroplanes that in 1942 Admiral Tovey, C-in-C Home Fleet, urged the Board of Admiralty to consider resigning en bloc if reinforcements could not be sent. (Naval criticism of resources diverted to Bomber Command for the bombing of German towns continued until the end of the war.) Meanwhile the Admiralty, having been forced to accept the loss of control over its aircraft and pilots until two years before the war, was reluctant to abandon the tried combination of air reconnaissance and naval gunnery. It seriously under-estimated not only the dangers of dive bombing and the aeroplane's role in convoy and warship defence, but also its strategic importance in naval battles, amphibious operations and attacks on enemy fleets in harbour, such as that by Swordfish on the Italian fleet in Taranto. Had World War I statistics been more carefully studied they would have shown that of merchant ships sunk in convoys in 1917 only 2 percent were sunk when air and sea escort were both present. This under-estimation of the carrier's role seems also to have been accompanied by an under-estimation of its vulnerability, for whether on patrol or accompanying convoys or battle fleets, the carrier required for its protection an effective destroyer screen and intelligence of enemy movements.

In 1939, in comparison with the US Navy's 1000 aircraft and Japan's 411, the Fleet Air Arm had only 159 aeroplanes, of which the performance of the majority was far from adequate. When the dual purpose Blackburn Skua was withdrawn, because of its failure to fulfil either role adequately, it was replaced as a fighter by maritime conversions of the Hurricane and Spitfire, but Britain continued without a properly effective dive bomber throughout the war and had to rely predominantly on the Americans (in 1945 60 percent of FAA dive bombers were American, compared with just under 50 percent of the 1336 aircraft of all types). The Japanese developed a dive bomber in 1934 and a maritime attack aircraft in 1937. Having in that year witnessed the horror of the Japanese dive bombing of Nanking, the British could perhaps be excused for showing a reluctance to develop such a vehicle of mass murder, leaving the pilot in no doubt as to the agonies he had inflicted. Less understandable, however, was the lack of a higher standard of training for the alternative form of maritime air attack, the complex launching of the aerial torpedo, peacetime tests for which were demonstrated with profuse numbers of aeroplanes – impossible to match in war. The USA used both torpedo aircraft and dive bombers in the Pacific, but they also were behind the Japanese in the development of maritime aircraft, for they did not possess an effective dive bomber until 1940, nor a fighter superior to that of the Japanese until 1943. In that year at the Battle of the Philippine Sea this modern fighter and new mode of ship defence to air attack gave them victory in the greatest carrier battle of the war. Not only had they twice as many aircraft as the Japanese, flown by pilots with a two year training, compared with Japanese replacement crews trained for only a quarter of the time, but they also had three times as many destroyers, squadrons of which, fitted with new fighter detector units, were deployed far out as an intercepting screen against attacking aircraft. One third of Japanese planes were lost in the first strike; in the second three quarters; in the third the pilots failed to find their target and in the fourth only 9 out of 82 aeroplanes survived. With 480 planes lost and 3 carriers sunk (2 to submarines) the Japanese Navy never recovered. The number of fleet carriers required for victory was formidable. By 1945 the British had 65 fleet and auxiliary carriers, while the USA had 17 fleet carriers, 10 light carriers and the balance of their 110 wartime built auxiliary carriers, 38 of which were sent to the UK.

The missile has recently added yet another dimension to sea battles. The story of the Falklands and the lessons drawn from it are told in the next chapter on amphibious operations, but many of the lessons concerning missiles were repeated in the Gulf, where this time the Allied Navies' amphibious role was ruse and support and where RN minesweepers had to be used to allow USN shore bombardment. Here 'The role of shore bombardment was given a new dimension by the sea-launched conventionally headed missile', while the use of the anti-missile missile emphasised again the traditional sequence in defence procurement, first the invention, then the antidote. A third lesson, learnt in both campaigns was, 'The success, admittedly against relatively weak opposition, of British weapons, some of them dismissed as toys by the too knowing', while the fourth was the use by the Royal Navy of helicopters to launch anti-ship missiles. Experience in ship defence against air attack in the Falklands showed that there is still a need for close range guns, such as the Bofors, as a back up to missiles, which depend on radar, satellites and computers and may suffer from saturation as well as from malfunction. The impact of the missile on any future sea battle will clearly be formidable and, so swift is the present advance in technology, that predictions about new weapons are out of date before they are made. It is for the experts only to predict, but both campaigns again demonstrated the continuity of basic naval strategy and tactics, as offensive and defensive inventions struggle to remain in balance.

While over the last centuries these developments in naval ships, aircraft and weapons were influencing battle tactics, so they also affected the nature of blockade, which has alternated between close and open, depending on the ships and weapons employed. Thus in 1914 Germany hoped Britain would impose a close blockade because there were submarines, mines and torpedo boats lying in wait for her on the hostile shore. In 1940, with German landings planned on the south coast, Churchill insisted that 40 watching destroyers were kept in the Channel in an open blockade, (rather than send more to the Western Approaches as convoy escorts – 'a choice between starvation and invasion'),while the RAF imposed a close blockade on transports assembling in enemy ports, trying at the same time to destroy them with bombs in the harbours. Here pilots met a furious fusilade, similar – in relation to the times –

to that which, three centuries earlier, had deterred Francis Drake, when, having burnt and shot up the first Spanish Armada in Cadiz, he drew back from launching another attack on ships protected by Lisbon's powerful harbour forts. Over the ensuing centuries the challenge of ever increasing port security was met by the British with a flexible three pronged strategy: either to close blockade the enemy fleet and transports into port, or to lie out from shore in an open blockade, ready to sink them if they ventured to escape or to mount raids of harassment upon enemy docks and ports to destroy ships, harbour installations and morale. Often, as now, they combined more than one of these tactics. During the eighteenth century Anson made the double claim that he would 'Keep the French in port and give them battle if they come out', while Hawke, having allowed the French to escape in a gale from Toulon during the Seven Years War, followed them to Quiberon Bay, where he swept in, 'In a rising gale under top gallant sails in headlong pursuit', a magnificent piece of seamanship rewarded not only with the destruction of the French fleet, but by historians' claims that he had invented the open blockade.

As ships became faster and ports more fiercely defended, the open blockade was more in favour. In the Revolutionary War and at the start of the Napoleonic War the primary aim of the blockade was to prevent invasion. By adopting the open blockade, Howe's chance encounter with the French led to victory at the Glorious First of June, while Jervis, after he was driven from the Mediterranean, imposed a loose blockade on Cadiz, which led to his victory at Cape St. Vincent. During the Napoleonic War Lord St. Vincent (as Jervis became), Admiral Cornwallis and Lord Nelson were all masters of the art. The first two lay before Brest and the entrance to the Channel, while Nelson at Toulon employed duplicity so effectively that historians have claimed his blockade was close, when he himself described it as open and said he was 'enticing the enemy to come out'. In the days of sail the gruelling routine of blockade required very high standards of leadership, which the Royal Navy had in abundance, for it broke many officers and men. Ships had to stand to in gales, cruise incessantly with crews constantly on watch in high winds, darkness or fog, while the need to revictual, clean off and repaint ships' bottoms necessitated stealthy returns to home port, where ships had to be heeled over or taken out of the water. This brief return home, later to be accepted under International Law as not lifting the blockade, could only be undertaken in foul weather when there was little danger of the enemy putting to sea, and every device was used, including sending signals to non existent ships, to convince the enemy of the squadron's feigned and continuing presence.

The setting up of an open blockade requires sufficient ships to challenge merchant shipping either at focal points on the sea lanes or lying off the approaches to an enemy port. After Trafalgar, the French had to rely on privateers, aided by Danes and Norwegians in small boats, to mount their Continental Blockade, which was imposed by soldiers at the ports, the primary aim being to bankrupt British exporters. The British answered the Berlin Decrees of 1806 – outlawing British goods – by Orders in Council, forbidding direct trade with Napoleon. In order to defend their shipping lanes and deny bases to the enemy, they captured islands all round the world, which enabled them to police the seas. At the same time Britain enforced her open blockade by insisting upon rights of search and putting pressure on the French with raids on enemy occupied coasts, followed by a full scale invasion on the Spanish Peninsular. British strategy was so successful that French financial houses began to fail and Napoleon had to stop burning British imports and allow the export of French wines to the UK. Without Russian participation he realised his blockade of Britain was doomed and, when the Czar withdrew, Napoleon set out on his march to Moscow in June 1812, knowing that the Royal Navy was now under threat, owing to the US declaration of war one week previously. Exasperated by interference with neutral shipping, and unable to use the fiction of 'broken voyage' to neutralise her trade with France, the USA had prohibited all trade with belligerents in 1809. Although, when this was lifted France had reciprocated, Britain continued with her rights of search under Orders in Council and lifted them too late to prevent the USA from joining the conflict. Britain now needed two Navies – one each side of the Atlantic – and only because Napoleon's Russian expedition failed could she move ships from Europe to properly blockade America. It seemed that the Royal Navy had met its match, for the US ships, mostly manned by privateers, outgunned and outstripped the British in almost every encounter, except in that between HMS Shannon and the USS Chesapeake in which Captain Broke achieved a notable victory. The expertise of the British and their tactic of flexible response soon, however, began to pay dividends and, in a raid of harassment and great effrontery, the Royal Navy sailed up the Patuxent River and set light to the White House and other government buildings in Washington. Slowly US commerce was worn down and exports fell. Britain emerged victorious and saved the world from dictatorship, but her blockade had endangered friendships and inspired the jealousy of nations, a lesson she did not forget and one which was to affect her position in the years to come.

Half a century later real attempts were made during the Crimean War to secure international agreement for the establishment of Rules, covering the right to 'Stop and Search' during blockade. The Declaration of Paris of 1856 said that, 'Blockades in order to be binding must be effective' and only contraband of war, carrying with it a presumption of guilt could be seized from neutral ships. Fifty three years later the unratified Treaty of London defined contraband as armaments, equipment, uniforms and any apparatus for manufacturing arms, while conditional contraband, requiring proof, was defined as anything which might be of use to naval or military forces and might prolong their resistance, including food. When in World War I Britain imposed a blockade on Germany and Austria, which brought privations to the protagonists in Europe, she kept neutral opinion this time on her side by an unobtrusive policy of 'Stop and search', which she did not enforce rigorously until the USA entered the war. In World War II the same pattern of contraband control points was followed – in Orkney, the Downs, Gibraltar, Haifa, Malta and Aden. In six weeks in 1939 338,000 tons of contraband were taken by three squadrons – a Channel Force at Portland, one in the Humber and the Northern

Patrol (which again, as in World War I was composed of old cruisers and AMCs, and covered the exits from the Atlantic). German coastal convoys were also attacked at night with limited success by small motor vessels, of which Southern Command had 300. Several times in both wars Britain relaxed her blockade in deference to neutral wishes. The blockade requiring the greatest tact was that imposed on French ports by Admiral Somerville in Gibraltar, a man with many French and Spanish contacts, who said that reactions to the Spanish blockade depended greatly on the Admiral in charge, fortunately a man known to him. During 1941 14 out of 32 Axis merchant ships crossing the Atlantic were intercepted and from April of that year to May 1942 only 4 out of 15 ships sailing from Japan to Germany got through. After that, with Allied counter measures in place, air and sea patrols working together spotted almost all ships running the blockade and brought them in. German attempts to ship cargo from the Far East therefore stopped in January 1944. By then the block-ade was virtually total.

Rigorous enforcement of a blockade can lead, however, to wider conflict. In 1940 there was a glaring gap in the Allied blockade of Germany and this led to the first amphibious operation of the war. Swedish iron ore was being run down Norwegian coastal waters to Germany. The British knew the trade must stop, but all requests to Norway having been turned down, they could not see how this could be done without precipitating a crisis. When the Admiralty sought permission to mine the waters the Foreign Office prevented it, but on April 5th 1940 permission was at last granted. It gave the Germans the excuse they were awaiting and on the 8th and 9th they launched the invasion of Norway – already fully prepared. As in Belgium and Holland, the Germans struck suddenly, without declaration of war, so that Britain and France had to go unprepared and at great speed to Norway's support. Planning was haphaz-ard; ships were carelessly loaded; there were reports of guns on one ship ammunition on another; transport liners lay at anchor with sailing orders delayed daily. By the time the Allies arrived in Norway the Germans had captured the airfields with catastrophic results. This blockade, imposed for unavoidable reasons if victory was to be won, precipitated a serious chain of circumstances, and led to the most disastrous amphibious operation to try and bring aid to a beleaguered and hopelessly outnumbered neutral nation.

CHAPTER XIII

THE ORDERED COMBINATION OF NAVAL, MILITARY AND AIR FORCE
AMPHIBIOUS OPERATIONS

The lessons learnt from the Norwegian debacle became the basis for the final plans by which victory in World War II was won. These lessons and principles were: first that there must be a prepared plan and detailed management for all amphibious landings, covering where and when transports, regiments and battalions were to land and what vehicles, equipment and supplies were to go to which ports and beaches. Second, that the invasion forces must have command of the sea and sufficient command of the air from land or sea based aircraft to bomb installations and defend the beachhead. Third, that gun bombardments from the sea could not be properly employed without command of the air because of the danger to ships. Fourth, that when a landing is planned in which all three services are involved success depends on co-operation between service commanders and one supreme leader taking decisions, if the plan needs to be substantially changed. A Director (later Chief) of Combined Operations was therefore appointed in June 1940. In Norway delays and procrastination had continued even upon disembarkation. Had there not been a delay before Admiral Whitworth's sinking of the German destroyers, crippled in Captain Warburton Lee's attack three days previously, and had troops been put ashore immediately after this second attack instead of waiting three weeks, Narvik might have been taken and North Norway held throughout the war, saving the lives of seamen serving on Russian convoys. The reason for the procrastination about landings was the difference of opinion between the General commanding land forces, who advised caution, and the Admiral, who wanted to land men at once. Eventually, it was the French ski troops who went in first, being the only ones properly equipped.

It has been claimed that it was the Elder Pitt who first saw that combined operations required combined leadership, but this is not so, for, earlier in British history, Drake's successful operations enjoyed unity of command. Drake's genius for speed, surprise, daring and flexibility made him a great leader of men. Ordered to rescue grain ships embargoed in Spanish ports, he not only made lightning attacks on Cadiz and other harbours to release vessels and burn enemy ships, but then, crossing the Atlantic, he sacked Santiago and went on to Cartagena, where, feigning a frontal attack, he took his troops in darkness to a place on the shore out of range of enemy guns and entered the town secretly from there. His expeditions established an English tradition of refusing to be intimidated and his capture of treasure had far reaching economic effects, causing the Bank of Seville to collapse and that of Venice to suffer strain. Nevertheless, despite Drake's genius, his last two amphibious operations foundered on delay and indecision between military and naval commanders, together with lack of judgement by statesmen as to what objectives were justified and attainable.

Two centuries were to go by before the Elder Pitt, endowed with a unique vision for the broader canvas and with Drake's gift for swift and resolute action, returned to office under Newcastle at a time when British morale was at the same low ebb as it was to be later in May 1940, when Churchill became Prime Minister. Everywhere British forces were in retreat, 'I think I can save England', said Pitt, 'and nobody else can'. Anxious to take pressure off his Prussian Allies he planned lightning raids on the French coast. A permanent Marine Corps had been established in 1755 and Marines were landed on Belle Isle off Brittany in 1761. Fortunate to have Anson as First Lord, for both men believed that successful defensive operations should conceal the possibility of attack, he nevertheless had to accept poor military appointments made without his sanction. Thus, although ships and harbours were set ablaze on these expeditions, disagreements and lack of co-ordination between the two services limited and endangered the success of the raids. Nevertheless a great naval tradition was established at this time – the absolute commitment of the Royal Navy to the evacuation of fighting units, one of the greatest strength of British amphibious warfare. At Cherbourg the Navy took on the Army's role of digging lines of entrenchment in order to embark troops and at St. Malo the hail of bullets on the beaches was so intense that Admiral Howe took the first embarkation boat in himself, in case his sailors flinched under fire.

The government learnt from its mistakes and so did the Chief of Staff, Brigadier James Wolfe, a young infantry officer chosen by Pitt (now Prime Minister) to lead the assault on Quebec, together with Admiral Saunders in charge of naval forces. The professional relationship between these two commanders was remarkable. Met in Newfoundland by the report that Admiral Durrell, disobeying commands, had allowed the French ships up the St. Lawrence after the ice melted, thus removing the element of surprise, Saunders navigated his largest men of war right up to the Isle d'Orleans before the Quebec Basin – following a channel which Durrell, with Cook as navigator, had marked with buoys. Popular belief pictures the assault on the Heights of Abraham as central to the campaign, but it was only after three months of trying to bring the French to action by skilful and complicated manoeuvres, landing and re-embarking troops where defences were weakest, that a frontal attack was conceived. Saunders provided vessels as stepping stones for each of these probing actions and, after the military had staged a diversionary bombardment of the city, he took his ships higher up the river so that the French lines could be attacked above Quebec. Wolfe was ill with fever and in his absence his subordinates decided to capitalise on this achievement and attack the city from there, but from his bed Wolfe, who had always withdrawn his men when under heavy fire, recommended a frontal attack, which fortunately the others rejected. Upon recovery, Wolfe in turn rejected his subordinate's plans and decided to scale the Heights. The French had destroyed the only perilous path, so a light raiding party went up first, followed by the main body of soldiers and lastly by the sailors, who hauled up the dismantled cannons by ropes thrown around the trees. (Although the prototype for the dismantling and re-assembly of the gun carriage – a competition feigned annually at the Royal Tournament – stems from the Boer War the tradition for such swift innovation goes back further). All this was achieved in the darkness of early dawn, the boats having floated silently down river without movement of oars on a racing tide, a very difficult landing to achieve. Perhaps it is axiomatic that Montcalm and Wolfe were both keen mathematicians, for the probing nature of the campaign displayed the qualities of imagination, precision and experiment required for this study at its higher levels.

The capture of Quebec set a great tradition for British combined operations to follow and half a century later, after a number of short harassment raids on the French coast during the Revolutionary Wars, at which time the Marines were given the title Royal, one of the greatest amphibious expeditions of all times was launched against Napoleon. All western continental Europe, with the exception of Sweden, had by now bowed the knee to Napoleon, either in defeat or fear. His Empire stretched to the gates of Russia and, in the East, to the captured Dutch colonies of Java and Sumatra, temporarily incorporating Alexandria and casting greedy eyes upon the Turkish Empire. It seemed the whole world would soon lie at his feet. 'Another year. Another deadly blow. Another mighty Empire overthrown. And we are left or shall be left alone. The last that dare to struggle with the Foe'. So it seemed to Wordsworth soon after Trafalgar, but as always with world conquerors it was not to be. Spain and Portugal now threw down the gauntlet and were able, on account of their mountainous terrain and three sided coastline, to wage a successful guerrilla war, supplied by the Royal Navy. In May 1808 the Spaniards rose in Cadiz and other parts of southern Spain in a national uprising and mobbed the British Admiral Cochrane in the streets to show their gratitude for his aid. Two British armies were successively landed on the peninsula; the first under Sir Arthur Wellesley drove the French out of Portugal, but the disembarkation of the second under Sir John Moore co-incided with Napoleon's arrival in Spain with a force five times larger. Retreating with starving, dying men over the mountains to Corunna, Moore was told the Royal Navy was delayed by bad weather, a delay of four days which cost him his life, sacrificed under French fire to ensure the safe embarkation of his troops. Valuable time had, however, been won for the guerrillas, who were not only provided with supplies by the Royal Navy but supported by actions more akin to those of today's Royal Marine Commandos – blowing bridges and trekking over mountains with ammunition and food.

In spite of its support for his campaign, and for the guerrillas, Wellington was critical of the Royal Navy, perhaps on account of the sacrifice of Sir John Moore's life and the delay of those four critical days. Yet it was sea power that had given his campaigns their incredible mobility, from the lines of Torres Vedras in Portugal, constructed after his second landing, to his final brilliant victory at Vittoria in the north. The Admiralty, while acknowledging his outstanding military genius, commented that he had little understanding of maritime matters and expected ships to lie at anchor in gales with insufficient shelter. During the next hundred and thirty years the Royal Navy had only limited opportunity in amphibious operations to retrieve any lost reputation for time keeping, real or imaginary, for although the Crimean War neutralised

Russian naval power in the Black Sea the campaign at Sebastopol was bogged down by mud and ineptitude, while that of Gallipoli in World War I was scarred by failure and seemingly useless sacrifice. Although the first landing at Sebastopol in 1854 on the northern side of the city were uncontested, delays and indecision soon set in, with commanders deciding to sail round from established northern positions to better harbours on the southern side, thus losing the combined advantage of time and surprise. Likewise at Gallipoli the enforced choice of unsatisfactory terrain, the administrative muddle and insufficient attention to detail among the military were again repeated, and here even the drinking water was not in plentiful supply. The survivors, particularly the young sixteen year old midshipmen, who took the heroic Anzacs into shore under a hail of bullets, with many boats losing their crew and soldiers almost before they grounded, were able to draw upon their experiences when they became flag officers in World War II and avoid the tragic error of allowing such unnecessary and terrible loss of life. One such was Admiral Sir Aubrey Mansergh, who, decorated as a midshipman at Gallipoli, served with US forces in the Second Solomons Campaign in World War II.

Thus, in 1942 and 1943, Churchill's hesitancy to accede to Russian and US pressure and land invasion forces on Normandy before 1944 was fully shared by British Chiefs of Staff, who did not wish to back an enterprise, the success of which must be in doubt. They preferred instead first to follow the historic pattern of flexible response and harassment raids to support their blockade and test out German defences, and then to create a tightening ring round Germany, before striking with invasion forces across the Channel. The first of these raids, on St. Nazaire in March 1942, also had the objective of putting out of action the biggest dry dock in the world, repair yard for convoy raiders. Over half the 621 men involved were RN personnel and, since St. Nazaire was one of the most heavily defended bases in Europe, one quarter of the total were killed and many more taken prisoner. The Campbeltown, an old Lease Lend destroyer, steamed across the Channel full of explosives and escorted by 2 destroyers, an MTB, MGB and flotilla of motor launches carrying Commandos. With the force floodlit and the full fury of the guns let loose, helmsman after helmsman were killed at the wheel of the Campbeltown, yet she rammed the caisson only four minutes late, while the Commandos stepped from their launches at almost point blank range. Around them boats were sinking and burning, and no fewer than 14 out of the 18 landing craft were lost. Yet all objectives were achieved; pumping stations, winding houses and lock gates were destroyed by the Commandos' explosives, leaving installations flooded, while the Campbeltown's cargo not being found she exploded after the appointed hour and blew the dry dock apart.

Then in August, in order to reduce pressure on the Russians, came the disastrous raid on Dieppe, chosen on account of docks, radar station and nearby airfield, where it was hoped to destroy large numbers of enemy aircraft on the ground. It was a frontal assault with wings, but there were high cliffs, narrow beaches and a heavily defended town. The Navy was uneasy – 'Centuries of experience and many failures had taught the Royal Navy the dangers of assault from the sea against intact defence works manned by an alerted garrison'. With over reliance on surprise, which was not achieved, with no previous aerial bombardment and no supporting fire by heavy naval guns the raid has been described as a, 'Sea parallel to the Charge of the Light Brigade'. The Commandos on the western flank were successful but the Germans on the east were alerted and poured murderous fire into the Royal Regiment of Canada. With the assault tanks in the centre stopped by a ditch, sea wall and road blocks, the fate of the infantry behind and of the Fusiliers Mount Royal in reserve was sealed, with rows of soldiers mown down by enemy guns. Under heavy fire the embarkation also was a harrowing experience with men rushing the boats. Casualties were high: 68 percent of the Canadians and 23 percent of the Commandos, while the Navy lost 550 men and the RAF 190. Yet many vital lessons had been learnt: that in any invasion ports must be avoided, that heavy naval gunnery must always support beachheads, that permanent naval assault forces must train with Military and Marines and that the plans of the three services must be co-ordinated beforehand. The only continuing argument was whether the hope of surprise should be sacrificed to the neutralisation of defences by previous aerial bombardment.

In that same month one of the most extraordinary and longest amphibious operations ever fought was being launched by the US Navy and Marines, aided at the outset by an Australian, New Zealand and British squadron commanded by a British Admiral. This was the retaking of the Southern Solomon Islands involving a small number of ground troops, against which Sir Alan Brooke and the British Chiefs of Staff warned, because of the dangers of escalation and sucking in large numbers of ships and aircraft. In their opinion, until the tide turned in the west, the Japanese should be held in a defensive ring, which should not get bogged down by limited offensives. Then, on July 5th 1942 the US Navy reported that the Japanese were building an airfield in the 'mud, slime and jungle' at Guadacanal, a neighbouring island to Tulagi, where they already had a seaplane base. This would act as a toll gate to Australia, possibly leading to another attempted seaborne assault on Port Moresby, and giving the Japanese air support in their overland advance to the port through Papua New Guinea, an advance started on July 21st and halted by the Australians. Because of this intelligence, confirmed by Australian coast watchers who had stayed behind among loyal and friendly islanders, the US Navy was given the go-ahead to recapture Tulagi and to land 16,000 Marines at Guadacanal, later increased to 19,000. Time for training was short and, with the most recent US amphibious operation in 1898, experience limited, so that, after a successful landing, everything went wrong. With the Japanese air base only 550 miles away the 3 US carriers were withdrawn at nightfall, together with supply ships, leaving the Marines with no protection from the air and without unloading vital equipment and supplies. Late inaccurate information from an Australian aircraft led the US Admiral in charge of amphibious forces to think no attack would take place that night. He therefore summoned Admiral Crutchley, the RN commander of the beachhead support group, to his flag ship to discuss the Task Force Admiral's withdrawal of carriers, just as the Japanese were about to strike. Allied naval forces had been at battle stations for 48 hours and were exhausted. They were also divided, one squadron patrolling between Guadacanal and Tulagi, while Crutchley's six cruisers and supporting destroyers were further split into two groups. No battle orders had been issued and, despite hearing gunfire, all were taken by surprise, so that four cruisers and one destroyer were sunk.

The stage was set for defeat, but in a miracle (repeated at the Battle of Leyte) the Japanese Admiral – with the Marines at his mercy – sailed away without firing a shot. The amphibious campaign that followed was one of the most heroic ever fought, with 10 land and 7 naval battles. The US Marines refused to be shifted, using abandoned Japanese equipment to set up a defence perimeter and get the airfield ready in double quick time. With control of the air, the US ruled the waves by day, supplying forces at will, while the Japanese, superior in night fighting, took command at dusk and ran men and naval supplies in the 'Tokyo Express' down the 'slot', the 600 mile waterway dividing the islands, which, with the life expectancy of a US warship being only three night patrols, soon became known as 'Ironbottom Sound'. The Japanese had no radar, but used huge binoculars and searchlights and powerful long-range Lance torpedoes. The US Navy had some radar, but was not fully trained in its use; there was too much talk over the TBS and, because the bridges were glassed-in, the only look-out with the naked eye in the open air was the rating below the bridge. While the Japanese approached in arrow formation, the Americans fought mostly in line ahead, placing themselves at a disadvantage because of the limited freedom between islands. Ships stopped and lines bunched and once, as cruisers wheeled, destroyers came between them and the enemy, with ships firing on each other. Almost always the destroyers were prevented from getting out in front and delivering their torpedoes in time.

By September the position was critical. The courage of the Americans was magnificent. Their errors, according to their official historian, were also in plentiful supply. Loss of the aircraft carrier Wasp now left them with only 2 carriers and 1 under repair compared with the Japanese 4. Because the Japanese controlled all adjacent waters they could bombard the Marines nightly, while US aircraft from Henderson field daily sank Japanese transports and forced them to supplement the transports with destroyers. On October 15th Admiral Nimitz reported, 'We are unable to control the sea in the Guadalcanal area... The situation is not hopeless but it is certainly critical'. On the 24th Roosevelt's message to the fleet recognised the 'limited offensive' had become one the USA could not afford to lose – Guadalcanal must be reinforced. Then came the Battle of Santa Cruz and the loss of another aircraft carrier, with damage inflicted on the last. On October 27th, therefore, came a request from the USA for a British carrier. With the invasion of North Africa taking place in November and every auxiliary carrier from the Atlantic now in the Mediterranean, the Admiralty signalled back, 'What are your dispositions?' But, in spite of advice not taken, no friend asked the British in vain, particularly one whose carrier, paradoxically the Wasp, had been lent to the British in their hour of need. She was one of two, which had twice flown off

Spitfires to Malta, when the island was struggling for its life in the spring of 1942. Nevertheless, Somerville did not wish to lose his only carrier in the Indian Ocean, so one month after the North African landings had been accomplished and in spite of the Sicilian and Italian landings already planned, the Home Fleet sent its only carrier, the modern Victorious, to the Pacific. She sailed on December 19th and Admiral Cunningham released the Formidable from the Mediterranean to take her place on receipt of the Admiralty's laconic signal, 'Two carriers with Force H is a luxury in view of the inactivity of the Italian fleet'.

In fact, the crisis in Guadalcanal came in November and December, simultaneous with the North African landings, but the knowledge that the Victorious was on her way no doubt helped to strengthen morale and her reinforced flight deck was invaluable when Allied Navies were later subjected to Kamikaze attacks. By now the Marines were battle weary and short of supplies and at the naval Battle of Guadacanal 2 US cruisers and 4 destroyers were sunk with all other ships damaged to a Japanese loss of only 1 battleship and 2 destroyers. Nevertheless, the Americans successfully reinforced their Marines and, with aircraft from Henderson field, prevented the Japanese from carrying out a bombardment and landing reinforcements and supplies. The Japanese now reversed priorities, but, although they got 2000 men ashore in the next attempt, they were made to retire without bombardment and, opposed by a US battleship with modern radar screen and accurate gunfire, they lost a battleship and destroyer to 3 US destroyers sunk. From then on they no longer used major warships to dispute these waters over which they had previously exercised night control and could only supply their beleaguered garrison with destroyers and submarines. Although the final Battle of Tassafarango was a naval victory for the Japanese, they had had enough of the contest and withdrew their ground forces. As in Norway, the holding of an adjacent airfield was the key to victory, but the British Chiefs of Staff had been correct in their predictions that a comparatively small amphibious landing might escalate so far in its demand for ships that there was a danger of its affecting the whole global strategy. Nevertheless, with the victories in Stalingrad and North Africa welcome to a weary world, the USA knew that the Japanese had also begun, albeit uncertainly, their long return journey to Japan.

Meanwhile, in the west the invasion of North Africa in November 1942 was the beginning of Germany's return to her heartland. Churchill, as has been said, favoured creating a tightening ring round Germany before striking across the Channel, and with this in view he proposed to Roosevelt in January 1942 that forces should be landed in North Africa, who would link up with the 8th Army and remove the Axis forces from the southern shores of the Mediterranean. The USA, whose Army had never faced the German blitzkrieg, were in favour of establishing a Normandy beachhead in 1942 (Operation Sledgehammer) and following it up with a full scale invasion the following year. In June 1942 Churchill told Roosevelt this was impossible. 'Neither Russian demands for the opening of a Second Front, nor American euphoria, which led to wild underestimation of the magnitude and complexity of the task, could disguise the fact that such an operation could not be mounted before 1943' at the earliest. Roosevelt was convinced – the troops anyway would have been mainly British – and gave decisive orders, unwelcome to the US Chiefs of Staff, that the Mediterranean would be the arena for the first strike against Hitler. On July 25th 1942 the decision to invade North Africa was, therefore, approved by the Combined Chiefs of Staff, and three weeks later General Eisenhower was appointed Allied C-in-C, with Admiral Sir Andrew Cunningham* Allied Naval Commander of the Expeditionary Force and Admiral Sir Bertram Ramsay, of Dunkirk fame, his Deputy.

US and British troops were to land at Algiers and Oran, the naval operations for which were to be entirely British, while a simultaneous assault was to be made on Casablanca by US forces crossing the Atlantic in their own ships and escorted by the US Navy. A British naval squadron was to lie off Casablanca, ready to support the US ships, which, when they crossed the meridian, would come under British naval control. The convoys for Oran and Algiers, sailing from Britain, assembled in the Bay before Gibraltar. In Captain Roskill's words, 'No waters… in the world, not even those which wash the shores of Britain itself, have played a greater part in her history and seen more of her maritime renown than these, where the rolling waves of the Atlantic approach the constricting passage of the Pillars of Hercules.' The organisation for the landings was prodigious, with its maritime forces totalling no less than 340 vessels, of which 170 were warships, a figure only achieved by milking off ships from other theatres, particularly the Home Fleet. Earlier in the autumn the 8th Army had attacked at El Alamein and, although a hastily organised and unsuccessful assault on Tobruk from the sea with meagre naval forces failed to relieve pressure upon them, the 8th Army broke through the German lines just four days before the North African landings on the 7th and 8th of November. The lessons learnt at Dieppe had been applied: secrecy this time had been secured; special groups of naval assault forces had been formed, each of which, with its own landing craft, sailed under a senior naval officer; responsibility for training and planning was co-ordinated by air, land and sea commanders; each section of the assault forces was controlled from a Headquarters Ship, often a liner; submarines marked positions seven miles out from shore, at which assault craft were lowered and from which they plied back and forth to the beachhead. Resistance from the Vichy French varied, some was light, some, particularly that of the French Navy, was determined and brave. All had ceased within three days and, although the Toulon fleet scuttled itself, a number of French ships crossed to the Allies, including one squadron impounded in Alexandria since 1940. It was fortunate that resistance was not heavier, for, with a sea rough, unpredictable and with a 'westerly set', a number of troops landed on the wrong beaches and in the words of their own historian some of the US landings were 'hit or miss' affairs. It was clear that more training and experience were required before the Normandy invasion was attempted.

* Later Lord Cunningham of Hyndehope, Bt, KT, GCB, KCB, CB, DSO.

Admiral Cunningham attributed the success of the amphibious landings to secrecy, planning, efficiency, training, co-operation between services, the base at Gibraltar, the 'determination and adaptability' of the Merchant Navy and the leadership of General Eisenhower; the only vital component not on the list being what Churchill described as his own 'profound contribution'. When, after the last Axis troops had surrendered in May, the Combined Chiefs of Staff met to discuss the next move, the USA again recommended France, but Churchill and the British Chiefs of Staff, anticipating the blood bath in which this could result unless mounted with undeniable superiority and professionalism, preferred to island hop to Sicily. 300,000 ground forces and just under 1000 German aircraft defended the island's mountainous terrain, supported by 375 aircraft at adjoining airfields and by the Italian airforce. Invasion forces made up a larger armada than that which sailed on D day for Normandy, totalling in all 2,500 naval and merchant ships, including landing craft. Allied convoys from the UK again assembled at Gibraltar and met those from Mediterranean ports 50 miles south of Malta, sailing to lowering positions on July 10th, 1943. Other troops sailed across the Narrows from Tunis in shore to shore landing craft. Force H provided a covering fleet of 4 battleships, 2 carriers, and a number of cruisers and destroyers, while a further battleship squadron staged a diversionary ruse. Admiral Ramsay's Eastern Task Force landed 115,000 British and Canadian troops, while US Admiral Hewitt commanded a smaller Western Task Force, which carried 66,000 men. Winds and high seas, together with the dumping of a corpse with false documents ('the man who never was'), secured surprise, and the enemy, who turned in early thinking there could be no invasion that night, woke too late to see forests of masts surrounding the beaches. All the lessons learnt in the previous landing were again put into effect: six flag officers, one for each section, lay off shore in the Headquarters Ships and senior officers of captain's rank sailed with their staffs in the Landing Ships Infantry (LSIs). Dukws were in use here for the first time and, equally at home on land or in shallow water, came to the rescue of landing craft stranded by uncharted sandbanks. Resistance was heaviest in one of the US sectors; and here where the sea was particularly rough, inexperienced crews wrecked 200 landing craft.

Within two days 80,000 men and 8,200 vehicles had been put ashore with minimum casualties and marked success. Here the only weak link in planning and communication was in the air, where, although the enemy were outnumbered by more than three to one and airfields and installations had been previously bombed, no specific object was mentioned in the Air Plan and US troops claimed that Air Chief Marshall Tedder's US Deputy concentrated more on the strategic task of destroying the Luftwaffe than on the tactical role of defending the beachheads. On the other hand the Royal Navy, who suffered more than the US Navy, but who had served off Norway, Dunkirk and Crete, thought it 'little short of miraculous' that ships could lie at anchor so close to enemy airfields with only slight losses. This want of communication and lack of forward thinking also led to tragedy, for, with take-off times for parachute drops and glider planes delayed by bad weather, blowing the aeroplanes far off course, Allied ships, lacking information, fired at unidentified aircraft, bringing many down. Some historians blame these same factors for the escape of Axis forces intact across the Straits to Italy, but this disregards the narrowness of the water (only 5½ miles across), the heavy gun emplacements on either shore, making air and sea activity hazardous, and the physical separation of the Supreme Commander in Algiers from his three C-in-Cs in Malta, Tunis and Sicily.

With Sicily taken, the USA, her eyes turned to New Guinea and the Central Solomons, began to move ships, landing craft and aircraft to the Pacific, urging Britain to do likewise to the Indian Ocean, where they wanted Lord Mountbatten to mount an amphibious assault on the Andaman Islands, while the British Army advanced on Burma and the Chinese moved in the North East. On July 21st 1943 Admiral Cunningham, knowing the British Chiefs of Staff needed sufficient forces in the Mediterranean for the invasion of Italy, countermanded orders issuing from the Washington Conference and told the C-in-C Levant to hold all landing craft pro tem. On the 26th, the Combined Chiefs of Staff ordered General Eisenhower to plan an Allied landing at Salerno, to take place a few days after the main army had crossed the Messina Straits into Italy, assuring him of all the necessary troops, ships and aircraft. The British, however, witnessing the continued movement of ships away from the Mediterranean, began making their own arrangements, and, since it proved impossible to hold the Levant landing craft longer, 10 troopships were brought from the UK to ferry both US and British personnel and Cunningham was told he could keep all his existing vessels and would be sent a further fleet carrier as well as escort carriers, cruisers, destroyers and smaller ships. Mussolini's fall from power made little or no difference to these plans. Hostilities continued for nearly three weeks under his successor and armistice negotiations were then so drawn out that the Germans were able to occupy Italy on a war footing – together with the strategic islands of Rhodes and Leros. It was not until September 11th that the Italian fleet tied up in Malta, 'Scrupulously honouring the arrangements entered into'. Three days previously the Salerno landings had taken place and news of the Armistice was broadcast during their crossing, giving the soldiers a false sense of security and hope.

Salerno lay at the extreme range of shore based one seater fighters operating from Sicily and Eisenhower was not enthusiastic about its choice. No long range fighters were to be released from escort duties over Germany and Air Marshall Tedder was told he could not have US Liberators or Fortress bombers to add weight to the neutralisation of airfields and communications. The British, therefore, devised a two tier system of defence – five escort carriers (one a repair ship with improvised flight deck) were withdrawn from the Atlantic to be placed in-shore under the command of Rear Admiral Vian. They carried 100 Seafires, maritime versions of the Spitfire, to provide continuous cover of 22 aircraft simultaneously over the beachheads, while their protection would come in turn from fleet carriers, lying further out with covering warships. Eisenhower thought the plan too risky and in the event more land based aircraft were provided, so that, although time over the beachhead was restricted to minutes, 32 additional fighters were present at any one time. This was merciful, for the Seafires were no match for the Dorniers. Light winds, combined with the slow speed of the carriers and their own fragile undercarriages, reduced their number after three days of 265 daily sorties to only 26 serviceable out of 100, with 10 lost. After the German counter attack on the sixth day had been repulsed, the escort carriers were withdrawn and the remaining Seafires flew from an impromptu airstrip constructed by the US in their sector.

Uncertainties about the supply of vessels and last minute hitches caused frequent changes of plan and ad hoc orders. Shortage of landing craft restricted the US in the southern sector to only one division, compared with the British two in the north, while the first US troops landed were not the veterans, who followed later from Sicily. Nevertheless a Western Task Force composed of 700 warships, merchant vessels and landing craft successfully ferried the troops into the bay, where flat plains were surrounded by hills divided by narrow valleys, bristling with gun emplacements. The Army again opted for surprise in preference to previous aerial and naval bombardment. This time, however, it was not achieved and the resulting combination of heavy artillery fire from the hills and shortage of landing craft meant that few tanks got ashore the first day, while in the US sector there was congestion on the beaches caused by inexperienced loading. In the north, although the British captured the port of Salerno and Montecorvino airfield, both were rendered unusable owing to constant heavy shelling and air attack. Disaster was not long in coming. On the 13th the Germans counter attacked and drove a two mile wide salient between the exhausted armies. It looked as if the troops, not yet established within a secure beachhead, might be hurled into the sea. With the position critical US General Mark Clark ordered the drawing up of plans to evacuate the American sector and transfer it to the British. In the view of the Royal Navy to evacuate men under heavy fire was suicidal, and Commodore Oliver, in command of the British assault force, appealed to Admiral Cunningham, who sent reinforcements from Tripoli in 3 cruisers, commanded by Rear Admiral Vian. Cunningham also ordered 2 battleships and more destroyers forward to add their weight to the gunnery bombardment of German tanks, with a further 2 capital ships standing by in reserve, while the RAF and Fleet Air Arm flew 1900 sorties in 24 hours. By the 14th the position had sufficiently stabilised for unloading to resume and by the 15th the Germans were halted. Kesselring said in his memoirs that he ordered retreat to avoid further naval bombardment. On the 17th the Allies were back on the offensive and were linking up with the 8th Army coming north, so that Naples was entered on the 1st of October.

Although Salerno was, 'One of the most fiercely and courageously contested beachheads of the war', the time scale was short and at sea only 4 destroyers, a minesweeper, a hospital ship, some landing craft and three merchantmen were lost. Nevertheless the Germans defended sufficiently long to extract their army from South Italy and this adversely affected hopes of a swift capture of Rome, about which objective there was no dispute among the Allies. Divergence arose over whether the Allies should advance into North

Italy, a plan favoured by the British (who remembered the fast trans-continental railway that had successfully run supplies and reinforcements between two German fronts in World War I),and supported by Eisenhower, or be content only with air bases far enough north to reach France and Germany, the view of US Chiefs of Staff. Either way the importance of the Mediterranean as a theatre of war had now diminished. After Salerno the Western Task Force was dissolved and the movement of US ships to the Pacific accelerated, where Japanese suicide resistance had transformed the policy of 'island hopping' into 'leapfrogging', requiring more ships and aircraft. The British also sent three large LSTs to South East Asia and dissolved Force H, which had grown from small beginnings into the vast force necessary to regain control of the Mediterranean: 6 battleships, 2 fleet carriers, 16 cruisers, 4 escort carriers, 2 monitors, 137 fleet and escort destroyers, 24 submarines, 2 HQ ships and 425 minesweepers, landing craft and smaller vessels, as well as 2 French cruisers, 7 destroyers and 9 submarines. 146 of these vessels now joined Somerville's Eastern Fleet which had been depleted to one old battleship, no carriers, 9 cruisers – of which only 4 were modern – and some destroyers and submarines. The remaining ships either rejoined the Home Fleet for the build up for Overlord, now fixed for May 1944, or remained in the Mediterranean, where the Combined Chiefs of Staff agreed that sufficient naval forces should be kept to support the Italian campaign and mount an amphibious landing on Southern France in May, an idea favoured by the Americans. There were also changes of leadership. Eisenhower, who depended for planning upon his C-in-C's and Chiefs of Staff, believing that he who makes plans should carry them out, was to their regret sent to be Supreme Commander of Overlord, while Cunningham, with his gift for resolute action in any crisis, became First Sea Lord, being replaced in the Mediterranean by Admiral John Cunningham

As predicted, the Germans headed for Cassino, 70 miles south of Rome, defended by rivers and mountains, where their firm hold for two months convinced General Alexander and the Chiefs of Staff of the need to land an amphibious force on their flank. Anzio was chosen, forty miles to the north – landings to be simultaneous with a push on the main front. Naval forces, which were giving gunnery support to the main armies from both seaboards, were now so stretched that they could only support one division and General Mark Clark, in command at Cassino, advised caution. The plan was temporarily shelved, to be revived again in January by Churchill, who proposed two divisions, dependent on finding more landing craft. Roosevelt responded by ordering the temporary retention of a number of these vessels earmarked for Overlord, and Churchill brought back all landing craft from South East Asia, where Mountbatten's plans for amphibious operations had so far been turned down. Mountbatten built up his own planning staff in Ceylon, causing some tension in his relationships with Admiral Somerville, who, although responsible to the Admiralty for fleet control, was under Mountbatten's orders for combined operations. With these vessels either back or on their way back, Admiral John Cunningham accepted responsibility for landing and supporting two divisions for 15 days. 'It would be precarious', he said, 'to land and maintain 3 divisions and impossible to do the same for 4'. Little did he know that he would be landing and supporting 7 divisions for 4 months.

The plan was a bold one. After capturing the Alban Hills, twenty miles inland astride the Allied route to Rome, thus cutting a main north/south road and railway, the Allied force could then threaten the rear of the German line or turn north for Rome, which was virtually undefended. Although by January 27th, eight days after the landing, 70,000 men and 237 tanks were ashore, it might have needed a military genius to have seized this opportunity, whereas US General Lucas, in command at Anzio, was old and cautious beyond his years, convinced he had been sent on a suicide mission. He was ordered by General Clark to 'advance to the Alban Hills', but to dig in before moving, leaving offensives to an 'undefined second phase'. The British landed in the north, the US in the south and a small contingent of US Rangers in the middle; the assault was on time, surprise complete and resistance minimal. Training, however, was short and build up of supplies slow. Beaches were heavily mined and the operation was aptly named Shingle, since gradients were so gradual that it was difficult to lower ramps and restrictions had to be placed on loads. The limited number of modern LSTs, fitted to carry assault craft, meant that Dukws had to be carried instead, which were slower. Nevertheless, by January 22nd 36,000 men were ashore with 3000 vehicles. Then the weather broke and ferocious gales closed the British beaches, so that it looked as if the main armour scheduled for the 27th might be delayed. In the centre, although the Rangers captured Anzio, unloading in the port was encumbered by debris and wrecks of landing craft destroyed by bombs and shells. Air support accompanied the convoys, but the plan to protect the beachhead by Spitfires flying from a steel impromptu landing strip was unworkable and tactical air support had to be given by aeroplanes flying from southern airfields. Seeing its opportunity the Luftwaffe changed to new tactics, coming in mainly at dusk and dawn, with planes using the half light to see targets, which were spotlighted with huge flares. Fighter bombers alternated with torpedo aircraft and new radio controlled glider bombs, which penetrated the wires of barrage balloons protecting ships. Judging these to be in danger, the British Admiral advised US Admiral Lowry in command of the Task Force to remove the cruisers at night. Admiral Lowry, 'Who had landed and supplied the troops with faultless efficiency' did not take kindly to the idea, but agreed after losses shot up – 4 destroyers, one well lit hospital ship (out of 3 bombed) going in 24 hours, together with smaller naval and merchant vessels. Although more AA ships arrived at once, the crews of the three ships fitted with electronic equipment to check the glider bombs were insufficiently trained, so that losses and injury continued, including a light cruiser and damage to the Warspite.

Massive air support had been relied upon to isolate the beachhead from advancing reinforcements but this did not take place on the scale expected. With ships under constant threat of air attack, there were also fewer requests for naval gunnery. Consequently by the 25th the Germans had reinforced in strength, so that probing patrols, which General Lucas was criticised for not sending out earlier, received heavy casualties. Almost all the Rangers were casualties and of 12 officers in three battalions of Green Jackets only 4 were alive by the 28th – the day on which Hitler ordered the extermination of the whole force. When the Allied attack started on the following day it was already too late and although British forces numbered 100,000, the Germans probably had more. It is claimed the Americans went forward too slowly but when the British pushed forward the Germans cut off the nose of the salient and took 900 prisoners. The position was critical. On February 2nd Admiral Lowry was replaced by a British Admiral, who made more use of naval gunnery, so that the German tanks were halted the following day. The lull was only temporary. Ten days later the Germans hurled themselves at the US sector, but this time they were halted by massive Allied air support, with very considerable casualties on both sides. On the 23rd General Lucas was replaced by his US Deputy and on March 3rd the German counter attack petered out. The battle then turned into trench warfare – the Navy supplying the beachhead with 3000 tons of supplies daily in February, and 5000 in March. Like Guadalcanal, Anzio had escalated into a contest which neither side could afford to lose. Had it succeeded in its ambitious form it would have shortened the war by months, demonstrating the mobility of amphibious warfare, but the stakes were high. As it was, it created a running sore in the enemy's side, sucking in 8 divisions, a number from France and Germany, thus reducing German strength in Normandy, a valuable contribution. While it is true that landings in the south of France had to be postponed from April to August, nevertheless on the 4th of June the Allies entered Rome, just two days before D day, a tremendous boost to morale and a tribute to the courage and determination of the men on the beachhead who had refused to give up the ground they had taken with such loss of life.

It is, of course, the Normandy landings which have captured the headlines of history and will continue to do so as long as the flame of freedom burns. Within two weeks nearly two thirds of a million men and 100,000 vehicles had been landed by a huge armada of ships and landing craft in what has been described as the 'final triumph of sea power'. Every lesson learnt in the previous landings was now put into effect, for the Allies knew that, had they been hurled back into the sea, the British promise made in 1940 to return and liberate Europe could not have been fulfilled. There would have been no second chance. The focal point for the invasion was a 50 mile beachhead with no port. To overcome this difficulty the British had invented and manufactured 2 Mulberry harbours, one for each sector. These were constructed out of concrete caissons 200 feet long, which, after being towed across the Channel, formed harbours 3½ miles long and stretching one mile out to sea with 3 entrances. It was an amazingly ambitious scheme, for which the roads and jetties of the previous beachheads provided prototypes only in small part. Inside the harbour were two floating roads and a jetty for coasters as well as two other piers for barges and landing craft. Since only 7 deep draught ships could be accommodated within the harbour, half a mile from the outer wall was a floating steel structure, within which more deep water was provided. Blockships were sunk to reinforce the caissons and provide more shore anchorage for smaller vessels. The harbours were the busiest in Europe until the 18th/19th June, when the US Mulberry was wrecked by a huge storm, which left only the breakwater blockships (known as gooseberries) intact, but by that time 314,514 US troops had been landed with 41,000 vehicles and 314,547 British troops, together with 54,000 vehicles.

Airborne landings were made behind the lines before D day. The tragedy of the failed parachute and airborne landings in Sicily was not this time allowed to deter the planners, but the pre-invasion timing eliminated the risk of mistaken identity. 13,000 US paratroopers were dropped the night before at the foot of the Cotentin peninsula and the British 6th Airborne Division was put down east of Caen. Complete air supremacy was established at 30 to 1 – not air superiority at 3 to 1 as in the Mediterranean – with Allied fighters alone numbering 171 squadrons. On the night before D day and again shortly after daylight a savage attack was made on the Luftwaffe and the 'fortress' wall, whose concrete gun emplacements made it the heaviest defended coast line in history. Roads and railways in France, Belgium and Germany were relentlessly bombed, 600 trains being forced to back track and all rail traffic between Paris and the Channel halted. This was not done on anything like the same scale in Italy and the price paid in German ability to reinforce there was high. Now, although the Germans brought in 1000 Luftwaffe planes they could not reinforce with the same lightening rapidity, and by the time the troops arrived the beachheads had been established. Immediately prior to H hour the beaches had also been subjected to a 45 minute bombardment and as the convoys approached the coast this was followed by a further bombardment from the sea by heavy naval guns from 5 battleships, 21 cruisers, 58 destroyers and a monitor ship. According to their official historian US Admiral King was 'tardy', as Admiral Lowry had been at Anzio, in supplying sufficient numbers of bombarding ships and the Royal Navy supplied the lion's share – 49 British ships, 22 US and 13 Commonwealth and Allied, mounting every dimension of gun from 16 to 4 inch and aided, as in Italy, by Spitfires, flying with escorts, spotting targets from the air.

As in previous landings, channels through the minefields were swept by minesweepers, going ahead of the assault convoys and marking channels with buoys, while other minesweepers cleared the assault areas. Here the mines extended right up the beachheads, and beyond the beaches was a casemated wall of concrete and mobile guns, with land mines planted behind them and a coil of barbed wire at the beaches' edge. Again two Naval Task Forces were responsible for the landings. The Eastern Task Force under Rear Admiral Sir Philip Vian landed the British troops, the Western Task Force under US Admiral Kirk landed the US troops. Lowering positions were marked by submarines – this time midgets – and tiny boats kept vigil at the spot. Within Operation Neptune (the naval arm of Overlord), there were 1213 warships, 864 merchant ships, 4126 landing ships and craft and 736 auxiliary vessels – US, British and Commonwealth, Dutch, French, Norwegian and Polish. The greatest danger to the armada came from U-boats, which had by now been fitted with effective schnorkels, making them formidable foes, and from motor torpedo boats, one man chariots and radio controlled explosive boats. In addition to the usual escort forces ten anti-submarine naval support groups were formed, aided by escort carriers and these were supported by 21 squadrons of the RAF. The motor torpedo boats were destroyed in harbour by Bomber Command and the other two ingenious devices failed to penetrate the naval screen protecting the beachhead. A great storm arose the day before, delaying sailing by 24 hours and not fully abating by the time of the landings. This contributed, as in Sicily, to surprise, as did the electronic blinding of the enemy, together with a massive and complex deception plan, unusual in its huge compass. A number of the first assault tanks were amphibious and included vehicles equipped to explode land mines. Also leading the assault were landing craft specially fitted with quick firing artillery and missiles – as well as rocket projectors, previously used at Anzio. All landings were successful, suffering only slight casualties, except on one US beachhead, where there was a strong sea running and heavy resistance, so that a number of landing craft and amphibious tanks were wrecked, including some equipped to clear obstacles. Cohesion was lost and shore obstacles were engulfed by the rising tide, causing further hazards. Nevertheless, despite heavy casualties, all objectives were achieved by nightfall. On the 26th June Cherbourg, the first port was taken; on 9th July Caen fell to the British and in the middle of August the Allies broke out of the beachhead.

Allied supply lines on the drive north and east were not, however, secure and one last and arguably the most heroic amphibious landing in World War II remains to be recounted – that on the island of Walcheren, which was almost a suicide mission for the Royal Navy. On October 5th the Admiralty said that it would not be possible to meet the Army's needs in the advance into the Ruhr without the port of Antwerp. As the British Army swept on north and east the only way of maintaining their supplies was to open the river Scheldt to all shipping, otherwise their lines of supply were long and unacceptably risky. The heavily mined river Scheldt splits into two arms and the West Scheldt narrows and leads to Antwerp. On its way it passes the island of Walcheren, on which stands the port of Flushing, and the promontory of South Beveland – both of which had to be captured to secure its passage. The RAF had breached the dykes surrounding the island of Walcheren, which was attached to South Beveland by a causeway. A three pronged assault was planned: the first across the causeway from South Beveland, the second across the river to Flushing and the third from the sea through the breached dyke, the assault troops for which were Commandos and Royal Marine Commandos. Their landing craft were to be flanked by others equipped with guns and rockets to give supporting fire. The landing at Flushing achieved surprise, but that from the sea took place later after the RAF had carried out attacks on the defences and here there were greater difficulties than at any other landing in the war. Only 7 out of the 27 landing craft were undamaged and very few tanks and fighting vehicles in the main landing force got ashore. The task of the naval crews of the supporting landing craft was to draw the German fire on the principle that, 'German gunners will aim at whoever is shooting at them'. If necessary their craft were to be beached and used as forts, pumping water into their tanks, which could be pumped out again in order to refloat. The naval personnel in these vessels acted with, 'Entire selflessness and devotion to duty', offering themselves as targets to the German fire, steaming on through eight foot waves under a hail of bullets and picking up survivors at point blank range. Many smashed on to the shore but only after supplies were safely unloaded. The RAF carried out an airdrop, but only 90 out of 500 aeroplanes got through safely. It was a tragic sacrifice of young lives and one for which a great debt is owed. The first ship entered the port of Antwerp on November 28th. The official history of the war argues that this sacrifice would not have been necessary if Antwerp had been secured before the headquarters of Admiral Ramsay and General Montgomery became separated. Then it would have been a truly combined operation and the Navy would not have been left to bear the brunt. It is the same argument as that put forward to explain the escape of Axis forces over the Straits of Messina – that until the supply lines of a military operation have been secured the command of all amphibious undertakings should remain combined. It was the judgement that the Elder Pitt had made two hundred years earlier.

In 1982 during the Falklands campaign command remained combined and here many of the difficulties encountered were anticipated by the Armed Services – that without strike aircraft, flying from shore or from conventional carriers, ships would be exposed to great risk if they acted to support ground forces. This risk was compounded by the absence of shipborne early warning aircraft, a capability which was lost when the Naval Gannets were phased out, exposing the destroyer screen to needless danger. David Brown in his history of the campaign emphasises a number of lessons learnt – the value of helicopters to fire missiles and to carry the air early warning radar (with which 3 Sea King helicopters were fitted before the end of the campaign); the vital role of submarines; the need for forward repair and maintenance ships; the important part played by naval missile and gunnery bombardments to support ground forces; the use of trawlers to land special forces; the need for more Bofors and Oerlikons for short range firing, (instead of the machine guns resorted to); the inadequacy of the 4.5 gun against larger calibre guns fired from ships, well protected from anti-ship missiles and only vulnerable to air or underwater attack, and lastly the shortcomings of medium range surface to air missiles against low flying aircraft,(Sea Wolf was the most effective weapon, but it was only fitted on 2 Task Force ships and was still in its infancy and suffering some teething problems). David Brown highlights the excellent performance of the Sea Harrier, without which the operation could not have been undertaken. The numbers tell their own story, for the battle group only had 20 Sea Harriers with no more arriving for three weeks (Keith Speed gives the figure 22 and adds a further 6 and 10 RAF Harriers which presumably arrived after the three week period had passed). The Argentinians had 120 Daggers, Sky Hawks and Super Etendards, the latter firing the Exocets which sank the Sheffield and Atlantic Conveyor. They flew 167 sorties in the first 5 days, 61 of which were turned back and 80 got through to attack. 16 Harriers were in the air in any one hour, 6 were lost, only 2 to enemy action. The success of the campaign, disregarding luck and the weakness of will of many Argentinians to fight, was due to the outstanding courage and expertise of all the Services involved. The problem is that lessons learnt can so easily be misinterpreted by press, public, and politicians. Because of the absence of a proper early warning system the only defence against low flying aircraft, which came in low to avoid the Sea Dart Missile, lay in the radar equipped picket ships (in this case destroyers) which exposed themselves at great risk in order to save the main force, as the US destroyers did at the Battle of the Philippine Sea. The escorts also exposed themselves to great danger in order to support the beachhead and, with insufficient air cover and no room to manoeuvre were sunk or damaged in the same way as they were in Norway. On the first day of the landings only 2 out of 7 ships were undamaged. One sank and only one of the 5 was still able to use its full armament. This is a deliberately extravagant and valiant use of warships and it is noteworthy that it had to be undertaken at a time when naval ships are in far too short supply. Keith Speed wrote shortly after the campaign that had there been more Sea Harriers for combat patrol the risks would have been lessened. As it was the Argentinians were forced to fly lower than the time setting of their bombs allowed, so that many did not explode. Speed also called for phalanx guns to be fitted to aircraft carriers and drew attention to the low melting point of aluminium, lessons immediately heeded.

The problem is that the pennies are too few to go round and the trouble is then exacerbated, as Keith Speed points out, by the 'corporate approach' of the Treasury – one Department saving money by moving the expense on to the account of another, instead of seeing the outlay of public funds in its totality, as was done in previous centuries. Also in a democracy there are more votes for politicians in providing hip replacements within the NHS than there are in providing meaningful defence except in time of war. The Falklands and the Gulf were a great tribute to all three Services for the efficiency that was achieved in spite of the cuts, over which they have no control, and for their outstanding courage. The psychological factor is that in both cases further cuts followed victory and this can be no way in which to reward excellence or provide effective defence for the nation. Together with the need for a proper number of naval ships protected by aircraft the Falklands campaign demonstrated again the great debt owed to the Merchant Navy for the provision of auxiliary ships and trained personnel to man them, but because of the decline in the size of the British merchant fleet a quarter of support ships were foreign (compared with 8 percent flying the British flag in the Gulf). In time of emergency these auxiliary ships include: aircraft and helicopter carriers, troop transports, rescue and hospital ships, minesweepers, drifters for net laying, liberty boats and reconnaissance craft. An island nation, which turns its back on its maritime past, loses not only impetus in manufacturing and earnings in foreign currency to enable it to prosper and so provide naval ships and aircraft for its defence, but also deprives itself of desperately needed auxiliary ships to come to its aid in time of conflict. Despite the dangers to which young men had been sometimes unnecessarily exposed in World War II, it appeared from the debates in Parliament as the armada sailed that these lessons had gone unheeded and that there was an alarming ignorance as to the risks involved.

CHAPTER XIV

A NEGLECTED STORY
SHIPBUILDING BEFORE THE FIRST WORLD WAR

In the eyes and the words of the poets, the oak represented both the hearts of the British sailors and the wood for her sailing ships, yet shipbuilding is a neglected part of British history, without which her maritime story is only half told. In spite of thousands of technical books on the mechanics of construction and individual accounts of particular areas and firms, no properly comprehensive history has been written and public support has been taken for granted. Encyclopaedias devote two or three lines to shipbuilding in principal ports and only now, when British shipbuilding is in danger of extinction, are 'coffee table' books on naval architecture beginning to appear in publication. A ship's grace of line is just as satisfying to the eye as that of great houses, cathedrals and castles and, unlike their terrestrial counterparts, ships 'Must stand upon and traverse the unsteady and unyielding ocean, climbing to the top of waves and pitching into their hollows, rolling violently and enduring storms, groundings and collisions', so that the genius required for their construction makes it infinitely surprising that no leading naval architect is, like William Adam and his two famous sons, a household name. Paintings of ships adorn maritime collections, but an exciting part of British history, profoundly influencing the progress of the British people, is either unrecorded or confined to local history bookshelves. Yet without the science of shipbuilding there would have been no Armada, no voyages of discovery, no age of sail, no Trafalgar, no tea or wool clippers racing each other to China or Australia, no dirty tramp steamers trading in every ocean and in two World Wars no survival of the British people or freedom of the world. The indissoluble partnership of shipowners, shipbuilders, managers and shipwrights provided the sense of purpose, new ideas, commercial strength and fresh horizons, while the close relationship between the naval and merchant fleets, dating from earliest times and cemented by the continuing support of government and parliament enabled Britain to retain a leading place as a maritime nation. The efficiency and very existence of both fleets were dependent upon a flourishing shipbuilding industry, with which they maintained the closest contact. From the age of Drake to that of Cunningham, captain and master handled their magnificent vessels with an intuitive judgement based on the knowledge of what that particular ship was built to do, so that seamanship, engineering and design were combined in expert performance. Unfortunately this close collaboration and support between seafarers, industry and government was increasingly undermined by subsidised foreign competition before and after both World Wars and with its absence has temporarily collapsed, let us pray not permanently, the shipbuilding industry of Great Britain.

The early history of British shipbuilding is bound up in the history of coastal towns and rivers: – Thames and Medway; Portsmouth; the Itchen and Beaulieu Rivers; Southampton; Bristol; Plymouth: Liverpool; Birkenhead; Barrow-on-

Furness, Tyne, Tees and Wear, and of course the Clyde. There were also a number of shipbuilding centres whose early history was never properly recorded, chief among which were some of the east coast Scottish ports from Inverness to Fife. In the days of wood and sail shipbuilding followed the forests, particularly those of oak, the favourite for ship construction. Warships had to withstand shot and remain at sea for months in gales and rough seas, so that only one in six of the oaks in the Royal Forests were fit for use in the Navy. These trees took a hundred years to mature and thus, inland from the Royal Dockyards, they were nurtured and monitored in the Royal Forests – the Forest of Dean, New Forest, Forest of Bere, Alice Holt, Ashdown Forest and others. Hampshire soil bred the best oaks and it was this that brought the shipbuilders to the Beaulieu River beside the New Forest and woods of the Montague family in the seventeenth and eighteenth centuries. Deck beams had to be fastened to the frame or ribs of the ships with right angled knees which could only be found in the junction of the trunk with the main branches, while other parts of the frame had to be cut to a radius requiring very large trees. Smaller parts and junctions were of elm; decks and walls were of beech. While the hulks of wooden ships lasted more than 50 years – the Victory being 40 years old when she fought at Trafalgar – the masts, which were a major task to erect, were of fir, coming predominantly from the Baltic and North America and lasting only ten years, a crucial factor in war. The keels were sheathed for protection, originally in soft wood, then in lead which was so heavy that it was changed to copper; bolts and fastenings were of home produced iron. When in the nineteenth century sail and wood gave way to iron, steel, and steam, new yards opened in the north or moved thither to be near the iron and coal mines, smelting furnaces and steel works – to Lancashire, the Mersey, Tyne, Tees and Wear, and the Clyde.

Little is known of shipbuilding in the Middle Ages beyond a few bare facts, such as that Henry V built ships at Southampton and Edward III at Kings Lynn and Hull, and that ships were built at such centres as Bristol, Chester, Dartmouth, Southampton and the Cinque Ports. In the social history books shipbuilding does not feature alongside the development of agriculture or the villages, the law, or cottage industries. The curtain therefore rises in England on the Thames and Medway at the time of the Tudors, while in Scotland, where ships traded in early days with Europe and the Mediterranean, very little information exists at all on the shipbuilding industry until the eighteenth and nineteenth centuries. Henry VII built ships at Portsmouth – where the Royal Dockyard opened in 1495 – and sometimes the later Tudors continued to build at both Rye and Portsmouth, but on the whole by Henry VIII's reign it was on the Thames, below London Bridge, that most of the shipbuilding for the crown took place. Between 1512 and the present day 5000 ships were built in two Royal Dockyards, Woolwich and Deptford, and in the 150 private yards, only a few of which lay up river between Hammersmith and Chiswick. On a summer evening in the sixteenth century the plip-plop of oars must have been a familiar sound to Londoners, as the monarch was rowed back in sunlight to Hampton Court from Greenwich. The opening lines of Shakespeare's immortal tribute to Cleopatra were no doubt as much inspired by his memories of the

Thames as they were by the history of Ancient Egypt. 'The barge she sat in, like a burnished throne, burnt on the water'. (This connection was perhaps also seen by the industry, for in 1844 an East Indiaman built in a Thames yard was named Cleopatra). Henry VIII watched the construction of his naval ships from Greenwich Palace. John Hawkins, sea captain and later naval Treasurer, chosen by Cecil to redesign Elizabeth's navy, performed his task from Whitehall, and from a house in Deptford Lord Howard of Effingham watched over the fitting out of his fleet that was to defeat the Armada. The efficiency of the Elizabethan Royal Dockyards was one of the most important reasons for victory at the Armada. All Elizabeth's warships were built and fitted out on the Thames and Peter Pett and Matthew Baker were the master shipwrights responsible for constructing 20 new ships and contracting with the Navy's Treasurer to fit out the fleet for a fixed sum. Although employed by the monarch, the Petts – father, two sons and grandsons – had their own private yards as well, as did another Elizabethan master shipwright, Richard Chapman.

The story of the Thames is intertwined with that of the Medway, which, because of its inaccessibility, offered unique facilities as a training ground for the Spanish and Dutch Wars. Elizabeth built most of her ships on the Thames, but Chatham Royal Dockyard began to build in 1586 and Sheerness Royal Dockyard in the following century. There were also eleven private yards on the Medway over the succeeding years, which were engaged in building and repairing, and from this river a number of voyages of discovery set sail in the reigns of Elizabeth and James I. James came from a Scotland well instructed in naval and maritime skills and he built merchant ships which could be used in war, as well as encouraging overseas voyages. Nevertheless, in spite of the arrival in London of Scottish shipwrights and men such as Thomas Penn from the West Country and other important English shipbuilders from the North, the Dutch at this time began to excel over the English in the quality of their ships. Charles I, his eyes always casting towards the continent and Roman Catholicism, only built ten warships in seventeen years and insufficient merchant vessels, so that it fell to Cromwell to rebuild the Navy, which he did mainly at the Royal Dockyards – six ships at Woolwich, four at Chatham, ten at Deptford and three at Portsmouth. This so emptied the national purse that after the Restoration Pepys endeavoured to bring public spending under control and prevent the fraud which always accompanies inadequacy of funding. He estimated it took 305 shipwrights to build one ship but unfortunately left no figure for the number required to refit. When William III arrived from Holland, he re-introduced the Elizabethan tradition of close co-operation between naval and merchant yards. Although he added Plymouth to the Royal Dockyards in 1694, over half the naval vessels launched in his reign were built in private yards. He thus re-imposed upon the Admiralty the need to scrutinise contracts and encouraged both parts of the shipbuilding industry to support each other.

Crowding the banks of the Thames in early days were rope and sail makers, suppliers of pitch and tar and all the other fringe industries that complement the making and fitting out of wooden sailing ships – 1000 blocks of elm were required for the rigging of one large warship for the Royal Navy, many of which continued to be built in Thames yards throughout the eighteenth century. Because they were well managed most of these firms operated at a profit, despite the fixed price contracts insisted upon by Lord Anson, First Lord of the Admiralty during the French wars when inflation trebled. Naval standards were meticulous and Anson's reforms in the Royal Dockyards and those of his successors in administration – Samuel Bentham, William Symonds and Isaac Watts – set the standards of excellence which private yards tried to achieve. A number of mansion houses were built within the yard gates at this time by owners or managers, who sought to identify with their men. Among these were the Johnsons at Blackwall, who, educated at Harrow and friends of Pitt, handed on their yard to other friends of Pitt's, who held a Grand Ball in the Moulding Loft. The Blackwall yard later merged with that at Wells, which was owned by the Duke of Bedford and had as its directors, three brothers – an MP, an Admiral and a picture collector. The close co-operation between the administrators of the naval yards and those of private firms continued in succeeding generations of private engineers. Among the remarkable group which gathered on the Thames a century later were Robert Stephenson from Newcastle, brother of George the famous railway inventor, and John Scott Russell, a graduate of St. Andrews and Glasgow, whose name featured as a leading proposer of the Great Exhibition of 1851. He found time as a shipbuilder to write books on design, demonstrating that speed was improved by hull length and movement of the bow through the water was eased by conformity to wave flow. Then there were the Napier cousins, David and Robert, who founded their own marine engine firms – David on the Thames, Robert at his home in Glasgow – and the brilliant and controversial Isambard Brunel, who designed the screw propelled Great Britain, which was built in Bristol. He also collaborated with Scott Russell on the Great Eastern, the largest merchant ship afloat and layer of the Atlantic cable, as well as on designs for submersible and semi-submersible ships. As wood gave way to iron and sail to steam, the old support industries on the banks of the Thames were replaced by sheds for the construction of marine engines and shops for cutting and rivetting steel plates. The dramatic growth in world trade and the developing importance of London as a port led to the excavation of the London docks and made available the large loop of the river at the Isle of Dogs for further maritime development. This brought more shipbuilders down from Newcastle and the north, one of whom was William Fairbairn, whose tow-vessels had already won fame on the Forth and Clyde Canal and who now put this experience to good use on the Thames, where in 1844 he built the first iron steamer to be classed A 1 by Lloyds, (the first iron ship having been accepted on to the Register seven years previously). What type of ships did these private yards on the Thames build? At the start there had been water ferries for the folk of London, barges for royalty, corporations and the rich, fishing smacks and skiffs, lifeboats and merchant and naval sailing ships. Later there were passenger vessels plying round British shores and across to the continent, East and West Indiamen, mail and packet steamers, naval ships, steam and sail yachts and tea and wool clippers. It was Richard Green of the Thames firm of his name, who, thumping the table after dinner, said of the US clippers, 'By Jove, we'll trump them'.

Thames yards had already faced competition more than a century earlier from other rivers and ports in Britain, for during the age of sail and wood private yards had begun to fan out all along the south coast, following the forests – at Cowes on the Isle of Wight, at Southampton and on the Itchen and Beaulieu Rivers, at Northam, Lymington, Bursildon and Bucklers Hard. A few smaller men o' war were built on the Beaulieu river at the end of the seventeenth century, but it was during the wars with France that shipwrights and builders came down to Bucklers Hard, of whom the most famous was Henry Adams, an Admiralty supervisor, transferred from Deptford in 1744. He built the warship Scorpion, which went with Wolffe to Quebec, and herring busses for the Society of Free British Fishery, formed to protect British fishing from the Dutch. By 1760 he had built 7 Royal Navy vessels – in partnership with a Deptford associate – and a number of East Indiamen. When peace came temporarily he survived because of his firm's diversity and his virtual monopoly on Beaulieu estate timber. When war resumed three of his ships were at Trafalgar, on one of which the news of Nelson's death was written. He died in 1805 aged 92, his son continuing the firm in lesser form until 1840. Adams was one of the most remarkable men in the history of British shipbuilding. If he was hard on his workforce he was, like a number of shipbuilders of the time, harder on himself in their interests, riding to London at the age of 81 to obtain Admiralty contracts. He spied their work in progress from a wide-windowed semi-circular room in the Master Builders House, using a telescope as his eyesight failed. Each workman had a number and could be summoned by the appropriate rings, climbing a rope ladder to the window to receive orders or reprimands. By the end of the French wars the yard at Bucklers Hard had built a total of 43 warships. Meanwhile, yet further west, Bristol, which lost much of its wooden shipbuilding to Liverpool in the eighteenth century, was chosen as the venue for the Royal Navy's first trials of the screw propeller, and once the Royal Navy had accepted the inevitability of the iron ship at the end of the Crimean War Bristol became an increasingly important centre for warship building. The Northam yard on the Itchen started in the seventeenth century (at which time all fitting out work was done in the Royal Dockyards) but most of the yards on the river opened during the Napoleonic Wars – Robert Adams built 5 naval craft at Chapel before going bankrupt in 1807. Southampton was still a small seaside town in 1830, but in the Victorian era it strove to become the Liverpool of the south, with Money Wigram at Northam building ships for P & O, Royal Mail and Union lines, all of whose vessels sailed from the port. William Summers started iron shipbuilding on the Solent in 1836 and then moved to Northam. Oswald and Mordaunt remained in Southampton building steamers, tugs and yachts, becoming the Southampton Naval Iron Works in 1899 and then being taken over by Thorneycroft in 1904.

The demand for space and proximity to iron ore and coal for smelting prompted expansion in the north – in Liverpool, Birkenhead, Barrow-in-

Furness, Tyneside, the Tees and Wear and the Clyde. Each of these centres had been building ships in the eighteenth century and a number had been in the industry longer. Liverpool launched ships in a small way in Elizabethan days, when letters of marque were issued to her captains, and, by the French wars at the end of the eighteenth century, was building an average of 20 ships a year, including 36 warships for the Royal Navy, cargo ships for the West and a few for the East Indies, slave traders (the only vessels exceeding 300 gross tons) and trading steamers, which plied across the Irish Sea. Some Liverpool merchants owned ships in co-operatives, with friends, who had no other shipping connections, joining together in speculative adventures. Liverpool trade, being westwards, was affected by US entry into the Napoleonic Wars and the abolition of slavery, but later the import of cotton for onward transmission to Manchester, trade in palm oil with West Africa and the transport of émigrés west made the port so busy that shipbuilding was driven over the river to Birkenhead, where the first iron merchant ship was built in 1828. Further north, where the Ulverston Canal opened in 1776, steps were taken to develop the port of Barrow to rival Liverpool in the emigrant trade with North America. Ocean-going shipbuilding at Barrow-in-Furness started in the 1860's with the founding of two companies, one of which, Barrow Shipbuilding, launched the second biggest merchant ship afloat at that time. Across on the north east coast Tyneside was building ocean-going ships by the eighteenth century, including four for Captain Cook, while shipbuilding on the Tees flourished in the American War of Independence and on the Wear in the Napoleonic era. Smiths Docks opened in Middlesborough in 1756 and built some of the first East Indiamen. Depending at the outset mainly on whalers and colliers, these north east yards soon expanded into building tugs, ferries, passenger liners, cargo vessels, tankers and warships. Meanwhile over the border on the east coast of Scotland there were flourishing shipbuilding yards in Aberdeen and in many of the Fife and Angus fishing and trading ports, which in the nineteenth century readily adapted from sail and wood to steam and iron. As in Dundee, in Arbroath and Montrose imports of flax and exports of linen caused a growth in shipbuilding, starting in the middle of the eighteenth century. By then these two burghs, like many others in Scotland, traded direct with the Baltic, the continent, the Mediterranean and occasionally with North America. A century later they each owned approximately 100 ships and built wooden ships of up to 800 gross tons. After that, however, when the linen boom came to an end, shipbuilding declined. In Fife, where it depended on the coal trade, shipbuilding converted to iron and steam and continued until quite recently. Across on the west, shipbuilding on Clydeside, which went back to the reign of Charles II, began to expand with the opening of Scotts of Greenock to build fishing smacks in 1711 and the deepening of the river in 1759. Thus Clydeside yards were well placed half a century later to take advantage of William Symington's revolutionary paddle steamer and the screw propeller, both of which were tested on the river. Soon they were building a wide range of vessels, including specialist ships of all kinds: ice breakers, tugs, ferries, overseas river craft, and even, during the Disruption of 1843, floating churches for the Free Church of

Scotland. With their first dry dock completed in 1858, orders were received for larger naval ships, tankers, and passenger and cargo vessels.

While these developments were taking place the Thames and Medway were taking an 'unconscionably long time in dying'. Although in the Napoleonic Wars half the berths in the Royal Dockyards were occupied in building, the Royal Navy still depended to a great extent upon private yards and its close connection with those on the Thames and Medway continued. Until 1860 all the naval ships built on the Thames were for the Royal Navy, but after that date many were exported. The Admiralty was reluctant to change from wood to iron and sail to steam, but once they saw change was inevitable they gave a lead in the new technologies by founding the first Apprenticeship Schools in the country at Chatham and Woolwich. They also blazed a trail by bringing to Chatham the Ship Design Committee of Assistant Master Shipwrights, who had qualified in the new RN School of Naval Architects at Portsmouth. Opening in 1812, it had closed and re-opened in South Kensington as the Royal School, moving to Greenwich in 1874, by when the civilian Institution of Naval Architects had also been founded in London. These developments came just in time to cope with the expansion in shipbuilding and introduction of new technology and ideas following the Crimean War, and, with the French Wars now a thing of the past, Chatham was chosen to build the first iron warship, the Achilles, launched in 1863. Seven years later the Admiralty constructed their first tank for testing models of proposed new designs, based on the inventions of William Froude, the father of applied hydrodynamics, and this was followed by the first commercial tank in 1893, the firm of Yarrow generously providing facilities for all competitors in 1911. 'Skilled workmanship, ' said Lord Wemyss recently, 'is more difficult to supply than plant'. Skills were what Britain then had in abundance and, with Bismarck's Germany replacing Austria as Russia's main ally, smaller nations overseas saw the ocean as their defence against the uncertain intentions of the Central Powers and flooded Britain with orders for torpedo boats and other naval craft, most of which never saw action. They had watched with alarm as the King of Prussia, just before being declared German Emperor in 1870, dramatically increased the size of his Imperial and Merchant Navies, starting to create a volunteer navy by inviting German shipowners to make their ships part of the Imperial Navy. A decade and a half later the Royal Navy increased its orders to private yards so that by 1911 over half the ships built on the Thames were naval craft. So impressed was Isaac Watts, Director of Naval Construction, by Scott Russell's launch of the SS Great Eastern that he embodied many of his ideas in the design of HMS Warrior, planned to be the greatest naval vessel afloat, and, with its graceful lines, the first to be developed as well as built by a private yard.

The need for space, deep water and access to raw materials was by now driving yards away from the Thames. Among those moving west to the Solent were famous names such as that of John Thorneycroft, an industrial revolution engineer of the third generation, among the first to have been trained at the new Regent Street Polytechnic, as well as attending Glasgow University and lectures at the Royal School of Naval Architecture. He built motor torpedo boats and destroyers for the Royal Navy, cargo vessels and river craft for emerging countries. To keep ahead of his competitors Thorneycroft also experimented with new methods of propulsion, hull resistance and stability and with innovations such as hydroplanes, air cushion vessels, anti-roll equipment and circular craft with surface piercing propellers. Also seeking deeper water and space, Yarrows moved north to Scotstoun on the Clyde, where 40 percent of their work was for the Royal Navy, 40 percent for export and 20 percent for British merchant shipping companies. While still on the Thames they had captured the African and Eastern markets with their river steamers, which could be taken to pieces, carried and reassembled, requiring only 15 inch draught and often capable of ascending rapids by using steam direct to the cylinders. They also built gunboats, two of which were in the rescue mission which arrived too late to save General Gordon at Khartoum. Meanwhile firms deciding to stay on the Thames diversified, even to the extent of building bridges, and concentrated on the lower end of the market, a number joining together in 1863 to promote Thames Barge Races to demonstrate their low running costs. In Britain 2000 barges were still afloat in the Channel in 1907 and 300 in 1945. Some other Thames firms seeking to promote economy in fuel, together with the ability to maintain schedules, specialised in building ships which functioned half by sail and half by steam, an idea again mooted today. Among Thames directors who continued to aim at the larger market while refusing to move, was Arnold Hill of the Thames Iron and Shipbuilding Company. Educated at Harrow, a school which imbued respect for the skills of the work place and consideration for those who exercised them, he did not wish to leave his East End home among his employees, knowing that the loss of their jobs would bring unemployment to the area. He inspired such loyalty in his men that ships were always delivered on time and he served them with such devotion that he continued with his work after becoming paralysed and even addressed a public meeting in Trafalgar Square from a stretcher. Nevertheless, his firm, affected by recession, went under in 1912. His type of employer, identifying so completely with his men, was rare then but rarer still in the years to come. Shipbuilding on the Thames was not finally extinguished until after World War I.

Meanwhile the great shipbuilding centres in the north of England were moving ahead and in 1835 Lloyd's referred to Sunderland as the, 'Most important shipbuilding centre in the country'. North east yards began by ship repairing and when starting to build were content with very small profits. The Tyne built its first steamboat in 1814 and by 1850, with the Cleveland Iron Ore Co. and Consett Iron Works opening in close proximity, the north east was building three quarters of a million gross tons a year. The change over to iron and steam had been forced upon the Newcastle shipbuilders by the introduction of the railways, which threatened to win the coal trade from the wooden sailing colliers. It was claimed these sailing ships took nearly two months to load, sail to London and unload their coal, but that one of the new steam driven iron ships could complete the journey in under a week. By 1855 eight Tyneside firms had followed the example of the go-ahead Palmer brothers, to, 'Whose yard men hastened to work', and who were building in iron and introducing rolled steel armour plating in HMS Terror. Many of the founders of these early firms came from simple backgrounds, but yet were able to raise sufficient finance to build iron ships on speculation. One of these was Andrew Leslie from the Shetlands who trained as a boilermaker in Aberdeen and, during the next thirty years, was commissioned to build 72 ships for British companies and 60 for the Russians. He was joined by Richard Hawthorne who began as a millwright and learnt his engineering on the light railways in the mines. Together they built general and specialised ships, including warships for the Royal and Russian Navies, ferries for the Great Lakes and refrigerated ships for New Zealand lamb. Equally tireless in his efforts to seek out new orders overseas, was John Wigham Richardson, who joined with Swan and Hunter, to create a firm renowned for flexibility in the face of adverse competition. One of their most famous ships was the Cunarder Mauretania, which won and held for many years the Blue Riband of the Atlantic and was then requisitioned, first to carry troops and then as a hospital ship at Gallipoli in World War I.

One of the greatest achievements of the north east yards was the invention of the turbine engine. At the Naval Review of 1897 a little ship, named Turbinia, steamed between the lines of grey warships. No patrol boat could catch her as she tore past the Royal Yacht at 34 knots, 'Kicking up white foam in her wake and suffering no vibrations'. She had been designed by a member of a Tyneside firm, one Charles Parsons, a younger son of the Earl of Rosse, an old Irish title. He had not been sent to school, but instead had been educated by leading scientists before attending Trinity College, Dublin and Cambridge University, after which he entered the firm of Armstrong and then set up his own Gateshead engineering partnership. He recognised, as Archimedes had demonstrated 2000 years before, that he could make an engine work faster by using the velocity of a jet of steam instead of its pressure to drive the pistons. He achieved the first satisfactory running of a turbine engine in 1884, after which he patented it and formed his own company for its production. Cunard installed the new turbine in its liners and by 1914 one half of the Royal Navy's ships were turbine driven. With the world caught up in battleship fever, the combined firm of Armstrong and Mitchell was by now building warships in their Elswick yard for the Chinese, Dutch, Austrian, Russian, Brazilian and Japanese navies, as well as for the Royal Navy – while continuing to build merchant ships in the old Mitchell yard. Like Parsons, Armstrong, although trained as a lawyer, was a keen engineer and he designed and built a rifled gun and supplied the British government with breech loaded guns, as well as exporting arms overseas. When the Japanese won their spectacular naval victories against the Russians in 1905 using long range gunnery, Armstrong's name sprang to fame, for his firm had built their battleships. Meanwhile in 1880 Armstrong Mitchell had experimented with the first steam propelled tanker and when it exploded, as did the second, their leading engineer, Henry Swan, designed and built a single skinned tanker, eliminating the possibility of oil seeping between layers of plates. At first Lloyd's refused to register these ships, but soon they received the highest classification and by 1920 Armstrong Mitchell had built a total of 120. By now Newcastle was a centre of world trade and, together with related ports, was producing a very substantial part of the world's shipping. It is said that Tyne workers in those days, 'Took as much interest in their craft as modern people do in football'.

Meanwhile on Clydeside, where the Royal Navy placed their first order in 1794 and the first iron ship was launched in 1818, the second Royal Navy iron-clad was built and not broken up until 1923. Here again, because of the river's proximity to Glasgow rich with the profits of sugar and tobacco, many new ships were sold either at design stage or after completion. Although at this time the old Scottish shipbuilding burghs of Aberdeen, Arbroath, Montrose, Dundee, Kirkcaldy, Burntisland and Kinghorn were still building their own large three masted sailing ships, either of wood, iron or composition – their bays filled with coasters and overseas traders – nevertheless for a number of reasons the main movement of the industry was to the Clyde and its estuary. For one thing Glasgow was the biggest port with a large pool of skilled and casual labour, and for another it was claimed the warmer climate made steel plates more malleable for processing and kinder to handlers. For nearly a century Hall and Hood of Aberdeen shared the Scottish clipper building market with the Clyde, launching the winning Thermopylae, to which the Clyde responded with the Cutty Sark in 1869. However, with the design of iron and steam ships growing more sophisticated, the need for training in mechanical and marine engineering was crucial to success and Glasgow had the foresight to step into the breach. It is said that English inventions sprang from improvisation and experiment rather than intellectual learning – George Stephenson taught himself to read at 17 and Pettit Smith developed the screw propeller on his farmyard pond – nevertheless the southern English shipbuilders benefited from the Royal Navy's Schools of Naval Architecture and Apprenticeship, as they did from the Institution of Naval Architects and later from the Polytechnics of London, while Newcastle also profited from its School of Naval Architecture at Kings College. The Universities of St. Andrews and Aberdeen would need to have opened departments of marine engineering if their adjacent ports were to retain a leading place in world shipbuilding. Instead, as Oxford University was to do in the next century when surrounded by the Cowley motor car works, they preserved their ancient traditions of humanism and developed skills in other scientific fields. Thus it was that the Clydeside fathers founded the Institution of Engineers and Shipbuilders of Scotland in 1857, sponsored the first professorship in Naval Architecture and Marine Engineering at Glasgow University in 1883 and started lectures in Marine Engineering at John Anderson's Technical College (later the University of Strathclyde). The great days of Clyde shipbuilding, described in George Blake's trilogy of novels, had begun.

Whereas Newcastle built its leading place on the transport of fuel and Liverpool on the movement of people and cotton, the Clyde concentrated for its advantage on the speed and reliability of Robert Napier's engines to launch some of the most famous ships in the world. Known as the father of Clyde shipbuilders and building his own first East Indiaman in 1835, Robert Napier produced engines so dependable that men set their watches by their time-keeping. All ship designers wanted fast ships, but while the Royal Navy put speed before economy, commercial companies wanted both advantages, with ships sliding easily through the water, meeting less resistance and consequently using less fuel. Above all they wanted reliability and to be able to maintain schedules in all seasons.(The twin turbine engine was later to satisfy both needs, with one engine for speed and one for economical cruising). The firms that settled on Clydeside derived an early benefit from Napier's genius which helped them to secure orders. In the century starting in 1860 Fairfields, renowned for rapid construction, combined with John Elder and built 180 vessels for the Royal Navy, as well as fast cargo and passenger vessels for Cunard and the Anchor Donaldson and Glen Lines. Scotts concentrated on fast merchant ships, including tankers – being the first firm to see that more oil could be carried by siting the superstructure of tankers aft – and before the First World War they built two turbine driven Dreadnoughts. Dennys, whose brilliant under-manager lectured on naval architecture in evening classes, built the first ocean going steel ship in 1879 (Lloyd's Register laying out the rules for building in steel nine years later) and also used the turbine engine in his design and construction of fast Channel steamers and modern ships for the Royal Navy. Meanwhile J and G Thomson had a wide US market, as well as building Royal Navy vessels and passenger ships for Cunard, including the largest steel ship afloat, second only in size to the Great Eastern. Taken over by John Brown, a leading Sheffield steel firm, the combined company built the most famous Cunarders of all, including the Lusitania, Acquitania, Queen Mary and Queens Elizabeth I and II and the Royal Yacht Britannia. When in 1903 the British Government, concerned at the expansion of the German Navies, approached Cunard with the offer of an annual subsidy of £150,000 and a loan of £2.6 million at two and three quarters percent if they would build fast liners available to the Royal Navy in time of war, the first of these were the sister ships Caronia (twin screwed and capable of 19½ knots) and the Carmania (with a new direct drive steam turbine achieving 20½ knots), both built on Clydeside. Then, after further consultation with the Director of Naval Construction, a number of other ships followed, including the Mauretania and Lusitania, which won the Blue Riband back from the Germans in 1907 and was torpedoed carrying civilian passengers on May 7th 1915. Two other companies engaged in the construction of fast passenger liners were Lithgows, who later purchased Fairfields and built for Cunard, and Cairds who built for P & O. By 1860 the Clyde was producing a very substantial share indeed of the nation's ships.

By the middle of the nineteenth century almost all Mersey shipbuilding had moved over the river from Liverpool to Birkenhead, where the firm of Laird was becoming famous. When William Laird came to Liverpool from Greenock in 1810 he became director of two shipping companies and agent for James Watt's steam engine, before buying land in Birkenhead for a harbour. While raising money for its construction, he founded an iron and boilermaking works and built the town of Birkenhead for his workers – a splendid prototype for later planners. Starting to build iron ships with his son John in 1828, he endeavoured to overcome prejudice by inviting the Astronomer Royal to carry out tests and make corrections to overcome the effect of metal on the compass. Building their first screw driven ship in 1838 the Lairds helped to promote the overland route to India, providing their own ships to Alexandria and from the Persian Gulf. By this time they were building P & O and cross-Channel steamers, cargo ships for the South American trade and dredgers and gunboats for the East India Company. Seeing their potential, the government decided in 1858 that Liverpool should complete the Birkenhead docks and appointed John Laird as government nominee. Meanwhile William's other son Macgregor was establishing trading posts in West Africa and, in spite of temporary imprisonment by the Africans, obtained orders for river steamers from Dr. Livingstone and other explorers, as well as establishing his own African Steam Navigation Company, taken over subsequently by Elder Dempster. Having built four gunboats for the Royal Navy, Lairds launched a speculative iron frigate, which, although rejected by the Navy, was sold to Mexico, where she performed admirably. Their prejudice against iron partially overcome, the Admiralty then ordered another iron frigate, which was converted into a troopship and sank after striking a rock off South Africa, the heroism of the soldiers, crew and passengers inspiring Sir Francis Doyle's famous poem THE LOSS OF THE BIRKENHEAD. John's sons, educated at Harrow, were all shipbuilders: William was a ship designer, John a French trained dockyard business administrator and Henry a draughtsman, also trained in the drawing office of a French shipbuilder. Building for Cunard, P & O, Inmans International and the Pacific Steam Navigation Company, the firm prided itself on the, 'Very fine lines and unusually fast turn of speed' of its ships. In 1885 came an order for four large RN warships, including the Royal Oak, and then for a number of torpedo boat destroyers. Having already enlarged their docks, Lairds then combined with Cammells, a Sheffield steel company, and carried out further modernisation – building a floating dock, more Royal Navy warships and passenger and train ferries before 1914.

Further up the coast but still in Lancashire, the Barrow Shipbuilding Company in the port of its name had by now become the Naval Construction and Armaments Company and was building large liners for Australia and New Zealand, as well as tankers and naval craft. The firm was then taken over by Edward Vickers and his two brilliant sons, Tom and Albert, who had been engaged in steel production in Sheffield, and who in 1888, in response to a request from the Admiralty, had installed plant for the construction of guns and armour plating. When Vickers took over Barrow Shipbuilding they also purchased the gun makers Maxim and Nordenfelt as well as Beardmore, the armour platers of Glasgow. They were now well placed to compete for naval orders, since they could both build ships and manufacture guns and armour, and at the request of the Admiralty they joined with Armstrongs to take over the firm of Whitehead Torpedoes to prevent the manufacture of these vital weapons from falling into foreign hands. Before 1914 Vickers built one

Dreadnought and the engine for another, as well as a number of other naval craft, including submarines. Some years before, the firm of Barrow Shipbuilding had experimented with submarines, but when the Turkish and Russian experimental vessels either suffered mishap or were wrecked the matter had lain dormant. Then 3 midget submarines were built in the USA by an Irish Fenian financed by US émigrés, who had the unusual idea (a type of attack not put into operation until World War II) of transporting them across the Atlantic and blowing up British ships in port. The US Navy saw the potential of these experiments and adopted the third model which, no longer in midget form, was built and marketed by a newly established firm, known as the Electric Boat Company. An agreement was made for Vickers to build and sell these boats in the UK under licence so that by 1903 five submarines had been launched by the Company. After considerable resistance from the older Admirals the RN developed a submarine arm and at the outbreak of war in 1914 Britain had 23 submarines to the German 21. Vickers, who were later to develop the Spitfire, were as forward looking in the air as they were on and under the sea and some of the merchant packet steamers built by the firm at this time were converted to seaplane carriers when war was declared.

Over the sea in Northern Ireland shipbuilding began at the mouth of the River Lagan, where improvements carried out in 1765 attracted William Ritchie from Ayrshire, who launched his first steamboat at Belfast in 1816. To improve port facilities a Board of Commissioners bought out the shipbuilders clustering round the harbour and moved them over the river to Queen's Island, where iron shipbuilding was started by Robert Hickson of the Belfast Iron Works. To this yard as manager came Edward Harland, an amateur engineer and scientist, friend of George Stephenson and apprentice to his brother Robert. The Harland family's friendship with Gustav Schwabe, a German Jewish business man with Manchester and Liverpool connections, brought in sufficient generous funding to buy Hickson out of ownership and also provided the second partner for the firm in the person of Schwabe's nephew Moritz Wolff. Being the owner of a ship management business, which imported cotton and silk from the Far East, Schwabe was in a position to introduce Harland and Wolff to the Bibby line, who subsequently ordered all their ships from them. Then, with the arrival of two more partners, William Pirrie (who began as a gentleman apprentice) and Walter Wilson (shortly to be replaced by his brother), the firm widened its base and began to acquire a reputation for strict discipline, above average pay for skilled workers and regional rather than national union agreements. This flexibility enabled them at the turn of the century to introduce a three-shift system and shorter working day, while other firms were hedged in by restrictive union working practices. Soon they were building for White Star (at half the normal commission), for P & O, and for Alfred Jones' African Steamship Company of Liverpool, to whom they offered attractive financial terms and in which Pirrie became a shareholder, later taking over Jones' shares as well. In two of the years immediately after 1890 Harland and Wolff built more ships than any other UK yard, but, when the liner conferences – or cartels – began to influence shipping policy, Pirrie

(Above) Stationers' Guild Ceremonial Thames Barge; (below) North East sailing collier unloading in London

The Victory, forty years old at Trafalgar, but modernised in extensive refits

Torpedoed oil tanker, 1941

Small craft fitting out; trawlers being prepared for Coast Patrol, August 1940

became unpopular for putting his firm before his patriotism. In company with American banker J.P. Morgan, White Star and two German shipping lines, he founded IMM (the International Maritime Marine Company) to take over the Atlantic route from Cunard. When the British Government reacted by giving subsidies to Cunard to build large liners, White Star responded by building even larger ones, including the Titanic. By now, Pirrie had extended his ownership of Harland and Wolff to seven more yards – in Southampton, Liverpool and Clydeside – and was in financial difficulties from which he was rescued by three 'lucky breaks'. First John Brown became a majority share-holder; second, he secured the licence to build the diesel engine in the UK (wresting this from Barclay and Curle and Swan Hunter, Wigham Richardson), and third, in 1917 he was appointed Controller General of Merchant Shipbuilding by Lloyd George, having already built a number of wartime standard ships in double quick time.

It may have seemed to some people towards the end of the nineteenth century that the sun would never set upon this expanding maritime trade, but already world needs were changing and recession was in the wind. In the first decades of the century the demand had been for passenger ships, whereas later, although a good proportion of that demand continued, there was a shift of emphasis towards large cargo ships to carry railway engines and machinery to help emerging countries develop their own infrastructure. This move to make them self-reliant meant that one day they would build their own ships and that trade in bulky commodities, such as engineering products and steel – which by 1900 was cheaper than iron – would eventually be reduced. Meanwhile at the end of the century the glut and recession cycle in shipbuilding recurred again, caused first by the Spanish American War of 1898, which sparked off a series of naval orders from South America, and then by the Boer War. Excessive building was followed by the recession of 1908/9, which coincided with labour troubles within the industry. Sparked off by changes in technology, they did not improve Britain's chances of maintaining her lead in world shipbuilding. In the days of rudimentary design and small yards, shipwrights held pride of place in an atmosphere of craft consciousness, in which every man was known by name, but after the iron and steam revolution – and again after the change over to steel for the construction of the hull – machine shops required larger sites, in which individuals lost their identity and there was a shift of importance towards mechanical engineers and men working in the new 'black' trades. Fairfields, for instance, covered 85 acres of Clydeside, comprising docks, machinery shops, fabrication sheds and assembly grounds for raw materials – 20 acres being devoted to engine works alone. Approved plans for ship construction went from the shipyard office to the tracing department and thence to the moulding loft, where they were usually drawn full size on the floor. Wooden templates (or moulds) were made for the various parts, includ-ing the armour plating for warships. New and complicated designs tended to promote the mechanical engineer at the expense of the craftsman and whereas, at the start of the iron and steam revolution, the shipwrights aligned the frame and laid the decks, now their pride of place was threatened by the boilermakers, responsible for the critical task of assembling and rivetting the plates of the hull. These plates were straightened, marked out to the correct size, capped and holes punched (or drilled in special cases). They were then rolled or pressed to the required shape and taken to the slipway for erection, rivetting and caulking.

It is hardly surprising, therefore, that by the second half of the nineteenth century the rivetters were the most highly paid craftsmen, followed by the platers, angle iron smiths, caulkers and holders up, all of whom belonged to the powerful Boilermakers Union, responsible for fabricating the hull. Their task finished, they were followed by blacksmiths, plumbers, coppersmiths, joiners, painters and electricians, much of whose work could take place after launch, where in a battleship there were still some hundreds of small parts to be fitted. The invention of the screw propeller subjected ships to further vibration stress and as they became longer and larger they needed cross-bracing to prevent structural distortion. All this promoted the boilermakers in importance and a further challenge came with the single skinned tanker, whose rivetted joints now had to keep in the oil as well as out the sea. When the shipwrights realised they were being downgraded they took work from the joiners, causing a three month stoppage. Thus began the demarcation disputes which have bedevilled the industry ever since. They were followed by similar troubles between the engineers and plumbers who fought over iron pipes. Meanwhile there was jealousy between the skilled and unskilled workforce. A typical way of working was for men to be in teams led by two craftsmen, who were paid twice as much as the labourers, while the apprentices' wages depended on time served. A major source of unrest was that some teams were paid on piece rates, some by time worked, while week-end work was rewarded at a different rate. All these variations led to inter-trade disputes, worsening labour relations and strikes, with owners watching profits turned to losses. No sooner had the well organised Boilermakers Union, who fined members for disobedience, secured a 5 year agreement in 1894 with north east employers, than the Trades Unions, asserting new powers bestowed by Parliament, undermined the agreement by reducing the differential between the skilled and the unskilled workers almost to half, while at the same time flexing their muscles by insisting upon maintaining the period of apprenticeship at 7 years. In 1896 Conciliation Boards were registered at the Board of Trade, establishing workers right to arbitration, and three years later the Shipbuilding Employers Federation was started to promote among other things, 'Interchange of information between employers and employed' in, 'Free and friendly communication' and to arrange, 'Equitable and fair settling of disputes'. As a result, in 1907/8, after a prolonged strike on Clydeside, where wages were lower than elsewhere, the Confederation of Shipbuilding and Engineering Unions and the Federation of Shipbuilding Employers swept away all previous sectional agreements and signed in Edinburgh a national agreement on wages and conditions.

Agreement, however, came too late, for the industry was then thrown into chaos by the recession of 1908/9 and all bargains were cancelled in order to survive. The precariousness of shipyard employment was never better illustrated. When times were hard and the employers wanted to cut wages the workers said 'No', and when times were good and the men wanted to increase wages the employers said 'No'. Alternating profits and bankruptcies were endemic to the industry and without the employers' right to hire and fire more firms would have gone to the wall. Then in three months after the 1908 recession was over orders picked up so quickly that the workforce was increased by 50 percent . Lack of security at the workplace was accompanied by poor working conditions, lagging behind those in other industries. In 1871 the working day was fixed at 9 hours, with a 53 hour week, but many firms which had switched to an 8 hour day by 1900 went bankrupt in the recession, so slender were the margins in lean times. Accidents and fatalities in the shipyards were covered by Lord Shaftesbury's Factory Acts and the Fatal Accidents Act of 1846, but safety regulations in shipyards were difficult to police, accidents often occurring far out on slipways. There were few medical facilities, (a situation not improved until the 1950's), and almost no welfare arrangement; in winter there were incidents of frostbite from the handling of cold steel; until World War II there were no canteens; it was not until the 1950's that mid morning breaks were accepted; and not until the 1960's that the employers agreed to fire on Fridays, giving a full week's pay. Nevertheless in old photographs the men look well fed, spruce and happy and there was great esprit de corps and a sense of identity with individual firms. Just as the Royal Navy had tested the different strengths of the then controversial screw propeller against the paddle wheel in an amusing tug of war, so did the Royal Dockyards now step into the breach caused by abrasive labour relations and organised races between gangs of rivetters working on each side of the first Dreadnoughts. Whichever team reached the target first was rewarded with a prize, turning bitterness to comradeship. In 1909, with the recession passed, employers and workers agreed to new procedures negotiated nationally for settling disputes over wages, with six months elapsing before changes were made and three years later both sides signed a National Demarcation Agreement, in which the Boilermakers refused to join.

The danger was that these altercations on the shop floor coincided with the greatest spurt in foreign shipbuilding which Britain had ever faced. In the twenty years prior to 1914 Britain's share of the world market fell by 20 percent. Hence Lord Wemyss' warning to the House of Lords on May 17th 1909. 'The question of invasion (and with hindsight Lord Wemyss could have added starvation) enters very largely into the question of foreign shipbuilding. As a very old man who may never speak again to this House I say it is the duty of the two Front Benches to put their heads together to see what can be done. If you had the courage, commonsense and justice to the country to do what ought to be done, the first effect would be that you would stop rival foreign shipbuilding '. How to stop subsidised foreign competition – that was the question that was now to confront British governments in the century to come. Having abandoned the Navigation Laws, which gave British shipbuilders an assured home market, how could the British compete with the protection, subsidies, cheap loans, taxation advantages and investment grants offered by nations abroad?

CHAPTER XV

DOWNHILL ALL THE WAY
SHIPBUILDING SINCE THE FIRST WORLD WAR

Within five years of Lord Wemyss' warning the First World War had broken out with longer hours and higher output, stretching industrial relations to the limit. Nearly 8 million tons of British shipping had to be replaced. Nevertheless, in spite of a shortage of steel, growing worse towards the end, and of skilled labour, diluted by military service, output was higher than ever before. In the north east yards 7856 vessels were repaired in dry dock and over 20,000 afloat. National launchings went up from a pre-war yearly average of two and a third million gross tons to nearly 4 million by the end of the war and between 1918 and 1920 5 million more gross tons were launched. In 1918 alone the firm of Harland and Wolff completed over 200,000 gross tons of shipping. Everywhere the men gave of their best and quality did not suffer, but the future of their crafts-manship was set in doubt by structural parts being prepared in steel yards and assembled and welded in berths to make 'standard' ships. (It was this anxiety about their post-war status that caused the Boilermakers to refuse to join an overtime agreement in 1923, which led to their expulsion from the Confederation of Shipbuilding and Engineering Unions). The war years also caused serious financial problems in the shipyards. After 1915 shipping, like other industries of national importance, was controlled by the state and, in order to stop profiteering, the government took 40 to 80 percent of profits above the Blue Book rates, which were based on the average profits made in the last years of peace. Although some fortunes were undoubtedly made, mostly before these arrangements were put in place in 1915, these rates were sometimes only a quar-ter of the amounts paid by the governments of neutral and Allied nations for similar compensation and services and they continued in force during the imme-diate post-war period when prices rose, making it impossible for industrialists to rebuild their capital base. Even when prices collapsed in 1920 Excess Profits Tax continued to be levied until 1921 on assessments from the previous year, (although, because of the high replacement costs faced by firms during the war, a proportion of this money was ultimately repaid). There were also post-war restrictions on the sale of ships, preventing owners from selling until prices had fallen and firms were under pressure from the banks.

As with earlier conflicts, the profits of neutral nations were vast, with no tax levied on firm's profits, provided they were reinvested in shipping. These nations also received and paid higher capital compensation for ships lost, creat-ing a danger of post-war over-capacity. Britain had lost a high percentage of her coal exports to neutrals and the carrying trade that went with it, as well as half her tramp trade, and this cut in demand for her shipping came at the time of a world wide glut, so that it was impossible for her to make good the loss. By the terms of the Armistice Britain was given the German Imperial and Merchant Navies, but, with the former scuttled, raised and turned back into German bullets ready for World War II, the latter, comprising 4 million gross tons, was not handed over until 1919 and consequently not put on the market until after prices had fallen. Some UK companies stretched themselves too far financially by taking a number of these ships and others held in reserve off the hands of the government, who for their part did not anticipate that the confiscation of German vessels would lead to renewed German shipbuilding on US loans. Meanwhile the USA, who had earlier seen her share of the world's carrying trade collapse as the result of her Civil War, and who had spearheaded the recent concept of mass fabrication for the rescue of the Allies, had increased her output so far that she was responsible for 86 percent of the growth in world tonnage between 1914 and 1921, half of which was built post-war. Lastly Japan had also been building during hostilities and had excess capacity as well. Britain should have cut her output in time, but the seriousness of the position was masked, first by port congestion and the need for repairs and conversions, and second by the fact that nearly half her 1920 orders came from overseas, many from Norway, so that in that year she was still building 35 percent of the world's tonnage. Prices rocketted and then, saturation point being reached in 1920, a slump followed, wages fell, two year old ships were sold for a quarter of the purchase price and the output of British merchant shipbuilding was cut by half. Thousands were thrown out of work and the industry was struck by sympathy strikes, stoppages and disputes.

Why did Britain not act at once to avert disaster? In previous crises great statesmen had stepped from the shadows to rescue her from them, but now wisdom and insight seemed to have been drained from government, diluting the old partnership between parliament, trade and the professions. War time cabinet government had been little short of dictatorship and now in the post-war period it was difficult for the nation to readjust and come to terms with the demands of labour, which, having found expression in its own parliamentary party, was giving voice to what it saw as exploitation of the shipyard and other industrial workers. On the other hand the debts facing Britain were vast, dwarfing previous problems, which placed power in the hands of Treasury officials. The war had cost the country an estimated £24,000 million, towards which Germany only paid one sixth of the reparations of £6,000 million, (partly on account of her debasing the currency) so that Britain ended the war in debt to the USA and then lost further economic headway by trying to bring stability to the world exchange in a unilateral return to the gold standard. Meanwhile, from 1925 US loans to Germany were twice the reparations paid, so that German shipbuilding could be easily subsidised. With funds earned during the war other nations were also subsidising their shipbuilding, causing further excess capacity and confusion. This created particular problems for the UK, which in 1914 had been producing 60 percent of the world's ships. Other countries recognised, even if Britain now did not, that the war had been won at sea as well as in the trenches and chose to subsidise shipbuilding rather than pour out hundreds of millions of pounds on the dole as Britain was doing. In earlier times the recession could have been eased by building for the Royal Navy, but now ten thousand men were sacked from the Royal Dockyards and the only large ships under construction were the battleship Nelson and the new County Class cruisers, nicknamed the Cherry

Trees, because their size and armaments had been cut down by George Washington! Restricted in this manner by the Washington Convention and by shortage of funds, the nation was also gripped by revulsion from war and exhaustion of mind and body. When, after Verdun parts of the French army mutinied, Britain had deliberately drawn German fire at Passchendaele, rather than risk awaiting the arrival of the main US army the following April. Those last months of suffering, following the catastrophic casualties of the Somme, had manifested themselves in hatred of war, and contributed to the labour troubles in industry, once it was understood that, freedom and justice apart, nothing had been gained on the positive side of the balance sheet except debts and unemployment.

Over-capacity in shipbuilding had followed the last three wars in the nineteenth century, but now the problem was exacerbated by the government not having taken the sinkings sufficiently seriously until 1917. Shipbuilders had then been asked to extend their facilities and, there being no response, a direct grant was given later that year. 'Nothing else can defeat us now', said Lloyd George, 'except a shortage of tonnage'. Thus by 1921 Britain had one third more capacity than in 1913, much of it provided in the last eighteen months of war. Had she acted at once to cut capacity and modernise the shipyards retained all might have been well, but instead the government and the industry drifted in indecision towards disaster. On the one hand the government excluded British shipbuilders from Export Credit Guarantees on grounds that it was not prudent to add to the world glut, while on the other, in order to avoid unemployment, it guaranteed loans to industry under the Trades Facilities and Loan Guarantee Acts, of which one third went to shipbuilding and later had to be repaid. In 1926 these loans were stopped and no further subsidies were given to shipping until the mid thirties, by which time defence needs were pressing, (the finishing of the Queen Mary for Cunard being the one exception). Meanwhile other countries, particularly Germany, Italy and Japan, pushed the UK out of shipping markets by providing subsidies, grants, low cost loans and relief from rates and taxes, so that their companies were able to modernise and build new ships. 70 percent of German shipping was under one cartel company and, although records do not reveal the extent of subsidies paid, the company was heavily indebted to the state and banks. Germany also set up a Rehabilitation Fund, which granted loans and subsidies for the replacement of ships, and this was followed in 1921 by a Shipbuilders Bank, which made advances at less than the Reichsbank rate. By these methods 3 million gross tons were built in Germany at virtually no cost to the owners and at three fifths of the UK price. In 1925 60 percent of German ships went for export, whereas by 1936 Britain imported more ships than she exported – Germany being responsible for one third of the figure and Holland for another third. Germany also supplied Italy, Japan, Scandinavia and Holland with machinery and cheap materials with which they could undercut the UK. The Italians were building warships; France, under a 1927 Act, was granting cheap loans to shipbuilders to whom she paid out millions of francs in subsidies, and, like the Germans, was building fast prestige liners; Holland was working double and treble shifts to the UK one; the Scandinavian countries were also providing shipping firms with state funds. Overseas the USA was giving subsidies to companies who maintained their new building programme and a US Maritime Commission paid the difference between building abroad and building at home, sometimes as much as 50 percent. In Japan the government and industrial banks were in partnership, the banks granting low interest loans and the government rendering them lower still by paying part of the interest. Moreover, in antithesis to over-hopeful Liberal expectations in 1848, other countries were now bringing in Navigations Laws, which operated against Britain. Germany imported Rumanian grain and in return exported manufactured goods, both in German ships. British coal, exported to Italy and France, was fetched in Italian or French ships and – with cheap subsidised Polish and German coal flooding the market and further exports lost owing to the prolonged miners strike – the British were in no position to dictate terms. German, French and Italian tramps were subsidised on mileage, whereas by 1933 the number of British tramps, now in competition with intermediate cargo liners, had been halved, with consequent knock-on effect on UK shipbuilding orders.

Britain at this time was also facing other problems, for alone among the nations of the world she had relied upon a volunteer army until 1916 and lost a generation of her finest young men. The effect of this loss was felt everywhere in the country, but in the labour intensive shipbuilding industry the ill results were compounded. Here the discipline was gone. There were sloppy working practices. Men arrived late and claimed for overtime. There was no planning or control of materials and poor costing led to the use of cost plus tenders, instead of fixed price contracts insisted upon in previous centuries. Large numbers of unions continued to co-exist. There were three or four craft unions concerned with construction and twenty one unions for skilled men in the finishing trades, as well as unions for those in the semi-skilled and unskilled bracket. Demarcation disputes continued and, after government control of war time wages had been lifted, there was an explosion of strikes. Lack of good working practices also affected management. There were too few skilled executives and managers and the number of students at the Institution of Naval Architects fell by three quarters. Until the recession employers did not reorganise their yards to produce efficient undercover welding, and Germany and other continental countries were ahead not only in this, but in the development and application of the diesel engine. The industry was also hit by the high price of steel, which pushed up prices of ships and continued until the devaluation of the pound. Before the war Britain imported cheap European steel, but now she was relying on her own supplies, which, owing to shortages, were subject to delays in delivery.

The government did not act until 1925, when it set up a Joint Enquiry into Foreign Competition and Conditions in the Shipbuilding Industry. This led to a Shipbuilding Conference to prevent undercutting and to the foundation of the National Shipbuilders' Security, under the chairmanship of Sir James Lithgow. Its task was to advise yards on how best to become viable and, if this failed, to reduce capacity by buying and closing unprofitable firms, with the proviso that they must not be reopened for 40 years. At last, in 1926/7 came an increase in world trade and measure of relief – first in the form of orders from the USA for

British coal to be carried in British ships, and then in an increase in the world's tanker fleet, with British yards, particularly in the north east, receiving a good proportion of the work. Meanwhile the employers, despite losses, had taken the risky and, in the circumstances, courageous step of agreeing a wage rise, which they could ill afford, linked to a new wage bargaining agreement, based on yard, local, central and general conferences, the substance of which held good until 1960. At the same time the period of apprenticeship was reduced to 5 years. This slight increase in demand together with better labour relations pushed Britain back up the shipbuilding league table and between 1927 and 1929 she was again producing one half of the world's ships. However, in 1929/30 there was a renewed decline in world trade and a drop in tanker demand due in part to the laying of pipe lines and, in spite of the return to Imperial Preference in 1931, by 1933 orders to yards had fallen to their lowest level since 1888. An Imperial Shipping Committee was set up to discuss the position of shipping in the Far East, where much trade had been lost to the Japanese and USA. At home Sir James Lithgow's association had meanwhile produced results – between 1930 and 1933 British shipbuilding capacity was reduced by one quarter and by the end of 1935 5 million gross tons of shipping had been scrapped. Spurred on by the anxiety caused by this retraction, British shipbuilding made considerable progress in researching and implementing the most economical ways to run a merchant fleet. This work was much needed, for, while world tonnage had increased by nearly a half since 1914, Britain's smaller fleet was earning only half the overseas currency earned in 1928 and needed to cut costs.

Until 1932 Naval Estimates continued to fall, but in that year Germany and Japan were the only countries in the world to increase their armaments by 3 percent and 52 percent respectively. The British government, seeing the writing on the wall, changed its policy and passed the Import Duties Act which, following in Gladstone's footsteps, allowed materials for shipbuilding and repairing into the country duty free. The following year – by which time 15 percent of the world tonnage laid up was British – the government at last introduced a scheme to help tramp shipping, which became law as the British Shipbuilding Assistance Act in 1935. A total of £2 million was given to tramp owners, provided there was no rate cutting, and £10 million was provided over 2 years for the building of new merchant ships, on condition that two million gross tons were scrapped for every one million built. Tempted by this Scrap and Build policy 50 ships were built with 97 percent of the cost coming from the government and in that year the National Shipbuilders Security ceased to sell off non profitable yards and instead put them on a care and maintenance basis. With rearmament in the UK beginning in 1934 and restrictions laid down by the Treaties of Washington and London coming to an end, one fifth of the work in shipbuilding was now for the Royal Navy, which drained off skilled men from civilian yards. This, together with the effects of death, unemployment and curtailment in the number of apprenticeships by the Unions, created a serious shortage of skills and consequent higher wages in civilian yards. In 1937, despite an increase in world trade, British launchings went down to 1600 from the average of 2250 for the years 1900 and 1920. Whereas since the war

Japanese shipping tonnage had trebled and US quadrupled, UK shipping fell from two fifths of the world's total to one quarter. Admittedly the number of very large UK vessels increased, but the number of medium sized ships decreased and continental trade vessels were hit hardest of all. To make matters worse, a public outcry against the private arms industry started in the USA and spread to the UK. A Royal Commission was appointed, which accepted the arguments of Sir Maurice Hankey (who was primarily responsible for the introduction of convoys in 1917) that government yards alone could not produce the capacity required in war. In 1938 – the year of Munich when Germany and Japan laid down more keels than the UK – a White Paper was published on merchant shipping. This proposed an operating subsidy for tramps (56 of which were now laid up) to bring them into line with foreign owners, and loans and grants for all shipowners, with particular emphasis upon passenger liners to meet foreign competition. In March 1939 yet further assistance was given and a special fund was set up to enable the government to purchase vessels for a reserve fleet. By September the world was again at war.

Part of the extant story of shipbuilding in World War II has already been told in Chapter V. Standardised 'Liberty' ships were built at speed to replace merchant vessels, but unlike World War I these had standard engines and component parts, but not necessarily standard hulls. Electric welding and flame cutting of steel were introduced into the yards, which cut time taken to build a ship by two thirds. In February 1940 all yards came under Admiralty control and a Controller of Merchant Shipbuilding and Repairs sat as a member of the Admiralty Board. During 1942/43 naval and merchant shipbuilding, repairing and refitting were the War Cabinet's main priority. British and overseas yards were asked to build large numbers of warships, together with standardised merchant ships and 1, 200 easy-to-assemble Liberty ships, and to convert between one and two hundred further captured vessels. The output was greater than in World War I, with a smaller workforce. There is no adequate explanation for the lack of proper accurate records of ships built and repaired during the war. The bombing of ports, docks and shipyards has been described in Chapter V and the effect it had on unloading and shipbuilding. Many Clydeside families had to be moved as a result of enemy action, which meant long journeys to work on top of 63 to 72-hour working weeks. Complaints are extant about too much paper work and thus it is evident that numerous records must have been lost or shredded, removing reliable accounts of one of the most memorable sagas of British history. A few figures emerge for individual areas: yards on the Wear built 240 merchant ships of 1½ million gross tons; 2000 new ships and 600 conversions were launched on the Clyde, where 5000 million gross tons of shipping were moved by tugs to assemble into convoys. To expedite production in Scotland there was a central drawing office sited in Glasgow and a headquarters for the assembly of parts in Edinburgh. Some records of individual firms have also survived. In six years of war Vickers built one battleship, 5 cruisers, 7 aircraft carriers, one monitor, 22 destroyers, 120 submarines, 60 landing craft and barges, 9 escort vessels, 10 merchant ships and a transport ferry. The story of how, in order to keep men working such long and unsocial hours, legally binding promises were given regarding working practices, which were difficult to honour after the war, is best told in the next chapter. Many yards were modernised in 1942/43 at a total cost of £6. 5 million, of which the government supplied £5 million from Lend Lease. Most of the UK work was on naval ships, while the US built the bulk of merchant ships and this created obvious difficulties when peace came in 1945. It seems extraordinary that no attempt has been made in the life time of the men involved to write a comprehensive history, but clearly it was an experience that most people wanted only to forget.

The years following World War II were different from the 1920's. Because of the inter-war recession there was now a reluctance to invest in new capacity. In 1945 there were 678 yards, employing nearly a quarter of a million men, of which 6 were very large indeed and 474 employed under 200 workers. Productivity was highest in the medium sized yards, employing between 500 and 800 men, where the relationship between the management and men was closest, and lack of investment was felt most keenly in the large capital intensive yards. As after every war there was an upsurge in shipbuilding worldwide and Britain in 1946 launched 464 ships of 2 million gross tons. As soon as possible, allowing for reconstruction, Germany, Japan and Scandinavia were once more building with state subsidies and soon German output was 40 percent higher than pre-war. In Britain the accumulated sterling balances held overseas initially brought orders for new ships from countries, who could not spend the balances outside the sterling area and these orders continued until 1955, when Thorneycroft made the highest profit in its history. In 1951 a Ship Mortgage Finance Company was set up to aid sales of British ships, which provided yards with orders for over 1000 ships of 6½ million gross tons but, as with other post-war UK schemes, by 1956 these loans were mainly going to foreigners building in British yards, defeating their main purpose. One problem was that, even if investment took place, the men, thinking they were safeguarding jobs, clung to old methods of working and demarcation between crafts. Financiers seeking profits could perhaps be excused for comparing the swift 'car plant' type of production lines in continental shipyards with the more conservative methods in British yards, where there was a reluctance to install new machinery. Here there were also shortages of experienced technical staff and union restrictions on the numbers of apprentice welders, together with strikes and demarcation disputes, which it was claimed added 5 percent to the cost of ships and contributed to late deliveries. Faced with delays caused by shortage of materials and with wage inflation and rising prices of steel and components over the three year period necessary to build a ship, yards were again opting for the accounting practice of 'cost plus' tenders rather than 'fixed price' contracts, so that there was little downward pressure upon costs. In 1947/48 there had been only half the steel required for shipbuilding, as well as shortages of paint, timber and hardware, so that shipbuilders could complete only just over half the orders placed. Then in 1949 the traditional discount to shipbuilders on the price of steel ended and prices consequently jumped.

Undoubtedly there were also misjudgements at this time. Seeing excess world capacity and not wishing to add to it, shipbuilders anticipated a demand for

tailor-made ships and returned to versatility rather than continuing with standardisation. They built luxury liners when the future of passenger travel was in
the air, dredgers when the future lay in deep sea ports and ferries when road
bridges and tunnels held the key to the development of internal transport.
Indebtedness and shortages of raw materials reduced their options. In 1949
Britain signed the Caltex Oil Agreement, by which US companies supplied
petrol to end its rationing and the UK reciprocated by building US oil tankers.
Consequently by 1955 50 percent of the post-1939 increase in the world's tanker
fleet was British, with tankers representing half her orders and the amount of oil
carried by UK ships quadrupling. This provided a lack of balance in her
merchant fleet, making her particularly vulnerable to the drop in oil production
and the rise in its price in 1973, followed by the re-opening of the Suez Canal for
the second time in 1975, all of which reduced the demand for long distance
tankers. During these years, although the world's dry cargo trade increased by
one third, the British share was only 10 percent and in 1956 the British
Government tried to persuade tramp owners to join together to create a sinking
fund, out of which traders could be compensated for laying up uncompetitive
ships. These included vessels which had either survived the war in a battered
state or been wartime standard-built and expensive to run. One innovation
during hostilities had been to pour asphalt between steel plates to give extra
bridge protection and this now added unnecessary weight to the ship. But with
tax allowances on new plant being withdrawn the previous year and with depreciation calculated at pre-war values, the heavily taxed shipowners could never
replace these ships and their trade was consequently lost. To make matters
worse, foreign countries were meanwhile again operating preferential navigational programmes, which included: reservation of coasting trade; grants and
subsidies; flag discrimination; preference shipping under foreign trade agreements and reduced custom, consular, and harbour charges. Because of the
continuing shortage of raw materials (particularly of steel) during the early
1950's Britain could not expand as fast as the rest of the world. Her predicament
was made much worse by the need to rearm at the time of the Korean War,
which brought back rationing of steel and other raw materials, as well as a
further jump in their price, while the crisis also created a new world wide
demand for ships of which other countries were able to take advantage.
Therefore, by 1954/55 Germany was again exporting more ships than the UK
and these exports represented half her total launches, compared with 70 percent
for Sweden and Japan and only 33 percent for Britain – with Holland also a
significant rival. There was very little action that Britain could take, for even by
1956 there was still less weight in British imports than before the war and the
lack of liquidity, which these import figures represented, placed her at an enormous disadvantage in her efforts to get back into the maritime race.

The real down turn came, however, between 1956 and 1958, when the USA
having invested in new technology in Japanese yards, placed substantial orders
there, so that by 1956 Japan's exports of ships were more than the total UK
launches for that year and she completed twice the tonnage. This new technology included not only flame profiling machines, but also the cutting of plates by

optical remote control computers, which could magnify the detail of the plans and which only a few British shipyards, including Vickers, had installed. Action now passed from the moulding loft to the drawing office and, once the design and drawing stages were past, there could be no more changes, so that the only workers needed were expert technicians and not craftsmen. Other changes were also taking place at this time; aluminium was now increasingly being used with steel for ship construction, making hulls lighter, while welded ships, with protective cantlings and some rivets to act as crack arrestors against the increased danger of brittle fracture, were becoming the norm, requiring indoor fabrication. In Britain there was lack of appreciation on the shop floor of the danger of this competition and instead workers concentrated on preserving old crafts, resisting new skills and insisting on annual rises in wages, so that productivity did not rise as it should have done. Then in 1956/7 came the first threatened national strike for thirty years. The employers decided to say 'No', but the Ministry of Labour set up a Court of Inquiry, which recommended giving 5 percent, which was the same proportion as that awarded in other industries. The employers agreed, provided assurances were given that there would be no more claims for a year and less demarcation. The Court refused to sanction these strings for skilled workers, for whom they recommended 5 percent free of obligations, but for the unskilled the Court recommended 6 percent, with strings laid down by the management. The result of this concession was little short of catastrophic. Wage policy in both World Wars had been dictated by the government, but whereas after World War I the number of strikes fell off after the General Strike in 1926, after World War II they increased in severity after the same time lag. The situation in the shipyards was not helped either by the shipwrights withdrawing from the National Agreement in 1958. Within two years of this strike, higher wages, increased bank rates, a credit squeeze and a drop in freight and ship prices were all having a disastrous effect. During the nineteen fifties and sixties there were ten times the number of days lost through strikes in UK shipbuilding than in any other sphere of manufacturing and higher prices were thus passed on to the consumer in this labour intensive industry. Since the end of the war the labour force had remained fairly constant. Now in 1959 it stood at just below 200,000 instead of a little above as in 1945. One third of this workforce were labourers, over one third craftsmen building the hull and under one third craftsmen engaged in fitting out. With the UK now only building 79 percent of its own ships, compared with 100 percent in 1951, Thorneycroft made its first loss since 1935. After 1960 the progress of British shipbuilding was all downhill, with the British percentage of world markets currently fluctuating between 2 and 4 percent. As always there were differences between individual areas. Clydeside concentrated on highly finished and specialised work, contributing one third to the total UK output; the north east, which had less equipment but a highly skilled workforce and good productivity, concentrated on economical tramps and the general market; Wear and Tees contributed one quarter of the total, the Tyne one sixth and the remaining areas another quarter.

During these years other nations, whose governments had helped industry to invest in new technology and whose shipyards were not troubled by strikes, rearmament or shortages of steel and finance forged ahead. While Japan in 1957 launched 2½ million gross tons, Germany launched 1½ million, Sweden ¾ of a million and the Netherlands half a million. In Japan 65 percent of the value of a ship being built was lent at low interest by the Development Bank, while an Import/Export Bank also gave 4 percent loans for ships for export. The German Federal and Länder governments and banks gave loans of up to 40 percent of the cost of a ship and allowed this investment to be set against tax. Many factory trawlers were built in Germany in this way at this time for the Russian fishing fleet. Korea was starting to build with similar state subsidies and the USA was establishing a new ship yard in Taiwan. Wages in Japan were then the lowest in the industrialised world; after which in order came Holland, Germany, UK, Norway, Denmark and Sweden, with the USA highest of all. The Swedes were able to maintain a leading position for a number of reasons. Building up a highly efficient repair business as well as building ships, their managers were mostly production engineers. They employed a ratio of 1 manager to 5 workers, compared with the British ratio of 1 to 10, and, 'Were earning an excellent reputation for sound purchasing of components, good choice of orders, runs of the same design, well organised and tidy yards and interchange of crafts'. Meanwhile Britain was turning away from the old structures of command – the foreman and the chargehand, 'Management's front line' – and was suffering from messy yards and low productivity. Ships were taking longer to build in the UK than in foreign yards, increasing the cost. 808 days was the average time taken to build a tanker in Britain, compared with 204 in Sweden, 307 in Germany and 414 in Italy. Yet ships were built in record time in wartime Britain. In Thorneycroft's annual general meetings during the 1960's, managing directors expressed astonishment at the number of stoppages and disputations in the face of the unprecedented improvement in working conditions carried out in 1964. Only the bravest of firms would have invested at this time and Thorneycroft was among the brave, but by the time the government acted to stimulate investment in 1964 with a £75 million Shipbuilding Credit Scheme – providing 80 percent of the cost of a ship in loans at 5 percent repayable over 10 years – it was too late for many firms – the markets had been captured by others. In 1958 the Japanese had established a further lead by cutting the prices of all their ships, whereas in Britain there was an 11 percent rise in wages in 1964/65, currently with the passing of the 1963 Contract of Employment Act and the ending of the employers' right to hire and fire with only an hour's notice – the traditional way of avoiding the worst results of recession in the shipbuilding industry.

It is easier to categorise the inter-war years – boom, recession, unemployment, rationalisation, the provision of subsidies and then renewed war – than it is to define the difficulties of the post-war years. Why was it all downhill? Without doubt, lack of liquidity was at the heart of the problem. Not only did it restrict investment in new plant and machinery, purchase of raw materials and expansion of facilities, but it led also to a number of changes in industrial structure. Whereas at one time accountants were the advisers to the directors, now they were on the board rather than the engineers, a factor amazing other members of the EEC, who did not understand the need in the UK financial scene for regular cash flow statements or a well presented balance sheet to a firm wanting to borrow from the bank. But the function of accountants is to cut waste – they do not understand the dynamics of industry, the need to be always moving forward, to be in the market place before the crowd. Who was now buying and selling in the market place? In the last century, it had been the head of the firm or his business partner or a member of his family, so that personal contact was maintained, consumer demand assessed and contracts more readily secured. Now, with the rationalisation of firms into large conglomerates these personal contacts were more difficult to sustain. Lack of liquidity was also a cause of the frequent changes in government policy – decision, counter decision, indecision. Not only were there changes of policy between opposing parties taking office, but there were changes within government and even within the lifetime of a single minister, a phenomenon particularly noticeable in defence, where continuity is vital. Here, firms, engaging in what appeared lucrative government contracts, were left to pick up debts and cut surplus capacity after the cancellation of such projects as the TSR II, on which billions of pounds had already been spent. Politics seemed to be becoming a separate power game, divorced from real life. While the nationalisation of an industry provided firms with compensation to enable them to diversify into other fields in which they had less experience, after a change-over of government they could find themselves re-possessed of the original enterprise, for which further scarce liquidity was required for reinvestment. Critics blamed ill-informed ministers, the civil service, back benchers, who would not listen nor act upon what they were told, and lastly the media, which, it was said, enlarged certain topics and blurred the real issues. Meanwhile complicated legislation poured from Westminster, couched in terms necessitating the employment of industrial lawyers to disentangle its complexities. While the Japanese forged ahead, combining their own methods with the best of those of their former adversaries, the British did not heed the lessons in leadership and organisation, which they had recently learnt at so great a cost.

What were these lessons? The word leadership comes from the leader ship, upon whose captain's judgement and experience everything depends, while the dictionary defines an organisation as having 'interdependent parts', of an 'organised whole'; which is 'prepared for activity' and is, 'a means of communicating vital information'. Certainly wartime experience demonstrated the need for vision and drive: first, a well thought out imaginative plan, tested for viability and then, with teamwork cementing together the interdependent parts, put into operation, after checking every detail to ensure the efficient coming together of the whole, with delegation and communication right down to the man at the 'sharp end'. No one should ever under-estimate the need for imagination in the original plan nor the efficiency required to execute it. The ski resort at Cairngorm had its birth in the wartime dream of a young naval officer seeing sails on Loch Morlich, but, without the expertise of those who came after, this idea would not have developed into the successful sailing and ski resort of today. Nor should anyone under-estimate the need for clear communication of the plan, demonstrated by all great wartime leaders, whose drive, efficiency and determination brought Allied plans to fruition. Perhaps when peace came the British thought too much in terms of the civil service attitudes to planning, the concept of a centralised bureaucracy, such as that which directed wartime shipbuilding, forgetting the important link these bodies had in the shipyards with the Service interpretation of planning – that he who makes or accepts responsibility for a plan must carry it through, making himself answerable for his actions and those of his delegates, thus enabling his superiors to pin point success or failure. If this is not kept in mind there is a danger in the words of Vickers of creating, 'A looking glass world, in which all plan and none produce' – a world in which there are too many chiefs and not enough men on the ground, with a top heavy structure, which becomes more expensive to run the closer it comes to the tip of the triangle.

How did post-war industry pick its leaders and decide the size of its units? Again, as in 1918, the best of the generation had been killed, and although in 1946 many young men with good war records went into industry, by 1948 a number had transferred to the professions, perhaps spurred on by the fear of creeping Socialist nationalisation. Later, industry thought it could pick young 'fliers' and put them on a fast track. Some firms insisted on a 'sandwich' course, giving students periods in industry during training, realising the importance of technical skills learnt in polytechnics and on the shop floor, without which language a leader cannot communicate with men, understand technical problems or generate innovative skills. Other firms took entrants from University in the usual way. Although statistics showed that it was in smaller organisations that chief executives had proper knowledge of conditions of work and markets, nevertheless, like a relentless juggernaut the movement continued towards large companies, in which the chairman could not know all matters concerning his business and was dependent on standards of communication among his staff. In these circumstances management became divorced from its workforce, and by the 1960's a mixture of Socialism and snobbery was forcing the two sides of industry apart, so that neither spoke the language nor understood the problems of the other. The need for trust, so vital a component of wartime leadership, began to give way to the abrasive confrontational style of the 1980's, which has not always produced results for which it was designed – the need for the workforce to identify with the firm, cut wage demands to zero and understand the wider issues. Unions and management blamed each other. Management felt the Unions had betrayed this trust in the strikes of the 1970's, caused by the increase in consumer prices after joining the EEC, coupled with a dash for growth. What perhaps they over-looked was that, in the second half of the century, the Unions had been left with only two main tasks, to raise wages and improve conditions of work. Even as late as World War I they were still responsible for weekly allowances for sick members and the payment of lump sums on marriage or death, but since 1947 the government had taken over these welfare functions, which encouraged Unions to become poachers rather than gamekeepers. Likewise in training Unions once set the standards for skills and controlled the length of apprenticeships. Wartime experience showed that training unlocked the door to greater expertise, improved morale, motivation, productivity and sense of purpose, and yet now training programmes, upon which the industrial future of the country depends, are fragmented, and do not expect nor obtain sufficiently high standards from young people. It was understandable that everyone wanted to forget the war, but there was no need to abandon centuries of experience. The vital word logistics – the importance of which should not be under-estimated – has two distinct roots and meanings, one military, the other 'pertaining to reasoning and calculation'. In World War I Harland and Wolff followed certain maxims regarding the logistics of materials and equipment in order to increase productivity: the introduction of expensive labour saving equipment, accompanied up by frequent touring of yards to see if it was being properly used and to correct hitches; the allocation of similar types of work contracts between yards in a group; the setting up of production lines within yards to produce the same type of ship; the synchronisation of parts; the delivery of materials only when required and lastly the vital need for order and tidiness, without which little can be achieved. Almost all these work practices and many others like them have been mirrored by Japanese industrial practices.

No one seemed able to cut through the jungle of industrial malaise. Men went to work because they were paid to do so, they did not run to work, as once it was claimed they had done to Palmer's yards, because they were interested in the ships to be launched. In 1965, after the return of a Labour government in two elections the previous year, the intervention of government into the shipbuilding industry, which had started in the late 1950's, acquired a new impetus. In that year there came an event which shook the whole shipbuilding world. John Elder, founded in 1834, which later became Fairfields – a firm famous for its Cunard, Anchor Donaldson and Glen Line ships – went into liquidation with a full order book. Although set up with help from government, industry and unions and in 1968 becoming part of Upper Clyde Shipbuilders, it was bankrupt again three and a half years later (at which time Govan Shipbuilders took over the yard). Startled into action by the first bankruptcy the government set up the Geddes Inquiry Committee, which, while acknowledging four reasons for maintaining a thriving shipbuilding industry – defence, shipping, balance of payments and employment – stated that the industry must be profitable and that to achieve this it must attack rising costs.

Although its diagnosis and aims were excellent the Report's main solution – to centralise the 27 yards building ships of over 5000 gross tons into larger groups – was impractical and unsuccessful. Geddes hoped this would provide more international 'muscle', improve planning and purchasing power, strengthen production management control and reduce costs of research and development, in which there should be more government involvement. Recognising that a quarter to a third of the cost of a ship comes from outside the yard, (with as many as 400 suppliers to one ship) the Committee recommended the standardisation of all component parts, to be sold at world prices, delivered on time and ordered by new group purchasing departments within the yards. Marine engine manufacturers should also be removed from parent shipbuilding companies and consolidated into groups, so that they could diversify. The lost romance of shipbuilding was mentioned, the need for greater efficiency and the difficulty of preparing reliable statistics, given the different tonnage yard sticks which Churchill criticised. The Report saw links between falling orders and declining numbers of ships registered under the British flag, a decrease from 88 to 71 percent in the first years of the sixties to only 38 percent in 1965. Stressing the need for a home market, it emphasised the extent of Japanese penetration into British markets in general. According to figures on Lloyd's Register, some of which were quoted in the Report, whereas in 1955 Britain had built 58 tankers and the Japanese 25 out of a world total of 217, in 1956 – after heavy US investment – the Japanese launched 62 to the British 46 out of a total of 233, while by 1960 the figures were 135 Japanese tankers to the British figure of 46 out a total of 335. Geddes pointed out that these new Japanese tankers were one fifth cheaper than their British counterparts and their bulk carriers one tenth cheaper, while only in dry cargo vessels, in which the British fleet had suffered such reductions, was the difference between the two nations' prices minimal. The Report did not mention that the Japanese were reported to be cutting prices by saving on thickness of scantlings – steel braces, enabling ships to withstand 'hogging', 'sagging' and other stresses caused by the weight of load and movement of waves – and that this could reduce the safety of their ships and the likelihood of their inclusion, if sold to a third country, on the register of Classification Societies such as Lloyd's, which demand high standards of safety. It also did not mention that this disparity in tanker price was particularly unwelcome to the British, because, since the 1949 Caltex Oil Agreement, Britain had been building a disproportionately large share of the world's tanker fleet compared with other types of vessels. It did point out, however, that, as the third biggest steel producer in the world, Japan's steel was cheaper and, since this accounted for one fifth of the cost of a ship, it was essential that British shipbuilders – as the largest consumers in the UK – were again given their traditional individual discount in steel, stopped in 1949. Pointing to the number of deep sea yards in Japan better suited to the building of giant tankers to sail round the Cape, it explained how this capturing by Japan of the increase in the tanker market, coupled with the UK credit squeeze, high bank rate, instability of sterling and increased wages after the 1957 strike, meant British firms could not recoup the investment made by borrowing with government encouragement in the late fifties.

On the subject of credit the Report stated that, whereas previously shipowners paid progress payments on ships building, now yards were often expected to finance this stage mainly themselves, making government credit of particular importance. Japan had a permanent subsidised credit system – firms raising finance at 5½ percent for 80 percent of the cost of a ship. The Report pointed to the boost in British orders, which a similar but temporary credit system in 1963 had produced and welcomed its reintroduction in 1965 for overseas buyers – calling for its extension to home buyers as well. (Since 1964 shipbuilders had also been enjoying zero rating customs duties for imported raw materials and components for exported ships and in 1965 this benefit was extended to the building of all ships). The Committee rejected a Scrap and Build policy as a permanent cure for British ills, because of the cross orders between home and abroad, and it also rejected specialist shipbuilding, on account of insufficient skilled labour. While stressing the long British shipbuilding traditions in certain areas, the great skill and intelligence of the labour force and the availability of naval orders the Report praised the smoother flow of work in overseas yards, the greater use of labour saving equipment, the higher standard of management and planning of work, the fewer number of unions, less industrial indiscipline, greater confidence in the economy and better sales promotion (almost all these attributes – with the exception of fewer unions – Britain had in the nineteenth century). In order to effect the necessary 15 percent reduction in costs Geddes suggested firms should become more market orientated and keep up continuous contact with potential customers by means of a Sales Department, as well as improving the image of the industry by keeping the public better informed. In matters of design the Committee stressed the need to look ahead, to provide good ship performance, to make economic use of materials and present something pleasing to the eye, (a skill sacrificed to commercialism). The prime need was to achieve a smooth flow of production with no bottlenecks, which, like traffic jams, build up with alarming speed behind late deliveries of parts, wild cat or other strikes, demarcation disputes and waiting between trades, caused by unions insisting upon only doing the work of their own craft. The Report listed British ills as industrial indiscipline; too many Unions (11 at fitting-out as compared to one main and one minor while building); wage rises; strikes; illiquidity; shortages of skilled men, apprentices, graduates and holders of Higher National Certificates, as well as of trained managers and foremen to keep up the flow of work on the shop floor and production lines. The Report also stressed the need to communicate vital information and to have better trained managers in accounting and office administration, who could provide monthly cash flow statements. Only by introducing wider training in skills and technology could more tasks be performed by all trades, with greater flexibility and interchange between unions.

All this was discerning data but in the main recommendations that the 27 larger firms should become 11 (later reduced to six), and that engine manufacturing firms, divorced from their shipbuilding parents, should be reduced to four, Geddes forgot that – human nature being what it is – two winning football or polo teams, artificially combined, make one losing one. There were good arguments for enabling engine firms to quote for independent work and for shipyards to specialise within groups to streamline production, but the problem was that each shipyard had its own working practices, labour arrangements and management method, and oil never mixes with water. Geddes also compared the 9 percent and 6 percent respectively, which represented the proportion of the total made by the small yards in Japan and Sweden with the 57 percent of total British output made by the 49 small yards in the UK. Although admitting that these smaller British specialist yards were doing the best – productivity being highest in firms of under a 1000 men – the Report assumed that, by reducing this number of small yards to Japanese levels, efficiency would follow. The traditions of the two countries were different. The British labour force was not used to working in vast conglomerates and one of the fundamental strengths of the British shipbuilding industry had been its family and local traditions. Geddes provided a carrot: a Shipbuilding Industry Board would be set up to act as consultant and provide loans to facilitate groupings and cash for firms to buy each other out. Those combining would have 75 percent of their costs paid in the first year, 50 percent in the second and twenty five in the third. Enormous sums of money were now poured into the industry. The SIB gave £43 million over 4 years to the large firms, while the government supplied £117 million as working capital, advances to liquidators and sums to meet losses. Nevertheless, the firms remained unprofitable, with inherited debts and unprofitable and penalty contracts, poor labour relations, demarcation disputes and each side of industry blaming each other for the mess. Only where the leadership was outstanding were results in individual firms brighter.

The Committee paid scant attention to the influence that naval shipbuilding had upon the industry since the days of King Alfred. It said that the Admiralty wished to continue to build in the Royal Dockyards in order to train its work-force – it did not mention the equally important reason of waiting between trades – and said that 11 out of the 23 larger naval ships (from an overall total of 78) had been built in this way in the last 11 years. It did not stress the leadership, which the Royal Dockyards had traditionally provided in setting standards for the industry, nor that the designs of many naval ships had originated in merchant ships nor the extent of the contribution of RN architects to merchant shipbuilding. Its attitude was ambivalent in the sense that it called for greater liaison with the Admiralty, while at the same time recommending naval specialisation in three yards under civilian control, so sounding the death knell to building in the Royal Dockyards by draining off its diminishing work. The end of a five hundred year tradition of building in the Royal Dockyards came about in 1969 and led to their privatisation in 1985, a further serious threat to the security of the Royal Navy and the country in time of war. Geddes did admit that the civilian yards, from which the naval work would now be creamed off, would not welcome this segregation, for not only had they derived benefits from working with naval research and design teams, but had also enjoyed the financial depend-ability of Admiralty orders, which were spread over a longer period and involved greater flexibility between design and finish. A serious instability at the heart of the Report was that, when assessing the importance of naval work to civilian shipbuilding and the link between them, it failed to rank Japan as a naval power. The truth is that for more than half a century Japan ranked among the first three naval powers in the world, currently recognising the need for a thriv-ing merchant marine and having more naval ships in her defence forces than Britain has in hers. In 1957 Japan had a merchant marine of only 4 million gross tons, whereas twenty years later it had risen in a steady climb to the astounding total of 41.5 million gross tons. Geddes also disregarded the enormous and inter-linked expansion of the Soviet merchant and naval fleets. In 1957 their merchant marine stood at 2.5 million gross tons, whereas by 1987 it had risen to 25 million, this rise being of course accompanied by an huge increase in the Soviet Navy.

The strong executive teams which Geddes expected to head the combined firms never materialised. Even if they had it is questionable whether the idea would have been suitable for an industry which for centuries had enjoyed close contact with a 'boss', who knew his job and lived either on or near his work. The largest group, formed in consequence of the Report and known as Upper Clyde Shipbuilders, consisted of Fairfields (now Govan), John Brown, Charles Connell, Alex Stephen and Yarrow, which later came out of the combination. Lower Clyde Shipbuilders were composed of two firms – Ferguson and Scott Lithgows. Swan Hunter and Wighan Richardson, Austin Pickersgill and Sunderland Shipbuilders went into the North East England group, while Vickers, Cammell Laird, Harland and Wolff, Thorneycroft and some others stood apart. These groups were unstable and firms moved in and out of them in a way not anticipated by Geddes. Had the plans for the marine engine groups been put into operation, it is possible they might have derived more benefit from consolidation than was the case with the shipyards. Large numbers of men were involved, since machinery makes up one third of the cost of the ship. Out of a total of 220,000 men employed in 1945 57,000 were employed in marine engineering, compared with 65,000 employed in shipbuilding, with the rest in ship repairing. The possibility of diversification for marine engine firms was welcome, for, although a number had been part of parent shipbuilding companies, probably the most inventive work had been carried out by individual firms operating on their own – after all Parsons had set up on his own to develop the turbine and Robert and David Napier had both run their own firms. During recent years the popularity of the gas turbine for very fast speeds has continued and the concept of twin turbines, for speed and cruising, has given the engine a fresh impetus, but the only British diesel design – the opposed piston engine of Doxford – passed its peak and went out of business. This was not due to lack of popularity, but more especially because the firm did not move sufficiently apace with advances in engine technology. After 1973 the rise in the price of oil made propulsive economy a first priority and the Danes, Germans and Japanese diesel firms all benefited from this increase in orders, whereas, although there are still a number of British firms making medium and smaller sized engines, the only large British based firm is now Kvaener and Kinkaid. In 1988/89 the government sold the Clark/Kincaid works out of state control to HLD, which bought the Fergus shipyard, and Kvaener then took a majority shareholding in the marine engine section of HLD. In 1945 Britain led the world in research and development in the field of marine engines, but just as shipbuilding depends for its success and survival on a home market, so does the manufacture of marine engines depend on shipbuilding for its existence. In this climate of decline the association of British firms, known as PAMETRADA, which was formed to conduct research and development, simply ceased to exist.

As the shipbuilding industry moved into this period of uncertainty and centralisation the government became increasingly involved as a shareholder and capital provider. In 1972 the Conservative government commissioned a Report by Hill Samuel into Upper Clyde Shipbuilders, which were in liquidation. Its tone reveals how far the battle had been lost. Everything had been tried and it seemed nothing could be done. Nevertheless, the Report stated that output of standard ships could be increased or doubled, provided £3.5 million was spent, although not until the fourth year of production would there be hope of viability. Because of the importance of the industry both economically and for defence, the government decided to spend further public money and some of the yards became as modern as any in Europe, but again luck was out and the following year the rise in oil price sparked off a drop in tanker orders. At the same time, because of the lack of orders, firms diversified into the construction of oil rigs, without fully assessing the difference in the skills and equipment required and many made a loss. The shipbuilding industry – by now conveniently grouped into conglomerates – thus became a ripe target for nationalisation by the next Labour government, with consequent fall-off in motivation and productivity. If the government even then had fixed its attention on a target of 10 to 15 percent of world capacity and had sold some yards and modernised others more of the industry might have been saved, but they did not. The decline therefore continued, until the industry had gone so far over the precipice that probably no rachet could have saved the majority of firms from their final fall.

Everyone, including foreign buyers, respected the men's skills but no one could explain their lack of motivation. Even the Labour government began to sell off some viable firms to overseas buyers, with the policy greatly accelerating under the Conservative government in the 1980's. While being shown round a nationalised yard building oil rigs in the south of Scotland, which had been beset by strikes, the writer was told by the chief executive, an experienced and fair minded man, 'The men are working better now'. Looking from the window two could be seen, with their hands in their pockets. After a continental buyer took over the firm he remarked to the writer how far ahead the British were in under-water welding techniques and how useful it was to his firm, (but not to them) that he could take this knowledge home. Under his leadership the yard was tidied and the men ran to lunch in squads, but on a day when completion of a contract was vital to obtaining further orders, the workforce took the day off to attend the funeral of a colleague, who died at work from natural causes. The director was mystified and sought an explanation, not understanding their extraordinary group loyalty or the reasons for it, 'Why don't they understand the need to meet a deadline?'. He was also amazed by the different, persuasive promises about pay made by British politicians, who, he said, confused the men and made management more difficult. At another shipyard also making oil rigs the under-manager described how the angry workforce had pinned him against a wall and how for minutes he wondered if he would escape. Yet managers, who relate on friendly, authoritative terms with their men, say that intimidation does not exist. 'Learn to think as the men do. Never allow them to take their problems outside the yard. Never allow yourself to be cornered'. In previous centuries, managers and owners lived either within the yard gates or only a short distance from them – a phenomenon also true of mine owners and managers – and this helped to reduce intimidation, since if there was violence it was impossible for them not to be affected by it also. In the absence of this contact it would seem that intimidation, like complacency and lack of morale, must surely have all been factors in decline. Finally, on to the scene in the 1970's and 80's stepped the asset strippers, the late stroll-on players, who created further mayhem on a stage already crowded with dying actors.

The Conservative Government, determined in the 1980's to end what they saw as a permanent drain upon the national purse, sold off the profitable yards first, including civilian yards building naval ships. By this time Britain was a member of the European Community and, when these negotiations were made with the Commission, the British government agreed, in return for being allowed to pay off past debts, not to allow these latter firms to receive the EC intervention grant. This grant, introduced as a counter to the Far Eastern threat, started at 25 percent in return for promises to cut capacity and employment. These bilateral restrictions were then dropped, aid rose to 28 percent of cost (equivalent to 35 percent of price under the UK aid system) and then was progressively reduced to the current 1992 ceiling of 9 percent for large ships and less for smaller ones. It has remained a running sore that these first firms to be privatised do not receive this credit, whereas others do, and legitimately they point out that they have no hope of competing with Japanese and German firms which are receiving this subsidy. Germany is also currently exporting ships to China with a subsidy, which because it comes under Development Aid is not prevented by EC rules, whereas North East Shipbuilders, among them Austin Pickersgill, one of the most modern yards in the world, must remain closed for five years and could not be sold when a buyer was eventually found. This was because, in the second wave of Conservative government sales, EC grants had been taken in the North East to set up alternative employment and the EC insisted they would have to be repaid if the yards re-opened within that period. These anomalies are a very serious threat to the country's future interests.

The result of these EC directives and the paying of subsidies, approved or disapproved of within EC rules, has meant (as in steel and coal) German dominance of European shipbuilding markets. German capacity currently stands at between 5 and 6 percent of world capacity, placing her in third place in the world league. Spain is only marginally behind, Denmark stands at 4 percent and the other West European countries, including Great Britain, at around 1 or 2 percent each. While the old Warsaw Pact countries build together about 12.5 percent of the world total, the Japanese have taken the position Great Britain once held, building about half of the world's ships. Other countries in the top league are Korea, until the war a Japanese suzerainty, Taiwan, the former Yugoslavia, China and Brazil. The USA, in spite of having introduced Navigation Laws known as the Jones Act and of giving subsidies to shipbuilding firms, has only built one merchant ship of any size since 1987, but has many yards building warships. Through the OECD the USA, seeing the extent of the Anglo-American crisis in shipbuilding, has initiated an attempt to stop subsidies in shipbuilding. The problem lies in the difficulty of enforcement. Subsidies trickle down through industrial banks and subsidiary firms within vast conglomerate cartels. Under Japanese law there is no need for individual companies to disclose accounts within the head holding group. Complete secrecy therefore can be maintained as to where the money originated – and this problem is not confined to Japan alone, but is shared in various degrees by other countries, including a number in the EC. Five years ago Britain lay seventh in the world league, but in the last two years she has fallen yet further behind. Apart from the effect this maritime decline has on all related industries, invisible earnings and the balance of payments – it raises serious questions of defence. In answer to questioning by the Geddes Committee, the Ministry of Defence said, 'They would not regard any governmental costs involved in supporting British merchant ship production as a proper charge on the defence vote'. The Report interpreted this as saying, 'We conclude that special effort by the country to maintain an uncompetitive shipbuilding industry could not be justified on defence grounds'. The two sentences have no obvious connection. Was the Report suggesting that, in addition to paying – in contradiction to what was first promised – for a part of the Trident programme, the Navy should pay for the nation's merchant shipbuilding programme? The idea is too fanciful to be taken seriously, but an island without a proper shipbuilding capacity has no defence policy worthy of the name.

Shipbuilding is initiated and motivated by orders from shipping owners, but they in turn are dependent on government policy and, in company with the shipbuilders, on levels of inflation of wages and prices and on standards of productivity. No one, politicians, owners or managers succeeded in getting across to the men employed in shipbuilding a proper sense of urgency. Owners sold their businesses. Managers retired early rather than risk heart failure caused by anxiety. The future of Britain as a trading country was at stake and yet the Trades Unions apparently could not (and some would say still cannot) see it, nor the men they led. Surely the only answer is for Britain to start again at the point where she came in, for there is money in the humble task of ship repairing and it is not perhaps fully realised by anyone but the experts that this requires a yet more skilled and experienced workforce than shipbuilding. Britain must recapture the lost romance of the industry and ask herself the question, 'Why did it die?'. Did it perish in those mountainous seas of the Battle of the Atlantic in the face of U-boat brutality, or when those magnificent ships became ugly conveyor belt products, whose lines give no satisfaction to the eye, remaining 'it' and never 'her'? Unfortunately the seller must provide, as Britain once did, what the world wants to buy and give her customers 'most favoured' status, but, given the wish to succeed, there is no reason why Britain should not use the knowledge won from her experience to circumvent the problems and re-establish her position in the maritime world.

One of the best ways to avoid the damage caused by inflation is to build smaller specialist ships, which require a shorter time scale to completion and for which Britain still has a satisfactory number of yards. Some container ships are currently being built of under 15,000 gross tons and, if sufficient passengers can be enticed back from air travel and share their journey with container cargo, then the future may present new opportunities for vessels, which require both speed and economy for fast turn around and quick economical cruising. Nevertheless some large ship capacity must remain for reasons of national security. Swan Hunter and Govan can build up to 70,000 gross tons and Harland and Wolff to

350,000 gross tons – and when Sunderland Shipbuilders re-opens as one day it surely will – (whoever heard of a Geordie who did not go to sea?) – the total would probably provide a sufficiently large capacity for future needs. If it is claimed the skills are now lacking to build the specialist ships that Swan Hunter is currently building then the skills must be retaught, for the intelligence is there, the traditions, the interest and the inventiveness. The British will always be innovators, but so many of their innovations have been largely developed by others, the jet aeroplane and hovercraft being recent examples, and it is here that a proper partnership between government and industry, particularly in research and development, will bear fruit. At the moment Fairy Brooke Marine are building one of three types of catamaran ferries – which can sail in a force 12 gale, achieve 32 knots and carry 450 passengers. Australia already has catamaran ferries at sea. Britain so often invents and other nations develop, but because Britain was too small a country to spend great resources on trials and development it was often the Royal Navy which, working closely with the shipbuilding industry, concentrated time and resources on testing tanks and preliminary trials. Without the Navy proving a good design, many developments would have been lost. An example now of this continuing co-operation is the consultancy firm set up by Yarrow to specialise in defence engineering and advanced naval architecture. Equally, without the merchant shipowners and shipbuilders pressing ahead, the Royal Navy would on a number of other occasions have fallen behind.

The Royal Navy, the Merchant Navy and the shipbuilding industry drew their inspiration from the same spring. That spring continually bubbling up with fresh water is the great love the British have for the sea. Is there any other race in the world whose coast is at all times of year speckled white with the sails of yachts and surf boarders? The British have suffered a set back and many men, not only in shipbuilding, have seen the things they gave their life to, broken, but that is no reason why they should not, with Kipling determination, which competitors and cynics call out-dated, 'Stoop and build 'em up with worn out tools'. The tragedy is that when we had the men, we did not have the tools – but then, in what may have appeared to some people the twilight of British shipbuilding, we had the tools, the docks and the fabrication sheds, but not apparently at any level (and some would say particularly at top level) the will to survive and to succeed. That remains for the future, in the same way as it has provided the history of the past. Already a renewed feeling of determination is beginning to stir in the wings, where the sites as well as the grass could be greener. The recent closure of Cammell Laird and the threatened closure of Swan Hunter impose upon the government the need to revise its maritime policy.

CHAPTER XVI

THE ONLY THING THE BRITISH LEARN FROM HISTORY IS THAT THE BRITISH LEARN NOTHING FROM HISTORY
THE STORY OF THE ROYAL DOCKYARDS

Ship repairing in peacetime is of no greater importance to the ordinary man than the repair of his car. Why should it be? To him it is the designer upon whose ability the running of the modern car or ship depends – the engineer who maintains it merely enables the product to function. But take instead the mechanic who repairs a vintage car or works in the pits of a racing track and one comes closer to understanding the complexities of ship repairing in wartime. Then the dockyard matey or civilian shipworker's task includes refitting, converting and repairing badly damaged and often old ships, some of which have come almost to the end of their life, and doing this under the continuous demand for speed. Even in peacetime safety at sea requires higher standards of vigilance than safety on land, for the sea gives no second chance. British merchant shipbuilders and repairers today call for enforced testing for older ships to improve safety, stimulate new building, bring the merchant and fishing fleets up to date and call in for repair a higher percentage of ships than current inspection at ports by DT officials. Shipping companies reply that most countries do not maintain such high standards of inspection – if they inspect at all – and that such testing would place British companies at further disadvantage. Also of concern is the shorter life and emerging defects of the modern welded ship, the life expectancy of which is at least one third shorter than that of its tailor made predecessors. Lloyd's Underwriters describe the current situation as 'ominous and disconcerting' – 'The losses of bulk carriers often in unexplained circumstances and with considerable loss of life continue in an alarming manner, increasingly the evidence is pointing to structural failure as the main culprit'. (Financial Times January 28th 1992). The problem is that structural failures in modern ships are almost impossible to predict, even upon closest inspection. Today's building techniques and computer based predictions providing optimum answers to constructional calculations, pose complex problems for surveying and maintenance, particularly for tankers and bulk carriers, transporting potentially dangerous cargoes. Modern lighter high tensile steel and thinner supporting flanges require more maintenance and repair to keep at bay the greatest enemy to steel ships in peacetime – corrosion and rust. Continual coating is essential, but often modern construction does not lend itself to easy application and with present fast turn around in port there is no time for on-going repair and maintenance work. Thus defects mount up almost unnoticed in a manner unfamiliar heretofore.

If the story of civilian shipbuilding has been neglected the story of civilian ship repairing has dropped into obscurity. For this reason and this reason only the writer has confined the history of ship repair to that of the Royal Dockyards, their beginnings and the vital contribution they made in times of conflict to winning the war at sea, both on account of the refits and repairs they carried out in their own yards and for the influence they had on the whole field of civilian ship repair. In peacetime the work of the Royal Dockyards has historically been to keep the fleet at a high level of efficiency – to undertake new building, refits, dockings, repairs, modernisations, the manufacture of replacement parts and structure and (until recently) to maintain the reserve fleet. Once hostilities have broken out ship repair becomes the second line of defence in the war at sea. A naval or merchant ship, broken-backed or with gaping holes torn in her deck or sides, limps back to port under her own steam or in tow, requiring instant attention. After an explosion by a mine a ship's hull is badly torn and distorted and requires replacement of damaged structure, wiring and machinery, while the rejoining of a broken-backed ship poses more problems than the building of a new one. High standards of expertise are required to accomplish such tasks, carried out in double-quick time in the filthy conditions of a damaged corroded hull. Gone now is the disinfected atmosphere of the modern fabrication shed; these jobs – whatever modern machinery is needed – must be undertaken 'mid the filthy aftermath of battle damage and the knowledge required is greater than that of the mechanic on the robot-controlled assembly line. If the reader recalls how many references to damaged naval and merchant ships there were in the previous chapters some small idea will be given of the pressure of work in wartime in both naval and civilian yards. In the spring of 1941 the shortage of seaworthy ships was so serious that Churchill instructed new building to be temporarily stopped in order to accommodate the back log of ship repairs. Although this directive was never precisely acted upon, civilian building and repairing yards were placed at this time under the control of the nearest Admiral Superintendent or Flag Officer in Charge and thus the Royal Dockyards and their trained staff became in a unique way the vanguard in command of the second line of defence in the war at sea. What would happen in any future emergency now that for the first time in 500 years the Royal Navy has been divorced from its own yards? How could it find in an emergency the expert knowledge to expand and operate its Dockyards for the very different pattern of usage required by war, no mind to embrace civilian ones as well? These questions remain unanswered.

It is no accident that the founding of the Navy and the start of a maritime policy were co-incidental with the founding of the Royal Dockyards, for the capability of a fleet depends upon the capability of its dockyards. Like all other stories of man's accomplishments this is not a record of uninterrupted success, but of success interspersed with periods of neglect and corruption, from which on each occasion the yards were rescued by the genius and dedication of men with gifts for organisation and instinct for ship design. Naval dockyards were efficient in times of naval supremacy, inefficient during periods of decline. Created by the Tudors – under whom they were superbly run – Portsmouth Royal Dockyard was opened in 1496, Henry VII constructing a dry dock there to refit his large merchant and naval ships, which had outgrown the berths in civilian yards and the shallower waters round Southampton. Henry VIII, wishing to build naval ships nearer London, founded two more Royal Dockyards –

Deptford in 1517 and Woolwich a year later – and was the first King to pay to have his fleet properly maintained in peacetime. By Elizabeth's reign, during which Chatham was opened in 1570 and given a dry dock a decade later, design, building, refitting and repairing were indissolubly linked with seamanship. One of Elizabeth's greatest seamen, John Hawkins, was also her greatest dockyard administrator. In her reign ship modernisation was so extensive that some vessels ran on into the reign of William III, setting a tradition of comprehensive refitting at half life, which the Navy followed until the defence cuts in the 1980's. Likewise the Treasurer, appointed by Elizabeth to supervise dockyard finances, administered them efficiently and economically. James I, on the other hand chose men 'unfit to manage or command'. This was the age of the master shipwright, but Phineas Pett – although a genius ship designer like his father, with the famous Victory and Ark Royal to his credit – was a dishonest, incapable administrator. He built his own ships with Crown materials and hired them back to James, who so admired his abilities as a designer that he rewarded instead of punishing him. Whereas dockyard pilfering under the Tudors had been petty, now 'authority took the lion's share'. Timber was over-ordered, stocks rotted and equipment was sold for profit. The organisation of the yards was so poor that men were ordered and counter-ordered by superiors, who did not understand the work. When the number of warships dramatically decreased, a Committee of Inquiry brought into being a Board of Navy Commissioners, among whose number was temporarily included the Lord High Admiral himself. Although Charles I, wishing to make his mark in maritime affairs, launched some large ships and transformed this Board into a Navy Office, which he later abolished, giving the post of Lord High Admiral to his own nominee, his autocratic rule alienated support in Parliament and in the maritime industries. Ships leaked, equipment was defective and fraud and theft became so rife that to stem the outflow of funds he leased Woolwich Dockyard to the East India Company.

Oliver Cromwell re-imposed discipline, disallowing the owning of private yards by master shipwrights in which they had feathered their nests, and appointing an Admiralty Committee of the Council of State to administer the dockyards, with a Commissioner in each yard answerable to it. This brought about efficient modernisation, but Cromwell's numerous launches and conversions of Dutch prizes left so many debts that Charles II had to make the deepest cuts in Navy and Dockyards. Hoping to save money he divided responsibility for fleet and support services into a 'customer and supplier' relationship, a policy popular again today. Cromwell's Admiralty Committee was abolished. The post of Lord High Admiral, which had lapsed, was recreated and given to his brother the Duke of York, with responsibility for building, refitting and repairing the fleet vested in a Navy Board, composed of Treasurer, Comptroller, Surveyor and Clerk. Starting as Clerk and later being appointed Secretary to the Admiralty, Pepys was not himself above receiving payment for the placing of contracts. He toured the Royal Dockyards – to which Harwich had now been added – in an attempt to cut waste. As always, however, the price paid for retrenchment was defeat. Lack of proper refitting and building caused obsolescence and fewer ships, allowing the Dutch to sail up the Medway, burning ships in harbour without the Royal Navy putting to sea. This ignominious defeat prompted another Committee of Inquiry, which made Peter Pett, Commissioner at Chatham, the scapegoat and replaced him with a younger member of his genius ship designing family, while Pepys appointed Anthony Deane, a first class ship designer free from scandal, to Portsmouth. With retrenchment giving way to proper principles of economy, Pepys endeavoured to standardise equipment in the Royal Dockyards and to eliminate the fraud, which, with the exception of the Commonwealth, had been endemic in the seventeenth century. He insisted upon methodical organisation and the restoration of discipline, which he pressed home with shrewdness and tact. Meanwhile Charles, realising responsibility for defeat lay in the cuts he had made, began to spend money on the Navy, building Sheerness Dockyard as an adjunct to Chatham and almost doubling the number of ships of the first three rates. Thus William III arrived in England to find an efficient fleet and dockyards, both of which he further strengthened by putting the post of Lord High Admiral back into the Board of Commissioners – known as the Lords Commissioner of the Board of Admiralty – and adding Plymouth (later Devonport) to his Royal Dockyards in 1694.

The siting of dockyards is vital to a maritime strategy, their importance varying according to their strategic significance in the accompanying international situation. Chatham had been important during the Dutch Wars; Portsmouth was to become so during the French; Devonport, opening on the Atlantic, led to the New World and gave sailors a wind in their backs coming up the Channel. The French Wars of the eighteenth century and the growing importance of the New World therefore not only tipped the balance towards Portsmouth and Devonport, but also demanded high standards of ocean going ships and seamen. During Lord Anson's tenure as First Lord, the administration of the Royal Dockyards was therefore reformed, their acreage increased, the skills of the workforce upgraded and knowledge of naval architecture improved. Although by mid century Britain had 100 ships of the line, there was a sudden call for more in the Seven Years War, which caused unseasoned timber to be used in building and repair, so that the vessels rotted. Thereafter timber was seasoned in water pits in the Royal Dockyards – for periods of up to 30 years for fir masts – and the need to keep a watchful eye on shipwrights repairing or refitting vessels meant that a Captain was never far from his ship while in dock. Certain alterations, for instance those to his living accommodation, could be carried out at his request. As well as encompassing docks, building slips and factory accommodation, the Royal Dockyards provided storage facilities for rigging, arming and loading vessels. Houses for dockyard mateys clustered round the dockyard walls, making self sufficient communities and, although working a 12 hour day, with almost no holidays and often working on Sundays, they had greater job security than their civilian counterparts, the Navy being reluctant to dismiss skilled shipwrights lest in emergency they would not find more. Dockyard mateys had other advantages as well, including piece work and over-time, rudimentary industrial injuries benefits and superannuation, and the right to take 'chips' (the ends of sawings). From about this time skilled craftsmen from UK yards could be asked to head shops or teams of craftsmen in dockyards opening overseas, of which the most important were Gibraltar, Port Mahon in Minorca and Port Royal in Jamaica.

Although between 1770 and 1790 over 30 magnificent vessels were added to the fleet, nevertheless a period of peace after the American War of Independence brought complacency. Thus, when in 1797 Britain found herself holding out alone against the might of revolutionary France allied with Spain, the Royal Navy faced mutiny at home. Pitt promised better conditions, the mutineers were quelled and Samuel Bentham, a reformer like his lawyer brother Jeremy, was made Inspector General of Naval Works to bring about improvements in the Royal Dockyards. A Committee of Inquiry was set up to investigate the current under-use of facilities, which caused the resignation amidst scandal of the First Lord of the Admiralty, Henry Dundas, First Viscount Melville. Bentham, who had toured continental yards in search of new ideas, introduced steam powered machinery, covered building slips and mechanical labour saving devices, engineered by Isambard Brunel. By 1815 the naval dockyards had become the largest industrial complex in the country, employing 15,000 men, an increase of 50 percent since the start of the Revolutionary and Napoleonic Wars. Dockyards were beginning to specialise either in building, refitting or repairing and some work was contracted out to civilian yards. Plymouth and Portsmouth were engaged mainly in repair and preparation of the fleet for war, while the Eastern dockyards concentrated primarily on building . Some new naval yards were opened on a temporary basis, one of which was Milford Haven – later moved over the river to Pembroke – while, as part of a chain of islands and bases established to stop privateering and piracy, further overseas naval yards were opened in Antigua, Bermuda, Bombay, Malta, Halifax and the Falkland Islands. This increase in maritime activity required an improved system of dockyard management unified under a single administration. The Navy Board was told to take a firmer grasp of its dockyards and see that accounting was employed as a tool of management to keep down costs. The Commissioners appointed by the Board to manage each Royal Dockyard were to be responsible for policy, control of wages and issue of regulations.

With the return of peace there was severe retrenchment and in 1832, at the time of parliamentary reform, all these arrangements were swept away. The Navy Boards were abolished and control of the Royal Navy was vested in four Naval Lords – the future Sea Lords – who were responsible for the administration of both fleet and dockyards. They were to have a direct link to the senior naval officers – the future Admiral Superintendents – who were to run the Royal Dockyards. Thus began a new era. Job security and training were improved and, with the opening of an Apprenticeship School, problems posed by the new technology were overcome. In 1859, while the Achilles was building in Chatham, it was considered impossible for shipwrights to do the armoured work and the ironsmiths, seeking to restrict numbers and claim a greater share of the work, refused to train more. With demarcation lines thus staked out, the Admiralty, refusing to be brow-beaten, re-employed the ship-wrights and trained them in the new skills, a lesson never forgotten by the workforce. The change-over to iron meant further alterations in the dockyards. Woolwich and Deptford were closed, modernisation began at Chatham and Portsmouth and the building of a yard at Haulbowline, an island in Cork harbour, was started in 1869 and became fully operational in 1894. Strategically placed for the Western Approaches, it provided the fleet with maintenance facilities and one very large dock and was of vital importance during World War I.

While the ironclads were building there was clamour for the privatisation of the Royal Dockyards, which occurs always during periods of naval decline and when new inventions and expensive modernisation and building programmes bring hope of profit to the entrepreneur. Financed by contractors, a lobby was formed to put pressure on Members of Parliament, and the suggestion was put forward that all naval dockyards should be closed and work transferred to civilian yards. Wiser heads prevailed, the government refused the offer and instead in 1890 the Admiralty appointed Lord Fisher as Admiral Superintendent, Portsmouth Dockyard. This appointment brought the Royal Dockyards into the twentieth century. 'He turned torpidity into zeal', speeded up ship construction, refits and repair and saved capital outlay and deprecia-tion. He was a 'stickler for standards', always addressing the men by name, a courtesy which had the added advantage of identifying them. While watching work in progress he would order a chair to be set out for him by the dry dock and had his meals served to him there. Lord Fisher's axioms were, 'Look for something where you can knock off a million' and 'When you are told a thing is impossible, that is the time to fight like the devil'. He never saved money by cutting corners, only by greater efficiency and his reforms successfully carried Britain's Navy and its dockyards through two World Wars. He revised the whole system of administration: separated dockyard and sea stores (the latter to be held in a different depot section of the port); developed standing contracts with suppliers; used commercial patterns wherever possible; reduced the number, type and description of articles and simplified the accounting system.

On leaving Portsmouth Lord Fisher was appointed Controller of the Royal Navy and Third Sea Lord in charge of building, arming, fitting out and repair-ing the fleet. He was a naval genius, concentrating on the need for speed, armour plating, range of guns, and the development of submarines and torpe-does. Under his administration the Admiral Superintendents' authority in the Royal Dockyards was supreme. They were to manage and give all orders both in dockyard and base, with armaments, coaling and stores under their command. When Fisher became professional head of the Navy in 1904 he used his knowledge of design and building to put in train a period of continuous building to match the German threat. In 1903 the decision was taken to build a major Royal Dockyard at Rosyth – with a near-by garden city to house dock-yard mateys. Construction did not start until 1909, by which time the number of dry docks had been increased to three. In addition to a range of factory buildings and oil storage facilities (enlarged now to hold a quarter of a million tons), there was an enclosed sea basin covering 56 acres, on the construction of which 2000 able seamen were employed during the war. The dockyard was not finished until 1916, after which 197 ships were dry docked before the end of the war. In 1917 Rosyth became the base for the Grand Fleet, unique in being able to offer it accommodation at all tides. In 1914 the workforce in all the Royal Dockyards was dramatically increased, hours of work lengthened and for the first time women were employed in a number of jobs, working on lathes, in acetylene welding and in the gun mounting, coppersmith and pattern shops. In this conflict damage to ships was caused less by gunnery than from explosions by mines and torpedoes. Some vessels were towed back with bows or sterns almost blown off, requiring virtual rebuilding. With allies and foes now inter-changed, specialisation in the various yards altered also. Shipbuilding ceased at Sheerness which, because of its strategic position, was now designated for repair and fleet maintenance only. As in the Napoleonic Wars, new dockyards opened along the trade routes and existing ones were updated. The dry docks at Malta and Gibraltar had been extended pre-war, a base in South Africa was opened at Simonstown and a floating dock was provided in Bermuda.

Although hours of work during the war were long, wages with overtime and bonuses were good. Thus, when peace brought retrenchment, recession and restrictions on new building, the Royal Dockyards were hit particularly hard. Thousands were thrown out of work; Rosyth and Pembroke were put on a Care and Maintenance basis; Sir Eric Geddes, a business man brought into government during the war and father of Sir Reay Geddes of the 1965 Report, recommended substantial naval cuts, which were nicknamed 'The Geddes axe'. Devonport, Chatham, Sheerness and Portsmouth had very little building work until well on in the 1930's and in 1929 the Hilton Committee, which had been appointed by the government, sought once more to privatise the Royal Dockyards. The Admiralty, realising the sword of Damocles hung above its head, set itself the task of discovering the most suitable type of naval officers to become Admiral Superintendents. One voice raised in 1929 was that of Lord Beatty, who said, 'After the Engineer-in-Chief the most important positions in the Naval Service of a technical and administrative order and dealing with questions for which the training of Engineering Officers under the common entry fits them are the posts of Admiral Superintendents'. In the same year, however, their Lordships rejected this suggestion and said that they had now, 'Definitely adopted a policy by which the selection for these posts will be made from officers who have shown a special capacity for and interest in administration'. Soon they were able to report that, 'The general state of affairs of the yards is considered very good, due in large measure to the Superintendents. The yards are run on good business lines and understand labour questions'. Recognising that the selection of Admiral Superintendents was the key factor in attaining the required efficiency, their Lordships then turned their urgent attention towards choosing the right men for the posts. They decided to opt for a combination of two qualities. They must be men who had, 'Organisation and administrative experience – who could also talk the language of engineering', in other words they must be able to set up an orderly structure, manage it efficiently and understand and impart technical knowledge. Recognising the important role the Royal Dockyards would play in hostilities, they decided to allow these men promotion to Vice Admiral, while remaining on the active list. They hoped in this way to attract them initially and keep them for 3 to 5 years, since their service would rank as 'good service' in the same way as service at sea. They said that if they could not succeed in doing this the plans for privatisation would rear their head once more . 'Unless the post of Admiral Superintendent can be made sufficiently attractive it will be necessary to again take into account the views of the Hilton Committee'. So important had the Royal Dockyards been at the turn of the century that in 1890, with the Great War on the horizon, Lord Fisher had been picked as the key man for a key job in Portsmouth Royal Dockyard and, benefiting from his knowledge of building and repair, went on to become Third and then First Sea Lord, whereas now, with the Second World War threatening, the Admiralty was working under the threat of privatisation. Where did the fault lie?

Although in 1939 Rosyth and Pembroke were still on a care and maintenance basis, the electrical distribution system at Portsmouth and Devonport had recently been modernised to enable employment of electro-welding and compressed air machine tools. Likewise, although Cork dockyard had been handed back to Eire by Treaty in 1938, taking with it control of the Western Approaches, naval work across the Irish Sea was transferred to Londonderry and Belfast, without whose loyalty the war would have been lost, for they controlled the entrance to the UK western ports via the Northern passage. In the dockyards work began at once on refitting and fitting out for war the Royal Fleet Auxiliaries and destroyer escorts – 200 of which were attended to in Devonport in 18 months. All the dockyard workforces were expanded, although not to the same extent as in previous wars, the percentage of increase at Devonport being only 15. Output thus depended on increased productivity. Women were again recruited and in Chatham they drove cranes and operated machinery. After her action with the Graf Spee at Montevideo, the Exeter returned to Devonport, from whence a year later bombing forced her to leave hurriedly with her refit uncompleted. The Ajax, also initially returning from Montevideo to Devonport, was refitted and repaired at Chatham, where she was only saved from destruction by being substituted for an old cruiser undergoing conversion, which the Luftwaffe mistook for their target and reported pulverised to a wreck. Many warships and rescue ships which assembled at Sheerness to evacuate the army from Dunkirk obtained succour in Chatham and Sheerness dockyards, enabling them to ply over the Channel to pick up men. Meanwhile, in April 1940 1,200 vessels assembled at Rosyth for the Norwegian campaign, a number of which returned damaged, including the battlecruiser Renown, after an encounter with the Scharnhorst and Gneisenau. Like Pembroke, also re-opened in September 1939, Rosyth was at a disadvantage, since its workforce, rising to between 5000 and 6000, was increased from a skeleton force of 750 virtually overnight. It normally takes two years to build up a dockyard workforce and twenty five to produce an effective foreman and generate the required efficiency and expertise at all levels of management and labour. Although the heads of shops and a number of foremen and charge-hands came to Rosyth from southern dockyards, particularly from Chatham, causing dilution of skills in that yard, the bulk of the workforce came from the ranks of the unemployed, having been rejected by other industries. Trawlers, ferries and steam yachts – recruited into minelaying, minesweeping and patrol teams and mostly manned by the RNR and RNVR – were the first casualties of mines and the Luftwaffe in Scottish waters. Then in November 1939 the cruiser Belfast broke her back by striking a mine in the Firth of Forth and was towed into Rosyth, where, after repairs, the hull remained 'out of true'. It was decided in June 1940 to send her down to Devonport in secrecy, where more suitable facilities were available for the extensive hull rebuilding that was required. She returned to operational service in October 1942 after a 28 month refit, with bulges added to strengthen her hull and improve stability. She is currently preserved as a museum secured alongside on the Thames south bank.

When serious air battles began over the Kent coast in summer 1940, Chatham received direct hits and more skilled men were sent north to Rosyth, which, apart from one costly German air raid in 1939, was considered a safer and more strategic haven. Lying under high ground, surrounded by barrage balloons on sea and land (30,000 of these balloons were manufactured by Dunlop during the war) the dockyard had the advantage of its situation at the head of a firth, on the mouth of which was Leuchars aerodrome, while its waters could be secured against attack by submarines. 'Rosyth', said an Admiralty communication, 'Must have consideration over southern yards... . Strategic considerations have amply proved the necessity for a naval dockyard in the north'. Skilled men coming from the south required accommodation and so, with Rosyth garden city otherwise occupied, valuable time had to be devoted to seeking local authority help and providing prefabricated housing, in spite of which some dockyard mateys had to travel from Edinburgh and the Fife burghs. By the autumn of 1940 the bombing had spread to Portsmouth, leaving Devonport as the only southern dockyard in comparative safety. Thither in November 1940 the destroyer Javelin was towed with her bow and stern blown off in action, leaving only 155 feet of her 353 foot hull. Four months later Devonport was also subjected to the fiercest of aerial attacks, with major devastation and men killed at work. During this and the following month, the old south yard was demolished, the cruiser Kent was hit in dock, workshops were destroyed and in the town whole streets were erased. It seemed for a time that the spirit of Plymouth might be broken by the ferocity of these nightly attacks, the intention of which was the complete destruction of the dockyard. This was a very anxious moment in the war at sea, but the people of Plymouth went firmly about their business and work in the dockyard contin-ued. Devonport's vulnerability, however, had now to be taken into account when allocating the future refits of capital ships.

Unfortunately there is no Official Report on the achievements of the Royal Dockyards during the war, except a five page document held by the National Maritime Museum. Time and time again the Admiralty referred to the need to stress their excellent record, but either no action was taken or the records have been shredded or lost. This explains the sketchiness of the chapters on modern times in the histories of the Royal Dockyards, which go into the minutest detail in times past, but produce few figures or information on the Second World War. Many of the relevant boxes at the Public Record Office are only sparsely filled and nothing can compensate for this loss to the nation. Among these papers is, however, an interesting correspondence between Mr. Bevin, Minister of Labour and National Service, and the Admiralty at the end of 1940, when Mr. Bevin was anxious about the supply of ships for military convoys to the Near and Middle East. It was at this time that the crisis caused by lack of skilled men in the shipyards became fully evident. Building skills required for naval ships were traditionally 30 percent higher than for merchant vessels and when it came to repair work the difference was yet more marked, but since the outbreak of war work on naval ships in private yards had been sucking in skilled men, who, because of the scarcity of skilled labour, were also needed urgently for merchant ship building and repair. (30,000 men were so engaged in 1939 and 100,000 by 1943). The Shaw Committee produced in 1940 a Report on the labour force in the Royal Dockyards, (which standing at 38,640 in 1939 rose to 48,370 by 1943, with half the increase being taken up by Rosyth alone). The Report defined only three divisions in the dockyard work-force – craftsmen, skilled and unskilled labourers – the former having higher pay and levels of entry, both as regards apprenticeship and examination. The Shaw Report pointed out that 14 percent of the workforce was 'established', which meant that they could be moved at the direction of the Admiralty to dockyards overseas or to other UK dockyards. They could also be moved on a voluntary basis to avoid air raids, which in some southern yards were totalling 24 a week. Thus in the first 12 months of war there had already been a wastage either abroad or to the forces of 12 percent and, with 30 or 40 ships in hand in each yard, this necessitated the recruitment of many men of lower calibre. 13,000 extra men were therefore required in the Royal Dockyards alone. The crisis of skills, about which the government had been repeatedly warned inter-war, had now arrived.

Early in 1941 the Ministry of Labour sent a Lloyd's assessor to make a report on the Naval Dockyards. This highlighted the problem of waiting between trades, which very few people outside the management of ship build-ing and ship repair yards and large engineering construction projects have ever understood. It was reported to be far worse in the private yards, where hulls could not be finished quickly enough and some highly skilled electricians were working 36 hours at a stretch and then not at all for weeks. The Admiralty replied that the concentration in the Royal Dockyards on repair work, with little new building being undertaken, had upset the balance of trades. The Lloyd's memorandum also criticised the men for 'idling', but the Admiralty replied that, 'As the assessor's visit coincided with night air attacks, idling during the day was the obvious result'. The naval view was that 'The dockyard workman on the whole is a thoroughly sound and reasonably hardworking man... From (reports of) officers of ships refitting at private ports idling is considerably worse there than in the Royal Dockyards'. The assessor had a number of criticisms about Rosyth, although he must have been aware that the men were mostly rejects from other industries – 'There are no more skilled men in Scotland', said the Admiralty. There were, said the assessor, subversive elements, who could only be dismissed if long drawn out Admiralty permission was obtained. The report picked four points for particular criticism: first, a shed beside one of the dry docks, which could have housed machinery, was being used as a tea canteen, allowing the men to break from their work without too long a walk (the reader will recall that there were no canteens in shipbuilding until the 1940's); second, there were too few women employed – the Admiral Superintendent's wife consequently qualified as a binoculars apprentice fitter to give a lead to other women; third, there was not enough disciplinary action to stop idling – the Admiral Superintendent's reaction was that inspections of work should no longer be carried out by foremen, but by a technically qualified Naval Commander accompanied by two policemen (a suggestion not taken seriously by the Admiralty); lastly, although absenteeism was only 2.3 percent, and could not be compared with the 7 percent average for private yards, nevertheless leave and absence figures at Rosyth were higher than in the other dockyards. Bearing in mind the men's 63 hour week and additional long travelling time, Rear Admiral Colin Cantlie's answer had been to work a six-and-a-half day week himself, with no holiday since the start of the war, and to site his modest one-storey office beside the dockyard gate, where late comers and early leavers could be spotted. Like Lord Gort in Malta, he and the Captain of the Dockyard bicycled to work. 'The Report', said the Admiralty, 'in addition to pointing out rightly the shortcomings, should have made some reference to the actual amount of work accomplished, since this is a record of which the yard as a whole feels proud'.

The report sparked off an acrimonious row between the Ministry of Labour and the Admiralty Director of Dockyards in Bath, who gave the Admiral Superintendents his complete support and said that valuable time had been wasted on ignorance. Mr. Bevin requested that men should be released from the Royal Dockyards for work in civil yards, a suggestion turned down by the Admiralty, who in return requested the termination of the assessor's appointment, referring, 'To his valueless but irritating comments'. 'The time of myself and other officers', said Admiral Talbot in Bath, 'has been wasted in having to reply to such ignorant and irresponsible criticism... It is not to be tolerated at the present time of national crisis'. Mr. Bevin then changed his ground and put forward the idea that the Ministry of Labour and the Admiralty should share responsibility for the work in the Royal Dockyards and private yards, a suggestion which the Admiralty said would, 'Entirely disorganize the work'. Bevin then came up with a third suggestion – that, in order to use the private building and repairing yards with greater efficiency, the Admiral Superintendents and Flag Officers in Charge should become responsible for all the private civil yards in their area, introducing a system of tribunals to preserve civilian status. At the apex of this huge complex was to be a Shipbuilding and Repair Control, with a Chairman appointed by the First Sea Lord and 2 representatives from

the Ministry of Labour among its members. This body was to have the power
to guarantee a working week, set wages and introduce payment by results. The
boilermakers were in favour of the plan, since it smacked of nationalisation,
but the Admiralty was not keen on the idea, seeing the danger of diluting naval
efficiency and being dragged into a wider range of industrial disputes than
those affecting their own yards. This time, however, their Lordships had little
alternative but to agree and the final words from the Director in Bath regarding
the complicated proposals, couched in civil service language were, 'I am afraid
I must concur without really understanding a word of it. I feel that someone
who can explain the business should take the earliest opportunity of visiting
the Flag Officers, and also find out what extra staff they require'. The Royal
Navy thus took over supervision and responsibility for the running of all civilian shipyards for the rest of the war and – with few exceptions – set up an
accounting base at each.

   This disagreement gave birth to the appointment of two liaison officers to
avoid future misunderstandings between the Admiralty and the Ministry of
Labour, relations between whom appear from now on to have remained good
until the end of the war. The Admiral Superintendents and Naval Officers in
Charge were not only good administrators, but, having no financial interest,
could intervene to calm disputes, where private management failed. An
account is extant among these papers of such an incident at Leith in the Firth
of Forth area in September 1943. 'The DSC (Director Shipyard Control –
which initials were added to the title of Admiral Superintendent) took action
concerning the Boilermakers, which, while theoretically unconstitutional, has
nevertheless been attended by the best result and has thus justified itself...
(There is) no doubt whatsoever that it was his bringing home to the men what
was involved that made the men receptive to the arguments of the delegates
that they would abide by the proper procedure and in the meantime resume
work'.

   The only figure for the number of repairs in the Royal Dockyards, which
emerges from the Public Records Office, misleads rather than informs. At
Sheerness they went up from 75 in 1938 to 293 in 1941. As a large number of
less urgent repairs had by this time been transferred from Sheerness and
Chatham to safer havens, the figure is distorted, as it would have been if statistics for 1940, including Dunkirk repairs, had been given instead. There is
fortunately, however, another account of work done in the Royal Dockyards,
since Sir Muirhead Bone, the Official War Artist, was sent to Rosyth for six
months in 1940 and 1941 and his drawings of Rosyth and other dockyards
appeared in the Illustrated London News and elsewhere. In World War I much
of his work had been concerned with the care of the wounded at the front – in
World War II it was primarily connected with the war at sea. His drawings
show how in the summer of 1940 the Hood arrived in Rosyth for refitting, to
be followed by the battleship King George V and Captain Vian's destroyer
Cossack. 'Amidst the clangour and hive-like activity of Rosyth Dockyard',
runs the caption, 'two famous ships of his Majesty's Navy are tended by expert
hands... The whole scene is redolent with grim reality'. All 5 battleships of the

King George V class were fitted out at Rosyth and the Warspite, damaged by mines, was repaired there and all her 15 inch guns replaced in 7 weeks. Further drawings published in the Illustrated London News on September 27th 1941 show Portsmouth Dockyard, 'With some of the little ships, which have played and are playing so important a part in the battle for the freedom of the seas'; the aircraft carrier Illustrious is seen being manoeuvred by tugs into the basin at John Brown's yard on Clydebank, while a troopship in dock in Rosyth is depicted with barrage balloons and gulls hovering overhead and battleships lying out in the Forth. Underneath are the words, 'Behind the spectacular deeds of the Royal Navy at sea lies the vast dockyard organisations of our land; from Rosyth in the north to Plymouth in the south are docks and harbours wherein maimed ships may find sanctuary and renewed vitality and others are equipped with their cargoes of merchandise, guns or men. Both (scenes) are alive with ceaseless activity; both are redolent with the spirit of grim determination common to those who work with British ships'.

Equally vital were repairs to merchant shipping, which were being damaged faster than they could be repaired, but, as already explained, details of this work are even harder to discover than those concerning naval ships. In June 1940 7 percent of the British cargo fleet was immobilised awaiting repair. By January 1941 this figure had risen to 13 percent, and in spite of a number of ships being repaired abroad this percentage remained stubbornly high. Shipowners applied to have their ships repaired in the shipyard of their choice, but by spring 1941 permission had to be given by the Naval Directors of Shipyard Control. Some idea of the formidable task faced by these men engaged in merchant ship repair is given by Sir Muirhead Bone's drawing in the Illustrated London News on March 8th 1941 of, 'A gallant little oil tanker'. Torpedoed and badly crippled, 'With green seas pouring through her broken hull, the ship was yet able to reach sanctuary thanks to the outstanding courage and skill of her officers and men. At one time feared a total loss, the tanker was duly repaired and is now at sea again. Surveying the original damage, one of her officers said to the artist, "This side looks as if the rats had been at her; it's not so bad on the other side, more like mice there"'. The words, 'Duly repaired' reflect the modest image of shipyard work – it was a job which had to be done – but, as with the Imperial Transport, a tanker with a new bow grafted on, these accomplishments were indeed, 'Triumphs of marine architecture'. In civil dockyards up and down the country, but particularly in those in the security of northern and western harbours, repairs were carried out in their hundreds of thousands. 35,000 ships were repaired, refitted and converted by 1943. In Liverpool a team of 20,000 worked round the clock in spite of enemy bombs. All-night working was not uncommon and men remained in the ships at their tasks during air raids. Although the Naval Officer commanding Tyne Station gives the figures for shipbuilding in yards within his control, there is no similar record of repairs. The same is true of the Clyde. These dockyard work-forces feel now and say in recently published books that their sacrifice and work are all forgotten. It is not that the British public do not wish to recognise their debt to these unseen and unsung men and women, but simply that they do not know what was accomplished. Part of this silence has been caused by the need at the time for secrecy about the movement of all ships, whether naval or merchant. 'Be like Dad', said the posters, 'Keep Mum'. This is precisely what was done, and perhaps partly on account of these instructions a large part of British history will consequently never be known.

References to naval repairs can of course be found in the log books of individual ships, but to build up from this a statistical account would be a formidable task. Periods of notable length in dockyard hands, however, are given in the 'pink slips'- the official records of the movement of ships held by the naval section of the MOD. Taking an average of refits for each year of war and comparing these with the average for 1938, it seems that substantial repairs, which included some refitting, went up by ten times during the war years. The efforts of the Royal Dockyards at home and overseas were not confined to meeting the needs of the Royal Navy alone. Ships of the Commonwealth and all the Allies, including American, Norwegian, Dutch, Polish, Free French and, more occasionally, Russian, all made good use of UK and overseas Dockyard facilities, imposing further demands upon their strained resources. Space does not permit an adequate account of the work done in the Royal Dockyard overseas at this time, all of which contained a nucleus of British skilled workers amongst the teams of local labour, nor of the work done in Commonwealth and US yards, particularly in Halifax in Canada. The heroic story of Malta with its five dry docks has already been told – and how by April 1942 they were all out of action with over 30 ships sunk in the harbour; Gibraltar offered a safer haven both for fleet repairs and as an assembly point for amphibious operations. Alexandria harbour, which received the Australian contingents via the Suez Canal, was hastily transformed into a naval dockyard in 1942 and, with a dry dock purchased from the Egyptians and a floating dock sent from the UK, repaired 3000 ships by the end of the war. With the fall of Hong Kong and Singapore and the vulnerability to air attack of Trincomalee and the Indian dockyards, Killindini at Mombasa was hurriedly given a floating dock and two depots ships and transformed into an effective base by Captain Hamley, formerly Captain of Rosyth Dockyard. Floating docks were also used in Iceland and later in the war in the Far East. Simonstown was always a key base and grew in importance after the Japanese entry into the war, while on the eastern and western shore of the Atlantic the dockyards at Fremantle, Bermuda and Halifax were working flat out, as was also Antigua, which had become a US Naval base after Lease Lend in September 1940. The official figure for the total number of refits of the Allied fleet, which took place in the Royal Dockyards at home and overseas, was 97,000 – an almost unbelievable figure did it come from any other source than the brief Official Report held in the National Maritime Museum.

As the war moved from the defensive to the offensive stage, so did the work in the Royal Dockyards alter. Towards the end of 1943 attention focused again on the dockyards in the south of England, which prepared the great Armada for Normandy. According to Philip MacDougall Portsmouth fitted out nearly a thousand miscellaneous assault craft and repaired over 400 ships in the two months following D day, while also providing expert help in the construction of Mulberry caissons and work for the headquarters of SHAEF. As well as undertaking work on the naval ships and auxiliary vessels required, Devonport constructed decoy sites for the luring of enemy aircraft on to the wrong targets, while Chatham did work for the Pluto pipeline and supplied welding equipment for land fighting vehicles and for the fitting out of shore establishments. By summer 1944 the concentration of the Admiralty and the Royal Dockyards turned to winning the war in the Far East, where the Royal Dockyards became the key to the fitting out of a vastly increased Naval Fleet. By this time Trincomalee had taken over from Kilindini as the forward base and, together with the four Indian dockyards, which Vice Admiral Colin Cantlie, Rosyth, was sent out to administer, formed the repair, refitting and assembly point for the enormous fleet that was now to form part of the invasion force for Japan – an invasion force that mercifully for the war-weary Western Allies was not required because of the dropping of the atomic bomb in August 1945.

The end of the war was followed by severe retrenchment. Orders were cancelled on the slipway and there were thousands of redundancies. Pembroke was closed in 1947, Sheerness in 1960. The closure of Malta in 1958 was decided against the wishes of the Maltese people, who formed a nationalised company to run the dockyard as a profitable commercial enterprise, lengthening the dry docks to take super tankers and bulk carriers. In the UK dockyards ships were refitted before being sold overseas. Mr. Bevin, now Foreign Secretary, wanted the Royal Dockyards to help repair the backlog of merchant ships, but they were fully employed fitting out and repairing the fleet, as well as maintaining the Reserve, which totalled over 250 vessels. By the following year the Admiralty was being pressed to contract out more shipbuilding to private yards, where merchant shipbuilding was falling off. Then came the worsening financial situation and shortages of steel, so the policy of 'Go Slow' was advocated by the government in the civilian yards in order to maintain the level of skills in employment by taking longer to build ships. Command in the Royal Dockyards remained with the Admiral Superintendents, who had authority over the dockyard and companion bases, which manned, moored and fuelled the ships. The Captains of the Dockyards continued to manage the movement and docking of ships and provide harbour services, while the senior Engineering and Electrical Engineering Managers were still Naval Officers, as were also the Assistants in the Engineering Department. It seemed during the late 1950's that life might be returning to normal but change was on the way. In 1964 Parliament debated the Defence Bill, by which the administration of the Armed Services was merged into one monolithic Ministry of Defence with three Departments, one for each Service, the Admiralty disappearing. Lord Attlee and a number of other Peers and politicians opposed the measure. He reminded the House of Lords of the efficiency of the wartime administration based on the traditional Service triumvirate and warned the government against tampering with tried methods. One of the unfortunate results of this Act was that dockyard mateys ceased to be employed by the Admiralty and became civil servants under the Civil Service Department of the MOD, which assumed control of all dockyard personnel, management and manpower levels, pay and conditions of service, thus taking away from management the ability to effectively manage and match resources to the load.

The effects of this change were exacerbated by the 1963 legislation on employment contracts, which removed the employers' right to hire and fire at will and to employ casual labour. This would have posed serious problems of cost in the Royal Dockyards even if warship building had continued there, but the Geddes Report recommended concentrating naval shipbuilding in a few specialist private warship yards, which ended new building in the Royal Dockyards in 1968. This was an example of the 'vicious circle' of which Disraeli had warned in 1848 – decisions taken in ignorance having a knock on effect on each other, so that the downward spiral of decline gathers a momentum that is virtually unstoppable. Seen against the enacted promise given by Mr. Bevin to uphold the demarcation between the skilled trades after the war, the cessation of building work, together with the elimination of the reserve fleet refits and the loss of the right to hire and fire labour, made the problems of balance of trades and waiting between trades in the Royal Dockyards virtually insoluble. Now the only long term projects to provide a reserve of manpower to meet the programme of trade peaks and at the same time to supply work during its troughs were the few refits and modernisations, which for this purpose were largely inadequate. Ways were discussed to solve the problem – either by employing flying squads of trained men going from yard to yard, unacceptable to their families; or training men in multiple skills, unacceptable to the Unions; or putting skilled men on to unskilled work, unacceptable to the craftsmen. Then in 1968 the Mallabar Committee, studying the future of the Royal Dockyards, recommended civilian management and the creation of a government Trading Fund to grant loans to the dockyards and fix financial targets. Between the wars the Admiralty had said of the Admiral Superintendents that 'They had run the dockyards on good business lines and understood labour relations'. Was this therefore simply a desire for change – the life blood of modern politics – or had the Navy lost its feeling for industrial relations, rejecting the modest wartime concept of leadership by example for a higher profile – flagged car, black ebony cane and gloves? Whatever the reason, Devonport led the way with a commercial manager, while Rosyth lagged behind, retaining its Admiral Superintendent almost to the end of MOD control.

While these changes were taking place modernisation of the four Royal Dockyards was going ahead. Devonport, which required virtual rebuilding after the war, was given a central office block and roofed frigate refitting complex, with lengthened docks and major workshop improvements. Portsmouth was provided with new shops and storage facilities, as well as improvements to the docks and refit areas. Modernisation of the conventional part of Rosyth dockyard followed, with a remarkable synchro lift being completed in 1980, to bring smaller ships right out of the water and slide them into a huge covered factory shed. When during the 1960's the airborne nuclear deterrent took to the sea and nuclear power became the propulsion for a number of submarines, Rosyth was chosen as the refitting base for Polaris and new acreage was later taken in to accommodate Trident. Chatham meanwhile received a complex for refitting nuclear powered submarines and Devonport was also updated as a modern operational base for nuclear powered submarines – with two dry docks, a wet berth and extensive support facilities. The promise that the cost of Polaris (now Trident) would come from a separate fund was, however, only kept in part – as was explained earlier – so that less money is left to provide conventional ships. 'The cuts which have been necessary in the surface ship programme in order to pay for Trident have undermined the necessity for a solid core programme of work for the dockyards'. (Naval evidence to the 1988/89 Public Accounts Committee).

Greater change, however, was to come for within 5 months of winning the 1979 election, plans were afoot in the Conservative government to change the status of the Royal Dockyards. Mr. Keith Speed, Under Secretary for the Royal Navy, set up a Dockyard Study Group, which drew attention to the number of levels of management and the amount of planning and paper work, which it claimed was coupled with insufficient supervision. It recommended, as the previous Mallabar Report had done, the provision of a loan to the Royal Dockyards from a government Trading Fund and the setting of financial targets to ensure a return on assets. The government accepted the Report and said an early announcement would be made. Then in 1981 the Defence White Paper heralded the closure of Chatham and Gibraltar dockyards, together with the major reduction of activities at Portsmouth, which was to be turned into a fleet support base. These reductions eliminated dockyard capacity roughly equal to the whole of the modernisation refit load of the Royal Dockyards. To balance this there were promises of increased activities at Devonport and Rosyth. The closure of Chatham in 1984, in spite of its recently installed nuclear powered submarine complex and of its being arguably the most experienced Royal Dockyard, was carried through in the teeth of opposition by Kent Members of Parliament more on a basis of local employment than on strategic need and, since the government had been elected on a strengthened defence policy, the nation accepted the policy on trust. The closure of Gibraltar, on the other hand, was bitterly opposed by the Gibraltarians, who saw a move on the part of the British government to abandon the base in the same way as Malta had previously been abandoned. Gibraltar acted as a port of call for NATO ships and was the last and vital British link safeguarding the security of trade routes to the East. Every assurance was given to the contrary and £23 million was given to the Gibraltar government to modernise the yard before it was handed over to Appledore to be run as a commercial enterprise, with an agreed amount of core naval work in refits and repairs. At the time of the author's visit there in 1986 the firm was making every effort to maintain the number of skilled men and train apprentices and attract new building to solve the problem of waiting between trades. However, in the Defence Estimates of 1984 the government announced that it intended to eliminate the major refits, which meant effectively modernisation at half life. This would not only reduce the amount of work done in the Royal Dockyards and exacerbate the problem of waiting between trades but would eventually, as in the time of Pepys, render the fleet obsolete and short of ships, unless further, more expensive building was proposed – an improbable outcome. In defence vote terms, the average cost of modernisation was about half that of a comparable new ship, so that, unless the naval element of the defence estimates was substantially increased, the number of operationally up-to-date ships would inevitably fall.

Declaring its intention to have some ships refitted commercially to compare costs, the government then turned its attention to shedding or reducing its financial responsibilities for the two remaining dockyards. When Charles I, for similar reasons, had leased Woolwich to the East India Company, he chose as lessees a private company, whose ships maintained the freedom of the seas for Britain east of Suez and whose officers were equal in rank to those of the Royal Navy. The government in the 1980's sought a formula to hive off the Royal Dockyards into commercial management, while safeguarding, so far as this 'leap in the dark' allowed, the efficiency of the fleet. The reader will recall that by this time the number of surface ships had so far dwindled that they had an operational strength equivalent to about two thirds of the escort, which set out to fight 13 merchant vessels through to Malta in August 1942. The government was able to enlist some naval support by arguing that if cuts were made in the support services more ships could be provided with the money saved. In fact, on account of continuing financial restrictions, the number of ships was then cut again in line with the reduced support facilities, producing a circle yet more vicious than any envisaged in the 1848 debates. The safety of the country in the event of conventional war was assumed, for there was a large US Navy to defend the Western Alliance and the existence of the seaborne nuclear deterrent discounted the threat of future invasion. In the Defence Open Government Document of 1985 the Secretary of State said that he would not contemplate keeping the Royal Dockyards in their present form, asserting their overmanning, inefficiency and absenteeism, which, in Devonport, was claimed to be 40 percent above the national average. Instead he offered 3 options of which one was Preferred. These were: full privatisation, rejected by all parties; a Trading Fund, favoured by most parties but rejected by the government because the dockyard workforce would remain within the constraints of the Civil Service and the Preferred Option – to lease the dockyards for 5, later extended to 7, years to commercial management, bringing the workforce out of Civil Service restraints and enabling redundancies to take place, for which the government could not be directly blamed. The government had three targets: to give local managers the right to manage (which they had before the ending of naval control in 1964 and the demise of the Admiral Superintendents), to introduce a customer/ supplier relationship (as in the time of Pepys) and to change from Civil Service to proper commercial accounting. Under the Preferred Option 70 percent of Royal Navy work would continue to go to the two remaining dockyards, but the Navy would retain the right to put the other 30 percent out to commercial tender in civil yards, should it so wish. In the first year the RN only availed themselves of this right to the extent of one ship, since commercial work available to the Royal Dockyards under their new management has been limited and the capacity to refit complex modern warships in UK private repairing yards was, and remains, very small – 5 percent before the loss of Chatham and Portsmouth.

The Public Accounts Committee and the Defence Select Committee directed considerable attention to the future of the Royal Dockyards between 1983 and 1989 and the latter was particularly critical of the time given for discussion – 11 weeks were reduced in some matters to only 2 because MOD papers were not available. It was not acceptable, said the Chairman, to suggest options were open and to invite parties to discuss them if these options in reality were closed. The government having stated that other countries, particularly the USA, had similar schemes, the Defence Select Committee hired a management consultancy company to investigate. As far as could be ascertained, the naval dockyards of these nine western nations all functioned under naval control and, although it was true that the USA did have some commercial management, this was confined to very small operations and found to be costly, owing to the supervision required. There are four main reasons, inter alia, why dockyard organisations of most Navies are kept under naval control. First, a Navy's dockyards are a vital and integral part of naval capability, directly responsive to the demands of the base commander and not simply providers of industrial output which can be bought by contract. Second, the dockyard managers are the only people, who by virtue of their professional knowledge and experience, can advise the Navy on the techniques of ship repair and how repairs and refitting cañ best be done. If this organisation remains part of the Navy, the advice given will always be that which is most economical for the Navy, whereas a private contractor will tend to advocate repair action giving him most profit and therefore the Navy most expense. Third, it is impossible to obtain and rigidly adhere to agreed fixed prices for contract refits, because much of the work required is found by surveys carried out in the middle of the refit. This emergent work may comprise 30 percent of the total and each extra has to be negotiated under pressure of time. A private contractor can claim dislocation and delay charges based on disruption of other work and because in all these circumstances it is easy for him to 'drive a horse and cart' through a fixed price contract, a great deal of non-productive effort has to be made by naval specification writers and overseers, who do not need to be employed if the dockyard is a part of the Navy. Fourth, a Navy which owns its dockyards does not have to pay a substantial profit margin on its refitting work.

Much evidence given to the Committees was critical of the Preferred Option, which it was felt spawned imponderables. Responsibilities for strategic planning and capital investment were to be retained by the Admiralty Board, while day-to-day running and short term investment would be under the control of commercial management. Disadvantages for the Royal Navy were summed up under four main headings: first, that commercial management might casualise the workforce, (which has to a certain extent happened with sub-contracting understandably taking the place of hiring and firing); second, that work might be moved off the yards altogether, so that the Navy would be ill-equipped in an emergency; third, that if naval work was required quickly the company, with its responsibility to shareholders, might not be able to oblige and lastly, that there could be delays in refitting the nuclear deterrent. Surprisingly, the threat to training schemes and apprenticeship schools was hardly raised in these Reports. Yet so vital was it to the RN that after its training ship was destroyed by fire in 1939 HMS Caledonia Training School for Artificers was given vitally scarce accommodation at Rosyth Dockyard throughout the war. Moreover the danger to the higher standards required for naval work failed also to become a central issue. However, in the Defence Select Committee Report of 1986/87 reference was made to a letter from Mr. Malcolm Rifkind, which said that, 'The number of apprentices training at the Dockyards under commercial management will primarily be determined by the contractors', and subsequently to a later statement by Lord Trefgarne at the Lords Committee stage of the Dockyard Services Bill on June 9th 1986 that, 'They will also have to be to the satisfaction of the Secretary of State'. There this matter, axiomatic to the whole debate, was left to rest.

Both Select Committees criticised the fact that, in spite of upheavals, savings would not be 'substantial', and the Public Accounts Committee felt that the MOD had exaggerated the financial benefits, particularly the costing of assets. The licence fee to commercial management for the use of equipment and assets posed further problems, since it had to be reduced for naval work and raised for commercial tenders, in order to avoid pushing down costs unnaturally to the detriment of other industries. Responsibility for redundancies – caused either by cuts in the naval programme or by improved methods of work – were still to be financed by the government and while the cost of handing over to commercial management would cause deficits for the first two years, competitive contracts might not be in place for four. It was calculated that £8 million would be saved annually if a Trading Fund was chosen, £15 million if a government owned PLC was created – the solution favoured by most witnesses – and £23 to £31 million if the yards were put under commercial management (although because of initial costs this target would not be reached for ten years). 'There is no point', said one witness, 'in getting value for money if our national security interests cannot be safeguarded'. The advantage claimed for the Preferred Option was that the Navy would only pay for refits and repairs and not for the running of the yards, so that resources would be released for front line ships, equipment and men, a hope not realised in the recent Options for Change.

The 1988/89 Public Accounts Committee pointed out that finding good managers to run commercialised dockyards and securing sufficient outside orders to keep the workforce employed and the dockyards profitable was not going to be easy. The Committee assessed that it was going to cost £60 million to hand over both dockyards to commercial management and stressed the absolute need for the Comptroller and Auditor General to have access to accounts, to ensure Parliamentary control. Redundancies were expected to reach 3, 400 at Devonport in 4 years and 1000 at Rosyth, while the figure for apprentices – the 'seed corn' of the industry – which had varied from 350 to 170 in the last 7 years, was now expected to remain at about 150. The Admiral, giving evidence on behalf of the RN, explained that when it came to the supply of skilled men he still had, 'Overall responsibility to protect long term strategic interests' and that if he saw a trade going below that which he believed necessary for war, he would have a right to step in. The Director General of Ship Refitting at Bath, who during the Civil Service interregnum had temporarily lost his title, would have an MOD staff, half of which would be at Bath and half at the dockyards. The latter would inspect the work, while Control in Bath would assess their own costs for comparison with the quoted commercial prices (the frequent wartime practice of captains staying close to their ships during refitting seems currently to have been abandoned). Although the Public Accounts Committee accepted that some improvements had already been made with line by line specifications introduced for work emerging after the ship was opened up, members nevertheless felt that the MOD was meeting a considerable challenge in trying to pin down contractors to specific prices for such work. What was required was a price per man per week for refitting, similar to Pepys' calculation of the men and months required for building a ship (in other words an ability for swift mathematical assessment, the importance of which was recognised by the Admiralty in the 1930's). The Committee concluded by expressing the view that all that had really been needed was greater authority for the managers to manage. They were met by the Admiral's explanation that this had proved impossible within Civil Service restraints. 'Under any government since the war there has never been a totally stable defence programme', said the Admiral, who also drew attention to the fact that this was the anniversary of the shooting of Admiral Byng (shot for his failure to prosecute a battle in which he had inadequate force, 'To save Ministers from popular indignation').

When in 1981, cuts were made in naval expenditure to meet John Nott's Defence Review, about half the country's ship repair capacity was destroyed. It was claimed that the Navy's teeth were being saved by cutting the tail, whereas in reality much of the blood stream was being eliminated, including the dockyard's modernisation capacity, which could only result – as it has done – in a progressive reduction of front line warships. The subsequent transfer of the remaining two dockyards to commercial management reduced the dockyards' responsiveness to the Navy's operational needs and created a contractual division, where financial control is difficult, wasteful in manpower and largely ineffective. What was required was a simple transfer, removing dockyard personnel from the Civil Service and making them a civilian repair force under naval control, which would have permitted effective management by the Service, whose needs require to be satisfied. Once the skilled workforce of a dockyard is dispersed and training lost it may never be possible to reassemble either. The close liaison between the sea-going Navy and Royal Dockyards was the glue that made indivisible the knowledge of design and operation of ships at sea. In order for the dockyard matey to accept naval control in war the Navy needs as much experience of the Trades Unions and of running a dockyard as the Trades Unions require of the Navy. Based on trust and respect the old Navy had a second-to-none tradition in man management. The Navy knew when to be flexible and when to be authoritarian – 'You can lead a horse to water', runs the proverb, 'but you cannot make him drink'. The Royal Dockyards were comparatively free from demarcation disputes because there was less division of specialised skills. Moreover the Naval Base and Royal Dockyards should never be uncoupled. The ship returns from sea to its base and there should be refitted, repaired, revictualled and refuelled, so that the men can be united for as long as possible with their wives and families.

In 1850 Admiral Sir George Byam Martin warned the House of Lords that they needed both Royal Dockyards and civilian yards, 'The safety of Britain depends on its shipwrights'. Few people understand the urgent need for ship repair until war is declared and ships return from the front line with shattered sides and mangled hulls, which no amount of fleet maintenance at sea can repair. Nearly 100 years later, in August 1939, the Admiral Superintendent and his Captain of the Dockyard, neither of whom had yet taken up their appointments were standing, dressed in civilian clothes, on high ground above the Dockyard looking out to sea. The Admiralty had given its assurance that Rosyth would have six months to build up an efficient workforce before receiving refits and complicated repairs. Nevertheless, they saw to their horror tugs, which had never coped before with any large ships, manoeuvring a large warship into the basin. No one had told them that she was coming. Would the men accomplish this task, no mind be able to tend the ship? When a dockyard is run down equipment and skills suffer and so also does the fabric of the buildings and indeed the site itself. In order to lay a cement base for what was to become the foundry for metal castings, sandy soil had to be excavated under the wooden floor. Here were found extensive rabbit warrens, stretching under great swathes of dockyard land. So entrenched were they that, despite every effort at control, they continued to maintain a right of habitation in the yard until well on in the war – often exercising themselves in broad daylight on the paths and roadways. Re-creating a dockyard in an emergency is a very much more formidable and expensive task than the cost of keeping one ticking over, in case emergency should arise. This is the sad truth that no one is able to believe, for it is perhaps rightly said that the only thing the British people learn from history is that the British learn nothing from history.

CHAPTER XVII

'BUT IT ROSE AFAR'
THE WILL TO SURVIVE

Although it is said that the British learn nothing from history, nevertheless in times of crisis there is no doubt they are inspired by great literature from their past, recalling courage and hope. 'A star was lost here', wrote Robert Browning in his poem Waring, 'but it rose afar'. Browning takes as his dramatic hero a young man about town who disappeared giving his friends no clue to his whereabouts. 'What's become of Waring?' they ask, 'Since he's given us all the slip?' No one has seen or heard of him, except the last to speak, who says casually, 'The last time I saw Waring... ' and in reply to eager questions he describes how he thinks he saw their friend, transformed into a bronzed young sailor and entrepreneur, stripped to the waist, sitting in a light skiff, sailing into Trieste harbour selling wines and commodities. The reader may remember that Browning chose for his setting the very port which in 1848 had been the most resistant to receiving British merchant ships. It was there, in what seemed an impossible environment, that he made his 'star' rise again. This is the adventurous spirit and determination not to be defeated that throughout the centuries inspired the British people and led them to great accomplishments. For this reason it cannot be right to end a book on a negative note. Even Charles Dickens was told by his publisher to add another chapter to Great Expectations in which his hero and heroine should meet again. But that was fiction. Nevertheless, at the saddest moment of British history – in August 1914 – an American wrote of London, 'All things are episodes to her vast experience. Always the tomorrows of London are greater than her todays'. The British are not out of the maritime race. They are only resting. Can a great nation, surrounded by the sea, nowhere far from its sound, smell and open horizon be relegated to a landward attachment to the continent, reached only through a Channel tunnel or on board a foreign ferry? Can Britain, through want of her own ships, be denied access to the vast expanses of the ocean, which its explorations were the first to chart in modern hydrography? The idea is preposterous. Yet, unless present policies are reversed, the British people will be cut off from the very life line which throughout the centuries has inspired and succoured them.

Three questions should be asked in conclusion about Britain's maritime decline. First, does it matter? Second, how did it happen. Third, what are the British people going to do about it? It has been repeatedly stated that an island is in a very strong position politically, economically and strategically if it has maritime forces, a merchant marine and a thriving shipbuilding industry, but it is in a very vulnerable position indeed if it is dependent on other nations to transport its goods, build its ships and defend its shores. Not only does the transport of its own goods bring security and savings in foreign currency, but the carrying trade contributes substantially to the balance of payments, with the cross trades in particular providing 59 percent in 1990 and 62 percent in 1991 of the total earnings from British shipping. 91.5 percent of imports and 97.5

percent of exports are carried by sea and even agriculture, the most basic of all our industries, would, without sea transport, collapse for want of fertilisers. The link between, on the one side, the manufacture of goods and extraction of minerals and, on the other, their transport to markets overseas has been neglected for so long that modern experts cannot conceive that the one could influence the other. Yet that link gives a freedom of choice and movement, which is denied to the non ship owner. The Newcastle shipbuilding industry was built upon the transport of coal and in the evidence given in 1848 to the Select Committee of the House of Lords, merchants testified to the connection between the successful export of manufactured goods and the owning and building of ships. To avoid the high price charged by liner conferences many exporters ran their own fleets and had agents in overseas ports, a practice now so lapsed that only senior citizens remember. It has been shown in this book how lack of maritime strength places Britain at the mercy of other nations and how in war and to maintain the peace the need for an island nation to have her own maritime forces within an alliance is paramount. This means not only suffi-cient naval and air forces, but merchant vessels, auxiliary and cargo, and ship-yards to replenish them. Yet Britain is currently short of between 300 and 400 ocean going ships, so that the question, 'From whence in an emergency, would they come?' cannot be answered. This not only endangers the strategy of the 90 day sealift reinforcement across the Atlantic, but also places in doubt the supply of trained personnel available to man RN ships in war. To help to remedy this deficiency the Government has now set up a Merchant Navy Reserve to provide volunteers from seafarers now in shore jobs and in the fishing fleet.

There is, however, another answer – hardly touched upon – to that first stark question, 'Does it matter?'. What if a nation's financial houses and institutions also depend upon its maritime interests? Take a walk through London's Square Mile and you will understand that not only is shipping itself a major invisible, but the City of London and indeed other cities and seaports throughout Great Britain depend upon her maritime trade for their very survival. Perhaps lay people do not realise that the City of London is the financial heart of a vast maritime trading organisation. Its whole wealth – a capital in every sense of the word – rests on the twin pillars of a merchant marine with which to earn its living and a Navy to guard its ships and shores. From British shores go out daily hundreds of ships to destinations all over the world. The bulk figures for the exports and imports which go overseas are nearly five times the figure for the rest of the EC. For this trade, 95 percent of which goes by sea, arrangements have to be made which involve the UK in countless maritime activities. Of these invisible earnings many of Britain's competitors are as envious as they were in the last century of the vast shipping opportunities that in 1848 she threw open to the world. Only in five of the years between 1796 and 1913 did Britain have a trading surplus in her current account, the balance was always made up from the invisibles, of which shipping has traditionally ranked as the highest provider. The shipowners are represented by the Chamber of Shipping and the British Motor Shipowners Association, but there are a host of other maritime service industries, which make substantial contributions to the balance of payments, including, the Classification Society of Lloyd's Register, the ship broking and chartering at the Baltic Exchange, Lloyd's Insurance, the work for safety at sea of the International Maritime Organisation, the legal contribution of the Commercial, Admiralty and Prize Courts, (all three of which date back to the Middle Ages), the International Chamber of Shipping, the International Tanker Owners Pollution Federation, CRISTAL Limited (which operates a compensation fund for the oil industry), and the more recent Society of International Gas Tanker and Terminal Operators. Moreover, approximately half the world's financial, commercial, shipping and freight income transactions are conducted by UK banks, and there are export houses, commodity markets and travel businesses, which, inter alia, make further valuable contributions to the invisibles, while having firm links with the maritime industries.

Before a ship sets out on a voyage administrative details have to be completed. It must have a flag to fly and a register on which its name appears. Ships may sail under the flag of their own country and be entered on its official register, the standards of which in Britain's case are very high; or they may sail under an off-shore flag of the same administration, requiring less stringent standards, (like the Norwegian second register – NIS); or if it is a British ship an off-shore flag of a Crown Dependency giving tax concessions, such as the Isle of Man; or the flag of a dependent territory, such as Gibraltar (or Hong Kong, to which special provisions now apply); or of a former dependent territory – like Cyprus; or under a foreign flag of pure convenience, such as that of Panama or Liberia. A ship may also be classed. Lloyd's Register in London is an independent, non profit-distributing international organisation, with no shareholders. Before the First World War Lloyd's classified a very high proportion of the world's vessels, and in 1966 the proportion was still just over a third of the total, but currently it is down to 21.4 percent so that the question can be asked whether a country which ceases to be maritime will continue to classify indefinitely a high proportion of the world's ships. There are about 45 Classification Societies in the world, of which 12, including Lloyd's, are members or associate members of the International Association of Classification Societies, founded in Hamburg in 1968. Classification is voluntary, but the issue of certain statutory certificates is largely dependent on classification surveys and most insurance policies include the clause 'warranted classification maintained'. Classification must not be confused with registration, which is a necessary requirement before a ship may fly a flag. If a ship does not comply with international standards of safety it should not be allowed to fly a flag and therefore should not sail. Unfortunately there are some countries in the world which allow ships not up to international requirements to sail under their flag. While national governments are responsible for standards of safety and for inspection, they can use the Classification Society inspectors for chosen matters. The Societies accept this delegated responsibility for warranting compliance with the regulations laid down by international bodies, such as the UN International Maritime Organisation (founded after World War II), the EC and the International Labour Organisation (founded after World War I). The Department of Transport carries out statutory inspections under the Merchant

Shipping Acts and checks to see if a ship meets with IMO standards and British domestic law. But they accept the Lloyd's mark for construction requirements and a Lloyd's certificate to show that the ship conforms to these regulations, which cover all matters concerning safety of life at sea (SOLAS), including the fixing of load lines, prevention of collisions, training, watchkeeping, search and rescue, fire protection, pollution, dumping, transport of passengers and carriage of dangerous materials. Lloyd's Register is authorised by 100 or so different administrations to carry out surveys for the issue of these safety certificates.

There are two main principles of ship classification. First, a ship should comply with standards of construction which ensure strength and reliability, taking into consideration future cargo, passengers carried and the loading machinery. Second, it should be adequately maintained throughout its life to ensure a continuing standard of strength. Only ships of the highest structural standard are accepted by Lloyd's Register. The Lloyd's designation 100A1 is preceded by the Maltese Cross and is the hall-mark of a first class ship. The mark A covers the building requirements, 1 covers anchoring and mooring equipment, 100 covers seagoing capability. If a shipowner wants a ship built to Lloyd's Register standards, he specifies this in his contract with the shipbuilder and inspection takes place of the plans, of the construction at the shipyard and of the materials and equipment. Approved plans must be adhered to, scantlings checked and welding examined. Maintenance of class status depends on periodical surveys in accordance with Lloyd's Rules, which have been updated to conform with invention over the centuries – be it iron (1855), steel (1888), special requirements for tankers (1925), or welded construction, the use of high tensile steels and other new techniques and materials. Special surveys are carried out every five years, but there are also intermediate surveys at half-time and annually, as well as surveys on dry docking, screwshafts and engines. On average there are approximately 350 surveyable items on each ship, and in its 255 world-wide offices Lloyd's carries teams of highly qualified surveyors to do this work. Currently attention is being directed towards the recent high casualties among bulk carriers during voyages in heavy weather and towards more stringent surveys of oil tankers, particularly older vessels. The age-old problem of longitudinal hull bending, due to the non-uniform distribution of weight and buoyancy remains, as do those concerning the required thickness of scantlings and corrosion of brackets and ballast spaces. With recent regulations requiring double hulls in new oil tankers, legislated for by the USA and, unless an alternative solution can be proved effective, called for also by IMO, the need for maintenance and inspection of spaces surrounding the cargo tanks will continue to demand special attention. The Classification Societies are in an unenviable dilemma. If they are too strict they drive ships off their register and if they are too lax they lose the credibility and influence expected of them. As well as carrying out its work on classifying ships, Lloyd's Register also publishes its famous Register of Ships, which starting in 1764 with 4,300 ships, now includes details of 78,000 merchant ships in the world over 100 gross tons, together with companion volumes on shipowners, shipbuilders, docks and offshore craft. It also publishes a Register of all classed yachts, built to approved plans under Lloyd's survey and periodically inspected, from which a yacht can disappear, be rebuilt, modernised and reappear sometimes years later and in a different country under the same name.

Other foreign currency earners among the 'invisibles' are the members of the Baltic Exchange, which starting like Lloyd's as a London coffee house in the eighteenth century, developed into a club with its own rules in 1823 and merged with the London Shipping Exchange in 1900. It moved to its present building in 1903, the architecture and decor of which is reminiscent of the magnificent state rooms of the trans-Atlantic liners. The trading floor walls are of marble, with marble columns supporting an ornate ceiling and there is an elevated and enclosed rostrum, from which the Exchange representative calls out the names of members, who are sought by others. The stone of the extension, an adjacent site rendered vacant by wartime bombs, was laid by Churchill in 1955 and the coffee house atmosphere is continued with catering facilities available. Nearly 1700 elected members can attend the floor of the Baltic Exchange, either as individuals or representing the 600 registered UK companies, which are themselves elected by members of the Board, all of whose business is related to world trade. These companies and individuals are engaged in numerous trading activities, the majority of which are maritime. They may buy and sell ships or they may hire them. The members may be brokers trading for ship owners, or they may be chartering agents. One group will be there on behalf of the owners, looking for cargoes for ships, another will be there on behalf of the merchants, looking for ships for cargoes. They may on the other hand be competitive brokers, representing on different occasions either owners or charterers. Brokers can only act for a principal; they can never act for themselves and they bind themselves to this in writing before starting to trade. Another group are the probationers, who are learning the business and must learn to comply with standards, including those of business dress. Members move freely about the floor exchanging conversation and circulars setting out the terms they are quoting or sit down to make agreements at the tables in the boxes surrounding the hall, divided from each other by wooden partitions. Ships can be chartered in three different ways – on voyage charter or on time charter or as bare boat. Voyage chartering involves a straightforward charter of a ship to carry cargo from one port to another at a negotiated rate, usually expressed in US dollars, although this can be varied. Time charter involves the hiring of a ship for an agreed duration, with the charterer paying the owner for the time taken, normally on the basis of a daily rate of hire. Under this arrangement, the daily running costs of the ship, such as crewing, victualling and insurance remain the owner's expense, whereas the voyage expenses, such as bunkers, port charges, canal dues and stevedoring are put to the time charterer's account. If the basis is bare boat the charterer effectively hires the hull of the ship, is responsible for crewing and for everything else, except the insurance of the vessel itself. The word 'charter-party' comes from the Latin charta partita, a contract divided, with each person holding their part.

Brokers in the Baltic Exchange also specialise in buying and selling ships. The larger firms have separate specialist departments concerned with the various aspects of their work – dry cargo, tankers, sale and purchase. About one half of all the world's purchase of ships is dealt with by the Exchange and two thirds of the world's bulk cargo is transported through dealings on the floor of the Exchange, whose contribution to 'invisible' earnings in 1991 was £801 million. The ships which are chartered or sold may be registered in any part of the world and the users trade globally. The Exchange is thus truly international. The Board of Directors lays down stringent rules, the first and most commanding being, 'Our word our bond'. It was this principle, together with the concept of fair play and justice, which was imposed in the Victorian era by rigorous train- ing over a wide jurisdiction in many areas of the world. The Exchange deals with severity with any member who does not conform to its standards. Discipline is strict and a member knows he is at peril if he does not obey the rules. Since many factors govern the market for ships – fluctuations in world trade, harvests, droughts, natural disasters, conflicts and political upheavals – steady nerves, provided by professionalism and training, are essential. Chartered shipbrokers help to train younger members and probationers to become experts not only in the skills of the Baltic Exchange, but in all the wider aspects of shipowning and shipping.

Also owing its origins to London life in the eighteenth century, Lloyd's Insurance, like Lloyd's Register, began in Edward Lloyd's coffee house, with a group of members taking premiums in return for which they pledged their personal fortunes upon the safe arrival of ships, relying for assessment of the risk upon the information supplied by Edward Lloyd and gleaned from the convivial and relaxed conversation in his coffee house. Insurance depends for success on good faith, the disclosure of all relevant information (uberrimae fidei) and also on first class intelligence and communications – which was covered by the publication of the news sheet, together with very high standards of surveying, aided by the classification provided by Lloyd's Register. At its commencement Lloyd's Insurance was engaged entirely in marine work, and for many years after it became the Society of Lloyd's – drawing up its own constitution in 1811 – it continued to publish a world wide news bulletin of the movement and loss of ships, known as Lloyd's List International. This task is now undertaken by Lloyd's of London Press, which is a subsidiary of the Society. Both organisations of Lloyd's – the Register and the Underwriters – played a significant part in getting Convoy Acts passed to lessen the risk of loss during war. After victory at the Battle of the Nile £38,000 was raised by Lloyd's Insurance for the relief of the wounded and for the dependents of those killed and awards of silver were also made to officers – a demonstration of gratitude repeated at Trafalgar. Increased trade after the Napoleonic Wars brought more demands for insurance and further regulation. By 1840 all the names appearing on a Lloyd's policy had to be elected members and in 1871 the Society was incorporated by Act of Parliament, to be followed by a succession of further Acts, the last of which, establishing a Council, was passed in 1982.

The trading room of Lloyd's is still dominated by the Lutine bell rung to notify members of important news – one ring for bad news, two for good. Whereas in the past the coffee house merchants signed policies themselves, the volume and complexity of modern business demands that each group or syndicate has a professional Lloyd's underwriter to accept insurance on its behalf. Members from 70 countries are grouped into approximately 400 syndicates, with each managed by a professional agent. Lloyd's brokers are the syndicate's only contact with the clients and they obtain business throughout the world, relying, as one of the most important sources of information for their assessment of marine risk, on Lloyd's List International. After taking the decision to insure, the underwriter giving the lead sets the premium and takes a proportion of the risk, sending the proposal on to other syndicates, who make their own judgement about whether or not to add their names. At one time Lloyd's insured nearly all the world's ships and this virtual monopoly is sometimes described as the 'old conspiracy', (insinuating, perhaps without intention, the existence of a new and opposing one). While it is true that often the same men built and insured the ships, sometimes making themselves responsible also for the carriage of goods, nevertheless this tightly knit system did ensure high standards of safety on the high seas with the minimum of risk, which was in the interests of all. 'Without Lloyd's and without its early marine background', which still provides a good slice of income, 'London would not be the world insurance centre that it is'. Marine insurance, which now accounts for only 15 percent of the total of Lloyd's insurance, was audited long before it was a statutory requirement and still provides a considerable contribution to the invisibles, a share of the market which other countries would dearly love to enjoy.

The virtual disappearance of the tailor-made low risk British flagged vessels, built to a very high standard and sailed by highly trained crews, has, however, now detrimentally affected the insurance market and created what could become a vicious spiral of dangerous under-cutting and increased risk. Flags of convenience originally earned this name because they did not set the same standards as would be insisted upon under the British flag, while modern ships are not built to last more than approximately ten years (almost half their previous life). Cutting costs in construction means that ships require more detailed inspection and even this does not yield all the information required. The Japanese insure their own ships; they also, like other countries in the Far East, export cut price ships which can end up on the register of an emerging country, unable to afford high standards of inspection. Another factor is the very fast turn around in port which provides little or no time for maintenance. Crews say that, even if there were time for repainting, connections and supports liable to rust are often situated immediately behind awkward fixtures, making them difficult to reach. A further danger to ships arises from machinery bulk loading of dry cargo by chute, causing raw materials, such as grain, to be forced down into the hold, creating stress and leaving the ship to set out on its voyage not stabilised. In assessing risk the problem for British insurers, both at Lloyd's and among other insurance companies (notably members of the Institute of London Underwriters) is that Britain has withdrawn too far from the maritime race to set the same high standards of construction and maintenance, for which she was once so famous, so that a greater degree of chance enters into contracts. Nevertheless, so long as she still registers one fifth of the world's ships her voice will be heard, and this voice is listened to also on account of the location here in London of IMO, the International Maritime Organisation, which is concerned with safety at sea.

The first international conference on Safety at Sea was held in 1914 as the result of the loss of the Titanic. IMO was born after the Second World War, when nations were once more reminded of those in peril on the sea. It was proposed that the work of ensuring safety should be put on an international footing through the agency of a permanent body of the United Nations. The Convention establishing the International Maritime Organisation was adopted in London in 1948 and came into effect in 1958. London was chosen for its situation and the first session was held in January 1959. The Organisation is presently composed of 137 members and two associate members, with an elected council and international secretariat. Its first convention in 1960 concerning safety of life at sea was a revised version of SOLAS (the initials standing for the words), and since then the Organisation has adopted more than 30 conventions and protocols. There are committees appointed for every department of maritime activity, which contribute to this governing principle. All types of merchant vessels come within IMO's remit, including fishing boats. In order for conventions to be ratified and enforced they must be accepted by a certain number of member countries, the percentage varying with the importance of the subject. Once ratified by the qualifying number, conventions are mandatory upon ratifying governments, which incorporate them into domestic law and set levels of liability. The organisation also issues recommendations and codes of safety, which act as guide lines for decision making.

Because of the increase in oil pollution, which has been the subject of a number of conventions, an international fund has been set up to provide compensation for victims, with contributions from oil importers to add to the sums already paid by shipowners under civil liability. The size of the response reflects the amount of oil transported, which has risen seven times since 1954. Particular regard has been paid to the Mediterranean, where pollution is high. Because of the importance of research in this field, IMO was instrumental in 1983 in setting up the first World Maritime University at Malmo in Sweden, which provides advanced training, from which 700 students have already graduated. There is also an International Maritime Academy at Trieste and an International Maritime Law Institute in Malta. One of IMO's present concerns is the increasing age of fleets, which – like economy building – is leading to greater casualty rates. Another anxiety is the widening of nationalities involved in crewing, which has highlighted the need for co-ordinating standards of crew competence. A convention has been introduced to establish minimum standards on certificates of training and watchkeeping. IMO's only means of enforcing conventions is through national legislation and governmental responsibility or, if the convention allows it, through port inspection. Ships not complying with rules, nor carrying the required certificates, can be prevented from sailing and, even if they do not belong to a ratifying nation, they come within IMO's jurisdiction when visiting countries which have ratified. Considerable success attended these policies – in 5 years starting in 1956 there were 156 collisions at sea, compared with less than a third of that figure in the 5 years starting in 1976, but the recent accidents involving tankers leave no room whatsoever for complacency. International interest in state port control received an impetus in 1982/83 when 19 European states signed a Memorandum of Understanding in Paris, the aim of which was to set up a system of port inspection to ensure IMO's safety standards were enforced. South America signed a similar agreement in 1992 and countries in the Pacific have an embryo agreement, which Canada may join.

English now forms the basis of the standard marine navigational vocabulary, as it does for the language of the air. This means that in the way flight instructions are given in English as well as in the language of the countries of departure and arrival of an aeroplane, so in the maritime world the same practice is followed. Likewise, English law exerts a considerable influence over mercantile and maritime international law. Perhaps in this context, British law is more apt, for over the centuries Scottish practices and precedents with regard to commercial law have made a significant contribution to the better functioning of the English system. English law, rising out of Anglo Saxon customs and from the witan (or King's wise men), is more flexible and open to development to accord with changing patterns of commerce, adapting also better to arbitration, than its continental counterparts, which absorbed more of the rigours of Roman law at the Renaissance. In early days in England and Scotland there was considerable overlapping between mercantile and maritime hearings and in the reorganisation of courts in the twentieth century both the Admiralty and Prize Courts have become, like the Commercial Court, part of the Queen's Bench. All three make valuable contributions to the country's invisible earnings. Lord Birkenhead is quoted as saying, 'Coke captured the law merchant for the common law, Holt retained it, Mansfield formally incorporated it into our system'. If, at the present time, disputes arise on a commercial contract the parties can either go to court, or, if a clause allows it, to arbitration – usually in London or New York. If London is chosen the matter will in all probability be dealt with by the London Maritime Arbitrators Association, which, although officially founded in 1960, has its roots in earlier history. If disputes go to court it will be to the Commercial Court, half of whose cases are now from abroad, without an English litigant, while in 80 percent of cases one side is foreign. These overseas litigants are not only from the Commonwealth. They come from everywhere, primarily in search of fairness. Lord Goff pointed out on February 4th 1992 in a debate in the House of Lords on the Carriage of Goods by Sea Bill that a very large number of contracts for the carriage of goods by sea are governed by English law. Although the ships' cargoes and the ports may have no connection with Britain, the contract may expressly state that it shall be governed by English law. 'London's role', said Lord Goff, 'in the making of these contracts and the settlement of disputes, which may arise from them, results in a significant contribution to our invisible earnings and helps to secure the status of London as the world's leading maritime centre and centre for the resolution of maritime disputes'.

The work of the Commercial Court goes back to antiquity. When during the age of exploration new markets opened overseas to supplement those in Europe, its hearings and practices became increasingly international. Mercantile disputes were settled in local fair and borough courts under the Statute of Merchants of 1283 and in the courts in the staple towns, which in 1353 were given exclusive jurisdiction over merchants trading within their boundaries. In these courts commercial custom was admissible as evidence and, although appeal was to the Court of Common Pleas, this flexibility gave the system a unique status. When Sir Edward Coke enhanced the Common Law Courts in the seventeenth century these local hearings were transferred to the King's Bench, where commercial evidence was not admissible and, although links with the City and Guildhall were maintained, strict procedure on evidence hampered merchants in the presentation of their cases. Lord Holt, Chief Justice of the King's Bench, therefore began in 1689 to accept evidence of mercantile custom and to consult merchants. Such was the position when Lord Mansfield, better known for his contribution to contract law, came down from Scotland to be Chief Justice of the King's Bench from 1756 to 1788. Starting a new commercial court in the Guildhall, he ensured that juries had commercial experience and he pronounced judgements laying down principles of commercial law, which became precedents. For a century this system flourished, but in 1865 commercial cases were returned to the Queen's Bench, where the resulting fall-off in applications was so marked that in 1891 there was an attempt to re-open the Guildhall sittings. The following year a huge majority of judges accepted the request of the Bar and Law Societies that there should be separate lists of court actions for commercial work. In 1894, with the Lord Chief Justice sympathetic to the idea, the judges used an inherent power to make the change without awaiting Parliament's approval and a year later the Commercial Court started producing law reports of its own. Parliamentary endorsement of the Court's separate and specialist nature finally came with the Administration of Justice Act in 1970 and the Supreme Court Act of 1981, when the Commercial, Admiralty and Prize Courts were officially absorbed into the Queen's Bench. The work of the Commercial Court multiplied three and a half times between 1975 and 1982 and the number of judges increased. Then between 1980 and 1985 it doubled, with a sixth judge added to the list in 1989.

Like the Commercial Court, the Admiralty and Prize Courts were international in their work and flexible in their attitude towards the admissibility of custom as evidence. At one time hearings in the Admiralty Courts encompassed mercantile disputes also and overlapped the work of the commercial courts. The Court of Admiralty was originally set up in the Middle Ages to deal with piracy on the high seas (now again on the increase in remoter seas) and Edward III was the first King to claim this exclusive right in the Channel, together with jurisdiction over spoil, flotsam and jetsam, derelict ships and British offenders on board ship. A Court of Admiralty sat then in each of the Cinque Ports and in the ports of the 3 Admirals of the North, South and West, but when, in 1391, the post of Lord High Admiral was created, lawyer deputies took over as judges, after which the hearings became so popular with merchants and mariners that the courts grew in number. Because of their creeping jurisdiction Richard II legislated to confine it to the seaward side of bridges and to maritime matters, but, when in the next century the local courts became superseded by the central High Court of Admiralty, judges continued, despite statutory disapproval, to deal with mercantile as well as maritime hearings. Then, with the opening of overseas markets in the age of exploration, Henry VIII recognised the Court's potential in an international forum and enlarged its civil jurisdiction to include charterparties and contracts made beyond the seas, while eliminating its criminal jurisdiction. The Court reached its zenith under Elizabeth, after which the lawyers at common law cast envious eyes upon its powers. Its wings were clipped by Coke's reforms and, the Restoration bringing no renewal of its powers, its work was permanently confined to matters arising on the high seas, such as salvage, derelict ships, collisions and injurious acts at sea. Meanwhile over the border in Scotland the circumstances of the local Admiralty courts in the Middle Ages were broadly similar, although the post of Lord High Admiral was hereditary. Sitting in seaports, they dealt with mercantile and maritime matters and were consolidated by Cromwell into the High Court of Admiralty, which, at the Act of Union, was merged into the Admiralty Court of Great Britain – the Scots retaining their judicial functions. The increase in British naval and merchant shipping during and after the French Wars brought a dramatic increase in maritime litigation before the Court of Admiralty and before the Prize Court, which functioned within its system.

To prevent the terrible attrition suffered on the sea during conflicts the Prize Court sprang into particular prominence in the second half of the nineteenth and early twentieth centuries, when attempts were made to internationalise the Humanitarian Law of the Sea. In the Middle Ages the Prize Court had been concerned with rights of capture, hearing whether ships were or were not neutral and whether they had been lawfully seized. At one time Admirals had on-the-spot rights of decision, but these were curtailed once professional lawyers sat as judges and further curtailed when jurisdiction was centralised in the High Court of Admiralty. In peacetime seizures, which were legitimate in war, became piracy and spoil, and the function of the Court was to ensure return to rightful owners. During Elizabeth's reign, when English traders insisted on their right to trade in the face of militant Spanish Catholicism, it was difficult at any time to know whether Spain and England were or were not in conflict and many Prize Court decisions must have offended overseas litigants. But by James I's reign the work of the court was respected internationally and many claimants were nations and foreign shipowners. The Court's disciplinary powers against its own illegal privateers were strengthened by Oliver Cromwell, who appointed Commissioners of Prizes to ensure the distribution of goods captured in war – an efficient system, bogged down by corruption in the time of Pepys. Faced by complicated decisions arising out of the sea battles of the French Wars, when the Rules of the Sea were formulated, the work of the Prize Court was gradually brought into line with that of Chancery and the Common Law. Judicial precedents and procedures were provided and followed, together with a proper appeal structure to the Privy Council. During the Napoleonic Wars merchant ships were not sunk on sight and afterwards it was hoped that order might be introduced into the carriage of goods at sea in time of war. In the idealistic words of Mr. Hume, during the debate on the Repeal of the Navigation Laws, 'Repeal would render it impossible for the system of maritime warfare – especially by privateers – to be carried on'. Such statements anticipated the Convention of a Humanitarian Law of the Sea in 1856. Efforts were made during the next century to internationalise the transport of neutral cargo during wars and this gave both Courts an enlarged role on the national and international stage. Jurisdiction and procedure in the Admiralty Court were revised and extended by Acts of Parliament and damage to cargo was brought within the powers of the Court, which could refer disputes to arbitration and enforce Conventions. The powers of the Prize Court were set out in the Naval Prize Act of 1864, which granted conditions for awarding prize bounty to officers and crew, a practice dating from earliest days and continuing (albeit in almost fictional form) until after World War II. In 1898 the Prize Court Rules were tightened up and published and after the attempts to create an International Prize Court foundered in 1912/13 great responsibility was placed upon the British Prize Court in World War I, when a captor had to prove a disputed case with papers, cargo documents and interrogatories. By 1918 the Prize Court in London had earned the reputation of being the, 'Most thorough and impartial tribunal of the kind in the world'. Yet, despite efforts in the Treaties of Washington and London to limit the savagery and piratical nature of war at sea, the Second World War released further brutality and acts of terrorism against merchant crews.

The contribution, direct or indirect, made to Britain's economy by all these maritime invisibles in the City of London is of immense importance. Experience shows that a country can carry forward a current account deficit for a limited time by dipping into gold or currency reserves or selling overseas assets or encouraging inward investment (or indeed by printing money), but that any of these policies carried to excess will eventually debase the currency. The contribution made by Britain's maritime legal services raises, however, another issue, for her expertise and leading position in international maritime law will be lost if she allows her seafaring role to be eroded further, and this will reduce her influence inter alia on the developing UN Law of the Sea. Britain has always played a leading role in this sphere, carrying on the traditions of earlier maritime powers – for the Romans fashioned and the Venetians developed a framework within which such Law was able to grow. Since World War II the UN has promulgated a number of Conventions on the Law of the Sea (UNCLOS), only four of which – put forward in 1958 – have received (in 1964) sufficient ratification or accession. These 1958 Conventions cover such matters as: the Territorial Sea surrounding nation states; the Contiguous 12-mile Zone which protects that area; the Continental Shelf, bringing rights of extraction and exploitation; and Fishing and Conservation. The 1982 Convention's wide-ranging articles extend to the High Seas, including the peaceful use of the sea bed: the recently introduced 200-mile Exclusive Economic Zone, covering fishing, conservation and similar matters (of which the provisions on conservation have so far produced only a dead letter), and such affairs as pollution, prevention of piracy and drug smuggling. Apart from the controversial matter of deep sea mining, which has held back the signature of the USA, and the controversial proposals for an International Seabed Authority and compulsory arbitration at an International Tribunal in Hamburg, the 1982 articles have not yet received sufficient ratification from nation states – the USA, the UK, France and Germany being four of the countries with reservations about the wisdom of some articles, but this does not mean that much has not already been adopted. The proposal to extend the Territorial Sea to 12 miles raises controversial issues concerning overlap of the Continental Shelf and the free passage of straits, which include those of Dover, Gibraltar and Hormuz, and reflect customary state practice. Britain gave a lead by incorporating into the Territorial Sea Act of 1987 free transit passage, in what was previously the High Seas, through the Dover Straits, the North Channel and the Shetland and Orkney Gap. Britain's leadership and expertise in these matters are invaluable – without the support of leading nations even a ratified Convention would be of little value – but her voice will not be listened to if she withdraws any further from her status as a maritime power, damaging not only her own interests, but the concept of justice world wide. On the one hand the Law of the Sea develops naturally as practice evolves and influences its future development, while on the other the Conventions contain ideas for the formation of new law, which may be adopted later.

The development of the Law of the Sea raises questions about its enforcement and the need to keep international waters safe from piracy and other forms of illicit interference. After World War II it has been the US Navy that has played this role, demonstrating in so doing the importance of seaborne air power in peacetime. But for how long will the USA shoulder this expensive and onerous burden? In the future it must increasingly be undertaken by a mix of maritime forces acting under the UN, or other peace keeping organisation, such as NATO, and in this Britain must play her part. The break up of the Soviet Empire is already causing problems of nationalism and ethnic chaos in the place of those previously posed by internationalism, so that the 'peace dividend' is largely squandered. Britain's primary reason for going overseas was to trade and that remains as true today, but successful trade requires stable conditions. In the last century Britain brought to a large part of the world a system of stable government and justice, as well as the benefits of modern medicine, education, sanitation and engineering and, although the developing world is now taking over the reins of government for itself, there is still a need to provide support for the Commonwealth and other friendly governments, within a system of alliances. Without overseas deep sea trade the island of Britain, with its slender primary resources and large population, faces economic stringency and disaster. Natural resources are in great demand and markets shrink if other people are always first and foremost in the market place to sell their wares.

The second question is more difficult to answer. If the decline in the maritime industries is of vital national importance, how did it happen? How could anything so important have come about almost by default? This book has set out some of the difficult decisions faced by successive governments: post-war lack of liquidity; the threat from the Soviet Empire; the upheavals of nationalism all over the world, caused by legitimate cries for self-government, and by terrorism of the far right and far left; strikes and lack of discipline at school, in the workplace and in public spending; the disturbing tariff walls erected in Europe with the creation of the EC – the need to be inside in order to trade locally and yet to be sufficiently outside to trade globally. Nevertheless, the question must be asked how far the decline in the merchant marine, in shipbuilding and in the Royal Navy could have been avoided by better judgement and greater wisdom on the part of those employed in Westminster and Whitehall. Although there appears to be a serious gap in knowledge and experience amongst MPs on the subject of defence, nevertheless no fewer that 80 percent of backbenchers signed an Early Day Motion on the need to reverse the decline of the Merchant Navy and this hardly indicates a lack of interest and knowledge. Harsh criticisms have been made of government and civil service – 'Ministers of Defence suffer from sea blindness', 'The closest the mandarins of Whitehall get to the sea is to watch the ducks swimming in the lakes in St. James Park'. It is also said that governments do not listen, not even to the House of Commons Select Committees, which they set up and which reduce the attendance in the Chamber for all but the most important debates. Many criticisms are true, others are exaggerated, but it would take another book to set out the reasons for any failure of post-war governments to provide vision and leadership. Many complex questions would have to be answered. Has the British system of checks and balances, set out in the last century by constitutionalists such as Bagehot, been temporarily thrown off balance? Is democracy still in her seat, or has the machinery of party politics forgotten the voice of the people and so lost the impetus coming from the grass roots? Is cabinet government and collective and ministerial responsibility currently effective, or have some Prime Ministers mirrored a presidential image? Are there too many junior government posts to allow backbenchers their necessary influence? Is there sufficient expertise in today's Parliament? In preceding centuries experts in wider fields became MPs late in life, the exceptions being statesmen like the Younger Pitt reared by his famous father. Have recent governments and Select Committees been misled by civil servants, who saw seafaring as just another type of everyday employment and method of transport? Has the attitude of the Treasury been too departmentalised? The questions are easy, but useful answers cannot be given within the contents of this book. Meanwhile information about government and Parliament available to the people is contained in fictional contributions in novel, radio or television form – none of which are designed to fill the ordinary reader with faith and enthusiasm for political life.

Perhaps today's problems are now so complex and far-reaching that it would take the wisdom of Solomon to unravel them; Solomon asked to be granted the gift of listening with understanding and the ability to discern between good and evil in what he was told. Repeated departures from the truth obviate this gift, and, although even Lord Salisbury acknowledged the need for governments sometimes to dissimulate, nevertheless in excess it clouds the issues and makes it difficult to find solutions. Likewise too much confrontation between parties loses the backing of a nation trying to pull together as a team. Back in the late forties, Joyce Grenfell, in the variety show Twopence Coloured imitated an American writing home from London. 'And, my dear they've got a government that simply isn't on their side'. The applause was deafening. With equal wit a taxi driver said to the writer, when passing the House of Commons nearly thirty years later, 'I hear they're going to pull the place down and build a kiddies' playground'. While opposition and choice are the essence of democracy, perpetual confrontation and argument about policies leaves the British people confused. Being tolerant and easy going they need a sense of urgency and direction in order to succeed, as well as working in a properly structured happy team with first class leadership. They also need a belief in themselves. If a nation has lived by the sea and derived so much of its trade and its history from over the oceans, it is a dangerous philosopher indeed who would endeavour to turn its head landward and command it to forget its past – insinuating as some do that its past is something of which to be ashamed. The reverse is the truth and the goodwill of the Commonwealth and of the territories overseas from which the British have withdrawn stands in stark contradiction to the sneers of the cynics.

So now the last question remains. What can be done to end Britain's maritime decline? First, the government should ensure that Britain is reserving as much shipping as her competitors. If other countries, 150 years after Britain's Repeal of her Navigation Laws, will not properly free their shipping to overseas competition, then Britain must return to the policy of her forebears. There can be no other answer. At last, because of the difficulty of monitoring that cabotage (coastal shipping) is genuinely free – particularly in the EC, where arrangements are made by a nod or a wink – the British government has taken powers under the 1988 Act to again restrict its coastal trade. In June 1992 the EC responded with a regulation to liberalise EC cabotage in a phased programme extended until 2004. On the 1st of January 1993 mainland and offshore trade will be free for Community members with vessels registered in and flying the flag of a member state. There are, however, derogations for cruise vessels, those carrying strategic products, or under 650 gross tons or regular passenger and ferry and island traffic, each of which have their own dates for the regulation coming into force. Likewise, if other countries reserve part of their ocean trade by the carriage of government cargo or national aid or by any other method, Britain must do the same, although any threat to her cross trades must first be carefully borne in mind. Again, under the Merchant Shipping Act 1988 there are powers to tax and impose charges if foreign governments or persons representing foreign governments pose a threat to UK shipping interests or those of any other state. Second, the age of the British-owned fleet should be reduced, for it is currently above the world average, standing in 1988 at 12.8 years, compared with 7.7 for Germany and 8.2 for Denmark, and in 1991 at 14.7 compared with 13.2 for the rest of the world. While the world rate for replacement is 8 percent, the rate for the UK is 4 percent – only Greece is lower. It is suggested by workers in the shipbuilding industry that to stimulate shipbuilding there should be an 'MOT' test for older ships, as is done with motor cars. In the case of cars the percentage of failure for older vehicles is high, stimulating repair, replacement and higher standards of safety. Because of overseas subsidised competition, the scheme for ships could be introduced concurrently with a temporary 'scrap and build' policy of grants for new building to soften hardship. It is argued on the other side that inspection, which is the task of Department of Transport Inspectors at ports, is currently adequate. But, although Britain has a greater number of inspectors than other countries, there are still too few to catch more than one in three of the offenders and there is little time to do more than check documents and spot obvious deficiencies.

Third, there should be government co-operation with the shipping industry to restore and improve training and cadetship and encourage young men back to sea. Maritime secondary schools and nautical training colleges and courses of study for Ordinary and Higher National Certificate must be maintained and if necessary re-started to ensure a revival of maritime skills. At last under the 1988 Act help has been given with repatriation of deep sea crews (where all serious training takes place), and one half of the £20,000 it costs to train for the first class certificate can now be reclaimed from the government. The turn around in cadet numbers, which have risen by 50 percent, is sufficient incentive for continuing government involvement. At one time it was believed that sea training was the finest education in the world, and that, even if a boy educated in one of these sea schools later earned his living in another way, the money had been well spent for he had been blessed with a preparation for life second to none. Perhaps attention should again be paid to the scheme started in 1890 to train young men under sail for Merchant Navy steam ships. Because of the growing scarcity of British recruits the arguments about nationality requirements for crews grow in stridency. At the present time the Master, First Officer and Chief Engineer must be British, Commonwealth or Irish, reflecting defence requirements, but the Junior Officers have no nationality requirements, although they must possess either British or Commonwealth certificates of competence, recognised by the dependent territories or the equivalent certificates from such seafaring countries as Norway or organisations such as NATO or the EC.

Fourth, the government must give tax concessions to shipping and shipbuilding in line with the rest of the world. It is hopeless to expect British firms to compete on equal terms with other foreign shipping companies which enjoy generous tax advantages. Germany, Norway and Denmark, to mention only three countries, have given huge tax breaks to partnership schemes and the only UK equivalent – the Business Expansion Scheme, (now to be phased out) which was shared with many firms on land – was minuscule in comparison in its contribution to the maritime industries. If other countries grant generous capital gains and corporation tax relief, then the UK must follow suit if its fleet is to remain competitive. The tax is not lost in a flagged in merchant fleet, for the government reclaims a large measure, whereas if a fleet is flagged out then tax is lost for ever. Likewise, by restoring the 100 percent capital allowance in the first year of a ship's life, as the practice is in Japan, Scandinavian and EC countries, British shipbuilding would be stimulated and the cost to the tax payer would be returned by earnings in foreign currency. 40 new ships are needed every year just to keep the age of the fleet at its present level and the second hand market could also be stimulated by allowing roll-over relief in corporation tax if a ship is sold and not immediately replaced. Many countries expressly encourage investment in the maritime industries by granting tax exemption for liquid reserves held for this purpose.

Fifth, the Netherlands, Norway, Greece, Denmark, Belgium and Sweden urge their citizens to go to sea by granting personal relief to seafarers on their own taxes and social security payments. Tax concessions in the UK were withdrawn at the end of the seventies, and although some welcome concessions have been made in the 1988 Act it can hardly be said that any of them have put the UK on a level playing field with other states. By fiscal incentives the government can usually achieve the ends it desires. Sixth, if other countries, such as Japan, South Korea, Germany, France, the Netherlands and Taiwan, grant low interest loans and subsidies to aid either the operation of ships or investment in shipbuilding, then these – properly supervised and not (as so often) used as a Pandora's Box – must be available in Britain as well. World trade has recently increased (although this year the recession has caused a drop), with a consequent upturn in shipbuilding of which Britain must take advantage. Seventh, there should be an on-going inquiry into ways in which costs at sea can be reduced. Speed is of the essence in cargo delivery and here there are revolutionary techniques in which Britain can and does lead. No sooner does an idea pop out of the pages of Jules Verne, than, like the jet propelled catamaran, it is already under test or in operation. Why, for instance, cannot ships running through strong winds generate sufficient power for turbines, thus reducing their fuel costs? Recently the drive for economy has relied on increased size, for above a certain number of deadweight tons the running costs are static. But a turning point may have been reached. With so many shipyards building large vessels now closed, the British have no alternative but to turn, as in the first Elizabethan days, to smaller ones. For nearly 200 years after the Armada ships of the line remained much the same size and still in Nelson's Navy the frigates were no larger than the average Elizabethan ship. Just as the days of the large warship, with the exception of the carrier, have now passed, so those of the large merchant ship – vulnerable to wave stress, strain, instability of uneven loading, and in war to torpedo, aircraft and mine – may also have reached their zenith. The age of smaller swifter passenger ferries and container ships carrying some passengers may yet be to come, for already there have been increases in passenger sea traffic, as people perhaps recognise again the therapeutic advantage of sea travel.

Eighth, despite its express omission in the 1988 Act, perhaps serious consideration should be given to the provision of a supplementary register, offering lower standards of entry. This has been spearheaded by Norway with its NIS Register, where there has recently been an increase of 16.2 million deadweight tons in one and a half years. Supplementary registers are now provided by an increasing number of countries and, although the Isle of Man is a safe haven for UK mainland ships, it only provides tax benefits, not an easing of other restrictions. Another way of increasing the number of British registered ships would be to recognise the temporary flagging in of foreign vessels and to allow the temporary flagging out of ships on the British register, provided only for limited duration. Foreign owned demise chartered ships could be registered in the UK during the period of their demise, while British ships chartered out could retain their UK identity. Regarding the contributions made by different categories of ships to foreign earnings, obviously those registered in the Isle of Man make the same contribution as those registered in mainland Britain, while there is a small drop in earnings in the case of vessels registered in the Commonwealth. If, on the other hand, vessels sail under a foreign flag, even if only time chartered, then there is a huge drop in earnings, which falls almost to zero for bare boat chartering. Likewise, if ships are wanted for strategic reasons, then again Isle of Man registration gives the same security as UK, but there is a drop of approximately half in Commonwealth availability, while if ships are registered in other countries they are not available at all. The directly owned UK fleet is now only 2.19 percent of the world fleet (expressed in deadweight tons) and these ships are spread over a number of registers. Of 151,000 merchant vessels of over 100 gross tons docking annually in UK ports those flying the British flag will soon aproach only 10 percent. Ninth, Britain should undoubtedly continue with her current vigorous efforts to try and make safety regulations international, so that the only differentials would then be those of wages and some social security payments. If safety regulations were to be set internationally, one country would not be at the competitive disadvantage of another. In Britain the Department of Transport issues Safe Manning Certificates and watches impotently while competitors in the North Sea operate more cheaply below these standards, where foreign penetration into the oil rig support fleet has now reached alarming proportions. Shipping cannot be regarded simply as transport – for an island nation it is indivisible from trade and the need for its protection remains as true today as heretofore. All nations protect their frontiers and because she is an island, Britain's 'Legions,' as Disraeli said, 'rest upon the waters'. Tenth and vitally important therefore Britain must have sufficient maritime forces to protect her shores, her trade and her overseas interests. In the last 3 years the RN paid off 30 major warships and over twice that number of other naval craft and auxiliaries, while ordering 2 Trident submarines, 3 frigates, a helicopter carrier and a supply craft.

The three leading shipbuilding nations of the world are now Japan, South Korea and Germany in that order, followed by Taiwan and the former Yugoslavia (where the most important yard is in Croatia), while Britain has slipped to 24th in the world order. The announcement of the closure of Cammell Laird in July is yet another nail in Britain's coffin for burial at sea, hammered in by government policy and EC authorisation of funds to East Germany, although Germany's position in the shipbuilding industry is already dominant. Britain is caught, as this book has said a number of times, on the horns of a dilemma. Her wealth began when her trade opened up with the New World and the East, the bulk of which was carried in her own ships, protected by the Navigation Laws dating back to the Middle Ages, widened and re-enacted by the Tudors and again in the seventeenth century. Even after these laws had been repealed she could – in the days of Empire and Commonwealth trading – sell her manufactured goods in return for farm produce, whereas now the EC countries, which supply her with food, expect to sell her their manufactured goods as well. The reader will recall that since 1957, when the Treaty of Rome was signed by the six founder members, she has slipped through the ratio of three to one in her export and import of manufactured goods and in the 1980's began to export fewer manufactured goods than she imported. This serious situation will not be eased by the continued undermining of GATT with tariffs and quotas and by the delays in the GATT talks on free trade, when the EC – responsible for 40 percent of world trade and represented on GATT by the Commission and not by individual countries – may not, even after six years, be able to break through US and French intransigence on agricultural protectionism to the detriment of world trade and the developing countries.

What is required above all is for a change of attitude on the part of the British people towards their maritime interests, together with a revival of will by government, parliament, people and press and a determination not to be netted in by EC restrictions and cut off from the open sea, which is Britain's lifeline. Many times in her history this island has been placed in jeopardy by policies pursued by or with regard to the continent, which have not been to her advantage. These problems are far from new. During Henry VIII's reign, Chancellor Wolsey's aggressive interpretation of the balance of power in Europe and his over-bearing personal ambitions towards the Papacy eventually weakened England's standing in the continental power game, over which Rome exerted much influence. Afterwards Henry relied on the twin pillars of his Parliament and his Navy to rebuild English status and strength and thus, under Edward and later under Elizabeth, while remaining an active European power, England took to the seas as well and regained her political and commercial stability. A century later at the height of the Stuart period, when she was weakened by internal strife, she became a pawn in another Roman Catholic continental power struggle, but starting under Charles II and developing under William III, she restored and built up her maritime trade and so escaped the dominance of Louis XIV's bureaucratic imperialism. Britain's natural assets have not changed, neither her harbours, her island position, nor her people. Her ships still operate in every corner of the world, albeit many built elsewhere, owned overseas and operating under a different flag. Much of the shipbroking of the world, shipping finance, marine insurance, freight income transactions, ship classification and maritime legal work is still done in Britain, while a host of maritime consultancies, publishing operations and specialist marine firms are scattered throughout the country. Britain still holds a number of face cards in her hand. The ace remains the genius and courage of her people, for, as dramatic as her periods of decline, has been her ability to recover. She must now do with urgency what she has done before – trade with and exert her influence in Europe and, at the same time restore her maritime position and maintain and expand her links with the Commonwealth. All that is needed is the sense of purpose and direction, the will and concentrated commitment to aim at the highest standards and to play those cards with her erstwhile consummate skill, together with the inspired leadership that has always been required to set that genius free.

EPILOGUE

No doubt the book should end there, but the thought is probably too simplistic, for this century has seen suffering on a grander scale than any before in modern history, and this of itself eventually inhibits enthusiasm and hope, particularly for the British who have made greater sacrifices than most nations for freedom's future. It seems that since the start of World War I an evil has crept across the world like the spreading veins in the grain of wood. Probably never before have so many people been working for good and so many for evil. The ending of the Pax Britannica has left a vacuum that has not yet been filled, while the drawing up of the Iron Curtain, which has brought light and liberty where there was previously darkness and fear, has encouraged some nations to splinter into smaller states, while others have huddled closer together into larger conglomerates. There is little leadership. Faced with upheavals where once there was order and with insufficient strength to make the same contribution as heretofore, the British have accepted a less dominant role. Are they as resolute as they once were, or are they less able to formulate policies in times of crisis and to take advantage of the opportunities in Europe and the wider world? If the metaphor is changed, although they still hold an ace, who holds the jokers?

In the early 1970's Lord Diplock made a speech in the Inns of Court. He drew attention to the transfer, under Article 177 of the Treaty of Rome, of the ultimate decisions of the judiciary – albeit within a restricted ambit – from the House of Lords to the Court of Justice in Luxembourg. This dilution of British freedom was considered then by Parliament and public to be of less importance than the arguments for strengthened defence and West European stability, which it was claimed Britain's membership would bring to the Community, and which were seen as vital to combat Soviet expansionism. Since then Communism has crumbled and the EEC is transforming itself into the EC, which aims at political, as well as economic Union – recent hair line referendum results throughout Europe indicating the caution of many people towards the Maastricht Treaty. Some citizens hope it will bring greater transparency and openness to EC government, others warn that it will create a European Union similar to the Zollverein which consolidated Germany, while others again see two opposing forces at work – a tug of war in which Chancellor Kohl and President Mitterand may have pulled the hardest. In recent discussions much reliance has been placed upon the doctrine of diffusion of central power or 'subsidiarity', which tried and failed to halt centralism and dictatorship in Italy and Germany in the 1930's. What seems certain is that, with ever closer integration, progressively greater power will concentrate upon the Court of Justice in Luxembourg. A student reading the Court's decision regarding the foreign fishermen, who bought British registered ex-fishing boats in order to claim fresh quotas for themselves, thus enabling them to fish in UK waters, might find it hard to fault the legal reasoning and Roman discipline in the judgement. The Court said that the 1988 UK legislation passed to prevent this intrusion offended Articles of the Treaty of Rome (7, 52, 58 and 221), enabling nationals of member states to set up firms anywhere in the EC, and thus entitling them to bring these boats back into service and claim quotas. The UK lawyers cited the 1894 and 1988 Merchant Shipping Acts for definition of nationality requirements and relied on the age-old device of going behind the whole document to seek justice. For centuries UK judges have on limited, or rare, occasions stated that, 'It cannot be the will of Parliament', when the rights of citizens have been taken away by over-strict legislation. These judgements force Parliament either to re-legislate or accept the decision as law. 'The Treaty', said the British representatives, 'cannot be interpreted so as to deprive the member states of competence to determine nationality of vessels and conditions relating to the nationality of owners'. The arguments failed. The Court refused to look at the wider issue of national quotas, which distorted their view, and gave judgement against the British. 'Having agreed with its Community partners on a system of fishing quotas, which would supposedly give fair protection to its fishing industry, the UK then found that other treaty provisions had been successfully used to circumvent and undermine that protection.' 'The law', said Lord Birkett, 'is not justice. It is man's interpretation of the ultimate ideal of justice'. In Britain, over a time-scale of hundreds of years, that approximation was steadily brought nearer to its target by relying on a series of devices to supplement the common and statute law, most of which were governed by equity, which on the continent had slightly different connotations. 'What can we do?', the British ask, 'We've joined a club in which most of the members are allowed to play different rules and there are too many jokers in the pack'.

The institutions of the EC rest upon four corner stones – Council (of Ministers), Commission, Parliament and Court, the first two of which make regulations and issue directives binding upon member states. The three articles of the Treaty of Rome, which set out the conditions under which state aid to industry can be granted (Articles 92, 93 and 94), allow flexibility in interpretation and give discretion to Council and Commission in their granting of permission for national subsidies to be channelled wherever they are most needed. The combined workings of these directives and UK government decisions have seldom, taken together, been in the best interests of British shipping or the shipbuilding industry, while industries, such as steel, shipping and shipbuilding, of certain other EC members, including Germany and France, have prospered. Shipbuilding Directive 90/684/EEC and its amendment of July 20th 1992 reveal legitimate loopholes that the Commission and Council can provide for nations intent on giving subsidies to shipbuilding. They also show the extent to which the EC has set its face against smaller firms, once the backbone of the British shipbuilding industry. Chapter VIII referred to the problems of hidden subsidies, those funds which 'trickle through' industrial banks and financial institutions into shipping companies and shipyards, in which continental banks are often shareholders. It described how, given the best will in the world, the Commission would find it difficult to stop these practices, which the decentralisation of German government exacerbates, just as it would the non-tariff barriers to trade which abound still throughout member states. The British sense of fair play, when they see tricks taken by these jokers, is wounded. They feel their government does not fight sufficiently hard for their interests, but they recognise that even if it did a number of other countries breach the rules by force of habit, whereas the British have been trained for generations to carry them out. Mr. Bangemann's recent calls for more sea and fresh water transport are viewed in some quarters with a degree of suspicion, for, with their already startling lead in European shipbuilding, it seems likely that any EC fleet or flag would be in danger of being dominated by the Germans. The UK is also critical of decisions reached by political bargains and not by choosing the best and fairest policy, although recognising the difficulty of bringing together the opposing concepts of partnership (a partner being one who plays a game on the same side) and competition (a competitor being a rival or opponent). Instead of shrugging off these problems as insoluble the British public should study these directives, regulations and judgements with care, resisting as far as is possible those that are eminently unworkable or unjust and recognising that they all are part of the framework of British life within the EC. The fact that they are not carried – as British statute law is carried – in public libraries explains their inaccessibility to ordinary people.

The Danes have been more succinct. 'Every time', they say, 'that you move a decision from national Parliaments to the Commission or the Council you move it from open democracy to secretive authoritarian bureaucracy and every time the decisions of these centres of EC rule make you change the laws of your own country you destroy the democracy, which for hundreds of years you have successfully and laboriously built up'. Britain has by far the longest experience of unbroken democracy of any nation in the world, dating from 1689. Also, despite post-war lapses and errors, her standing in the wider world is higher than she herself probably appreciates. It reflects the character and ability of her people and therefore the continuing number of aces she holds in her hand. Nevertheless she faces very unpalatable options. That most sensitive of all areas, the mouth of the Scheldt and the Rhine Delta, which the reader will remember she has for centuries struggled to keep free from foreign domination for the sake of her trade, lies at the very heart of the EC. 54 percent of Britain's trade is now with Europe. When 150 years ago she repealed her Navigation Laws, one of the reasons for so doing was her concern for the revolutions then sweeping the continent. These were a mixture of democratic, radical and to a lesser extent Communist forces, but they were in large part caused by the inability of continental governments to bring down in time the barriers of 'secretive authoritarian bureaucracy'. Britain escaped those revolutions because of her democratic institutions and her ability always to find a middle way and a fairer and more just solution. Had the nations of continental Europe listened before 1848 to the voice of their peoples, Britain would not have needed to make the sacrifice that Repeal eventually entailed, nor would she have needed to pour out her blood and her wealth in two World Wars to ensure that democracy survived. Were they to listen now they would concentrate less on bureaucracy, blinkered law, summitry, secrecy and centralism and instead encourage their peoples to use their freedom to endeavour to create a properly fair and truly common market and to promote in the wider world the 'maintenance of justice among men and nations'. Alas, it may not be only the British who learn nothing from history.

BIBLIOGRAPHY

CHAPTER ONE

Cornewall Jones, R. J. *The British Merchant Service*. Sampson, Low, Marston and Co. London. 1898.

Hurd, A. (Ed) *Britain's Merchant Navy*. Odhams Press. London. 1943.

Kemp, P. (Ed) *History of the Royal Navy*. Arthur Barker. London. 1969.

Kirkcaldy, A. W. *British Shipping*. David and Charles. London. 1970.

Lindsay, W. S. *History of British Merchant Shipping and Ancient Commerce*. Sampson and Low. London. 1874.

Lipson, E. *Economic History of England*. Vols. II and III. The Age of Mercantilism. A. and C. Black. London. 1961.

Lloyd, C. *The Nation and the Navy*. Cresset Press. London. 1954.

Padfield, P. *Tide of Empires*. Vols. I and II. Kegan Paul. London. 1979 and 1982.

Salzman, L. F. *English trade in the Middle Ages*. H. Pordes. London. 1964.

Trevelyan, G. M. *History of England*. Longmans. London. 1926.

Trevelyan, G. M. *English Social History*. Longmans. London. 1942.

Trevelyan, G. M. *England Under the Stewarts*. Methuen. London. 1949.

The Statutes of the Realm. Vols. I to IX. Printed by Command of HMG. London. MDCCCX-MDCCCXXII.

Act and Ordinances of the Interregnum 1642-1660. HMSO. London. 1911.

CHAPTER TWO

Allen, J. *The Navigation Laws of Great Britain*. Bailing Bros. London. 1849.

Bird, A. *The Damnable Duke of Cumberland*. Barrie and Rockcliff. London. 1966.

Disraeli, B. *Lord George Bentinck: A Political Biography*. Colburn. London. 1852.

Flenley, R., and Spencer, R. *Modern German History*. Dent. London. 1968.

Kent, J. *Racing life of Lord George Bentinck*. Blackwood. London. 1893.

M. Mann, *A Particular Duty: Canadian Rebellions 1837-1839*. Russel. Salisbury. 1986.

House of Commons. Hansard Parliamentary Debates. Third Series. 1847-1848. Vols. XCVI-CV.

CHAPTER THREE

Briggs, J. H. *Naval Administrations: The Experience of 65 Years*. Sampson, Low, Marston and Co. London. 1887.

Cantlie Stewart, J. *The Quality of Mercy*. George, Allen and Unwin. London. 1983.

Hope, R. *A New History of British Shipping*. John Murray. London. 1990.

Lindsay, W. S. *History of British Merchant Shipping and Ancient Commerce*. (see above).

Vice, A. *Financier at Sea*. Merlin Books. Braunton. 1985.

Annual Statement of the Navigation and Shipping for the United Kingdom

for the year 1874. Eyre and Spottiswoode. HMSO. London. 1875.
Annual Statement of the Navigation and Shipping for the United Kingdom
    for the year 1886. HMSO. London. 1887.
Annual Statement of the Navigation and Shipping for the United Kingdom
    for the year 1911. HMSO. London. 1911.
Annual Statement of the Trade of the United Kingdom with foreign
    Countries for the year 1883. Eyre and Spottiswoode. London. 1884.
House of Commons. Hansard Parliamentary Debates (as above).
A List of Her Majesty's Ships of Foreign Vessels of War in Commission on
    Foreign Stations. January 1880. Eyre and Spottiswoode for HMSO.
    London. 1880.
A List of Her Majesty's Ships of Foreign Vessels of War in Commission on
    Foreign Stations. January 1885. Eyre and Spottiswoode for HMSO.
    London. 1885.

CHAPTER FOUR

Hurd, A. *Official History of the War: The Merchant Navy*. John Murray.
    London. 1929.

CHAPTER FIVE

Behrens, C. *Merchant Shipping and the Demands of War*. HMSO. London.
    1955.
Hay, D. *War under the Red Ensign: The Merchant Navy 1939-1945*. Jane's.
    London. 1982.
Hurd, A. (Ed) *Britain's Merchant Navy*. Odhams Press. London. 1943.
Konings, C. *Queen Elizabeth at War*. P. Stephens. Wellingborough. 1985.
Padfield, Peter. *Dönitz: The Last Fuhrer*. Gollancz. London. 1984.
Roskill, S. W. *The Merchant Fleet at War: 1939–1945*. Collins. London.
    1962.
Slader, J. *The Red Duster at War*. William Kimber. London. 1988.
D. Thomson, *The Atlantic Star: 1939–45*. W. H. Allen. London. 1990.

CHAPTERS SIX, SEVEN AND EIGHT

Cairncross, A. *Years of Recovery*. Methuen. London. 1985.
Cairncross, A. *The Price of War*. Blackwell. Oxford. 1986.
Cairncross, A., and Smythe, C. *A Country to Play with (Level of Industry
    Negotiations in London and Berlin)*. 1945-46. Gerards Cross. 1987.
Cairncross, A., and Watts, P. *The Economics Section*. Routledge. London and
    New York. 1989.
Churchill, Winston. S. *Second World War: Vol. II. Their Finest Hour*.
    Cassell. London. 1949.
Colville, J. *The Fringes of Power*. Hodder and Stoughton. London. 1985.
De Conde, A. (Ed) *Encyclopaedia of American Foreign Policy*. Vol. II.
    Charles Schribners. New York. 1978.
Donovan, R. J. *The Second Victory*. Madison Books. New York. 1987.
Eatwell, J. *Whatever happened to Britain?* BBC. London. 1982.
Ernest Bevin: Unskilled Labourer and World Statesman. SPA Books. 1981.
Kennedy, J. *Why England Slept*. Hutchinson. London. 1940.

Tipton, F., and Aldrich, R. *An Economic and Social History of Europe.* Macmillan. London. 1987.
Williams, A. *Western Europe Economy.* Hutchinson. London. 1987.
Wise, M. *The Common Fisheries Policy of the European Community.* Methuen. London. 1984.
Yao-Su Hu. *Industrial Banking and Special Credit Institutions: A comparative study.* Policy Studies Institute. London. 1984.

Treaty Series. No 1. (1931) International Treaty for the Limitation and Reduction of Naval Armaments. HMSO. London. 1931. Cmd 3758.
Exchange of Notes between US President and the Marquis of Lothian, regarding US destroyers and naval and air facilities for the US and British Transatlantic Territories. Washington. Sept. 2nd 1940, Aug. 14th 1941, Sept. 3rd 1942.
Parliamentary Papers. Treaty Series. No. 2. (1941) Lend Lease. Cmd 6259.
Joint Declaration by the President of the USA and Mr Winston Churchill, representing HMG in the United Kingdom, known as the Atlantic Charter. August 14th. 1941. Cmd 6321. Parliamentary Session 1941-1942.
Mutual Aid Agreement. Feb. 23rd 1942. Agreement between the government of the United Kingdom and the United States of America on the principles applying to Mutual Aid in the prosecution of the war against aggression. 1941/42. Cmd 6341.
Aid to Russia. July 4th 1942. Alliance in the War against Hitlerite Germany and her Associates in Europe and providing also for collaboration and mutual assistance thereafter. Concluded between the UK and the Union of Soviet Socialist Republics. Cmd. 6368. Parliamentary Session 1941-1942.
Annual Abstract of Statistics. 1957. No. 94., 1967. No. 104., 1981. No. 118., 1985. No. 122., 1986. No. 123., 1987. No. 124. Central Statistical Office. HMSO. London. 1958.
Annual Statement of 1957 Trade of the United Kingdom with Commonwealth Countries and Foreign Countries. HMSO. London. 1959.
Evidence from the Scottish Fishing Federation to the House of Lords Select Committee on the European Communities, 1992/3. 2nd Report. Review of the Common Fisheries Policy with Evidence. House of Lords. Paper 9. 1992. HMSO. London.

House of Commons. Hansard Parliamentary Debates. 1954/5. Vol. 537. Feb. 14 - March 4. P 882 and following.

CHAPTERS NINE TO THIRTEEN
Beatty, D. *Our Admiral: A Biography of Admiral of the Fleet Earl Beatty.* W. H. Allen. London. 1980.
Blumenson, M. *Anzio: The Gamble that failed.* Weidenfeld and Nicholson. London. 1963.
Brooke, G. *Singapore's Dunkirk.* Lee Cooper. London. 1989.
Brown, David. *Mountbatten as First Sea Lord.* R. U. S. I. Defence Studies Journal. June 1986.
Brown, D. *The Royal Navy and the Falklands War.* Leo Cooper. London. 1987.

Bryant, A. *The Turn of the Tide*. (Based on the diaries of Field Marshal, The Viscount Alanbrooke). Collins. London. 1957.

Campbell, I., and Macintyre, D. *The Kola Run*. Frederick Muller. London. 1959.

Corbett, J. S. *Drake and the Tudor Navy*. Vols. I and II. Longmans Green. London. 1898 and 1912.

Corbett, J. S. *England in the Seven Years War*. Longmans Green. London. 1918.

Corbett, J. S. *Some Principles of Maritime Strategy*. Longmans Green. London. 1911.

Corbett, J. S. *The Successors of Drake*. Longmans Green. London. 1900.

Corbett, J. S. (Ed) *Fighting Instructions 1530-1816*. Navy Records Society. 1905.

Janes Fighting Ships. 1903, 1913, 1919, 1938, 1947, 1948, 1968, 1986, 1987, 1991. Jane's Publishing Co. London.

Kemp, Peter (Ed) *The History of the Royal Navy*. Arthur Barker. London. 1969.

Macintyre, D. *Aircraft Carrier: The Majestic Weapon*. Macdonald. London. 1968.

Macintyre, D. *The Battle for the Mediterranean*. Batsford. London. 1964.

Macintyre, D. *The Battle for the Pacific*. Batsford. London. 1966.

Macintyre, D. *Battle of the Atlantic*. Batsford. London. 1961.

Macintyre, D. *Fighting Admiral: The Life and Battles of Admiral of the Fleet, Sir James Somerville*. Evans Bros. London. 1961.

Macintyre, D. *Fighting Ships and Seamen*. Evans Bros. London. 1963.

Macintyre, D. *Jutland*. Evans Bros. London. 1957.

Macintyre, D. *Narvik*. Evans Bros. London. 1959.

Macintyre, D. *The Naval War against Hitler*. Batsford. London. 1971.

Macintyre, D. *U-Boat Killer*. Seeley Service. London. 1976.

Macintyre, D., and Baillie, B. *The Man of War*. Methuen. London. 1968.

Marcus, G. J. *Hearts of Oak*. Oxford University Press. 1975.

Marcus, G. J. *A Naval History of England: The Formative Years*. Longmans. London. 1961.

Marcus, G. J. *A Naval History of England: The Age of Nelson*. G. Allen and Unwin. London. 1971.

Morison, Samuel Eliot. *The Two Ocean War*. Little Brown and Co. Boston. 1963.

Padfield, Peter. *Dönitz: The Last Fuhrer*. (See above).

Roskill, S. W. *The War at Sea: 1939-45*. 3 Vols. HMSO. London. 1956.

Schindler and Toman, (Eds). *Laws of Armed Conflict*. Sijhhoff and Noordhoff. Rockville, Maryland. 1981.

Schofield, B. *British Sea Power: Naval Policy in the Twentieth Century*. Batsford. London. 1967.

Speed, K. *Sea Change: The Battle of the Falklands and the Future of Britain's Navy*. Ashgrove Press. Bristol. 1982.

Verney, P. *Anzio: An Unexpected Fury*. Batsford. London. 1978.

Report of the Sub Committee of Imperial Defence on the Vulnerability of

Capital Ships to Air Attack. HMSO. London. 1936.
Parliamentary Papers. Treaty Series. Misc. No 6. (1908) Cd 4175.
Parliamentary Papers. Treaty Series. Misc. No 4. (1909) Cd 4554.
Treaty Series No 56. (1924) Cmd 2037.
Treaty Series No 1. (1931) Cmd 3758.
Treaty Series No 36. (1937) Cmd 5561.
Defence Outline of Future Policy. 1956-1957. Cmmd 124. XXIII 489.

House of Commons. Hansard Parliamentary Debates. 1908-1912. Fourth and
   Fifth Series. Vols. CLXXXIII-XLVIII.

CHAPTERS FOURTEEN AND FIFTEEN

Banbury, P. *Shipbuilders on the Thames and Medway*. David and Charles.
   Newton Abbot. 1971.
Blake, G. *British Ships and Shipbuilders*. Collins. London. 1946.
Brown, R. Stewart *Liverpool Ships in the Eighteenth Century*. Liverpool
   University Press. 1932.
Builders of Great Ships. Cammell Laird and Co. Birkenhead. 1959.
Castle, C. *Better by Yards*. Murdoch, Carberry. Erskine. 1988.
Clark, T. *A Century of Shipbuilding*. Dalesman Books. Clapham. 1971.
Clarke, J. *Power on Land and Sea: 160 Years of Industrial Enterprise on
   Tyneside*. Clavering Press. Newcastle.
Dougan, D. *The History of North East Shipbuilding*. G. Allen and Unwin.
   London. 1968.
Evans, H. *Vickers against the Odds: 1956/77*. Hodder and Stoughton.
   London. 1978.
The Fairfield Shipbuilding and Engineering Works: History of the Company.
   The Strand. London. 1909.
Gale, A. *The Restructuring of the UK Shipbuilding Industry: 1977-1990*.
   Southampton University. 1988.
Harris, J. *Liverpool and Merseyside*. Frank Cass. London. 1969.
Holland, A. J. *Bucklers Hard*. Kenneth Mason. 1985.
Jones, L. *Shipbuilding in Britain*. University of Wales. Cardiff. 1957.
Konings, C. *Queen Elizabeth at War: HM Transport 1939-45*. Patrick
   Stephens. Wellingborough. 1985.
Moss, M., and Hume, J. *Shipbuilders to the World: 125 years of Harland and
   Wolff, Belfast, 1861-1986*. Belfast. 1986.
Parkinson. *The Economics of Shipbuilding in the United Kingdom*.
   Cambridge University Press. 1960.
Rance, A. *Shipbuilding in Victorian Southampton*. Southampton University.
   1981.
Scott, J. *Vickers: A history*. Weidenfeld and Nicholson. London. 1962.
Thorneycroft, J. *100 Years of Specialised Shipbuilding and Engineering*. K.
   G. Barnaby. 1964.
Walker, F. *Song of the Clyde: A History of Clyde Shipbuilding*. Patrick
   Stephens. Cambridge. 1984.
Whale, D. *The Liners of Liverpool*. Countrywise. Wirral. 1986.

House of Lords Select Committee on the European Communities. 28th
    Report. Community Shipping Measures. House of Lords Paper.
    1987/1990. No. 90.
Report on British Shipping. HMSO. London. 1990.
Shipbuilding Inquiry Committee 1965-66. R. M. Geddes. HMSO. London.
    Cmmd 2937.
Shipbuilding on the Upper Clyde. Hill Samuel. HMSO. London. 1972.
    Cmmd 4918.

House of Lords. Hansard Parliamentary Debates. 5th Series. 1908/9. Vol. 1.
    16th Feb–May 26th.

CHAPTER SIXTEEN

Bacon, R. H. *Lord Fisher*. Hodder and Stoughton. London. 1929.
Dockland History Project. *Mersey Ship Repairers*. University of Liverpool.
    1988.
Macdougall, P. *Chatham Dockyard Story*. Rochester Press. 1981.
Macdougall, P. *Royal Dockyards*. David and Charles. Newton Abbot. 1982.
Morris, R. *The Royal Dockyards during the Revolutionary and Napoleonic
    Wars*. Leicester University Press. 1983.
Tanner, J. *Samuel Pepys and the Royal Navy*. Cambridge University Press.
    1920.
Illustrated London News. 1939-1942.

Defence Select Committee on the future of the Royal Dockyards. House of
    Commons Papers. No. 453. 1984/5., No. 258. 1985/86., No. 15. 1986/7.
Public Accounts Committee Control of Dockyards. Operation and
    Manpower. House of Commons Papers. No 342. 1983/4., No. 440.
    1984/5., No. 286. 1985/6., No. 55. 1988/9. (Ministry of Defence Transfer
    of Royal Dockyards to Commercial Management).
Official Papers, Public Record Office, Kew, London. Adm. 1. 10997, 11103,
    11108, 11243, 12066, 12081, 15780, 17091, 19056. Adm. 116. 4587,
    5649, 6724.

CHAPTER SEVENTEEN

Bowman, M.J., and Harris, J. *Multilateral Treaties*. Compiled at Nottingham
    University. Butterworth. London. 1984.
Clarke, W. *Britain's Invisible Earnings: Report of the Committee of Invisible
    Exports*. British National Export Council. London. 1967.
Colman, A. *The practice and Procedure of the Commercial Court*. Lloyds of
    London Press. London. 1990.
Halsburys Laws of England. Vol. I. Butterworth. London. 1973.
Howe, M. *Europe and the Constitution after Maastricht*. Nelson and Pollard.
    Oxford. 1993.
Kiralfy, A. K. R. *Potter's Historical Introduction to English Law*. Sweet and
    Maxwell. London. 1958.
Roscoe, E. S. *History of the High Court of Admiralty*. Lloyds. London. 1924.
Trade Reports of City Institutions.

INDEX

ABDA Command, 136, 146
Aberdeen, Earl of, 26
Aberdeen, 41, 209, 212, 213, trawlers, 51,
(and see shipbuilding centres)
Aden, 67, 184, Gulf of, 121, 178
Admiralty, 9, 13–15, 48, 161, 166, 167, 173,
174, 181, 185, 188, 192, 197, 201, 206, 208,
210, 215, 225, 243, 246–256, 262, Board of,
225, 259, Lords Commissioner of, 9, 244,
Controller of the RN, 246, Court, 13, 265,
271–274, First Lord, 14, 187, 207, 245, Sea
Lords, 245, 247, 248, 252, First Sea Lord,
51, 137, 160, 161, 248, 252, Third Sea Lord,
246, 248, Lord High Admiral, 3, 6, 243, 244,
272, (see under Navy Board and Royal
Dockyards)
Adriatic Sea, 3, 30
Africa, 4, 7, 9, 19, 21, 40, 71, 97, 163, 211,
(see under East, North, South and West)
Air power and defences, 52, 57, 63–71, 78–80,
119, 122–137, 140–151, 154–161, 165–169,
180–185, 190–203, 248–254, Bombing of
German cities, 92, 141, 181, Bombing of
UK and Commonwealth ports and cities, 63,
64, 68, 85, 127–130, 141–148, 190, 225,
249, 253, Glider and wireless controlled
bombs, 198, Barrage balloons, 198, 249,
253, (and see under German Luftwaffe, RAF
and FAA)
Air Ministry, 180, Joint Committee with
Admiralty, 167, (and see under RAF)
Alexander, Field Marshall, Earl of Tunis, 128,
197
Allied naval and merchant ships, 52–76,
142–151, 158–169, 178, 190–203, 254
America, 4, 8, 9, 15–17, 205, 244, (and see
under USA)
Amphibious operations, 70–76, 120, 133,
162–166, 178, 180–203, Anzio, 197–201,
Crimea, 189, Falklands, 109, 182, 202, 203,
Gallipoli, 52, 53, 177, 189, Guadalcanal,
132, 190–192, 199, Normandy (Operation
Overlord and Neptune), 73, 76, 178, 189,
193–202, 254, 255, North Africa (Operation
Torch), 70, 71, 76, 162–167, 191–194,
Norway, 123, 125, 133, 136, 185, 186, 248,
Quebec, 187, Reggio, 74, Salerno, 74, 195,
196, Sicily (Operation Husky), 72, 166, 194,
195, 201, Spanish Peninsula, 184, 188,
Amphibious Raids, 183, 187–199, Belle Isle,
187, Cherbourg, 187, Dieppe, 189, 190, St.
Malo, 187, St. Nazaire, 189
Anne, Queen, 12, 13
Anson, Admiral Lord, 14, 172–175, 180, 183,
187, 244
ANZAC Command, 146
Arctic, Ocean, 68, 159–161, 167, North Pole,
4, N.W. Passage, 7, l4, N.E. Passage, 4
Argentine Air Force, 202, 203, River Plate,
124
Atlantic Ocean, 3, 7, 14, 37–44, 52–57, 61–81,
108, 111, 114, 120–125, 130–135, 139–143,
154–188, 193, 212, 217, (and see under
South Atlantic), Battle of the, 50, 61–76,
122, 152–169, 239, (and see under
Convoys), Cable, 207, Charter, 81, 94, 98
Attlee, Rt Hon Earl, 86, 87, 91, 255
Auchinleck, Field Marshall Sir Claude, 128
Australia, 14, 23, 29, 33, 37–44, 67–69, 97,
136, 144–149, 163, 164, 178, 189, 190, 215,
240, 254; regions and provinces, Botany
Bay, 14, N.S. Wales, 14; cities and ports,
Adelaide, 43, Darwin, 68, 145, Fremantle,
164, 254, Melbourne, 41, Perth, 43; Anzacs,
149, 189, 254, (and see under RAN and
Commonwealth)
Austria, 15, 30, 32, 43–45, 94, 153, 178, 184,
210; cities, Vienna, 30
Bahamas, 80
Baltic Exchange, 15, 42, 265–268, (and see
under ship broking and chartering)
Baltic Sea, 3, 14, 15, 30, 125, 178, 209
Bank of England, 13, 21, 85
Barents Sea, 5, 68, 131, 159–163, 168, 178,
180
Barham, Admiral, Lord, 124
Barry, Rear Admiral, C.B., 163
Battenburg, Prince Louis of, 48
Bear Island, 159, 161
Beatty, Admiral Sir D., 123, 177, 247
Belgium, 32, 51–59, 62, 63, 87, 104, 105,
140–142, 185, 200–202; cities and ports,
Antwerp, 2, 8, 28, 201, 202, Bruges, 2, 54,
Brussels, 98, 117, Ostend, 57, 141,
Zeebrugge, 57; rivers, Scheldt, 141, 201,
283; shipping, 63; subsidies and tax conces-
sions, 104, 278, 279; fishing, 111, (and see
Netherlands)
Bengal, Bay of, 68, 147
Bentinck, Lord George, 21, 24–28, 31, 32, 45
Beresford, Admiral Lord Charles, 45, 51
Bermuda, 8, 79, 80, 109, 158, 245, 247, 254
Beveridge Report, 84
Bevin, Rt Hon. Ernest, 87, 90, 250, 255, 256
Biscay, Bay of, 153, 179
Bismark, Prince, 38, 175, 210
Black Sea, 189
Blockade, by air, 141, 157, 182, land, (Berlin
Decrees), 16, 183, sea, 9, 11, 13, 15–17, 38,
49–57, 60–75, 120, 124, 125, 139, 152, 160,
179–185, open, 50, 56, 124, 182–185, close,
50, 51, 124, 182, 183, principles of,
Continuous Voyage, 9, 16, 50, Stop and
Search, 179, 180, 184, enforced by, Channel
Force, 184, Humber Force, 184, Northern
Patrol, (Tenth Cruiser Squadron) 38, 53, 57,
184, 185, contraband, 11, 13, 16, 50, 53, 57,
154, 184, (and see Orders in Council)
Blue Book, 58, 220
Blue Riband, 38, 42, 212, 214
Borneo, 145
Boscawen, Admiral E., 172